Literature for Young Children

Supporting Emergent Literacy, Ages 0–8

Sixth Edition

Cyndi Giorgis
University of Nevada, Las Vegas

Joan I. Glazer
Rhode Island College

Allyn & Bacon
is an imprint of

PEARSON

Boston | New York | San Francisco
Mexico City | Montreal | Toronto | London | Madrid | Munich | Paris
Hong Kong | Singapore | Tokyo | Cape Town | Sydney

Vice President and Executive Publisher: Jeffery W. Johnston
Executive Editor: Linda Ashe Bishop
Editorial Assistant: Demetrius Hall
Senior Managing Editor: Pamela D. Bennett
Project Manager: Kerry J. Rubadue
Production Coordination: Aptara
Design Coordinator: Diane C. Lorenzo
Photo Coordinator: Sandy Schaefer
Cover Design: Diane C. Lorenzo
Cover Image: Kane/Miller Book Publishers
Operations Specialist: Matt Ottenweller
Director of Marketing: Quinn Perkson
Marketing Coordinator: Brian Mounts

For related titles and support materials, visit our online catalog at www.pearsonhighered.com.

Between the time website information is gathered and then published, it is not unusual for some sites to have closed. Also, the transcription of URLs can result in typographical errors. The publisher would appreciate notification where these errors occur so that they may be corrected in subsequent editions.

Library of Congress Cataloging-in-Publication Data

Giorgis, Cyndi.
  Literature for young Children: supporting emergent literacy ages 0-8 / Cyndi Giorgis, Joan I. Glazer.—6th ed.
    p. cm.
Glazer's name appears first on the previous edition.
Includes bibliographical references and indexes.
ISBN-13: 978-0-13-240504-1
ISBN-10:   0-13-240504-0
1. Children—Books and reading—United States.   2. Children's literature—Study and teaching (Early childhood)—United States.   I. Glazer, Joan I.   II. Title.
Z1037.A1G573 2009
028.5'5—dc22

2008015403

10 9 8 7 6 5 4 3   STO 12 11 10

Allyn & Bacon
is an imprint of

PEARSON

Preface

Literature for Young Children: Supporting Emergent Literacy, Ages 0–8 is written for early childhood teachers and child-care professionals to help them learn to recognize high-quality children's literature and use it effectively to support emerging literacy development in infants (age 0–12 months), toddlers (ages 12–24 months), preschoolers (ages 2–4), and primary-age children (ages 5–8). The text not only exposes the literary merits of early childhood literature but also explains how to use children's literature as a teaching tool, offering a myriad of developmentally appropriate strategies for sharing literature with young children.

The Sixth Edition provides:

- An evaluation of various genres and criteria for selecting and using high-quality literature with young children.
- Discussions of classic and contemporary literature appropriate for infants, toddlers, preschoolers, and primary-age children.
- Explanations and strategies to demonstrate how literature supports the development of children's language, cognitive skills, personality, social and moral development, and aesthetic and creative development.
- Effective strategies for sharing literature to support emerging literacy skills.
- National professional standards aligned with state and local standards for early childhood literacy.
- Suggestions for integrating a variety of literature into the early childhood curriculum.
- Educational theory and research pertinent to the topic of each chapter.
- Strategies to extend learning beyond the chapter's focus.
- Developmental goals, teaching suggestions, and recommended literature gathered together and presented in a table format.

New to This Edition:

- Boxed lists of developmentally appropriate books featured throughout chapters to present extensive examples of literature aligned to chapter concepts.
- Inclusion of literature appropriate for infants and toddlers.
- Children's responses to literature.
- Web sites related to authors, illustrators, organizations, and other information about children's literature.
- Detailed explanations of how to implement a yearlong theme and the literature that supports it.

ORGANIZATION OF THE TEXT

The first three chapters introduce the range of literacy typically developed with young children, demonstrate how standards of literacy excellence can be applied, and provide suggestions for child-care professionals and teachers working with parents to select good literature. Chapter 4 focuses on the successful integration of literature into the curriculum, whereas Chapters 5 through 9 center on how literature addresses the development of children—their language, their personality, and their cognitive, moral, social, and creative skills. The final chapter, Chapter 10, presents a detailed, step-by-step look at how to use one specific book with toddlers and preschoolers and one with primary-age children.

ACKNOWLEDGMENTS

I am grateful to a number of individuals who assisted me in the revision of this text: graduate assistants Alicia Walsh and Meredith Swift, who assisted me in finding information and working on permissions; Megan Sloan, Elysha O'Brien, Sophie Ladd, and Maury Lowe, who allowed me to use their students' responses to literature; and my friends and colleagues at the University of Nevada, Las Vegas, who were always there for me with encouragement or a brownie—whichever I needed at the moment.

I am also thankful to my editor, Linda Bishop, who provided patience, critical editorial advice, and ongoing enthusiasm and support for this book, and to my reviewers, Anna Bolling, California State University–Stanislaus; Kathryn M. Brimmer, University of Wisconsin–Whitewater; Larry Browning, Baylor University; Karen Coats, Illinois State University; and Carol J. Fuhler, Iowa State University, who offered much needed direction.

And, finally, I would like to acknowledge and thank my mother, Donna Zanetti, for a lifetime of love and support. I know that I never would have accomplished what I have, both personally and professionally, without her guidance.

Cyndi Giorgis

Contents

About the Authors

Cyndi Giorgis is a Professor at the University of Nevada Las Vegas, where she teaches courses in children's and young adult literature. She is a former elementary classroom teacher and school librarian. She has served on both the Newbery, Caldecott and Geisel Award committees and is a former coeditor of *The Reading Teacher's* Children's Books review column. She is currently the coeditor of the *Journal of Children's Literature.* Dr. Giorgis was elected to the board of the Children's Literature Assembly and the Children's Literature Special Interest Group of the International Reading Association. She has served on the National Council of Teachers of English Notable Books in the Language Arts committee, and IRA's Notable Books for a Global Society and was a regional coordinator for IRA's Teachers' Choices. She has published numerous articles in professional journals and has presented at national and international conferences on reader response, art, and design of picture books and integrating literature into the elementary and secondary curriculum. Dr. Giorgis is a recipient of the International Reading Association's Arbuthnot Award for Outstanding Professor of Children's and Young Adult Literature.

Joan I. Glazer is Professor Emerita of Education at Rhode Island College, where she teaches courses in children's literature, language arts, and reading. She has taught at the elementary school level, served as a Head Start supervisor, and worked as an educational consultant for numerous school districts. She spent the 2002–2003 academic year in Norway as a Fulbright Scholar, visiting more than 60 schools to present teacher workshops and demonstration lessons focusing on American Studies. She is a past president of the United States Board on Books for Young People, a past Executive Committee member of the International Board on Books for Young People, and is the current president of the board that oversees the publication of *Bookbird: A Journal of International Children's Literature.* Dr. Glazer has been honored with the Distinguished Teacher Award from the Feinstein School of Education and Human Development at Rhode Island College, was the first holder of the Thorp Professorship for Scholarship, and has received the school's Award for Service.

Literature for Young Children

Supporting Emergent Literacy, Ages 0-8

CHAPTER ONE

MIYA, Age 7
Response to *Amazing Grace*

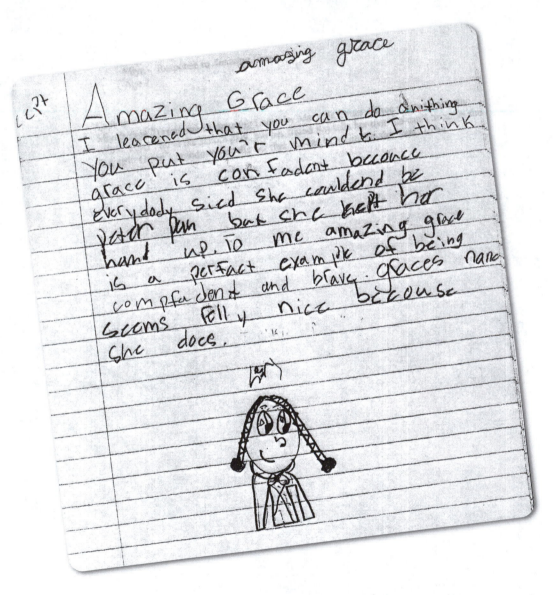

Miya's (age 7) response to *Amazing Grace* by Mary Hoffman.
Grace wants to play the role of Peter Pan in the school play, but her
friend Raj tells her that she can't because she is a girl. Grace's
grandmother tells her that she can be whatever she wants to be.

Defining Literature for Young Children

The primary goal of a literature program focused on infants, toddlers, preschoolers, kindergarteners, and children in first through third grades is the creation of a positive attitude toward literature. Children form attitudes about literature based on their individual experiences with books and with learning to read. Children who enjoy and value literature will continue to read and will find a lifelong source of emotional and intellectual enrichment. Teachers of young children in preschool through grade 3, childcare providers, and parents are in an ideal position to help create such an attitude.

This book is designed to demonstrate the many ways in which literature can and does support the goals of early childhood education. It also illustrates how books can be presented so that children develop and maintain a positive attitude toward literary experiences. Before seeing how literature contributes to the achievement of developmental goals, however, it is essential that you first be aware of the wide range of stories, poems, and informational books currently available for young children and that you be able to select from these the best in terms of literary quality. This first chapter is devoted to defining types of literature and the second chapter, to describing criteria for selecting quality literature. In addition, sections are included on children's preferences and responses to literature and suggestions for assisting parents in selecting books and book-related media.

THE RANGE OF LITERATURE

Several categorization systems are used to describe and classify books; within each are occasional differences of opinion among experts about the placement or labeling of books. Children's books frequently are classified in one of two ways, either by their format or by their genre.

Format

The format of a book is its general makeup. This includes the size, shape, type of binding, arrangement of illustrations, endpapers, cover, paper quality, typography, and spacing. A description of the format of the Caldecott Award winning picture book *My Friend Rabbit* (Rohmann, 2002), a story of a well-intentioned Rabbit who accidentally tosses Mouse's new airplane high into a tree, would include that it is a hardcover book measuring 11 inches wide and 8 ¼ inches high. The book cover depicts Rabbit holding an airplane with Mouse sitting inside. Bright grassy green endpapers are revealed once the book is opened. The title page shows Rabbit and Mouse with a large gift box that once contained the airplane. Throughout the story, Rohmann utilizes double-page, full-color relief prints framed in black. The book format changes at one point in the story requiring readers to tilt the book vertically to view the climactic spread that shows a stack of very annoyed animals sitting on each other's backs. At the top of the heap, Rabbit is holding Squirrel in an attempt to retrieve the airplane wedged in the tree. This nearly wordless book makes occasional use of black text in an easy-to-read font. Heavy, high-quality paper and a sturdy binding make this humorous book durable.

Many children's books are available in hardcover and paperback editions as well as board books. Eric Carle's *The Very Hungry Caterpillar* (1994) board book measures 5 inches wide by 4 inches high and is perfect for little hands. Paperbacks are less expensive, thus bringing quality literature within the economic reach of more families. However, they are generally not as durable as hardcover books. Also, a paperback edition of a picture book may differ in size from the original. Robert McCloskey's classic *Make Way for Ducklings* (1941) paperback edition is approximately one third the size of the original Caldecott Medal winner. This would greatly affect the ability of a group of children to view McCloskey's expressive illustrations, which might impact their enjoyment and response to the story. Another Caldecott Medal winner, *Hey, Al* (1986) by Arthur Yorinks, utilizes the endpapers to assist in telling the story of a janitor who lives in a dingy apartment in Manhattan with his dog Eddie. One day both dog and man are given the opportunity to experience a place with no worries and no cares. The front endpapers of the book are a drab tan color, whereas the final end

Rohmann conveys a story of patience and loyalty through comically expressive illustrations.
(Illustration copyright Eric Rohmann from *My Friend Rabbit*. Used with permission of Roaring Book Press.)

pages are a vibrant yellow. Although the hardcover edition contains this clever story-telling device, the paperback version does not.

Another component to consider when assessing the quality of a book is the binding. Repeated readings of a book with an inadequate binding may soon leave a book that resembles a loose-leaf notebook. The use of inferior paper can dull otherwise colorful illustrations (which is often the case with paperback books). Even the placement of illustrations on the page is important. If eight Mother Goose rhymes are crowded together on a single page, with illustrations scattered randomly to fill the white spaces, young children may be confused about which illustration goes with which verse.

Unusual Formats   Some books stand out because of their unusual format. In *The Very Busy Spider* (1984) by Eric Carle, each strand of the web is raised on the paper, so we not only see but also feel the web as it develops from outer edge and spokes to its full pattern of concentric circles. In Carle's *The Very Clumsy Click Beetle* (1999), the sound of clicking as the beetle completes three graceful somersaults is heard near the conclusion of the story, thanks to an electronic chip embedded in the endpapers and powered by a replaceable battery. The format and the repetitious text in both books encourage a child's active participation.

Joseph Had a Little Overcoat (Taback, 2000), but it was full of holes—just like this clever retelling of a Yiddish folktale that received the Caldecott Medal. When Joseph's coat became too old and shabby he didn't want to throw it out, so he made it into a jacket. When that became worn, he fashioned a vest from it. As the story goes on and things become ragged, each subsequent item that Joseph made became smaller and smaller. As children turn the pages, they can use the die-cut holes to predict what Joseph will be making next from his amazing overcoat.

Janet and Allan Ahlberg encourage participation through another unusual format. They have created three books that have pages constructed as envelopes with letters inside. *The Jolly Postman or Other People's Letters* (1986) is the story of the postman who goes around on his bicycle delivering letters addressed to storybook characters. The various types of mail he delivers include an advertisement from "Hobgoblin Supplies Ltd" that is addressed to the "Occupant" of the Gingerbread Bungalow; Baby Bear's invitation to Goldilocks' party; and a letter to the wolf received from the attorneys representing Red Riding Hood. In *the Jolly Christmas Postman* (1991), the same postman delivers Christmas gifts and messages, again to storybook characters but this time with small puzzles and games, including a foldout show for the postman from Santa. In *The Jolly Pocket Postman* (1995), the postman shrinks in size to visit Storyland, where he meets Alice in Wonderland and joins Dorothy on her quest to Oz. The book contains glittery maps and a miniature magnifying glass to help readers keep an eye on the tiny postman. Katharine Holabird's story about a delightful mouse ballerina utilizes a similar format in *Angelina Ballerina's Invitation to the Ballet* (2003). Angelina wins two tickets to the ballet, but none of her friends can go because they've all received mail of their own. Six envelopes bound into the book contain invitations, letters, cards, and a Cindermouse ballet poster. Teachers and caregivers using Ahlberg's or Holabird's books have found it helpful to make photocopies of the letters and games as insurance against loss or damage.

Format should be used to make the literature more effective. In *The Very Busy Spider,* the raised web reinforces the growing pattern of the web and complements the patterning of the language. In *My Friend Rabbit,* Rohmann uses wordless and sometimes empty frames to create a comic effect while allowing the huge animals to make sudden entrances from the side or the top of the page. This technique artfully captures the expressions on the animals' faces. Format should be used to enhance, but not detract from, the presentation of the story in a picture book. Format classifications are used regularly to identify types of books. The most common are toy and board books, wordless picture books, picture books, beginning-to-read books, and chapter books.

Toy and Board Books Toy books are books with some special device for involving readers. Some have portions that children can feel. Infants and toddlers enjoy tickling the mischievous pink pig in *Tickle the Pig* (Davis, 2001). This interactive book contains various textures that invite little fingers to touch and feel. Van Fleet's *Fuzzy Yellow Ducklings* (1995) also uses a tactile approach as it presents the concepts of colors and shapes. Young listeners can touch the sticky pink frog tongue shaped like a line. Still other books have pop-up figures that come to life as the page is turned or various flaps are lifted or pulled. Eric Hill's stories about Spot, a friendly and inquisitive puppy, have been popular with toddlers for more than two decades. In *Spot's Playtime Pop-Up* (Hill, 2007), bright, bold colors and large, sturdy pages depict the pup and his friends playing with his toys. The "Spot" lift-the-flap stories engage toddlers' attention as they answer the questions the text poses and then lift the flap or pull the tab to reveal the answers. Robert Sabuda's counting book, *Cookie Count* (1997), brings gasps of surprise and delight as his intricate paper engineering twists and twirls plate after plate of cookies, culminating in a gingerbread house with 10 windows. Children can count the number of cookies and also search for the same number of mice, each wearing a baker's hat, as the numbers go from 1 to 10.

Toy books are generally best suited for use with individual children rather than groups. Many are not sturdy enough for repeated use; even when durable, they require that children take turns. Some, such as flip books, can be used by only one child at a time. In some flip books, the reader must skim through the pages rapidly to get the effect of animation and "see" the story. Only the person holding the book is positioned to see the full appearance of changes in the drawings from page to page. Other flip book formats are designed with pages cut into segments. *Flip-a-Face: Colors* (SAMI, 2006) contains pages cut into fourths for four different portions of the face and head. Purple glasses? Flip the page and now they are green. This flip book, appropriate for ages 1–3, introduces or reinforces colors.

Board books are printed on heavy cardboard and are often laminated. They are designed for babies and toddlers who are just learning to handle books. Because of the stiffness of the pages, they can be grasped and turned more easily than lighter weight pages, and they are less likely to tear. Some board books are cut in the shape of their topic, such as vehicles or animals.

Board books vary greatly in quality, from those with inaccurate information and overly cute language and characters, to those of moderate quality (the vast majority of books), to some very fine works by authors such as Eric Hill, Tana Hoban, Karen Katz, Leo Lionni, Helen Oxenbury, Nancy Tafuri, and Rosemary Wells. Good board books give clear pictures for the child to use in naming, have simple direct plots, are accurate in text and illustration, and are appropriate in content for children from 0 to 3 years of age. Helen Oxenbury's *All Fall Down* (1999) is an excellent example of a quality board book. The text is only four lines, with a catchy rhythm and rhyme. A group of toddlers is pictured running around, bouncing on the bed, then all tumbling down on the bed. The clear and uncluttered illustrations capture the action and enjoyment of the four youngsters, who seem to run and bounce in time with the text.

Many board books have been created from books originally published as picture books. They may use all the text and illustrations, excerpt certain sections, or rewrite and simplify the text. Some make the transition well, but others do not. Changing the size of the illustrations, say from 10 inches by 11 inches to 4 inches by 5 inches, may cause detail to be lost. A 2-year-old may not understand content that was written for a child 8 or 9 years old. For example, Tomie dePaola's *Stega Nona* (1997), the humorous story of a magic pasta-making pot, works well in a picture book format, but the smaller board book contains extensive text on each page and diminishes both the quality and effectiveness of the illustrations. Generally speaking, it is better to wait until a child can appreciate a particular story than to reduce it in size for a younger audience. When assessing a board book, look at it as a new publication and judge it for its own merit.

Recommended Board Books for Children Ages 0–3

Bauer, Marion Dane. (2002). *Toes, Ears, and Nose!* Ill. Karen Katz. New York: Little Simon.

Boynton, Sandra. (2000). *Pajama Time!* New York: Workman.

Carle, Eric. (2007). *My Very First Book of Animal Sounds.* New York: Philomel.

Katz, Karen. (2003). *Counting Kisses: A Kiss and Read Book.* New York: Little Simon.

Kubler, Annie. (2005). *Itsy Bitsy Spider: A Sign and Sing Along.* Swindon, UK: Child's Play.

Lewis, Kevin. (2006). *My Truck is Stuck.* Ill. Daniel Kirk. New York: Hyperion.

Taback, Simms. (2006). *Peek-a-Boo Who?* San Francisco: Blue Apple/Chronicle.

Yolen, Jane. (2006). *How Do Dinosaurs Learn Their Colors?* Ill. Mark Teague. New York: Scholastic.

Wordless Picture Books   Wordless picture books are exactly what the name implies. They are books that have no text and present their story through illustrations only. Wordless picture books can be used to develop language and thinking skills in young children. They assist very young children in becoming accustomed to the left-to-right pattern of reading. More importantly, these books enhance emergent readers' ability to detect sequence, identify details, note cause-and-effect relationships, make judgments, determine main ideas, and make inferences. A wordless book that encourages readers to engage in these types of skills is Pat Schories's *Breakfast for Jack* (2004), which introduces Jack, an appealing orange-and-white terrier, who just wants to be fed amid the weekday morning rush. As the humans around him scurry to eat breakfast, get dressed, and rush out the door, Schories's watercolor illustrations convey Jack's bewilderment at being neglected. *The Red Book* (Lehman, 2004) tells the story of a reader who gets lost, literally, in a book. On her way to school, a young girl spies a book's red cover sticking out of a snowdrift and picks it up. Once at school, the girl opens the book and finds a series of square illustrations depicting a map, then an island, then a beach, and, finally, a boy. As the wordless story continues, each character stumbles across his or her enchanted red book. Other illustrators such as Mitsumasa Anno, Jeannie Baker, Eric Rohmann, and David Wiesner also create wordless picture books with visual stories that engage readers and encourage interaction with the book.

There are also books that contain very little text and are termed nearly wordless. Peggy Rathmann's *10 Minutes till Bedtime* (1998) is a nearly wordless book featuring a father's countdown to bedtime just as a slew of hamsters arrive for the "10-Minute Bedtime Tour." The tour bus heads to the kitchen for animal crackers, stops in the bathroom for brushing teeth, and cruises to the bedroom for a story. Finally, it is bedtime, and the hamsters climb back into numerous vehicles, taking along a variety of collected souvenirs. The ongoing countdown to bedtime and the antics of the hamsters engage readers in a story that conveys zaniness and spry illustrations.

Wordless and nearly wordless books vary in complexity. Tana Hoban's *Look Book* (1997) focuses on attention to detail, because only a small portion of an image shows through a small, die-cut circle on the page. The pages are black, making a clear frame for what is shown. When the cut page is turned, the full object shows. For example, odd brown loops with white speckles are revealed to be large, soft pretzels. Hoban provides a second photograph to show the pretzels on a street vendor's display. The book can be used as a visual guessing game—what is it that we are seeing? Viewers begin paying attention to color, texture, and pattern, and the predictable structure of *Look Book* gives it coherence. In *Sector 7* (1999), David Wiesner utilizes frames and panels to assist the reader's eyes in moving across and down the page to follow the sequence of the story. On a foggy day, a boy is visiting the Empire State Building during a class field trip. He befriends a cloud and is soon whisked away to Sector 7 and the Cloud Dispatch Center, which resembles a train station indicating arrivals and departures. The clouds complain that they are tired of their boring shapes, so the boy creates new blueprints for them. Unfortunately, the dispatchers are not pleased with the new shapes, and the boy is escorted back to his classmates. However, a few changes still remain in the skies over Manhattan that surprise cats at windows and children below.

Not all wordless picture books are for very young children. *The Red Book* and *Sector 7* are examples of wordless picture books that are appropriate for primary-grade students because they must "read" detailed illustrations and also read words such as terminals, arrivals, and assignment station. Many wordless and nearly wordless books are excellent for children in grades 1 through 3 because they promote higher level thinking skills. You must evaluate the level of understanding required for these books, just as you would for books with text.

Wordless picture books can also be used to encourage English-language learners to create or narrate their own text (Hadaway, Vardell, & Young, 2002). These books are excellent sources for "storytelling, developing oral fluency, assessing visual literacy, and developing language skills" (p. 69).

Recommended Wordless (Or Nearly Wordless) Books

Anno, Mitsumasa. (2004). *Anno's Spain*. New York: Philomel.

Armstrong, Jennifer. (2006). *Once Upon a Banana*. Ill. David Small. New York: Simon & Schuster.

Baker, Jeannie. (2004). *Home*. New York: Greenwillow.

Day, Alexandra. (1998). *Follow Carl*. New York: Farrar, Straus & Giroux.

Lehman, Barbara. (2006). *The Museum Trip*. Boston: Houghton Mifflin.

McCully, Emily Arnold. (2001). *Four Hungry Kittens*. New York: Dial.

Rohmann, Eric. (1994). *Time Flies*. New York: Crown.

Schories, Pat. (2004). *Jack and the Missing Piece*. Asheville, NC: Front Street.

Sis, Peter. (2000). *Dinosaur*. New York: Greenwillow.

Spier, Peter. (1982). *Rain*. Garden City, NY: Doubleday.

Wiesner, David. (2006). *Flotsam*. New York: Clarion.

Weitzman, Jacqueline Preiss, & Glasser, Robin Preiss. (2002). *You Can't Take a Balloon into the Museum of Fine Arts*. New York: Dial.

Picture Books   Picture books are those books in which the text and illustration work in concert to create meaning. Picture books are a format (form/design) and not a genre (content), although sometime the term *genre* is used to describe picture books as a whole. The format or the physical aspect of picture books is what makes them distinct within the field of children's literature. Generally picture books are 32 pages, although some titles may include 24 or 48 pages. The illustrations integrate with the narrative to bring the story to a conclusion. The overall design of the picture book serves to build a relationship between the text and the illustrations; this includes the front matter, back matter, and the book jacket.

Kevin Henkes's *A Good Day* (2007) is an excellent example of picture book for young children. The book jacket depicts the story's creatures, in four separate boxes, which are experiencing a bad day. The title and author's name on the book jacket appear in raised letters. If the book jacket is removed, readers will discover stripes of the watercolor palette used throughout the book. Inside, the brown endpapers complement the thick brown lines that border each interior illustration and character. The font is also in brown. Brief text tells the story of four creatures and the reasons why

Henkes uses brief text and full-page pastel hued illustrations in this gentle story that introduces young children to ways of dealing with life's small disappointments.
(Copyright © 2007 by Kevin Henkes. Used by permission of HarperCollins Publishers.)

they are having a bad day: A bird loses his favorite feather, a dog gets her leash tangled in a fence, a fox loses his mother, and a squirrel drops her nut. But then . . . all these bad days turn to good ones as the squirrel finds a bigger nut, the fox finds his mother, the dog untangles the leash, and the bird forgets the feather as he flies higher than ever before. Each full-page pastel-hued illustration depicts an expressive character as things go from bad to good. The final page shows a young girl with a yellow feather tucked behind her ear and reveals the interrelatedness of this circular story's characters.

The illustrations match the spirit of the text in *A Good Day*. The pictures are filled with emotion, show the dilemma of each situation, and extend the story. The first page of text includes well-chosen words, "It was a bad day . . . ," to set the stage, whereas the sunny watercolors allow the child to absorb each scene in its entirety with the turn of a page. This deceptively simple work reassures young children that with a little luck, determination, and persistence, things can work out. The story is also one that elicits responses from children as they recognize that there are ways to deal with life's small disappointments.

In *The Stray Dog* (2001), Marc Simont's art and narrative play off each other strategically to convey a story of humor and compassion. "It was a great day for a picnic," begins Simont's story, as the double-page spread following the title page shows the family packing up the car with a basket and a blanket. While picnicking in the country, a scruffy stray dog appears. The boy and girl spend the afternoon playing with him and even name him Willy. The children, however, are heartbroken when their parents will not let them take the stray dog back to their city home. During the week, all the family can do is to think about Willy, which Simont depicts poignantly through a series of vignettes, which show each family member brooding and preoccupied. Finally, Saturday arrives, and the family goes in search of their furry friend. Unfortunately, the dogcatcher has spied Willy first, and the boy and girl react quickly to claim the dog as their own. Simont's watercolor illustrations tell a story that engages children's attention. He effectively utilizes white space to illustrate the loneliness of the dog and the expansiveness of the landscape. The colors are muted earth tones, except for the concluding page, which shows Willy enveloped by red as he sleeps on his new bed.

Because the *picture book* denotes a format, it is important to remember that these books are not indicative of an interest level or the reading ability of young children. Students at all grade levels enjoy listening to and reading picture books. The topics that are presented vary in complexity and parents, caregivers, and teachers should preread them before sharing the books to determine if the topic is appropriate for the ages of the children.

Concept books   A specialized type of picture book is the concept book—a book that explicates a general idea or concept by presenting many specific examples of it. Ann D. Carlson (1991) defines a concept book as one that is intended for young children under the age of five and focuses on colors, shapes, numbers and counting, and the alphabet. As children acquire language, they are often able to say words before they have a complete understanding of their meanings. Concept books assist young children in gaining this understanding.

Names of colors are simple concepts, which children around 15 months and older can grasp (Carlson, 1991). Books intended to teach the names of basic colors, such as red, blue, yellow, green, etc., are appropriate for toddlers and preschoolers. A book about colors for a toddler will show an object or objects labeled with the color word. *Red, Blue, Yellow Shoe* (1986) by Tana Hoban is a board book that has a photograph of the object, a dot of that color, and the word printed in the color it names.

The photographs are of familiar objects: an orange, a blue mitten, and a black cat. The pictures have a clean and spacious look, good for use in naming activities as well as for color recognition.

Pink is for crow . . . white is for blueberry . . . yellow is for pine tree. George Shannon's *White is for Blueberry* (2005) provides a playful guessing game that invites young readers and listeners to ponder one statement after another. It won't be too confusing because, once the page is turned, the mystery reveals itself. "White is for blueberry when the blueberry is still too young to pick." The color-saturated illustrations add to both the guessing and the enjoyment of this unique concept book that encourages children to make their own predictions and connections.

Author Bill Martin, Jr., and illustrator Steven Kellogg introduce both color and number concepts through cartoonish illustrations and a rhyming text. Four brave and curious mice go exploring, "In the dark, dark woods/there is a dark, dark house." In *A Beasty Story* (1999), the daring mice creep down a dark, dark red staircase to a cellar with dark, dark blue walls until they eventually discover a dark, dark green bottle containing a "beast" that floats away. The large-print text appears at the top of each page and reinforces the color name by printing the concept word in that color. The repetitive language also adds to the appeal for reading this story aloud to children.

Still other concept books combine ideas. *Red Is a Dragon: A Book of Colors* by Roseanne Thong (2001) introduces many objects that are Asian in origin. A Chinese American girl provides rhyming descriptions of the variety of colors she sees around her. Red is the dragon in the Chinese New Year parade, green is a bracelet made of jade, and yellow are the taxis on her street. Each color is featured on a double-page spread that celebrates family festivals and rituals.

Concept books often explain relationships. There are books that illustrate the concept of opposites, show the meanings of comparative terms, or match parts of animals to the whole. Leo and Diane Dillon have reillustrated Margaret Wise Brown's timeless story, *Two Little Trains* (2001). Beginning with the cover illustration, the sleek, horizontal illustrations chronicle the parallel journeys of two trains heading west. One train is streamlined, whereas the other is small and old. Each train encounters rivers, hills, snow, and dust storms, but neither is disillusioned in its efforts. Upon closer inspection, children recognize that one train is the real thing and the other is a toy. The trains appear to be different but have many characteristics in common.

Everyone's favorite mouse, Maisy, introduces opposites in a kaleidoscopic concept book, *Maisy Big, Maisy Small: A Book of Opposites* (Cousins, 2007). Maisy's fast, she's slow, she's messy, she's clean. She also demonstrates thick and thin, tall and short, young and old, wiggly and straight. The large text is easy to read, and the vibrant colors leap off the page. Laura Vaccaro Seeger's *Black? White! Day? Night!* (2006) uses a question-answer format and full-page lift-the-flaps to present 18 opposites. Younger children will be delighted as they discover the clever transformation of a black bat that turns out to be the upturned mouth of a white ghost or the tiny bug that becomes the eye of the huge elephant. Primary grade readers will enjoy anticipating and analyzing the process itself as each question (over?) yields the unexpected answer (under!). Each flap is a different bold color so children won't miss the next opposite being presented.

Alphabet and counting books are two of the most popular types of concept books. As with other picture books, these are written at many levels of sophistication. You cannot assume that the subject matter automatically makes them appropriate for children just learning to recognize letters or learning to count. You must consider a child's level of development and the purpose for using the book as they begin sharing alphabet and counting books.

If you want children to recognize letters and to see how they are formed, then you might select *Wildflower ABC: An Alphabet of Potato Prints* (1997) by Diana Pomeroy or *Flora McDonnell's ABC* (McDonnell, 1997). Initial letter recognition is best served by a book that shows both uppercase and lowercase letters, which these books do. *Wildflower ABC* shows an upper- and a lowercase letter beside the name of each flower, and *Flora McDonnell's ABC* shows a large animal or object paired with a small one for each letter, with both uppercase and lowercase letters.

Recommended Alphabet Books

Catalanotto, Peter. (2002). *Matthew A.B.C.* New York: Atheneum.

Cronin, Doreen. (2005). *Click, Clack, Quackity-Quack: An Alphabetical Adventure.* Ill. Betsy Lewin. New York: Atheneum.

Ernst, Lisa Campbell. (2004). *The Turn-Around, Upside-Down Alphabet Book.* New York: Simon & Schuster.

Fleming, Denise. (2002). *Alphabet under Construction.* New York: Holt.

Lindbergh, Reeve. (1997). *The Awful Aardvarks Go to School.* New York: Viking.

MacDonald, Ross. (2003). *Achoo! Bang! Crash!: The Noisy Alphabet.* Brookfield, CT: Roaring Brook.

MacDonald, Suse. (2005). *Edward Lear's A Was Once an Apple Pie.* New York: Orchard.

Rose, Deborah Lee. (2000). *Into the A, B, Sea.* Ill. Steve Jenkins. New York: Scholastic.

Seeger, Laura Vaccaro. (2003). *The Hidden Alphabet.* Brookfield, CT: Roaring Brook.

Slate, Joseph. (2006). *Miss Bindergarten Celebrates the Last Day of Kindergarten.* Ill. Ashley Wolff. New York: Dutton.

If you want children to explore the sounds that letters make, you must be particularly careful that the objects illustrated are those that give the usual sounds of the letters. For example, *C* should not be illustrated with a chicken, because even though chicken begins with a *c*, children hear the sound of the *ch* blend. You should also check that the pictures could not be given different names by young children—the rabbit for *R* being called a bunny, for instance. *Brian Wildsmith's ABC* (Wildsmith, 1996) features letter names and the sounds they make as initial letters. Wildsmith uses words with which small children are familiar, such as *apple, butterfly, cat, dog*, and *elephant*. This book is also available in Spanish and contains 10 illustrations that are different from the English edition to accommodate language differences.

Sometimes an alphabet book follows a theme. *Gone Wild: An Endangered Animal Alphabet* (McLimans, 2006) is a Caldecott Honor book that is organized as a conventional alphabet book, but the letters and topic are far from ordinary. Twenty-six endangered animals are shown through red silhouettes, and their physical characteristics are incorporated into the shape of the letter with which the animal begins. For example, the *H* for Bushman Hare has ears at the top, two round circles as eyes midway down, and a cutout resembling a nose that appears on the bar across the middle. An accompanying box on each page includes a small stylized red-and-white image of the animal plus information about its class, habitat, range, threats, and status as an endangered animal.

For other books, the alphabet may be a way of organizing content, and it is the content, not the fact that it is an alphabet book, that determines its choice. Alma Flor Ada's *Gathering the Sun: An Alphabet in Spanish and English* (1997) is a collection of poetry about the lives of migrant farm workers, with the Spanish text determining the placement. Thus *A* is represented by *arboles* (trees) and *Z* by *zanahoria* (carrot). You would choose to use this book for its outstanding short poems, for its depiction of the lives of the farm workers and the honor in their work, or for its text in both Spanish and English more than for its usefulness as an alphabet book.

Choose alphabet books based on their special attributes and with an eye toward how children might use them. Shannon's *Tomorrow's Alphabet* (1996) makes the alphabet a guessing game about what comes next. The *B* is for "eggs," tomorrow's "birds," and *I* is for "water," tomorrow's "ice cubes." *I Spy: An Alphabet in Art* (Micklethwait, 1992) presents objects for letters of the alphabet through paintings by artists such as Magritte, Picasso, Botticelli, and Goya. Alert children will be able to locate several objects in each painting related to the corresponding letter. This gallery of great paintings will prompt questions while increasing knowledge of art styles and periods.

All the alphabet books discussed present well-crafted illustrations using photography, painting, or graphic arts, and all of them may stimulate discussion between you and a child about the objects or scenes presented. Very young children may look at a single illustration and name it. Eight-year-olds may look at a page filled with action, hidden letters, or objects and test their own observation skills.

Counting books often follow the same format as alphabet books. The books shows a numeral, the word, and a picture illustrating the number, with one number per page. Books for babies and toddlers concentrate on number recognition and matching a numeral or number word to the correct number of objects. Clarity of illustrations is essential, for these children are checking their skill at counting and their understanding of its concept. Introduce children to counting through the use of concrete objects, and continue this use of manipulatives as they progress through the primary grades and as you present counting books and other materials to them. George Lyon's *Counting on the Woods* (1998) uses color photographs of plants and animals, all identified in captions, to represent clearly the numbers 1 through 10. Arlene Alda's *1 2 3: What Do You See?* (Alda, 1998) focuses attention on the shape of the numeral, captured in photographs of natural and everyday objects. A stork's legs form a 4; a wisp of curly hair, a 6; a conch shell, a 9. Numerals from 1 to 10 are shown at the side or bottom of each page, with the numeral in the photograph highlighted by its large size and its color. Children can look for objects or parts of objects themselves that form numerals.

Counting books, like alphabet books, can also incorporate humor into the learning of concepts. Mrs. Tuttle has 20 dalmatians in her obedience class, and they are all named Daisy. *Daisy 1, 2, 3* (Catalanotto, 2003) is a canine counting book with plenty of visual humor, such as Daisy the Diva with her nine security guards or Cinderella Daisy, who must be home by midnight. Bill Grossman's *My Little Sister Ate One Hare* (1996) tells everything that the sibling ate in this rib-tickling counting story with a surprise twist.

Lois Ehlert's *Fish Eyes: A Book You Can Count On* (1990) adds several elements to basic counting. Using the premise that if the author were a fish, she would swim far into the ocean and see, first, one green fish, then two jumping fish, and so on through 10, each page states that the number of fish seen, "plus me," makes ____, and the next number is stated, thus introducing both the concept and the language of addition. The "me" is a tiny black fish on each double-page spread. The fish seen are in patterned neon colors shown on a deep blue background, with the eyes cut out so that colors from the previous and the next page show through. The endpapers, title page, and introductory and concluding pages have many fish, allowing for counting to higher numbers and counting by category—such as black fish or fish with blue eyes. Individual pages throughout the book can also be used for categorization and counting, using the number of dots or stripes on a fish or the number of fins.

Recommended Counting Books

Baker, Keith. (1999). *Quack and Count*. San Diego, CA: Harcourt Brace.

Bang, Molly. (1997/1983). *Diez, Nueve, Ocho/Ten, Nine, Eight*. Translated by Clarita Kohen. New York: Greenwillow.

Cousins, Lucy. (1997). *Count with Maisy*. Cambridge, MA: Candlewick.

Martin, Bill, Jr. (2004). *Chicka Chicka 1, 2, 3*. Ill. Lois Ehlert. New York: Simon & Schuster.

Reiser, Lynn. (2003). *Ten Puppies*. New York: Greenwillow.

Root, Phyllis. (2003). *One Duck Stuck*. Cambridge, MA: Candlewick.

Counting the First 100 Days of School

Carlson, Nancy. (2005). *Henry's 100 Days of Kindergarten*. New York: Viking.

Cuyler, Margery. (2000). *100th Day Worries*. New York: Simon & Schuster.

Franco, Betsy. (2004). *Counting Our Way to the 100th Day*. Ill. Steve Salerno. New York: McElderry.

Rockwell, Anne. (2002). *100 School Days*. Ill. Lizzy Rockwell. New York: HarperCollins.

Slate, Joseph. (1998). *Miss Bindergarten Celebrates the 100th Day of Kindergarten*. Ill. Ashley Wolff. New York: Dutton.

Wells, Rosemary. (2000). *Emily's First 100 Days of School*. New York: Hyperion.

As with alphabet books, some counting books tell a story around the numbers or use the number format as an organizing theme. Hutchins's *1 Hunter* (1982) tells its story in the illustrations, as the one hunter, complete in safari outfit with pith helmet, stalks through the jungle, staring so intently ahead that he misses seeing all the animals—until he turns around, that is, and is so frightened upon seeing the entire menagerie that he runs off down the path. *Moja Means One* (Feelings, 1971), subtitled *Swahili Counting Book*, organizes information about East African village life around the listing of a numeral and the Swahili word for it. The author writes in her introduction to the book that she hopes boys and girls of African origin will learn both to count in Swahili and to know something of their heritage.

There are counting books that require a fair amount of counting competence and test, rather than teach, the concept. *When Sheep Cannot Sleep* (Kitamura, 1986) seldom mentions numbers but tells what one sheep named Woody does when he cannot sleep. He goes for a walk and chases a butterfly; sees two ladybugs; notices "some" owls (there are three); and so forth. If you're wondering whether he ever does get to sleep, be assured that he does. This sheep that cannot sleep finally lies down in bed and thinks about his relatives. The child looking at this book must first identify the organizing scheme and then find and count the objects that are named in the context of the story.

Anno's Counting Book (Anno, 1977) is as much a book on categorizing as it is a counting book. The numeral is shown beside each double-page illustration, but within the illustration are objects that must be categorized into groups before they can be counted. Thus "four" has four buildings (three houses and a church) but eight trees (four evergreen and four deciduous). The illustrations, which also show seasonal changes, lend themselves to discussion about how objects might be categorized, what is happening in each illustration, and the need for a system of enumeration.

When you select counting books, keep in mind what you expect them to accomplish and the child's level of comprehension. Toddlers enjoy interacting with books and pointing to different things that they can name. Although these concept books may appear simple, they often become favorites because of their bold colors and photographs or paintings of familiar, everyday items. Preschool-age children are gaining proficiency in counting, so books selected for 3- and 4-year-olds should allow them to focus on learning this skill. For primary grade students, the objective is often to reinforce the ability to count as well as other mathematical operations. Literature that contains stories about counting as well as addition, subtraction, counting by twos, etc., can introduce or reinforce this learning.

Beginning-to-Read Books   Publishers use labels such as I Can Read, Read Alone, Step into Reading, and Easy-to-Read to denote books that have a limited vocabulary and regulated sentence length. These factors contribute to the ease with which material can be read and are designed for beginning readers. Attention is given to the number of difficult words, but the writing is not done from a standardized word list, as are some stories in basal readers. Beginning-to-read books are excellent choices for children just learning to read independently and are used for this purpose, rather than for reading aloud to children.

Skilled writers are able to work within the constraints of vocabulary and sentence-length restrictions to produce interesting and well-written stories. There is no need to limit the topics of easy-reading books. They can explore poetry, such as Jack Prelutsky's *My Parents Think I'm Sleeping* (2007). They can read about historical incidents in books like *The 18 Penny Goose* (Walker, 1998), in which young Letty and her family must leave their farm to escape approaching British soldiers during the Revolutionary War, or in a biography of Rosa Parks (Parks with Haskins, 1998), which explores the beginnings of the civil rights movement in the United States. They can laugh at and be challenged by the riddles, filled with language play and puns, in *Dino Riddles* (Hall, 2002). They can read about characters that might be having similar experiences such as *Amanda Pig, First Grader* (Van Leeuwen, 2007), who is excited to learn how to read and knows that this year she won't have to take naps. They can scare themselves with the tales in Alvin Schwartz's *In a Dark, Dark Room* (1984), a collection of classic ghost stories often told on Halloween or around a campfire at night.

There is no need for writers to use an "Oh! Oh! Look! Look! Look!" style of writing. Arnold Lobel has captured the natural cadence of speech in *Frog and Toad Are Friends* (1970). Frog arrives at Toad's house and knocks on the door:

"Toad, Toad," shouted Frog, "wake up. It is spring!"

"Blah," said a voice from inside the house.

"Toad, Toad!" cried Frog. "The sun is shining! The snow is melting. Wake up!"

"I am not here," said the voice.   *(pp. 4–5)*

In this classic, well-written early chapter book, the sentences are short and the vocabulary is easy, but the humor shines through.

Young independent readers can begin to make friends with book characters such as Frog and Toad, getting to know them well through the several books that feature their adventures. Enjoying one book leads to reading another. Cynthia Rylant's series of easy-reading books about Henry and his dog Mudge, James Howe's books about Pinky and Rex, or Erica Silverman's stories about Cowgirl Kate and her horse Cocoa are filled with natural-sounding dialogue, fast action, and humor. They capture children's imaginations by developing characters and themes effectively and by using language creatively.

Theodor Seuss Geisel Award

The Theodor Seuss Geisel Award was established in 2004 by the Association of Library Science to Children, a division of the American Library Association, to honor the most distinguished contribution to the body of American children's literature known as the beginning reader books. Geisel created the category of beginning-to-read books with the *Cat in the Hat* (1957). In response to an article that appeared in *Life Magazine,* John Hersey suggested that Dr. Seuss was just the person to write a more interesting book for beginning readers (Chatton, 2007). Geisel took "The List" of controlled vocabulary insisted upon by the publishers of basal readers at the time, and created his story with only these simple words.

The charge of the Theodor Seuss Geisel Award committee is to explore the wide range of books published for children PreK–Grade 2 that were published during the calendar year. The books chosen to receive the award should be distinguished, offer child appeal, and support the beginning reader. The following books have been selected as Geisel Award winners and Honor books.

2007 Medal Winner
Zelda and Ivy: The Runaways by Laura McGee Kvasnosky. Cambridge, MA: Candlewick.

The fox sisters want to avoid the dreaded cucumber sandwiches Dad is preparing. They also engage in writing and trying to create their own time capsule.

2007 Honor Books
Mercy Watson Goes for a Ride by Kate DiCamillo. Ill. Chris Van Dusen. Cambridge, MA: Candlewick.

Mr. Watson's pig, the "porcine wonder," finally gets behind the wheel of a 1959 pink convertible. DiCamillo's superb, dialogue-filled, 14-chapter story is a humorous delight, and Van Dusen's retro-style illustrations are engaging and fun.

Move Over, Rover! by Karen Beaumont. Ill. Jane Dyer. San Diego, CA: Harcourt.

Beaumont's patterned cumulative text is expanded by Dyer's watercolors, which contain context clues, to tell the story of creatures from squirrel to skunk seeking shelter by squeezing into Rover's doghouse.

Not a Box by Antoinette Portis. New York: HarperCollins.

Imagination is the focus of this appealing picture about a bunny playing with, in, and on a cardboard box.

2006 Medal Winner
Henry and Mudge and the Great Grandpas by Cynthia Rylant, Ill. Suçie Stevenson, New York: Simon & Schuster.

Henry and his lovable dog, Mudge, visit Great Grandpa Bill in the house where he lives with lots of other grandpas.

2006 Honor Books
Hi! Fly Guy by Tedd Arnold. New York: Cartwheel Books/Scholastic.

A boy decides that a fly, which he names Buzz, is the perfect pet.

A Splendid Friend, Indeed by Suzanne Bloom. Honesdale, PA: Boyds Mills Press.

Goose becomes a real nuisance when he takes Polar Bear's book and his writing and asks persistent questions.

Cowgirl Kate and Cocoa by Erica Silverman. Ill. Betsy Lewin. San Diego, CA: Harcourt.

Set on a cattle ranch, this beginning chapter book tells four spirited stories about a young cowgirl, Kate, and her beloved talking horse, Cocoa.

Amanda Pig and the Really Hot Day by Jean Van Leeuwen. Ill. Ann Schweninger. New York: Dial.

Amanda and her brother Oliver try to endure a really hot day by building a fort and selling lemonade through four episodic chapters.

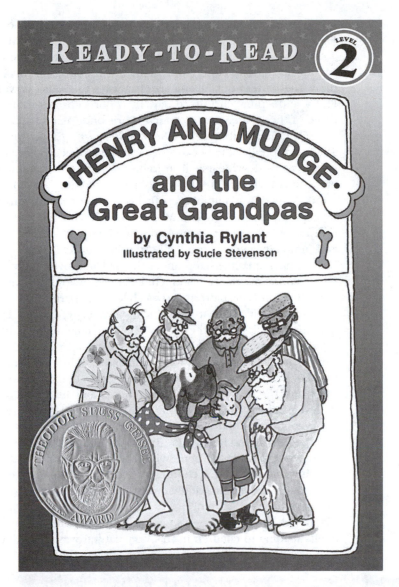

Rylant's easy-to-read chapter book was honored as the first Geisel Award winner.
(Reprinted with the permission of Simon & Schuster Books for Young Readers, an imprint of Simon & Schuster Children's Publishing Division from *Henry and Mudge and the Great Grandpas* by Cynthia Rylant, illustrated by Sucie Stevenson. Illustrations copyright © 2005 Sucie Stevenson.)

Predictable books   Predictable books have a structure that allows children to predict with some accuracy what will happen next. Sometimes that structure is in the repetition of a similar refrain. Those children familiar with *Brown Bear, Brown Bear, What Do You See?* (Martin, 1983) will be excited by the fourth and final collaboration of Bill Martin, Jr., and Eric Carle, *Baby Bear, Baby Bear, What Do You See?* (2007). This predictable story is written using the same appealing cadence as the previous book as it introduces a sequence of animals such as a red fox, blue heron, and striped skunk. Carle's signature collage illustrations capture the true sense of the animal while effectively using white space and color.

Sometimes the predictability is in the structure of the story itself. Denise Fleming's *Mama Cat Has Three Kittens* (1998) shows Mama Cat engaged in many activities. When she washes her paws, or walks along a stone wall, or chases leaves, two of her kittens, Fluffy and Skinny, always do the same; but the third kitten, Boris, naps. The pattern of the language is always the same as well. However, when Mama, Fluffy, and Skinny curl up to nap, then Boris springs into action and pounces on all three of them. After that, of course, Boris once again naps.

Cumulative tales, such as *Bearsie Bear and the Surprise Sleepover Party* (Waber, 1997), are predictable because what has happened before is repeated with each new event. In this story, Bearsie Bear, in his nice warm bed, is snuggled down under the covers when one by one, a series of animals comes and asks for shelter from the snow and wind. Bearsie Bear admits each, finally sharing his bed with Goosie Goose, Foxie Fox, Piggie Pig, Cowsie Cow, and Moosie Moose. With each new animal, the whole lineup is repeated. The pattern is broken when Porkie Porcupine declares it a sleepover party and jumps into bed, causing all the others to leave. The problem is resolved first by Bearsie having Porkie sleep under the bed and inviting the others to return, and then, when Porkie expresses his loneliness, by allowing him back in as long as he doesn't "thrash about." This pattern allows children to participate in the reading or telling.

Predictable books are valuable for a variety of reasons. First, they encourage participation by children as they listen. *Do You Ears Hang Low?* (Church, 2002) can be repeated or sung; *Bearsie Bear* can easily engage children in speaking the parts of the various animals. Second, they can stimulate children to begin learning to read naturally. Children learn the words easily, and then begin to match the words they are saying with the words on the page. They can do this as they listen and as they look at the book on their own. They gain quick control over a story and the words used to tell it, which gives them confidence in their ability to learn to read. Many of the current books published in large format and labeled Big Books are predictable stories. The large format allows the teacher to share the book with a group of children and lets each child see and follow the print. In this way, children are encouraged to learn first to "read" whole refrains, then sentences, and then individual words. Childcare providers and parents provide the same stimulus for learning to read when they sit next to a child and share a book so that the child can see the print as the adult reads. In fact, it was from parents and other adults reading to children in this very natural way that educators came to realize the importance and potential of working with big books.

Recommended Predictable Books

Asch, Frank. (1982). *Happy Birthday, Moon.* New York: Simon & Schuster.

Burningham, John. (1971). *Mr. Gumpy's Outing.* New York: Holt.

Carle, Eric. (2002). *"Slowly, Slowly, Slowy," said the Sloth.* New York: Philomel.

Fox, Mem. (2002). *The Magic Hat.* Ill. Tricia Tusa. San Diego, CA: Harcourt.

Lindbergh, Reeve. (1990). *The Day the Goose Got Loose.* Ill. Steven Kellogg. New York: Dial.

Martin, Bill, Jr. (1991). *Polar Bear, Polar Bear, What Do You Hear?* Ill. Eric Carle. New York: Holt.

Numeroff, Laura Joffe. (1998). *If You Give a Pig a Pancake.* Ill. Felicia Bond. New York: HarperCollins.

Root, Phyllis. (1998). *One Duck Stuck.* Ill. Jane Chapman. Cambridge, MA: Candlewick.

Waite, Judy. (1998). *Mouse, Look Out!* Ill. Norma Burgin. New York: Dutton.

Ziefert, Harriet. (1998). *I Swapped My Dog.* Ill. Emily Bolam. Boston: Houghton Mifflin.

Predictable books are also extremely useful in helping children for whom English is their second language learn the sounds, cadences, and meanings of English sentences and words. The emphasis on meaning, the use of context, and the enjoyment produced by good literature combine to provide both incentive and the tools needed for second-language learning.

Chapter Books Chapter books, as the name indicates, are books with chapters. The format has importance for primary-grade children because it provides a transition between picture books and novels. The reading level is similar to that in many picture books, but the stories are longer, and text predominates. Often the plot is episodic, with a character having a different adventure in each chapter. This is true in Ann Cameron's stories about Julian and about Huey. In *More Stories Huey Tells* (Cameron, 1997), the first chapter relates Huey's attempts to doctor his sunflowers when they begin to turn brown. He tries those things that seem reasonable to him—sugar because his father had told him that plants' leaves made sugar, coffee because that works for his father in the mornings, and even vitamins. He borrows Julian's radio so the plants can have music. Although he is not successful in changing the looks of his sunflowers, he does learn that they are going to seed, and he can save some of the seeds and grow new sunflowers next spring. Chapter 2 has a completely new plot about Julian's birthday and the basketball he is to share, but once again it involves both Huey and Julian.

Other chapter books have a continuous plot line, requiring that the child remember what has happened and who the characters are over several days of reading. In Claudia Mills's $7 \times 9 = Trouble!$ (2002), Wilson Williams is certain he will be the only third-grader unable to pass his times-tables tests by the end of the school year. In fact, he believes he won't even pass them by the end of fifth grade! But with plenty of encouragement from his parents and younger brother, coupled with a few helpful hints from a classmate, Wilson works hard and achieves his goal. Added to his math anxiety are the challenges presented when Wilson's class's beloved and adventuresome hamster disappears. G. Brian Karas's black-and-white illustrations complement this engaging, short chapter book that holds great appeal as a class read-aloud or for independent reading. The 10 chapters in this humorous book form a continuous story that is more involved than the narratives in most picture books.

Often, chapter books, whose intended audience is children in grades 1 through 3, are series books. Readers delight in the antics of humorous characters such as Junie B. Jones, Horrible Harry, Cam Jansen, Judy Moody, Amber Brown, or Jake Drake. Primary-grade children return to these books because they are familiar with the main characters and the writing styles. These series books are generally the ones that children select for their independent reading.

Format alone, however, is not a guide to the difficulty of a book. There are some picture books that are appropriate for toddlers and others that require the maturity of a sixth-grader for any real understanding to occur. Some beginning-to-read books are divided into chapters. Look carefully, not only at format but also at content and writing style as you select books to share with children.

Literature-Based Media

Many literature selections for children are now available through various media formats—audiocassette, CD, video, film, CD-ROM, and DVD. Children see stories animated on television, particularly the very popular *Arthur* series, using the books by

Marc Brown featuring Arthur (an aardvark), Francine, his friend, and the energetic D.W., his little sister (http://pbskids.org/arthur). They have traveled with *The Magic School Bus,* stories that combine fantasy and science education by Joanna Cole and Bruce Degan, joining Ms. Frizzle as she takes them on trips to the solar system or traveling through the bloodstream. They see iconographic techniques, in which the camera zooms in and out on various portions of an illustration, giving the sensation of motion, used for some of the sharing of books on *Reading Rainbow* (http://pbskids.org/readingrainbow). The growing penetration of technology in our lives has had a significant effect on individuals of all ages, including young children (Shamir & Korat, 2006). One reason is that numerous children's books have been adapted for film and television. These videos and DVDs are available for purchase, so many children are viewing them at home or in libraries.

CD-ROMs often add an interactive quality to the stories presented. In some presentations, the child clicks on various objects in the story to see the motion and sound connected with them. In others, children make choices about the format before beginning the presentation, clicking on the language they prefer, on whether they want words to be highlighted as a story is read, or if they want to view text at all. Some stories follow the "choose your own adventure" format, in which the action stops at various points within the story, and children select in which direction they would like the plot to turn. Children may make those choices by taking the role of one of the characters and manipulating that character through different settings. This is done particularly in mystery stories, where the viewer acts as detective.

The increasing popularity of media based on literature and the development of computer technology have vastly expanded the ways in which children may experience literature.

Genre

Although *format* refers to the physical qualities of a book, *genre* refers to the content—what is said and how it is said. The major genre classifications are poetry and prose.

Poetry   This genre is better understood in practice than by definition. An attempt may be made to differentiate between poetry and prose by saying that poetry rhymes—but blank verse does not rhyme. It may be said that poetry has a depth of emotion and an imaginative quality—but so does some prose. It may be said that the sound of poetry is pleasing and that the meaning often comes from the sound as well as the words; certainly, rhythm plays an important role in poetry. Concrete poetry, however, which is shaped like its subject, needs to be seen rather than heard. It may be said that poetry relies on figurative language, yet there are narrative poems without a single simile or metaphor. The best that can be done is to list poetry's characteristics, recognizing that any one poem will not have all of them, and that almost any one of them may be present in prose also.

A large part of young children's poetry experience may be with Mother Goose rhymes, although children are not being exposed to them as much as they have been in the past. Also in this genre are books with collections of poems and single poems illustrated in picture-book format. There is verse as well, rhymed but lacking the depth of emotion and compactness of language of quality poetry. Lucille Clifton, Rebecca Kae Dotlich, Douglas Florian, Kristine O'Connell George, Eloise Greenfield, Lee Bennett Hopkins, Karla Kuskin, Myra Cohn Livingston, Eve Merriam, Jack Prelutsky, Alice Schertle, and Jane Yolen are well-known poets whose writing is generally appropriate for young children.

Prose   Prose is divided into nonfiction and fiction, with nonfiction the factual work and fiction the invented work. Each of these is further subdivided.

Nonfiction   Nonfiction includes informational books and biography. Informational books are designed to tell about a specific subject—such as stars, colonial times, or how to build a dollhouse. Sometimes the information is conveyed in story form, with child characters sharing their knowledge about a subject or with the use of *you* and *we* to make it more personal. At other times the information is presented directly, organized by topic. In *Actual Size* (Jenkins, 2004), each spread presents a new animal or two for readers to discover. There are also interesting facts and physical dimensions. The colorful collage illustrations display either the entire animal at their actual size or some physical aspect that will fit on a page, such as an African elephant's foot or a few 4-inch-long teeth of a great white shark. Concept books are related to informational books in that they, too, deal with facts as building blocks, but concept books tend to be simpler.

A biography is a story of a person's life or a segment of that person's life. Authentic biographies use only statements that the person is known to have made and base all incidents on recorded happenings. Doreen Rappaport weaves in Dr. King's own words in *Martin's Big Words: The Life of Dr. Martin Luther King, Jr.* (2001). This stunning picture-book biography provides an ideal introduction to this leader and his works that is appropriate for a range of audiences. Fictionalized biographies may dramatize incidents and dialogues, having the person say what he or she is likely to have said and filling in gaps in information with plausible events. Only probable dialogue and events may be added. Otherwise, the book ceases to be a biography and is classified instead as biographical fiction.

Fiction   Fiction includes all stories that are created from an author's imagination, even though they may be based on real happenings. If the story could happen now or could have happened in the past, it is called realism. If the setting is present day, the genre is contemporary realism; if the setting is in the past, it is historical fiction. The Geisel Award–winning *Henry and Mudge and the Great Grandpas* and *7 × 9 = Trouble!* are contemporary realism because they have a present-day setting and could happen. *Sarah Plain and Tall* (MacLachlan, 1985) is about a Maine woman moving to the Midwest after answering an ad from a widower with two children who is looking for a wife, and *Miss Rumphius* (Cooney, 1982) travels to faraway places until she returns home to do something to make the world more beautiful. Both are set in the past and are considered historical fiction.

If the story includes any actions that could not happen in the world as we know it today, the book is categorized as fantasy. *Frog and Toad Are Friends* is fantasy because animals do not talk and move like humans. This is also true of *My Friend Rabbit.*

Traditional literature—folktales, fairy tales, epics, myths, and legends, which began in the oral tradition of storytelling—is a rich source of stories for children. The tales were adapted by various storytellers to fit particular audiences. With their quick action and clear portrayal of good and evil, folktales have survived for generations in a number of versions. Some have been told in single picture-book editions, whereas others appear in collections. The book's title page will often indicate that the tale is "retold by" or "adapted by" an author or illustrator because the original authors are unknown.

Genre and format are two separate systems for categorizing books. *My Friend Rabbit* and *Frog and Toad Are Friends* are the same genre, fantasy, but they represent different formats: wordless picture book and beginning-to-read book. *Miss Rumphius* and *Martin's Big Words* are both in a picture-book format, but they are different genres—the first is historical fiction and the second is biography.

It is useful to know ways of categorizing books to provide a variety of formats and of genres for your students. Knowing these methods may also be useful as you look for books in a library. For example, folktales and poetry are sometimes classified by genre and appear in the nonfiction section of the library. At other times, folktales and poetry in picture-book format are shelved with the picture books. You should check the online catalog for the location of specific folktales and poetry books.

CHILDREN'S PREFERENCES IN LITERATURE

The topic of children's preferences in literature has been more fully researched for intermediate-grade children than for children ages 0–8. In looking at what is available, though, you should keep several cautions in mind. First, these research results—and others like them—tell what children as a group appear to like. They do not indicate what an individual child will like. They provide a starting point, a suggestion—not an answer. Second, although a survey of preferences helps educators judge the content and type of literature children may enjoy, it is not a guide to literary quality. Teachers must work both with what they know of children and with what they know of literature as they select books.

In general, sex differences in reading interest may appear for children as early as kindergarten (Dutro, 2001/2002). Primary-school children, both boys and girls, enjoy stories about personified animals, about nature, about children their age or slightly older, and about daily life and familiar experiences (Monson & Sebesta, 1991). They prefer illustrations that adults would term *representational,* as opposed to abstract, when they are judging pictures apart from text. Although they generally prefer color illustrations over black and white, a researcher did a study with primary children choosing books in their own classroom, she found that some books in black and white had special meaning for certain children (Kiefer, 1983). Any book, due to a certain combination of content and type of illustration, may become a favorite.

Thus, isolating a single factor has not proven to be a reliable method of predicting children's responses to a specific book. You may want to observe the children you teach to see which books they prefer and what patterns of response they exhibit. Some teachers conduct interest surveys within their own classes, determining what interests the children have in common and finding individual interests that can be matched with appropriate literature. Many teachers find that books that are humorous are very popular with their classes.

You may also want to read each year's "Children's Choices" results. Under the direction of a joint committee of the International Reading Association and the Children's Book Council, a list of books is selected from those published during the current year. They are chosen for literary quality and for diversity of types and subjects. The list is then sent to teams of educators, who share the books with children. The children vote on their favorites, and each year the list of winners is published in the October issue of *The Reading Teacher* and is available online at http://www.cbcbooks.org.

Children learn to appreciate poetry by being exposed to and immersed in it during their formative years (Zeece, 1998). When poetry is an integral part of a children's literary experience, it provides a powerful, creative, and effective mechanism by which ideas and feelings are identified, shared, and celebrated (p. 101). Often, if children like the topic of the poem, they like the poem, too. If they dislike the subject, they dislike the poem about it. Children may have difficulty in comprehending figurative language, tending to interpret it literally, which may result in some rather strange conceptions of what the poem is about. But their favorite poems often have strong rhythm and rhyme and are frequently narrative in form.

Perhaps one of the most consistent findings of all the studies is that young children enjoy literature, both prose and poetry. Teachers, parents and childcare providers have the opportunity to extend this enjoyment, to broaden children's taste in literature, and to plan literature experiences in such a way that goals of early childhood education are supported.

Be aware also that there is a social dimension to children's literary preferences. Children will respond to the attitudes of other children and of the adults who are presenting books (Hickman, 1983). When a teacher shows that he or she enjoys a book and encourages children to look at or read it, the climate is set for a positive response. When a parent or childcare provider makes the environment conducive to looking at and sharing books, children are more likely to do so. Even the way in which the book is presented may become associated with the book itself. Care should be taken to share books in ways that are enjoyable for children.

Children and the Literary Experience

Each individual who reads or listens to a work of literature helps to create for himself or herself the meaning of that work. Whether adults or children, we bring our own expectations, experiences, and backgrounds to whatever we read. Louise Rosenblatt (1978) describes experiencing literature as a transaction, a two-way process between a reader and a text. The reader comes to the work having made a decision, whether conscious or unconscious, about whether the reading is to be done primarily to gain information or primarily for enjoyment. A reader may read a textbook or manual with the express purpose of learning certain facts or how to do something. The reading is a means to an end. At other times, a reader may approach a story or a poem simply for

Gordon E. Rowley

As readers, we bring our expectations and backgrounds to what we read.

the pleasure of reading. There is no attempt during the reading to remember particular facts, no specific search for information. Reading and responding are ends in themselves. The literary experience for young children is generally of this second type. They listen to stories and poems, responding to the rhythm of the language, the excitement of the plot, and the feelings evoked. Infants will squeal with delight or point to pictures with familiar objects, children, toddler age and up, can express their responses in art, in discussion, and in drama, but they are not listening to engage in the activities. Childcare professionals and teachers help reinforce the importance of responding to literature as a pleasurable experience by providing opportunities for children to share their interpretations and responses in open-ended activities and discussions. When very specific recall questions about facts within a story are employed regularly following story reading, children begin listening to stories as if they were for information only.

In addition to approaching reading material with a preconceived idea of its purpose, a reader also helps to create the meaning of a text by interacting with it. The author contributes the piece of literature, having selected a topic and developed it with conscious choice of style. The reader contributes meaning to that literature by making inferences and generalizations based on his or her own thoughts, feelings, and memories. A story may mean different things to different people or to the same person at different ages. In one childcare center the adults knew that the caterpillar in a book they read became the butterfly at the end because they understood the process of metamorphosis. The children said that the character was the same, but they based their conclusion on the fact that the caterpillar and the butterfly had the same face in the illustrations.

An author may control some responses by using characters or words that generally evoke a particular reaction. Other responses, however, come from the individual. A child listening to *Dr. De Soto* (Steig, 1982), a story about a mouse who is a dentist and usually treats only small animals, may have heard enough stories about foxes to know immediately that the fox who appears begging for help will be dangerous. The child may also expect the fox to try some clever trick. Thus, the author's use of character matches the reader's expectation. One child may respond to the story with sympathy for Dr. De Soto, who is portrayed as a conscientious dentist who cares about his patients. Another child, perhaps having recently experienced pain in a dentist's office, may see Dr. De Soto as the antagonist and secretly hope that the fox will have the dentist for dinner.

Selecting literature to share with children means being aware of the child as reader or listener. Begin choosing books using what you know of children's preferences and of their developmental levels. The second half of the formula is selecting books of literary excellence, which is discussed in chapter 2.

Helping Parents Select Literature

As a childcare professional or primary-grade teacher, it is likely that you will find yourself being asked many questions by parents who value your experience. One topic of concern for parents is the selection of books and media appropriate for their children. There are various ways that you, individually, and the school or center where you work can assist parents. It is helpful to describe for parents the type of books that are generally appropriate for particular developmental levels and to show them examples of such books. For infants and toddlers up to 2 years of age, toy and board books are often good choices. Board books are durable, and young hands can turn the pages. They allow the children, who are in a stage of exploring the world through the senses—they will taste as well as look at a book—to participate actively. The pictures should be clear and uncluttered, ones that can be identified by the child and discussed by parent and child together. Helen Oxenbury's set of *I Can, I Hear, I See,* and *I Touch* (1995a, b, c, d) are good examples of board books that present clear illustrations of familiar objects and activities. Children of this age also respond to the sounds of language, and this is the time to introduce Mother Goose rhymes and books with patterned language.

Children from ages 2 to 5 can follow simple plots and are beginning to develop a sense of story. It is a good time to share books that have clear plots, such as *Trashy Town* (Zimmerman, 1999), in which Mr. Gilly is a trash collector who has the enviable task of driving the big blue garbage truck. Mr. Gilly collects garbage from the school, the park, and the pizza parlor. After Mr. Gilly has cleaned up the town, he takes his load of garbage to the dump and then goes home to take a bath. Preschoolers will enjoy the refrain: "dump it in, smash it down, drive around the Trashy Town." The story is clear, and it depicts a job with which young children are familiar and can understand.

Children from 2 to 5 years old are in a period of rapid growth in language. They respond to rhythm and repetition in language. This is a time to present traditional literature that has refrains or cumulative plot structure, such as *The Three Little Pigs*, *The Gingerbread Boy,* and *The Three Billy Goats Gruff.* Children can repeat the refrains, clap to the rhythm of the words, and participate as they hear the story read or told.

Children from 5 to 8 years are able to follow more complex stories that may have subplots. They are beginning to be able to distinguish between fantasy and reality, to generalize, to recognize different points of view, and to read for themselves. They notice details in both text and illustrations. This is a time to present a wide variety of picture books, some that are fantasy and some that are realism. Children still enjoy traditional tales with tales such as *Snow White, Rumpelstiltskin,* and *Cinderella* being favorites. Beginning-to-read books such as the *Henry and Mudge* series (Rylant) or early chapter books such as the Mercy Watson series (Di Camililo) give a new reader a chance to feel successful and to use his or her new skills. However, encourage parents to continue reading aloud to their children during this period, because many of the books enjoyed by primary-grade children are still above their reading level. In addition, the sharing of literature provides a period of closeness between parent and child.

You, as a teacher or childcare provider, will also be in a position to show the parents examples of what is being shared in the school or center. This can be done in a parent conference, where you can encourage the parent to browse through the room library, or by showing parents books, videos or DVDs, or CDs that have special appeal to their children. Children. Allow children to take books and media home to read or view with their parents, or send books home with suggestions of appropriate activities that parents might do with their children or topics related to the book that they might discuss.

A school or center can provide ways for parents to see what literature is available, either through special workshops or through a book fair. If teachers or childcare professionals are present at these functions, they can talk with the parents about appropriate literature. They may also have some input in the selection of which books will be discussed at a workshop or offered for sale at a book fair.

Schools or centers can also provide materials to parents that will aid them in selecting books and give suggestions for using books with their children. *Best Books for Children: Preschool through Grade 6* (Barr & Gillespie, 2005), *What Should I Read Aloud* (Anderson, 2007) and *The Read-Aloud Handbook* (Trelease, 2006) include annotated lists of books appropriate for young children. *How to Get Your Child to Love Reading: For Ravenous and Reluctant Readers Alike* (2003) by former teacher and school librarian Esme Raji Codell provides hundreds of easy and inventive ideas, innovative projects, creative activities, and inspiring suggestions that have been shared, tried, and proven with children from birth through eighth grade. Having these reference books available for parents to borrow would both build goodwill and encourage parents to select quality literature. The International Reading Association has a series of brochures for parents, including *Explore the Playground of Books: Tips for Parents* (1998) and *Making the Reading–Writing Connections: Tips for Parents of Young Learners* (1999), which give excellent advice in a very readable format and are available in English and Spanish at http://www.reading.org/publications/brochures/brochures.html. Teachers could make book lists available to parents as well. Local children's bookstores and public libraries can often help in providing book lists and brochures. Book lists are also available through the American Library Association at http://www.ala.org. Lists of recommended wordless books, concept books, predictable books, alphabet, counting, and beginning-to-read books are located throughout this chapter. Internet sites that give book reviews include http://www.kidsread.com and online bookstores.

Encourage parents to use their local libraries. They may find that story hours are presented on a regular basis. They can also find out what their children enjoy and provide a stimulus for reading if they take their children with them to the library and have the children select books themselves. The parent may also select some books so that there are a variety of types of literature to be shared at home. Young children can learn to browse at bookstores, seeing what appeals to them and handling books carefully. One mother boasts that her 4-year-old can occupy himself with books in a bookstore for 30 to 40 minutes. Of course, this is a mother who likes to read herself, who is hooked on bookstores, and who has shared both her love of literature and her interest in seeing new books with her child. When the child becomes restless, they leave the store, so that it remains a pleasant experience for them both.

Let parents know the importance of children owning books themselves. They might want to see which books are popular with their children and then buy those. They might also begin by purchasing books that are classics, such as Mother Goose and various fairy tales. A good collection of children's poetry is a necessity, too—*20th Century Children's Poetry* (Prelutsky, 1999), *The Random House Book of Poetry for Children* (Prelutsky, 1983), *Sing a Song of Popcorn: Every Child's Book of Poems* (de Regniers et al., 1988), and *Here's a Little Poem: A Very First Book of Poetry* (Yolen, 2007) are four good choices. Parents can designate a special place for the books so that the child knows that these are his or her books, a private library. Parents may purchase paperbacks as well as hardcover books. Parents might also look into magazine subscriptions or book clubs, so that new reading material will be arrivic on a regular basis. Some parents buy cassettes or CDs so that their children can hear favorite stories read again and again. For families who have a CD or cassette player in their car, listening to stories provides a valuable diversion during family trips.

Finally, talk with parents about techniques of reading aloud to children. Because they are reading to only one or two children at a time, they have the opportunity to listen to the children's responses during the story and to have them point to objects and words and take part in the reading. They should set the stage for reading by finding a quiet place, helping the child get comfortable, and holding the book so that the child can see the illustrations. Parents should begin the reading by letting the child look at the cover of the book and make comments about the story within, and during the reading they should encourage the child to respond. The child should have some control over the reading, perhaps turning the pages so that the listener determines when he or she is ready to continue. The child should also have the opportunity to select which books he or she would like to hear. If the child becomes restless, the parent should end the session. Children should be encouraged to talk about what they have heard and to participate as fully as possible in the sharing of books and poetry. In *Reading Magic: Why Reading Aloud to Our Children Will Change Their Lives Forever* (2001), best-selling picture-book author Mem Fox highlights the benefits of reading to preschoolers, even newborns, and gives suggestions for helping children to learn to read by themselves. Parents who share literature with their children are providing a base of understanding about the reading process, about human relations, and about the enjoyment that books can bring. You should give them all the help and encouragement you can.

SUMMARY

This book is designed to show the many ways in which literature can and does support the goals of early childhood education. At the center of any literature program for children is the literature itself and its contribution to the development of children's imaginations. Beyond this, reading regularly to children and engaging them in active response to literature supports their language, intellectual, personality, social, moral, aesthetic, and creative development.

To plan a literature program, you need to know what literature is available for children. Books for children vary in format and in genre. *Format* refers both to the physical features of a book, such as its paper, binding, and typography, and to the ratio and relationship of text and illustrations. *Genre* refers to the type of literature, whether prose or poetry, fiction or nonfiction, realism or fantasy. Teachers and childcare professionals may want to use research results about children's preferences in literature as a guide to the initial selection of literature to present, but they need to keep in mind that any one book or poem is a combination of many elements and that preferences will vary from individual to individual. In addition, each individual helps to create the meaning of a work through his or her own background, which influences that person's interpretation of what the author has written. From the wide range of literature available, teachers and childcare providers will select for sharing only what is of high literary merit.

You will be in a position to provide valuable assistance to parents in selecting books for their children. Information about which books are being used in the school or center, publications for parents, booklists, and techniques for sharing literature with the children will help parents give their children a rich literary background.

Extending Your Learning

1. Locate a hardcover and a paperback edition of the same book, such as *Make Way for Ducklings,* and compare the differences in both text and illustration and look at design features such as book covers and endpapers.

2. Go to both a bookstore and a drugstore or grocery store. Assess the range and quality of books for infants, toddlers, preschoolers and primary-grade children in each of the settings.

3. Rank five wordless or nearly wordless picture books by level of difficulty. Tell how you ranked each one.

4. Explain how you might use a specific alphabet, counting, or other concept book with a young child. Try to read board books and picture books in preparing for this extended learning activity.

5. Read collections of poetry by at least three of the poets mentioned in this chapter. Select poems that you would enjoy sharing with children.

6. Do an Internet search under the names of three authors or illustrators of books for young children.

7. Search the Internet for suggestions of books and activities that a parent and child might do together at home.

8. Create a database of books, videos or DVDs, and Web sites that you would suggest to parents.

REFERENCES

Professional References Cited

Anderson, Nancy. (2007). *What should I read aloud?* Newark, DE: International Reading Association.

Barr, Catherine and Gillespie, John. (2005). *Best books for children: Preschool through grade 6.* (8th ed.). Westport, CT: Libraries Unlimited.

Carlson, Ann. D. (1991). *The preschooler and the library.* Metuchen, NJ: Scarecrow.

Chatton, B. (2007). On beyond the *Cat in the hat*: Theodor Seuss Geisel Award-winning books for beginning readers. *Journal of Children's Literature, 33*(1), 47–51.

Codell, E. R. (2003). *How to get your child to love reading: For ravenous and reluctant readers alike.* New York: Algonquin.

Dutro, Elizabeth. (2001/2002). "But that's a girls' book!": Exploring gender boundaries in children's reading practices. *The Reading Teacher, 55*(4), 376–84.

Fox, M. (2001). *Reading magic: Why reading aloud to our children will change their lives forever.* San Diego, CA: Harvest Books/Harcourt.

Hadaway, N., Vardell, S. M., & Young, T. (2002). *Literature-based instruction with English language learners.* Boston: Allyn and Bacon.

Hickman, J. (1983). Everything considered: Response to literature in an elementary school setting. *Journal of Research and Development in Education, 16,* 8–13.

International Reading Association: Parent Brochures. (November, 1998). Retrieved February 25, 2008, from http://www.reading.org/resources/tools/parent.html

Kiefer, B. (1983). The responses of children in a combination first/second grade classroom to picture books in a variety of artistic styles. *Journal of Research and Development in Education, 13,* 14–20.

Monson, D., & Sebesta, S. (1991). Reading preferences. In J. Floor, J. Jensen, D. Lapp, & J. Squire (Eds.), *Handbook of Research on Teaching the English Language Arts* (pp. 664–673). New York: Macmillan.

Rosenblatt, L. (1978). *The reader, the text, the poem.* Carbondale: Southern Illinois University Press.

Shamir, A. & Korat, O. (2006). How to select CD-ROM storybooks for young children: The teacher's role. *The Reading Teacher, 59*(6), 532–543.

Trelease, J. (2006). *The read aloud handbook* (6th ed.). New York: Penguin.

Zeece, Pauline Davey. (1998). Dancing Words: Poetry for Young Children. *Early Childhood Education Journal, 26*(2), 101–106.

Children's Literature Cited

Ada, Alma Flor. (1997). *Gathering the Sun: An Alphabet in Spanish and English.* Ill. Simon Silva. English translation by Rosa Zubizarreta. New York: Lothrop.

Ahlberg, Janet, & Ahlberg, Allen. (1986). *The Jolly Postman.* Boston: Little, Brown.

Ahlberg, Janet, & Ahlberg, Allen. (1991). *The Jolly Christmas Postman.* Boston: Little, Brown.

Ahlberg, Janet, & Ahlberg, Allen. (1995). *The Jolly Pocket Postman.* Boston: Little, Brown.

Alda, Arlene. (1998). *Arlene Alda's 1 2 3: What Do You See?* Berkeley, CA: Tricycle.

Anno, Mitsumasa. (1977). *Anno's Counting Book.* New York: Crowell.

Brown, Margaret Wise. (2001). *Two Little Trains.* Ill. Leo and Diane Dillon. New York: HarperCollins.

Cameron, Ann. (1997). *More Stories Huey Tells.* Ill. Lis Toft. New York: Farrar, Straus & Giroux.

Carle, Eric. (1984). *The Very Busy Spider.* New York: Philomel.

Carle, Eric. (1994). *The Very Hungry Caterpillar* (board book). New York: Philomel.

Carle, Eric. (1999). *The Very Clumsy Click Beetle.* New York: Philomel.

Catalanotto, Peter. (2003). *Daisy 1, 2, 3.* New York: Atheneum.

Church, Caroline Jayne. (2002). *Do You Ears Hang Low?* New York: Scholastic.

Cooney, Barbara. (1982). *Miss Rumphius.* New York: Viking.

Cousins, Lucy. (2007). Maisy Big, Maisy Small: A Book of Opposites, New York: Walker.

Davis, Edith Kunhardt. (2001). *Tickle the Pig.* New York: Golden Books.

De Regniers, Beatrice Schenk. (1988). *Sing a Song of Popcorn: Every Child's Book of Poems.* New York: Scholastic.

dePaola, Tomie. (1997). *Strega Nona.* New York: Little Simon.

Ehlert, Lois. (1990). *Fish Eyes: A Book You Can Count On.* San Diego: Harcourt.

Feelings, Muriel. (1971). *Moja Means One.* Ill. Tom Feelings. New York: Dial.

Fleming, Denise. (1998). *Mama Cat Has Three Kittens.* New York: Holt.

Grossman, Bill. (1996). *My Little Sister Ate One Hare.* Ill. Kevin Hawkes. New York: Crown.

Hall, Katy. (2002). *Dino Riddles.* Ill. Nicole Rubel. New York: Dial.

Henkes, Kevin. (2007). *A Good Day.* New York: Greenwillow.

Hill, Eric. (2007). *Spot's Playtime Pop-Up.* New York: Putnam.

Hoban, Tana. (1986). *Red, Blue, Yellow Shoe.* New York: Greenwillow.

Hoban, Tana. (1997). *Look Book.* New York: Greenwillow.

Holabird, K. (2003). *Angelina Ballerina's Invitation to the Ballet.* Ill. Helen Craig. Middleton, WI: Pleasant Company.

Hutchins, Pat. (1982). *1 Hunter.* New York: Greenwillow.

Jenkins, Steve. (2004). *Actual Size.* Boston: Houghton Mifflin.

Kitamura, Satoshi. (1986). *When Sheep Cannot Sleep.* New York: Farrar, Straus & Giroux.

Lehman, Barbara. (2004). *The Red Book.* Boston: Houghton Mifflin.

Lobel, Arnold. (1970). *Frog and Toad Are Friends.* New York: Harper.

Lyon, George. (1998). *Counting on the Woods.* Ill. Ann Olson. New York: DK Publishing, Inc.

MacLachlan, Patricia. (1985). *Sarah Plain and Tall.* New York: HarperCollins.

Martin, Bill Jr. (1983). *Brown Bear, Brown Bear, What Do You See?* Ill Eric Carle. New York: Holt.

Martin, Bill, Jr. (1999). *A Beasty Story.* Ill. Steven Kellogg. San Diego, CA: Harcourt.

Martin, Bill, Jr. (2007). *Baby Bear, Baby Bear, What Do You See?* Ill. Eric Carle. New York: Holt.

McCloskey, Robert. (1941). *Make Way for Ducklings.* New York: Viking.

McDonnell, Flora. (1997). *Flora McDonnell's ABC.* Cambridge, MA: Candlewick.

McLimans, David. (2006). *Gone Wild: An Endangered Animal Alphabet.* New York: Walker.

Micklethwait, Lucy. (1992). *I Spy: An Alphabet in Art.* New York: Greenwillow.

Mills, Claudia. (2002). *7 × 9 = Trouble!* New York: Farrar, Straus & Giroux.

Oxenbury, Helen. (1995a). *I Can.* Cambridge, MA: Candlewick.

Oxenbury, Helen. (1995b). *I Hear.* Cambridge, MA: Candlewick.

Oxenbury, Helen. (1995c). *I See.* Cambridge, MA: Candlewick.

Oxenbury, Helen. (1995d). *I Touch.* Cambridge, MA: Candlewick.

Oxenbury, Helen. (1999). *All Fall Down.* New York: Little Simon.

Parks, Rosa with Haskins, Jim. (1998). *I Am Rosa Parks.* Ill. Wil Clay. New York: Dial.

Pomeroy, Diana. (1997). *Wildflower ABC: An Alphabet of Potato Prints.* San Diego: Harcourt.

Prelutsky, Jack. (1983). *The Random House Book of Poetry for Children.* Ill. Arnold Lobel. New York: Random House.

Prelutsky, Jack. (1999). *20th Century Children's Poetry.* Ill. Meilo So. New York: Random House.

Prelutsky, Jack. (2007). *My Parents Think I'm Sleeping.* Ill Yossi Abolafia. New York: HarperCollins.

Rappaport, Doreen. (2001). *Martin's Big Words: The Life of Dr. Martin Luther King, Jr.* Ill. Bryan Collier. New York: Hyperion.

Rathmann, Peggy. (1998). *10 Minutes till Bedtime.* New York: Putnam.

Rohmann, Eric. (2002). *My Friend Rabbit.* Brookfield, CT: Roaring Brook Press.

Rylant, Cynthia. (1998). *Henry and Mudge and the Starry Night: The Seventeenth Book of Their Adventures.* Ill. Suçie Stevenson. New York: Simon.

Sabuda, Robert. (1997). *Cookie Count: A Tasty Pop-Up.* New York: Simon & Schuster.

SAMI. (2006). *Flip-a-Face: Colors.* San Francisco: Blue Apple/Chronicle.

Schories, Pat. (2004). *Breakfast for Jack.* Asheville, NC: Front Street.

Schwartz, Alvin. (1984). *In a Dark, Dark Room.* Ill. Dirk Zimmer. New York: Harper.

Seeger, Laura Vaccaro. (2006). *Black? White! Day? Night!* New Milford, CT: Roaring Brook Press.

Seuss, Dr. (1957). *The Cat in the Hat.* New York: Random House.

Shannon, George. (1996). *Tomorrow's Alphabet.* Ill. Donald Crews. New York: Greenwillow.

Shannon, George. (2005). *White is for Blueberry.* Ill. Laura Dronzek. New York: Greenwillow.

Simont, Marc. (2001). *The Stray Dog.* New York: HarperCollins.

Steig, William. (1982). *Dr. De Soto.* New York: Farrar, Straus & Giroux.

Taback, Simms. (2000). *Joseph Had a Little Overcoat.* New York: Viking.

Thong, Roseanne. (2001). *Red Is a Dragon: A Book of Colors.* Ill. Grace Lin. San Francisco: Chronicle.

Van Fleet, Matthew. (1995). *Fuzzy Yellow Ducklings.* New York: Dial.

Van Leeuwen, Jean. (2007). *Amanda Pig, First Grader.* Ill. Ann Schweninger. New York: Dial.

Waber, Bernard. (1997). *Bearsie Bear and the Surprise Sleepover Party.* Boston: Houghton Mifflin.

Walker, Sally. (1998). *The 18 Penny Goose.* Ill. Ellen Beier. New York: HarperCollins.

Wiesner, David. (1999). *Sector 7.* New York: Clarion.

Wildsmith, Brian. (1996). *Brian Wildsmith's ABC.* Long Island City, NY: Star Bright.

Yolen, Jane. (2007). *Here's a Little Poem: A Very First Book of Poetry.* Cambridge, MA: Candlewick.

Yorinks, A. (1986). *Hey, Al.* Ill. R. Egielski. New York: Farrar, Straus & Giroux.

Zimmerman, Andrea & Clemesha, David. (1999). *Trashy Town.* Ill. Dan Yaccarino. New York: HarperCollins.

CHAPTER TWO

JENSYN, Age 4
Sharks

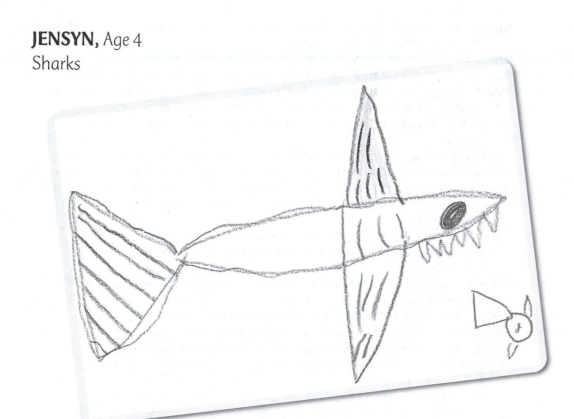

Jensyn (age 4) became obsessed with sea and shark books over a year ago and it still hasn't subsided. Some of her favorite nonfiction books are *Sharks and Other Dangers of the Deep* by Simon Mugford (2005); *Rub-a-dub-dub* by Linda Ashman (2003), *Faucet Fish* by Fay Robinson (2005); and *A House for Hermit Crab* by Eric Carle (1997). Jensyn said that "the little fish doesn't know the shark is coming to get him." She demonstrated her knowledge that the shark is the predator in most cases. Jensyn illustrates the perspective of both shark and fish.

Evaluating Literature for Children

Books shared with children should represent the best by both literary and artistic standards. Some help in judging books can be found in reviews of new books that appear in journals such as *The Horn Book, Language Arts, The Reading Teacher,* and *School Library Journal* or in publications devoted entirely to book reviews, such as *Publisher's Weekly* and *Booklist.* Reading these will allow you to see how some critics apply literary criteria. The Caldecott Award, given each year by a committee of the American Library Association to the illustrator of the most distinguished American picture book for children, records what one group of school and public librarians, children's literature educators, and book reviewers consider to be outstanding illustrations. A list of the Caldecott winners and honor books is given in the appendix. The Theodor Seuss Geisel Award is also presented by the American Library Association and recognizes beginning-to-read books. Chapter 1 presented the Geisel Award winners and honor books. Because libraries tend to purchase books that librarians judge to be of literary merit, talking with local librarians may help you discover how they apply standards of literary excellence.

But rather than rely totally on others' opinions, learn to evaluate children's books for yourself. This skill will enable you to feel secure using a book you haven't heard about from others and is requisite for you to be able to help children develop taste in literature.

EVALUATING FICTION

Literary Elements

One way of analyzing fiction is to look at the literary elements that make up the selection. Strengths and weaknesses in plot, setting, characterization, theme, and style of writing can be identified.

Plot   The plot of a story is what happens in it. In *Knuffle Bunny: A Cautionary Tale* (Willems, 2004), toddler Trixie eagerly accompanies her daddy on an errand. They walk down the block and through the park and finally arrive at the laundromat. There, Trixie helps put the laundry into the washing machine and even gets to put the money into the coin slots. On their walk home, Trixie suddenly realizes something and desperately attempts to communicate with her daddy. "Aggle, flaggle, klabble." But her daddy doesn't understand and soon both Trixie and her daddy are frustrated and unhappy. Once they arrive home, Trixie's mommy asks, "Where's Knuffle Bunny?" Immediately, the entire family scurries back to the laundromat to rescue the beloved bunny, prompting Trixie to utter her first words, "Knuffle Bunny!!!"

A good plot is interesting. It builds suspense so that the reader will want to know what is going to happen next. This story builds: from the introduction, in which Trixie and her daddy are off to do an errand, to accomplishing the task, to the universal signs of toddler distress. Trixie's daddy reacts the way that most parents do when a child is having a trantrum in a public place—he picks up his bawling child and carries her home. The climax occurs when child and bunny are reunited and Trixie speaks her first recognizable words.

A good plot builds logically. There are causal relationships that connect the events, and these are plausible within the context of the story. Even though many children may not have experienced venturing to a laundromat, they will relate to the situation of a treasured stuffed animal that is lost or left behind. The cause and effect of Trixie becoming upset and her daddy telling her not to be "fussy" is also plausible.

Plots in picture books and chapter books vary in complexity. There may be only one problem or several to be solved. There may be 2 characters or 20. Occasionally, there will be parallel plots, two story lines weaving together by the conclusion. However simple or complex the plot is, the events should be logically related to one another.

Setting   Setting, where and when a story takes place, should be an integral part of the story, not just a backdrop that could be changed without affecting the plot. The setting for *Knuffle Bunny* is a contemporary Brooklyn neighborhood and, more importantly, the laundromat. In this case, the setting is such that it allows Trixie and her daddy to walk through the park and past a school to arrive at their destination. Willems uses sepia-toned photographs of his neighborhood, framed in pale green, superimposed with bright cartoon drawings of the characters.

If the story has a specific setting, with the exact time and place identified, the description should be accurate. Other settings may be more generally depicted as being located in a town, in the country, or "long ago in a faraway land." Even when location is not precisely spelled out, the reader should be given a taste of what life is like at the place and at that time.

Characterization   Characterization, how the author portrays each character, is often what makes a book memorable. Children know Madeline, Olivia, Arthur, Curious George, Junie B. Jones, and Horrible Harry because these characters are clearly delineated. The reader knows what they like and dislike, how they will behave in a given situation, and what is special about them. They have more than one dimension, so the reader can respond to the many aspects of their personalities. There are some likable things they do or think and some not so likable. A good author lets the reader know about characters by showing what they do, what they think, or what they say and sometimes by showing what others say or think about them or how they are treated.

Even though Trixie communicates in what some might term hilarious gibberish, readers still understand her wide-eyed pleasure at putting the coins in the washing machine, her annoyance with her clueless father, and her sheer joy in being reunited with Knuffle Bunny. They will also recognize that daddy is responding to her, first with patience and then with total exasperation. It's clear that toddler and father have a loving relationship, even when things sometimes go wrong. This relationship is depicted once again in *Knuffle Bunny Too: A Case of Mistaken Identity* (2007).

In some stories the characters change or develop as a result of what has happened to them. It is difficult to have much character development in books for young children, simply because the stories are fairly short in both picture-book and chapter-book formats. There is little time to fully delineate a character, then have a believable change take place.

Theme   The theme of a book is its underlying idea. It may be a general theme, such as friendship or courage, or it may be more specific and stated in sentence form, such as, "Even though persons seem alike, each one is unique" or "We should make our own decisions, and not let others make them for us." A story may have no theme, one theme, or more than one theme. One idea underlying *Knuffle Bunny* is the inability to communicate with others. Another is that of cherished items being lost. None of these themes intrudes on the plot. If there is a theme, it should be an integral part of the story but should not overpower the story. There should be no need for closing comments by the author to make certain the theme is understood clearly.

Style of Writing   The style of writing—which words are chosen and how they are arranged—helps create the mood of the story. Willems sometimes uses short sentences along with speech bubbles to emphasize action and feeling.

> Aggle flaggle klabble! said Trixie again.
> Blaggle plabble! Wumby flappy?! Snurp.
> "Now please don't get fussy," said her daddy.
> Well she had no choice . . .
> Trixie bawled. Waaaa!
> She went boneless.
> She did everything she could to show how unhappy she was.   *(n.p.)*

The vocabulary gives a full picture of what is happening in a succinct manner. What reader or listener won't have a visual image of the physical reaction of going "boneless"?

There is humor in the story, both in text and illustrations. On the title pages, three framed illustrations show Trixie's parents getting married, when she was a newborn, and finally being transported in a baby carrier. At the laundromat, Trixie "helps" her daddy put laundry into the machine by dancing around wearing a pair of pants on her head, a sock on one hand, a bra in the other. Even Trixie's ongoing efforts to convey her loss to her father presents some comedic moments. Readers of Willems's other books, particularly *Don't Let the Pigeon Drive the Bus* (2003) will notice that as the family members go in pursuit of the bunny, they pass by a man wearing a pigeon shirt. The characters' faces and actions in *Knuffle Bunny* are highly expressive and corroborate the succinct text.

Other authors, especially in chapter books, may use descriptive passages that achieve the same end of advancing the plot but give a tale a slower pace. The style should be appropriate to the story being told. It should appear so natural that readers are not distracted by it and are scarcely aware of how it is functioning.

Plot, setting, characterization, theme, and style should be mutually compatible, each complementing the others. In addition to these marks of good writing, books for children should be free of stereotypes and of condescension in tone. Stereotypes generally

The plot, setting, characterization, and illustrations in a picture book should be mutually compatible.
(From KNUFFLE BUNNY by Mo Willems. Text and illustrations copyright © 2004 by Mo Willems. Reprinted by Permission of Hyperion Books for Children. All Rights Reserved.)

indicate poor writing and are intellectually and socially offensive. Stereotypes present a person not as an individual, but as a representative of a group whose members are deemed to possess the same characteristics. A condescending tone should be avoided because it is an insult to children.

Coherence

Another way of evaluating fiction is to look at the overall coherence of the story. There should be a sense of completeness when the book is finished. The author has taken or created an incident, developed it, and structured it. The story will not have the lags, random happenings, or intrusions that characterize real life. It should flow in a meaningful way, with each part related to other parts and to the whole. Storytelling is recognized as one of the ways in which we make sense of our lives and the lives of others.

Coherence depends on a carefully structured plot and compatibility between the individual elements of plot, setting, characterization, theme, and style of writing. *Knuffle Bunny: A Cautionary Tale* works because the plot revolves around the frustration Trixie feels in trying to communicate with her daddy. The brief dialogue and characters' actions reinforce elements of characterization and advance the plot. The style of writing and the illustrations contribute to the understanding of the characters and to the mood of the entire story. The book presents a coherent whole.

Just Right Stew (English, 1998) uses a different but equally effective structure. Victoria, who tells the story, is sitting on the kitchen floor as Mama and Aunt Rose cook a special birthday dinner for her grandmother, Big Mama. They are discussing the pot of oxtail stew that needs something else to taste like the stew Big Mama makes. Rose suggests dill, so they send Victoria to get some from Cousin Shug. This begins the pattern. Rose and Mama think of spices that might be the missing ingredient and send Victoria to get them. Then, as other aunts arrive, each adds what she believes to be the needed spice. Finally, Big Mama herself slips into the kitchen and adds sugar, the secret ingredient that only she and Victoria know. The stew is a success, and all relax once Big Mama announces at the table that this is the best stew she's ever tasted. The structure is repetitive, with each unsuccessful attempt to fix the stew adding to the suspense and to the humor, until Big Mama herself makes the stew perfect. The ending is particularly satisfying because of the surprise element that Victoria has known all along what needed to be added.

Literary elements reinforce one another. The repetition of the plot is echoed in the comments of the characters, as when one adds an ingredient, another always expresses doubt that the solution has been found. The variety of the comments adds interest, and the ways the statements are phrased fit with the delineation of the characters and the action of the story. Miss Helena, the elderly neighbor who lives alone and always wants to give Victoria candy, ponders and says slowly that she doesn't think she's heard of lemon pepper in oxtail stew. Mama, in contrast, shouts that it "ain't cumin" when her sister Violet, having arrived in a rush, insists that it is and wants to add cumin herself.

When you finish a book, first ask yourself if you have a sense of satisfaction, of a complete experience. Then go back and look at a book carefully to discern what it is that has or has not given coherence to the work as a whole.

Integrity

Good children's literature contains freshness and honesty. It may touch children's emotions; it may stimulate their imaginations. It may make them think about new ideas or think about old ideas in new ways. The child's world is expanded through the inventiveness of the author and the illustrator. *Knuffle Bunny: A Cautionary Tale* uses concise, humorous, and deftly told narrative to relate the frustration of a toddler not being able to communicate with one parent, whereas the other parent recognizes the dilemma immediately. *Just Right Stew* takes a family gathering and builds it into a mystery to be solved and a study in human relations. All bring a creative approach to their topics and an honest presentation of the story.

EVALUATING NONFICTION

Standards for nonfiction and biography should be applied as rigorously as are standards for fiction. Like fiction, nonfiction should be well written and interesting as well as accurate.

Organization

Good writing in nonfiction is clear and informative. There is a careful and logical organization to the material being presented. The table of contents and index that are standard in nonfiction for older readers are sometimes omitted in books for young children, and the text may appear more like a story than a textbook. The organization, however, should follow a pattern that helps to make the content understandable to younger readers.

Vivian French, in *Growing Frogs* (2000), which is available in hardcover, paperback and big book formats, uses a narrative that provides a chronological approach to her topic. She describes the process for collecting frog spawn, placing it in a fish tank with pond water, watching the eggs hatching into tadpoles, and seeing how tadpoles eventually turn into frogs. French carefully indicates the passage of time through both text and illustration. Gail Gibbons, in *Marshes & Swamps* (1998b), uses a pattern of general to specific and then back to general. First, she defines both marshes and swamps as forms of wetlands, then she writes about freshwater marshes and saltwater marshes and, finally, freshwater swamps and mangrove swamps. Each example is described in detail, with examples of the plants and animals that live in that ecosystem. She concludes by describing the importance of wetlands and how they can be protected. A flowchart of *Growing Frogs* would be a single line with items on it; a chart of *Marshes & Swamps* would have a single line (wetlands) branching into two lines (marshes and swamps); then these two would branch again, each into freshwater and saltwater. Finally, all would join into a single line at the conclusion. Both patterns and organizations are clear and logical.

Nonfiction books have changed over the past decade in regard to format, font, quality of illustrations, and subject matter. *Surprising Sharks* (Davies, 2003) presents an interesting topic by organizing information about sharks according to size, shape, and behavior. Varying print size emphasizes concepts and creates drama and aesthetic interest. Sharks are well labeled with interesting facts about each one. James Croft's acrylic and pastel illustrations on double-page spreads illustrate the exapansiveness of the ocean. The drawing of the shark both inside and out will certainly capture children's attention and prompt drawings of their own. Davies also includes an index and additional facts about sharks at the conclusion of the book. Author Laurence Pringle approaches the same subject very differently. *Sharks! Strange and Wonderful* (2001) contains realistic acrylic paintings by Meryl Henderson with lighter shades of blue. The text is not as brief as *Surprising Sharks* and the font does not vary. The information is clearly written, and many more sharks are included. Pringle focuses on their physical capabilities and behaviors, their importance in the food chain, and the problems faced from human overfishing. This book is intended for a little older audience and does not contain a table of contents or index. The Davies book is a good introduction to sharks for toddlers and preschoolers because it contains less text and bright, colorful illustrations. The Pringle book is a good choice for primary-grade students who might use it for research as well as enjoyment.

Accurate Presentation of Facts

Factual accuracy is one of the most important criteria to consider when choosing nonfiction books. Nonfiction for any age level should not contain misinformation nor oversimplify a topic to the point of inaccuracy. Look at concept books for infants and toddlers with the same critical eye that you use for all nonfiction. These beginning informational books should be accurate in the information they give and in the examples they use to illustrate a concept. Nonfiction picture-book author and illustrator Gail Gibbons is known for her succinct text and colorful watercolor illustrations. *The Art Box* (1998a) introduces the contents of an art box and describes the different tools and supplies artists use to create their work. It is clear that Gibbons's focus is on basic tools artists use rather than attempting to present all tools and supplies. It is understandable that extensive information is omitted in this picture book for very young children.

Look for what is excluded as well as what is included. Although not a direct misstatement of fact, leaving out essential information can be just as misleading. Authors writing about broad topics must make choices, of course, and it is impossible to include everything. Nicola Davies and Laurence Pringle, the two authors who wrote about sharks, had to select specific facts about sharks, and in some cases they chose different ones.

Nonfiction should be clear about when a statement is of a factual nature and when it is an opinion or a value position. The difficulty arises when an author gives an opinion as though it were fact. In one book, for example, an author writing about beavers states that many have been killed for their fur, then writes that this is sad, and continues to say that beaver dams help control floods, embedding her opinion among the facts and using the same tone and style of writing to express it. The reason for the sadness about beavers being killed is not stated. It might be implied from the text that the reason is that their dams are needed for flood control. Some people might agree with the sadness but base it on a value position that says that the killing of animals is wrong. Still others might worry that beavers might become extinct. Value positions related to nonfiction need to be included because they are a part of understanding a topic, but they should be identified as such.

Two other problems that sometimes occur in nonfiction are the inclusion of anthropomorphism and teleological explanations. Anthropomorphism is the giving of human feelings and thoughts to animals or to inanimate objects. Some illustrations in *Surprising Sharks* show slightly anthropomorphized creatures but not to an extent that readers cannot glean basic anatomical features. If Davies had indicated that a shark "felt" this way, it would not be acceptable in a book of nonfiction. Teleological explanations assume that all of nature works according to one grand plan, often with "Mother Nature" guiding it. Whatever happens, it is because that is the way Mother Nature works. If you find yourself saying, "Isn't that cute?" about a nonfiction picture book, you should reevaluate it.

Finally, be aware that fiction books may also be used to present factual information that you might expect to find only in a book of nonfiction. The books by Joanna Cole and Bruce Degen about a magic school bus delight children with their stories while presenting accurate and detailed information. In *The Magic School Bus and the Science Fair Expedition* (2006), Ms. Frizzle and her students travel back in time to visit a variety of scientists. The science fair projects aren't going well, especially when Ralphie's ants escape and the other students are lacking in ideas for their own projects. Ms. Frizzle suggests a trip to a nearby museum for inspiration. There they discover a cardboard school bus, and they are off on yet another wild, but educational, adventure. As in previous books in this series, homework pages provide concrete information on scientific inquiry and speech bubbles add a bit of humor to the story. In *The Magic School Bus and the Electric Field Trip* (1998), Ms. Frizzle takes her class through high-voltage wires from a power plant to the library, to Jo's Diner, and to Phoebe's house. They learn about electricity as a source of light and of heat and how electricity powers motors. The fantasy of the trip and accurate science information are combined. Author Cole and illustrator Degen have expanded Ms. Frizzle's quest for learning into the area of social studies by traveling back in time to ancient China in *Ms. Frizzle's Adventures: Imperial China* (2005). These types of books demand a double evaluation—one for their effectiveness as a fiction story and another for the accuracy of the facts presented.

Current Information

Books of nonfiction that you use should present current information. You should pay attention to the copyright date and the data themselves. Obviously some areas are changing more quickly than others, and so the topic itself may alert you. It is no surprise to find that a book on computers, *How to Talk to Your Computer* (Simon, 1985), is outdated in terms of today's computer usage. It is not factually inaccurate, but the emphasis is on computer languages and programming. A more recent book that focuses on electronic communications, e-mail, and the Internet would be more useful. When a field is changing rapidly, it is particularly important to select recently published books and to alert children to the date of publication when you are using books that are older.

However, an "old" topic does not mean that new information is not being acquired and that recent information is not necessary. Aliki has written many carefully researched books about dinosaurs. In *My Visit to the Dinosaurs* (1969), her protagonist describes seeing the skeleton of a brontosaurus. Later there is an illustration of how the brontosaurus is thought to have looked and accompanying text. In a 1981 book, *Digging Up Dinosaurs* (Aliki, 1981), the character sees a skeleton of a dinosaur in a museum and says that she has seen an apatosaurus. In one small drawing the dinosaur is labeled "apatosaurus," with "brontosaurus" in parentheses, and in a cartoon speech balloon, the character explains that although apatosaurus is its real name, some people call it a brontosaurus. By 1988, Aliki referred to it only as apatosaurus (*Dinosaur Bones,* Aliki, 1988). This alteration in terminology reflects new knowledge about a subject we may not think of as "changing" and demonstrates the need to be aware of when a nonfiction book was published, no matter what the topic. Children can locate other books about dinosaurs, such as *Boy, Were We Wrong About Dinosaurs!* (Kudlinski, 2005), with more recent copyright dates and then compare that information with Aliki's books as well.

EVALUATING POETRY

Poetry takes careful reading. There is a compactness of language—every word counts. The sound of the language as it is read aloud is vital. The rhythm should be strong and natural. Even free verse, with no rhyme, has a rhythm to it. The rhyme, if it is a rhyming poem, should have a pattern. There may be a steady beat, as in "The Little Turtle," by Vachel Lindsay (1986).

> There was a little turtle,
> He lived in a box,
> He swam in a puddle,
> He climbed on the rocks.
> He snapped at a mosquito,
> He snapped at a flea,
> He snapped at a minnow,
> And he snapped at me.
> He caught the mosquito,
> He caught the flea,
> He caught the minnow,
> But he didn't catch me.

p. 20

Here the rhythm seems to sing. The poet has used language for its sound as well as for its meaning. This may be one of the reasons why this poem and others like it are considered classics and have been introduced to young children by both parents and teachers.

The rhyme in poems should not take precedence over the meaning. That is, words should not be stated in awkward order just so the last words will rhyme. Nor should there be lines included because they rhyme that would not make sense if found in a prose selection.

The language in poetry should be fresh. It may show a new way of looking at something or a new way of telling about it. Poetry often uses figurative language and makes comparisons. It relies heavily on imagery, describing how experiences are perceived by the senses. Read poems to see if the comparison and descriptions make sense and if they are vivid.

The literary standards by which poetry for children is judged are no less demanding than those for adult poetry. A poem that is poor by adult standards is poor for children as well. Nor is there any need to talk down to children, or to make poems cute or easy. To do so is to show a basic disrespect for the child reader or listener. Teachers have a responsibility to children to select poems that have literary merit.

EVALUATING ILLUSTRATIONS

In *The Potential of Picturebooks* (1995), Barbara Kiefer writes that critics must begin with the verbal text of a picture book when they are judging it because that is where the artist usually begins. However, "once we have some idea of the theme of the book, the motifs and moods, characters, setting, and events, we can evaluate how well the artist has chosen artistic elements, principles, and conventions to convey those meanings visually and how those artistic or stylistic choices have contributed to the overall aesthetic experience of the book" (p. 120). This is what you will be doing as you select picture books, looking at the overall effectiveness of the total book. And as you look at a variety of books more carefully, you will become better at analyzing the art as well as the text.

Proximity to Text

Illustrations in a picture book should be near the text they depict, either on the same page or on the opposite page. Children look at the picture as the story is being read and, if they are reading the book by themselves, may use the pictures as clues to meaning. If the story is to be unified, then text and illustrations must appear together. In books of poetry, the illustration should be tied to the poem by its placement on the page as well as by its content. This is particularly true if several poems appear on a single page.

Developing the Text

Illustrations should match both the description and the action in the text. When the text says that Trixie has gone "boneless," the reader sees the toddler hanging limp in her father's arms. The illustrator, however, is free to add any actions or details that might extend the story, develop the setting, or enhance the characterization. In his text, Willems doesn't describe the people he and Trixie pass to and from the laundromat, but by viewing the pages carefully, the reader gains insight as to the setting as well as humor.

The illustrator need not show everything that is mentioned in the text. The basic criterion is that there be no conflict between text and illustration. Sometimes illustrations can be confusing rather than helpful, even if there is no direct conflict. For example, illustrations that combine realism with fantasy when the text does not or that portray elements of setting that are inconsistent with one another make comprehension of the story more difficult.

Capturing the Emotional Link

Canadian illustrator Ian Wallace explains how he attempts to capture the emotional link that ties the reader to the story:

> To discover the emotional link of a story, the illustrator must understand all levels on which the story functions: intellectual, physical, psychological, and spiritual. This link is then made by a variety of means: appropriate media, color, changing perspectives, shape of the illustrations, shape of the book, style of type, white space around the type and each of the drawings, and the position of each character in relation to one another. Nothing must be left to chance. *(1989, p. 7)*

David Shannon's semiautobiographical story, *No, David!* (1998) clearly depict David's emotions whether he is being told to "Be quiet," "Not in the house, David," or

Shannon uses energetic and wacky full-color acrylic paintings to portray a lively and imaginative boy whose stick-figure body conveys every nuance of anger, exuberance, defiance, and, best of all, the reassurance of his mother's love.

(Cover illustration from NO, DAVID! By David Shannon. Copyright © 1998 by David Shannon. Reprinted by permission of Scholastic Inc.)

"No, no, no." Although many of David's emotions are shown on his face, the reader can infer other emotions as David gleefully runs naked down the street (being shown only from behind) or when he sits dejectedly in the corner facing the wall for "time out." Children know immediately how David is feeling and will want to offer their own stories about misbehaving.

As you examine the art in children's books, consider those aspects of art that develop an emotional link between story and reader. That is, see if the media, colors, changing perspectives, style of illustration, use of white space, and shape of the book and illustrations assist in telling the story well.

Materials developed by John Stewig (1988) for teaching children about illustrations indicate that children are frequently directed to look at a particular illustration and say what they notice about it. This is a good beginning for anyone assessing the art in a picture book. What stands out? What do you notice about the colors being used? Are they intense? Subdued? Natural? Arbitrary? What do you notice about lines? Are they thin or thick, straight or curved, harsh or soft? What about shapes? Do they overlap/Do some dominate? What is unique about the illustrations? Do they add humor? Imply action? What is the effect of the illustrations?

When readers view Ian Falconer's illustrations of *Olivia* (2000), an irresistible pig with limitless energy, they will notice that she is constantly on the move while showcasing her talents and dreaming big dreams. Falconer's charcoal illustrations with dollops of bright red are highly amusing. When the text states, "She is *very* good at wearing people out," we see Olivia engaged in a variety of activities through 13 black-and-white vignettes, with an occasional splash of red. Falconer illustrates Olivia's ongoing sense of movement until eventually, "She even wears herself out." The artist uses lines to convey Olivia's movement and emotion. These lines also enable the readers' eyes to move across the page. The use of white space is effective in displaying the vignettes and the full scenes. The focus is always on Olivia, and that is simply the story's theme.

The illustrations in *Olivia* are effective as art and in combination with the brief text. The style and the medium are highly unique and eye-catching. The spacious design of the book, the clever illustrations, the humorous storyline, and the opportunity for readers to see a little of themselves in Olivia make this Caldecott Honor book one to revisit for repeated readings. *Olivia* makes the emotional link that Wallace describes. It is true to the mood and content of the text, blending words and pictures effectively. The cartoon-style illustrations of *Knuffle Bunny* are suited to that humorous story, yet are completely different in style and technique from *Olivia*.

Think for a minute of how you picture the character of Goldilocks and what you think the bears look like. If you look at the illustrations from three versions of *Goldilocks and the Three Bears,* you will see that each presents the story through a different style. First look at Jan Brett's (1987) version, which incorporates numerous details into her illustrations as well as into the borders, clothing, and expressions of the characters. Then view the old-fashioned illustrations in Jim Aylesworth's version of *Goldilocks and the Three Bears* (2003), illustrated by Barbara McClintock, which feature hilariously exaggerated facial expressions within delicate framed borders. Finally, explore the oil-over-acrylic paintings that enhance the story in *Goldilocks and the Three Bears* (2007), written by Caralyn Buehner and illustrated by Mark Buehner. This time the yellow-haired visitor is a rope-jumping Goldilocks wearing cowboy boots. As you read the three retellings, you will find that they differ in tone and language. The Brett and Aylesworth versions use more traditional wording; Buehner uses more contemporary wording and invites readers to find the hidden cat, rabbit, and Tyrannosaurus rex in each picture. Brett's and Aylesworth's Goldilocks liked the porridge so much that she "ate" it all up; Buehner's "devours" it.

Brett's bears go for a walk, rather matter-of-factly, while their porridge is cooling. Aylesworth's bears leave by the front door as the porridge is cooling off on their kitchen table, and Buehner's Mama Bear cooks a new pot of porridge (soon after Goldilocks skedaddles), which Papa and Baby Bear exclaim is "just right." Each set of illustrations is compatible with the story as told, and all three sets extend and enhance the text.

Appropriateness of Illustrations

The purpose for which the book was designed can help define criteria for evaluating the illustrations. In alphabet books, used particularly with toddlers to name objects, the illustrations should be clear and uncluttered. If the alphabet book is designed to emphasize the sound or sounds made by each letter, then the illustrations must be accurate. That is, *s* should not be represented by an object such as shoe, because even though the word does begin with *s,* it is the sound of the *sh* blend that children hear. If the book is designed to help children learn to count and recognize numerals, then the illustrations must show the objects clearly. The child should know what is to be counted. There should be no confusing background, no questions about whether it is the bugs or the legs on the bugs to be counted. In nonfiction, the illustrations must help convey the facts or concepts being presented. This means that diagrams must make a concept clearer, that photographs must convey information as well as beauty, and that drawings must help the reader understand. Illustrations in nonfiction can be categorized by the degree of representationality (Kerper, 1998). Photographs, for example, are usually highly representational, showing the object's features as they appear naturally. Diagrams that combine pictures with labels are less representational and more abstract, and tables and charts are the least representational and the most abstract. Kerper writes that

> Nonfiction books for young children frequently contain visual displays such as photographs and pictures that fall at the high level of representationality end of the continuum. Their closer connection to the real world makes them appropriate for the cognitive development of the intended audience.   *(1998, p. 64)*

Photographs should be of high technical quality. For example, Peter Greste uses a high-speed photographic technique to capture *Owen and Mzee: The True Story of a Remarkable Friendship* (Hatkoff, 2006), which tells of a baby hippo befriended by a 130-year-old tortoise following the 2004 tsunami. Bruce McMillan explains in his foreword to *Salmon Summer* (1998) that the pictures were taken in the Kodiak National Wildlife Refuge in the summer of 1996. He stayed at a fishing camp with the family he photographed in this story of 9-year-old Alex, a native Aleut, as he and his family fished for salmon.

Diagrams vary in complexity, from simple labeling of objects or parts of objects to cutaway or cross-sectional drawings. They should clarify or extend the information in the text. Of particular interest in nonfiction is the way in which scale is shown or whether it is shown at all. In *Poison Dart Frogs* (1998), Dewey gives the sizes of three different kinds of these frogs and then illustrates them above a ruler, with a notation that the scale is in inches. The frogs are thus shown life size. Often an artist will include in the illustration something whose size is known—such as a hand holding a baby mouse or a car parked next to a redwood tree—or may label the size of the object. The illustrations help the reader visualize not only the subject itself but also the subject in context.

Captions, although not essential, can make photographs, diagrams, maps, tables, and other ways of presenting data much clearer to the reader. They may also help to

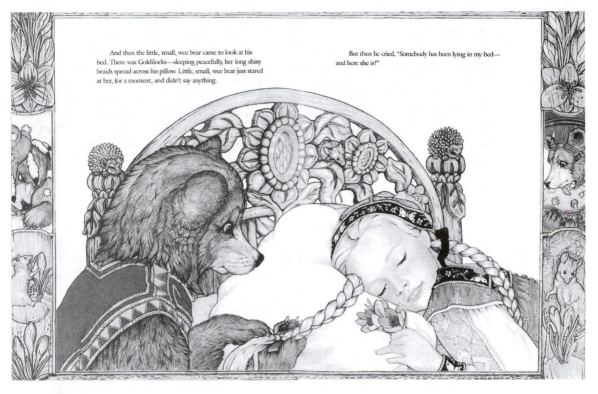

And then the little, small, wee bear came to look at his bed. There was Goldilocks—sleeping peacefully, her long shiny braids spread across his pillow. Little, small, wee bear just stared at her, for a moment, and didn't say anything.

But then he cried, "Somebody has been lying in my bed—and here she is!"

Notice the details included in this illustration.
(Illustration by Jan Brett reprinted by permission of G.P. Putnam's Sons from GOLDILOCKS and the Three Bears, © 1987 by Jan Brett.)

capture the reader's interest. Davies and Pringle provide captions alongside the illustrations and drawings of sharks that indicate the name and size of the creatures as well as the role that the skin, fins, and gills serve.

When you evaluate the illustrations in a nonfiction book, you may want to think of the ways you plan to share the book with children. Think about whether the book can help the children to become careful observers and interpreters of visual data.

Illustrations are central to the success of all picture books. They should be evaluated carefully, because they are a basic component of a young child's literary and artistic education. In chapter books, illustrations should add to the enjoyment of reading the book but should not distract the reader. Illustrations in chapter books are used primarily to break up the text and are generally not critical to the meaning of the story.

EVALUATING INTERACTIVE LITERATURE ON **CD-ROM**

The National Association for the Education of Young Children has taken the position that computer software can enhance children's development but notes that it should not take the place of books, blocks, and other more traditional early childhood materials (Walter, 1997). This reflects the opinion of many early childhood educators, torn between excitement at the potential of the medium and concern that it not replace the warmth and sharing involved in the personal sharing of literature.

When looking at stories on CD-ROM, a first criterion is whether the content is age appropriate. Look at the understanding level required just as you would in selecting a book. Look to see also if it can be run easily by a child if you are planning to have one or two children engaged with it on their own. Are the directions understandable? Can the children figure out how to go forward, go back, and access special features? Assess the technical quality. Are voices clear and understandable, and is the animation smooth? Picture children viewing the story. Will they be engaged in thinking and feeling as they participate in the story or just engaging in passive point-and-click activities?

One key criterion, however, is whether the CD makes good use of the special attributes of the medium. Terri Butler writes:

> Be aware, first of all, that this is a medium about doing. The most successful CD-ROMs are those that make the best use of the medium's potential for movement, action, sound, and music—a potential it shares with video. But unlike video, what you see is not all you get. At the click of a mouse, there are surprises just waiting to happen, whether it's a puzzle to put together in that famous Parisian house covered with vines, or discovering that French-fried fudge is the favorite food of Dr. Seuss's Fiffer-feffer-feffs.
>
> These surprises—the "hot buttons" built into the disk's program—are key to any good CD-ROM. They can summon a sound effect or a song, a problem to solve, or a game to play. When used well they broaden a story's potential to educate and entertain. And yes, they mean we've gone beyond a faithful rendering of the book—in some cases, way beyond. *(1997, p. 219)*

In the CD-ROM version of *Stellaluna* (2006) based on the book by Janell Cannon, there are 14 interactive pages as well as a "bat" science quiz. The style of illustrations is faithful to the original illustrations. In the CDs based on the Arthur books by Marc Brown, such as *Arthur's Reading Games* (2000), the illustrations match the originals here as well. Animation moves the story along. However, if the child clicks on all the hot-button choices given, he or she may slow down the story considerably. The buttons can keep the child very actively involved but can also dilute the force of the narrative. When you are selecting a CD for a literary experience, you should assess the narrative flow of the story. Do the choices given enhance the story? That is, do they add interest, give information, or provide entertainment in a way that is consistent with both the plot and the mood of the literature? A serious story interrupted with funny sounds loses its impact, whereas a humorous story with those same sounds could be very effective. Characterization may be augmented if the voice given the character fits or may be confused if it doesn't. Hyperlinks may add depth to nonfiction by letting children select which aspects of a topic are of most interest to them or dilute the topic if they are only peripherally related.

Finally, look for CDs that may have special meaning for the children with whom you work. Many offer the text in both English and Spanish, for example, which is useful for many second-language learners. Some include word processing so that students can make notes as they interact. Some highlight text as it is read, encouraging reading development. Some allow a child to read and then play back his or her reading. In this rapidly developing field, there are likely to be more and more options, making evaluation more complex. A good CD, like a good book, should provide a child with both enjoyment and new understandings.

SUMMARY

Books shared with children should be the very best available based on literary and artistic standards. It is necessary, therefore, that childcare providers and teachers be able to judge the quality of children's books. You can evaluate fiction by assessing the effectiveness of the literary elements of plot, setting, characterization, theme, and style of writing as well as how the elements are integrated to provide a unified whole. You should judge nonfiction for factual accuracy, current information, and clear differentiation between fact and opinion. The organization and choice of material affect the quality of nonfiction.

You can evaluate poetry for children on freshness and compactness of language, use of rhythm and rhyme, and emotional content. You can judge illustrations for appropriateness of style and medium to the mood and content of the text, for how well they extend the text, and for their artistic quality. Illustrations in nonfiction should present information clearly and accurately. Reading many picture books with a critical eye will help you to develop skill in assessing texts and illustrations. Books on CD-ROM should engage the child and use the medium to advantage, while still maintaining the narrative flow of the story.

Extending Your Learning

1. Read a recently published children's book and write your own comments about it. Locate two published reviews of the book. Reviews of children's books appear in journals such as *Language Arts, The Reading Teacher, The Horn Book, School Library Journal, Publisher's Weekly* and *Booklist.*

2. Using the same criteria as were applied to *Knuffle Bunny: A Cautionary Tale,* to evaluate a picture book of your choice.

3. Compare the illustrations in any two winners of the Caldecott Award. Look at the choice of media, the style of art, and the effectiveness of the illustrations in helping to tell the story.

4. What do you see as the role of CD-ROMs for young children? Select a CD and evaluate it for its ease of use, its technical quality, its reproduction of book illustrations, and its level of enjoyment for children.

REFERENCES

Professional References Cited

Butler, T. (1997). Tale-spinning: Children's books on CD-ROM. *The Horn Book, 2,* 219–224.

Kerper, R. (1998). Choosing quality nonfiction literature: Features for assessing and visualizing information. In R. Bamford & J. Kirsto (Eds.), *Making facts come alive: Choosing quality nonfiction literature K–8* (pp. 55–74). Norwood, MA: Christopher-Gordon.

Kiefer, B. (1995). *The potential of picturebooks: From visual literacy to aesthetic understanding.* Columbus, OH: Merrill Prentice Hall.

Stewig, J. (1988). *Reading pictures, exploring illustrations with children.* New Berlin, WI: The Resourceful Educator.

Wallace, I. (1989). The emotional link. *The New Advocate, 2,* 75–82.

Walter, V. (1997). Starting early: Multimedia for the tricycle set. *Book Links, 5,* 26–33.

Children's Literature Cited

Aylesworth, Jim. (2003). *Goldilocks and the Three Bears.* Ill. Barbara McClintock. New York: Scholastic.

Aliki. (1969). *My Visit to the Dinosaurs.* New York: Crowell.

Aliki. (1981). *Digging Up Dinosaurs.* New York: Harper.

Aliki. (1988). *Dinosaur Bones.* New York: Crowell.

Brett, Jan. (1987). *Goldilocks and the Three Bears.* New York: Dodd.

Brown, Marc. (2000). *Arthur's Reading Games.* Novato, CA: The Learning Company.

Buehner, Caralyn. (2007). *Goldilocks and the Three Bears.* Ill. Mark Buehner. New York: Dial.

Cole, Joanna. (1998). *The Magic School Bus and the Electric Field Trip.* Ill. Bruce Degen. New York: Scholastic.

Cole, Joanna. (2005). *Ms. Frizzle's Adventures: Imperial China.* Ill. Bruce Degen. New York: Scholastic.

Cole, Joanna. (2006). *The Magic School Bus and the Science Fair Expedition.* Ill. Bruce Degen. New York: Scholastic.

Davies, Nicola. (2003). *Surprising Sharks.* Ill. James Croft. Cambridge, MA: Candlewick.

Dewey, Jennifer Owings. (1998). *Poison Dart Frogs.* Honesdale, PA: Boyds Mills.

English, Karen. (1998). *Just Right Stew.* Ill. Anna Rich. Honesdale, PA: Boyds Mills.

Falconer, Ian. (2000). *Olivia.* New York: Atheneum.

French, Vivian. (2000). *Growing Frogs.* Ill. Alison Bartlett. Cambridge, MA: Candlewick.

Gibbons, Gail. (1998a). *The Art Box.* New York: Holiday House.

Gibbons, Gail. (1998b). *Marshes & Swamps.* New York: Holiday House.

Hatkoff, Isabella, & Hatkoff, Craig. (2006). *Owen & Mzee: The Story of a Remarkable Friendship.* Photos. Peter Greste. New York: Scholastic.

Kudlinski, Kathleen V. (2005). *Boy, Were We Wrong About Dinosaurs.* Ill. S. D. Schindler. New York: Dutton.

Lindsay, Vachel. (1986). "The Little Turtle." In *Read Aloud Rhymes for the Very Young* by Jack Prelutsky. New York: Knopf.

McMillan, Bruce. (1998). *Salmon Summer*. Boston: Houghton Mifflin.
Pringle, Laurence. (2001). *Sharks! Strange and Wonderful.* Ill. Meryl Henderson. Honesdale, PA: Boyds Mills.
Shannon, David. (1998). *No, David!* New York: Scholastic.
Simon, Seymour. (1985). *How to Talk to Your Computer*. Ill. Barbara & Ed Emberley. New York: Crowell.
Stellaluna. CD-ROM. The Learning Company, 2006.
Willems, Mo. (2003). *Don't Let the Pigeon Drive the Bus.* New York: Hyperion.
Willems, Mo. (2004). *Knuffle Bunny: A Cautionary Tale.* New York: Hyperion.
Willems, Mo. (2007). *Knuffle Bunny Too: A Case of Mistaken Identity.* New York: Hyperion.

Recommended Professional Resources for Book Selection

Barr, K., & Gillespie, J. T. (2005). *Best books for children: Preschool through grade 6* (8th ed.). Westport, CT: Libraries Unlimited.
Hansen-Krening, N., Aoki, E., & Mizokawa, D. T. (2003). *Kaleidoscope: A multicultural booklist for grades K–8* (4th ed.). Urbana, IL: National Council of Teachers of English.
Lima, C. W., & Lima, J. A. (2005). *A to zoo: Subject access to children's picture books* (7th ed.). Westport, CT: Bowker-Greenwood.
Odean, K. (2003). *Great books for babies and toddlers: More than 500 recommended books for your child's first three years.* New York: Ballantine.
Post, A. D., Scott, M., & Theberge, M. (2000). *Celebrating children's choices: 25 years of children's favorite books.* Newark, DE: International Reading Assocation.
Silvey, A. (2004). *100 best books for children.* Boston: Houghton Miflfin.
Trelease, J. (2006). *The read aloud handbook* (6th ed.). New York: Penguin.

CHAPTER THREE

TATUM & ROBBIE, Age 5
The Pumpkin Book by Gail Gibbons

Tatum and Robbie's (both age 5) teacher read aloud
The Pumpkin Book by Gail Gibbons (1999) to her first grade
students. They demonstrated their learning about pumpkins
through a written response and received positive feedback from
Megan Sloan, their teacher.

Sharing Literature

The voice of a young child asking an adult to "read it again" is proof of the pleasure that can come from literature shared aloud. Much of what children enjoy hearing, they are unable to read themselves. Picture storybooks, usually written on a third-grade or higher readability level, are inaccessible to preschool and many primary-grade children without someone to present them. And poetry, even more than prose, needs to be read aloud by a skilled reader. Such a reader can emphasize the meaning and the rhythm of the words, having passed the stage of struggling simply to recognize and pronounce the words. A smooth presentation shows children the power that literature can have.

You may choose to read a story or tell it. If you tell it, you may want to let your voice alone carry the tale, or you may want to use a feltboard or other visual aid. You may also share literature through CD-ROMs, audiobooks, films, videos, or DVDs. Throughout the year, you will have the opportunity to share literature in a variety of ways.

READING ALOUD

Finding the Right Book

As you begin looking through books or poems to choose one to share with children, you should consider several factors. One aspect, of course, is the quality of the material itself. Using the criteria presented in chapter 2, assess the literary merit of the story, eliminating from consideration any books that are of poor quality.

Story time with infants and toddlers works best as a one-on-one activity (Honig, 2004). Choose a board book with a large, colorful picture on each page. Honig indicates that babies enjoy pictures of familiar items from their daily lives, such as an adult dressing or feeding a baby, a baby in a crib kicking at a mobile, or a baby rolling a ball or crawling toward a pet (p. 25). Sharing books with very young children helps them to learn to listen, to attend, and to relate stories to their own lives.

The purpose for reading to infants and toddlers may differ from the purpose for reading aloud to preschoolers and primary-grade children. Suppose you are working with a group of 3- and 4-year-olds. It is the beginning of the year, and you and the children are just getting to know one another. You decide you will begin story time by telling some stories you think they will have heard at home. You want the children to feel comfortable with you, and this will help you establish rapport. You also want this experience to lead into a sharing of similar stories that the children may not have heard. You decide to work with traditional literature.

The two stories that you will tell are *The Three Bears* and *The Three Little Pigs.* Both are folktales that use patterns of three and have a repetition of phrases and events. Now you need to select two or three similar folktales to share on succeeding days. These should also contain clear action, an appealing repetition of language, and only a few characters. You may begin by looking on the computer at the library and talking with the librarian about possible choices. You might look in texts or reference books about children's literature. *Children's Literature in the Elementary School* by Huck, Kiefer, Hepler, and Hickman (2006) has a section on traditional literature that groups tales by motif and by country of origin. You might look in sources that list books for children. The *Subject Guide to Children's Books in Print* (2008), for instance, lists all the children's books currently in print under subject headings. There are no annotations, so you would need to find the actual books to obtain further information about them. However, the titles alone may jog your memory about appropriate stories.

Other useful references are the *Children's Catalog* (2006), generally available in the children's section of public libraries as well as school libraries. *The Horn Book Guide,* issued twice each year, gives short, critical annotations for all hardcover trade children's and young adult books published in the United States during the preceding 6-month period. They are listed within categories and indexed by author, title, and subject. *The Horn Book Guide Online* contains more than 65,000 reviews of books published over the past two decades. You can search this database by author, title, subject, and bibliographic data as well as by the rating given it in the original *Horn Book* review.

The Bank Street Bookstore, an online initiative of the Bank Street College of Education (www.bankstreetbook.com), classifies children's books under such headings as adoption, beginning readers, families, pirates, poetry, and seasons. You can also sign up to receive the online Bank Street newsletter to inform you about new books. Other online bookstores have lists created by consumers and also have searchable features.

If you check a variety of listings, you will find many book titles from which to choose. Some teachers keep a database or card file of books that they have used successfully. They add to it as they learn of new titles and explore new areas with their classes. In this way, they have personal listings readily available. New teachers sometimes find it helpful to talk with other teachers and librarians. They often find that colleagues are an abundant source of information.

Using these sources, you have selected titles and gathered books to read and preview. In addition to sharing the traditional stories of *The Three Bears* and *The Three Little Pigs,* you have decided to also share *The Little Red Hen* and found 10 versions or variants listed, 6 of which the library owns. You are also going to look at *Deep in the Forest* (Turkle, 1976). You read through the books, keeping in mind your purposes and assessing the literary and artistic quality of each selection as well as the appropriateness of the story for preschoolers. You choose *The Little Red Hen,* illustrated by Byron Barton (1993), because it has bright bold colors and tells the old, familiar story with striking simplicity. The library also has a big-book version of Barton's story, which makes it appealing to share with a group of children. You locate and read another version of *The Little Red Hen*, this time retold with beautifully crafted water-color illustrations by Jerry Pinkney (2006). Because the second version is lengthier and the illustrations are more detailed, you decide to wait until later in the year to read it. Pinkney's version will be better appreciated by the children when they have had a little more experience with literature and are able to attend to a story for a longer period of time. It's also a good idea to revisit stories later in the year and add to children's knowledge of books.

The next two books you select are *The Little Red Hen* (1973) by Paul Galdone and *Deep in the Forest* by Brinton Turkle (1976). You plan to read the second version of *The Little Red Hen* to show how one tale maintains its structure but varies in details with each retelling and different illustrations. The Barton version has a pig, duck, and cat that refuse to assist the Little Red Hen. The intense colors and vivid images also assist in telling the story. Galdone's version has a cat, a dog, and a mouse who watch while the Little Red Hen plants wheat and finally bakes a cake. The muted tones of the watercolor illustrations provide a very different visual experience.

Deep in the Forest is a wordless picture book in which a bear cub enters a cabin in the woods to find a table with three chairs and three bowls, in the standard small, medium, and large sizes of *Goldilocks and the Three Bears.* The story reverses the characters, because it is the young girl who returns to find a cub in her bed and her cabin in disarray. You choose this story because you think the children will delight in grasping what has happened to the story and because it will elicit discussion of the structure of the tale as the children point out the changes.

You also find versions of *Goldilocks and the Three Bears* with very different styles of illustrations by Jan Brett (1987), Jim Aylesworth (2003) and Carolyn Buehner (2007). You plan to bring them in together and tell the children that you have three books in which different artists have drawn pictures to go with a story they know. Can they tell from the covers what the story is? You will leave these books for the children to look at on their own, listen for their comments, and see if they ask you to read the stories.

You have chosen carefully, keeping both your purposes and the children's needs and interests in mind. You have also noted that the books you are planning to share with the group are large enough for the children to see the illustrations clearly as you read. If they were not, you would need to share the books with only one or two children at a time or perhaps use a video or DVD that would allow all the children to see.

Of course, there are some instances when children may not need to see the illustrations as the story is being read. They may listen to familiar Mother Goose rhymes and only later look at the illustrations. In an illustrated book with few pictures, the teacher may decide to show the illustrations by walking around so that children get a closer view. With only a few pictures, this does not create much of an interruption in the story.

Creating a Positive Environment

You will want to share the books in a way that invites children to enter into the experience wholeheartedly. Reading well orally is basic to this. It is often helpful to read the selection aloud yourself before sharing it with children of any age.

Being familiar with the material will eliminate any stumbling over unusual words. It will also give you a chance to rehearse any special voices you may want to

David Mager/Pearson Learning Photo Studio

When reading aloud, hold the book so children can see the illustrations.

use for different characters. If you are reading poetry, it will allow you to plan where the breaks should be so that you keep the meaning intact.

It may be useful to get feedback on your skill in reading aloud. One way of doing this is to audiotape or videotape yourself. As you listen to the tape or watch the video, ask several questions. Am I enunciating clearly? That is, are my words distinct? Is the volume pleasant, loud enough to be heard without straining, yet not uncomfortably loud? Am I reading at a speed that allows the listener to comprehend easily? Does the expression in my voice move the story along and make it more interesting? If the answer to any of these is no, then perhaps you should practice the same story several times, concentrating on improving areas of weakness.

Another way to get feedback is to ask a friend to observe you as you read to a group of children. Ask the friend to answer the same questions you would ask of yourself if listening to a tape. In addition, ask the friend to tell you if you are looking up as you read and making eye contact with the children.

When you read aloud to infants, hold the book within the child's visual range and turn the pages slowly. As you read aloud to children 18 months and older try to hold the book so that they can see the illustrations as you read. Some teachers accomplish this by holding the book to one side as they read. Others look down over the top of the book, reading the print upside down. Because text and illustrations together create meaning, it is imperative that you read the text while showing the illustrations at the same time. Otherwise, the meaning-making experience becomes disjointed and sometimes frustrating to young children, who often rely on visual images to engage them and to enhance their understanding of the story.

Being familiar with the content of the book through having read it aloud frees you to make more eye contact with the children and share in their enjoyment of the story. It allows you to see children's responses—what amuses them, for example, or if any of them are getting tired of listening.

After each reading, perhaps formally but usually informally, evaluate your sharing of the book. If all went well, remember what you did that contributed to the successful experience. If problems occurred, try to analyze why they happened and what might be done to avoid them in the future. For example, if the fire bell rang in the middle of the story, there is little you could have done to prevent it. But if the story was interrupted by one child kicking another, you might have seen the two poking at each other with increasing frequency if you had looked up more often. A look from you with a shake of your head or separating the children as you showed illustrations in the book might have prevented the incident.

Whether for a small group or the total class, plan the setting so that it will be as easy as possible for the children to pay attention. This means trying to find a quiet place to read. If there is going to be extraneous noise, move so that your voice and the noise are not coming from the same direction and competing with each other. Place yourself so that children can focus on you and on the book. Put their backs to any movement that may be distracting. If there is a strong light source, such as a window, have the children's backs to it also. Light shining on you and on the book will make both easily seen; light shining behind you and the book may have children squinting at a silhouette.

If you know the children are likely to be restless, plan how you will help them calm down. Perhaps you can say a few poems together, have the children each tell one thing they heard on the playground, or do two or three finger plays. Let children know what your expectations are. If story time is to be a quiet time for listening, praise such behavior. If you want children to hold their comments until the conclusion of a story, remind them of this when you begin.

A set time for story hour, particularly for young children, lets them know it is an important part of the day. It also gives them some control over the situation because they know what the pattern is. You may want to have a rule that says they may leave the story circle if they wish, but they are not to make noise, talk, or in any way distract those who are listening. Or you may want to establish a pattern in which all children stay for the entire story. For primary-grade children, you may want to have a set time but incorporate reading aloud during other times of the day by reading books that support the curriculum.

Think about contingencies that may arise. A comment that you are certain to hear at least once is, "I've heard it before." Be prepared to respond with a comment such as, "Don't tell how it ends," or "See if you notice anything in the story this time that you didn't when you heard it before." This acknowledges the child's remark, yet avoids a lengthy discussion about whether he or she wants to hear it again.

Plan how you will introduce the book. Some teachers give the title and author at the beginning; others do it at the end. At some time, however, children should be told the title, author, and illustrator. This helps establish the idea that books are written by real people and also assists in making connections with other books that may have been shared written or illustrated by those individuals.

Helping Children Construct Meaning

There are many ways to build interest in and enhance the comprehension of a book you are about to read. You might ask children to make some guesses or predictions about the story from the title or from the picture on the cover. Before sharing *The Little Red Hen,* you might ask the children to look at the cover and tell what they think the Little Red Hen likes to do. For *Goldilocks and the Three Bears,* children might answer the question, "What differences do you see among the three bears shown on the cover?" Introductory comments set the stage for the story and can be used to guide children's learning. Having them listen for special things encourages careful listening. Having them guess what will happen fosters logical thinking about cause and effect.

Narrative Structure   Children develop a sense of story—an idea of how events are sequenced and are interrelated. This comes in part from hearing many stories, but also from teachers and childcare providers who talk with children about what they have heard. Sipe (1998) found that the first- and second-graders who responded to picture books read aloud engaged in five conceptual categories of responses. They talked about the elements of literature, such as plot, characterization, and sequence, and how the illustrations influenced their understanding. They compared the story being read aloud with other stories they had heard. They connected the story to their own lives. They lost themselves in the story, and, finally, they used it as a base for their own creative activities. This suggests that even young children can be part of a community that understands and responds to literature, even to fairly sophisticated techniques such as foreshadowing.

Sipe also noted that the teachers exhibited scaffolding behavior—that is, they engaged in practices that supported and encouraged the children's understanding. They mediated the stories for the children, pacing the reading appropriately and adding expression to their voices. They modeled how discussion could progress and managed it in ways that elicited more talk. They helped children make links between the stories and took a stance in which they, too, wondered about events in the books. And, finally, they were aware of and used the teachable moments, often taking children's comments to higher levels of abstraction.

Books read aloud provide the perfect time for talking about how stories are structured. This may well come during the story reading. For many children, it is helpful to make a visual representation of the structure of the story, a sort of flowchart of events or arrows showing which events cause others. These are usually most effective when constructed by the children and teacher together, so that explanation and conversation accompany the charting, but they should not be done too frequently.

Visual Literacy   Visual literacy is the ability to gain meaning from visual images. For children viewing picture books, this means interpreting the nontextual elements—the illustrations, the endpapers, and the title page. John Stewig (1992) sees three steps in sharing books with children in a way that encourages the development of visual literacy. First, have children bring their own background to bear on what they see. Have them tell what they notice and how it compares with what they have experienced. Second, have them pay attention to individual units within the larger unit; perhaps look at the use of color in an illustration or see how the endpapers relate to the text. Third, ask the children to make aesthetic judgments about the relative merits of one picture book over another and give their reasons for their conclusions.

Your discussions about books will most likely involve both narrative structure and visual literacy, because both contribute to meaning. If you are going to discuss a book, questions should be developed and written down. If you plan extension activities, you will need to have materials and directions ready. If you plan no follow-up, then you may simply say, "And that's the story of Trixie losing her favorite stuffed animal," or "There are other books by Mo Willems. Would you like to hear another story by him?" If you do ask the children what they would like to hear, be prepared to honor their response. If they say yes, then plan to read what they want. If they say no, skip the book for now, even though you may know it is excellent literature.

Many teachers or caregivers display the book they have just finished reading in a special place. Children then know where to find it if they want to read it themselves or look at the pictures. This practice also gives the teacher a chance to judge the reaction of children to particular books. Some may sit unopened; others may be in constant demand.

Although reading aloud is probably the most frequently used method of sharing literature with children, other ways are also effective. One of these is storytelling.

STORYTELLING

Finding the Right Story

In selecting a story to tell, either with or without visuals, you will use many of the same criteria that you use to select books to read aloud. You want it to be good literature, and you want it to match the interest and understanding level of the audience. But there are other criteria to consider. The story should have a fairly compact plot, with much action. It should also have a strong beginning and a satisfying conclusion. Natural dialogue will keep the story moving and add interest, although having too many characters speak can make a story difficult for both teller and listener to follow. Because folktales originated in oral, rather than written, form, they are excellent for telling. They are not the only "tellable" tales, of course, but they are a logical place to begin.

Some qualities may make a story better read than told. Examples are descriptive language that is an integral part of the story or exact dialogue that is essential to the meaning or mood. The storyteller tells the tale in his or her own words; so if specific language is needed and it is more than can be memorized, the teller might be better off choosing another story.

The story should be one that you like. If you spend the time to learn it, you will want to tell it more than once. It should be a story that you think will appeal to many groups of children. You can build a repertoire of stories by learning three or four each year.

Storytelling for babies to 2-year-olds encompasses rhymes and songs such as Itsy-Bitsy Spider or Pat-a-Cake. Children ages 2 to 5 years old are considered to be in the age of repetition. They enjoy stories that have repetitive plots, such as *The Three Little Pigs* and *The Gingerbread Boy,* or *The Little Red Hen.* Repeated lines keep the children oriented to the sequence of the story. Children also enjoy taking part in the telling themselves, saying the refrain with the storyteller or engaging in motions to accompany the story. If you are working with preschool youngsters, you might want to learn a story like *We're Going on a Bear Hunt* (Rosen, 1989). Rosen demonstrates the motions for the story at www.youtube.com watch?v=ytc042WAz4s. that you can learn and children can perform as the tale is being told.

Children ages 6 to 9 are what Briggs and Wagner (1979) consider to be in the "age of fancy." From about ages 7 to 9 is the period of peak interest in fairy tales. These children are able to distinguish fantasy from reality. They can tolerate the violence because they know the story is make-believe. They expect the evil characters to be punished and the good to be rewarded, a pattern of justice that exists in most fairy tales. You may find that you know many fairy tales already. In this case, a quick review and practice might be all the preparation you need.

A popular visual aid that you can use effectively by classroom and childcare storytellers is the felt or flannel board. This is a board, usually masonite, plywood, or stiff cardboard, that is covered with cloth, usually felt or flannel. Characters and bits of setting are placed on the board as the story is told. To select stories for felt-board storytelling, keep in mind the space on the board and how much you can manipulate at one time. There will not be room for a cast of thousands. Even for only eight different characters, if you must use them in several different groupings or appear in the story randomly rather than in a patterned sequence, you may end up giving all your attention to finding the right characters at the right time and be unable to concentrate on telling the story well. English-language learners also benefit from the visual aspect of using felt-board stories.

When first beginning to tell stories to toddlers, choose short stories that they will know and invite their participation. Before telling a complete story, start with short and familiar nursery rhymes such as "Hey, Diddle Diddle," "Little Miss Muffet," or "The Itsy-Bitsy Spider." The initial fascination with the flannel board is often the flannel pieces themselves. Use pieces that are large and simple; if possible, be sure they are made out of washable materials. Tactile one-year-olds love to touch and "smooch" the pieces (Church, 2002). Once they begin to understand the process of a story being told, then move on to fairy tales such as *The Gingerbread Man*. The repetitive phrase "Run, run as fast as you can. You can't catch me. I'm the Gingerbread Man" is one that children quickly learn. The key with toddlers is to keep them engaged by participation.

For 3- to 5-year-olds, look for stories that have a fairly simple plot, perhaps either cumulative or repetitive. Think about what can be used to give the idea of the story. Neither setting nor characters need to be exact in detail. The story itself should be simple enough to work well. Choose a clear plot, with a limited number of characters. In sharing Eric Carle's *The Very Hungry Caterpillar* (1981), listeners hear how the caterpillar ate through a variety of fruit and other food until he eventually formed a cocoon around himself. The pattern makes the story easy for children to follow and the repetitive phrase engages them, and once he has eaten through a food item, it no longer needs to be placed on the felt board.

Creating a Positive Environment

In storytelling, as in reading aloud, it is essential that the children be able to see the presenter. One of the rewards of storytelling is that you can maintain constant eye contact with the children. You can adapt the story to their reactions. You can show that you find the tale amusing, or sad, or quietly beautiful.

Some teachers and caregivers use a puppet to introduce stories that they are going to tell. It may be a hand puppet that comes to the session, hidden in a pocket or a bag. The teacher or caregiver wakes the puppet, and the two may have a brief conversation about the story, or the puppet may talk directly to the children. It is one way of setting the stage for storytelling. The puppet is put away during the telling and perhaps recalled at the conclusion.

Recommended Literature for Storytelling or Flannel-Board Stories

Aylesworth, Jim. (1998). *The Gingerbread Man*. Ill. Barbara McClintock. New York: Scholastic.

Barrett, Judy. (1978). *Cloud with a Chance of Meatballs*. Ill. Ron Barrett. New York: Atheneum.

Beaumont, Karen. (2006). *Move Over, Rover*. Ill. Jane Dyer. San Diego, CA: Harcourt.

Brett, Jan. (1989). *The Mitten*. New York: Putnam.

Brown, Marcia. (1974). *Stone Soup*. New York: Scribner's.

French, Vivian. (2006). *Henny Penny*. Ill. Sophie Windham. New York: Bloomsbury.

McCloskey, Robert. (1948). *Blueberries for Sal*. New York: Viking.

Morgan, Pierr. (1990). *The Turnip*. New York: Philomel.

Numeroff, Laura Joffe. (1985). *If You Give a Mouse a Cookie*. Ill. Felicia Bond. New York: HarperCollins.

Slobodkina, Esphyr. (1947). *Caps for Sale*. New York: HarperCollins.

Winter, Jeanette. (2000). *The House that Jack Built*. New York: Dial.

Wood, Audrey. (1984). *The Napping House*. Ill. Don Wood. San Diego, CA: Harcourt.

If you are going to use a felt board, decide whether you want it propped up on an easel or a chair. Think about where it will be in relation to the children's eye level. Will they be able to see it comfortably? Also, plan where you will stand or sit. It will need to be a place where you can reach the board, reach the characters, and see the children.

You can judge the reaction of your audience as you tell a story.

Preparing to tell a story usually takes more time than preparing to read a story. You may wonder where you will find the time to do this preparation or whether you have the talent to tell a story well. It may help to keep in mind that your audience is not expecting a professional storyteller. You need not spend hours in getting ready, nor should you expect to have a perfect presentation every times. Just do the best you can, improving as you gain experience.

It is useful to know how others learn a story and then adapt it to individual situations. Few storytellers memorize a story word for word. Most make note of the basic sequences of action—what happens when. They may memorize the opening sentence and the concluding sentence and any refrains that are part of the story, but the rest they tell in their own words. They begin by reading the story over several times, getting a sense of the story as a whole. Then they may list the action on a sheet of paper or on note cards. Storytellers use these lists to set the action in their minds and to refresh their memories when they have not told that particular story for awhile. These lists are not used during the storytelling itself.

Some storytellers visualize the story, picturing in their minds the setting, characters, and how the action progresses. This picture helps them remember and is also useful as they begin to describe the scene or tell about a character.

When intially beginning to tell stories, one such as *If You Give a Mouse a Cookie* (Numeroff, 1985) that has straightforward action and text that is easily learned is a good place to begin your storytelling. Stack the objects that the mouse wants in order and then place them on the flannel board as you tell the story. Not only will children be able to participate in the storytelling (because they will surely know the story), but they will also want to use the felt pieces to retell the story for themselves.

If the story is longer or has more action or characters, you might want to create brief notes that remind you of the story's action or the next character to appear. Some storytellers make a series of note cards denoting the basic action of the story. The cards give the sequence of action, but they don't give the flavor of the story. Reading

Spencer Grant/PhotoEdit Inc.

Practicing a story before you share it with young children allows you to follow its sequence but adapt its wordiness and length to fit the needs of young listeners.

the story over and over does this. Keep in mind that the story is enhanced by sound and refrains.

Now practice saying the story aloud. You will be able to identify any rough spots in the telling. Some teachers practice telling stories as they drive or do chores around the house. Once you have mastered the story, you can recall it by going over your note cards quickly and perhaps saying it once or twice to yourself.

Using a felt board to tell a story shortens one part of the preparation and lengthens another. Learning the story will probably take less time, because by stacking the figures in the order they appear, you give yourself clues to the story's sequence. If you were telling *The Very Hungry Caterpillar* with a felt board, you would see each food item in order. Some childcare providers keep the figures faceup in a pile; others put them facedown so the numbers that mark the sequence will show on the back. A brief synopsis of the story can be kept in a folder with the figures. This provides a quick review before each telling.

The preparation will be lengthened by making the figures themselves. They can be cut from felt or made from paper with sandpaper or felt pieces glued to the back so they will adhere to the board. Velcro can also be used for sticking figures to the board. Many storytellers make characters from pellon, a type of interfacing available at fabric stores. Figures can be traced onto it and then colored in with crayon, felt-tip markers, or liquid embroidery. Pellon figures tend to be more durable than those constructed from paper. The felt board itself is covered with cloth, generally a dark, solid color that provides a background for many stories. You can experiment with different backings and methods of making characters to find the ones that suit you best.

It is necessary to practice using the figures as you rehearse the story. Set the board up exactly as you plan to use it with children. Experiment with the angle of the board to ensure that the characters will not fall to the floor easily. Adjust the board or add more backing to the figures so the story can proceed smoothly when you tell it to the children. If necessary, rough up the back of the characters with an emery board or fine sandpaper. Decide where to put the characters so the children will not see them before they are placed on the felt board. You may want to keep them in a box or behind the board.

When you have completed the story, take a minute to evaluate your presentation. After you have told three or four stories to a group of children, you might ask them to tell which stories they liked best and why. Putting their impressions into words will help children compare stories to see how tales are alike and different. It may also give you some insight into your own presentations. If they tell you that they liked *Goldilocks and the Three Bears* because you used different voices for each of the bears, you know your expression and voice quality were effective. If they cannot remember any of the events in the story, then either the presentation or the selection of the tale for those children was a problem. Perhaps there were distractions during the telling of the story. The children may be able to tell about the fight on the playground outside the window instead of the story. Perhaps the story was too complicated or too long for that group. They simply may have lost interest and have been unable to follow what was happening from the beginning. Analyzing past presentations will help you improve future storytelling.

Helping Children Construct Meaning

Telling stories well is key to helping children develop understanding. There are many similarities, obviously, between reading a story and telling a story, but there are differences also.

Narrative Structure   The requirements of storytelling to young children, especially when using a felt board, mean that sequence is a prime concern. Thus it makes sense to focus on this area of story structure. Stories can be retold by having children come up and select the figure that should go next on the felt board and adding the appropriate text or by moving figures around. You might also have them listen to a story and then decide what characters would be needed to tell it as a felt-board story. Children are thus identifying the key characters.

Some stories may be told twice, allowing the children to become familiar with the sequence and to master any refrains so that they can say them with the teacher. The same is true as children learn motions to accompany the telling or if they sing during the telling as a part of the story. If the children are taking turns participating in or retelling the story, let them know when the session is about to end. Comments such as, "Let's hear from two more people before we stop," or "Teddy, we'll let you be the last one to tell our story for today," give children a sense of conclusion rather than interruption.

Visual Literacy   As with looking at illustrations in picture books, children will look at how the teacher or childcare provider has represented elements of the story visually if a felt board is used. Often it will be in less detail, so that rather than looking at the subtleties, as in an illustration, they will look at the symbolic nature of the representation. The children themselves might suggest what objects are central to the plot and thus necessary for the retelling or how the setting could be suggested with only a few objects. If they were telling a cumulative tale, such as *The Jacket I Wear in the*

Snow (Neitzel, 1989), the objects are clear—each piece of clothing that the child puts on. They will be addressing the question of how visual elements contribute to understanding.

SHARING LITERATURE THROUGH MEDIA

Finding the Right Media

The number and range of audiovisual materials, particularly CD-ROMs, is expanding rapidly. Some companies have been in the business of producing DVDs and audio-books based on children's stories for many years. Among these are Weston Woods Studios, Recorded Books, Spoken Arts, and Live Oak Media. Sending for their and other companies' catalogs may give you an idea of what is currently available. Also, Reading Rainbow sells its programs on videocassettes. On their Web site, the nonprofit corporation Coalition for Quality Children's Media has reviews of media that its experts and the children who have participated recommend. Information about books in media format is also readily available in publishers' book catalogs and on their Internet sites. A useful reference book is *Bowker's Complete Video Directory* (2007).

The proliferation of CD-ROMs that are literature related means that it is necessary first to read how the company describes the material on its package or in advertising and then to actually preview the material. It is more likely that an electronic version of *Stellaluna* (2006) will have more literary merit than Teletubbies, although that is not guaranteed. However, a package that tells you that beginning readers will love filling in the blanks and "learning about adjectives, nouns, and verbs" because the exercises are based on a popular children's book is no more than an electronic workbook.

Sound and action and, with CDs, interaction should engage the viewer in a literary experience that brings the narrative to life. Your purpose should also guide you in the selection of media. Perhaps you want to share a book with the total class, but it is so small that they could not see the illustrations. A video or DVD will overcome this problem. If you have been introducing the work of several poets, your class could listen to recordings of these poets reading some of their own poetry. It may be that you want a cassette or CD you can leave in the listening center for children to play themselves. Children can then elect to hear their favorite stories or poems again and again. If you want to encourage children to follow along in a book while listening to the text being read, then you will probably want a recording that has a sound to mark the turning of each page. This will help beginning readers keep their places. Another option is to select tapes and CDs that show the text as it is read. Being clear in your own mind about the purpose for using the media will help you select the most appropriate type.

Preview the material before you share it with the children. Assess the quality of the audiovisual material just as you do print materials. Generally speaking, media or an interactive format cannot rescue a book that was of poor quality originally. If you know that the book version is of literary merit, you will still need to evaluate the media version. The medium should be appropriate to the story. A recording may fit very well with a story that has many descriptive passages because children can visualize the picture in their minds as they listen to the words. On the other hand, a recording may prove confusing to children if several speakers utter dialogue from a book and the voices are difficult to distinguish.

Check the technical quality of the production. Voices should be clear and easily understood. In live-action films or videos, lips and voices should be synchronized. Prints and pictures should be distinct and in focus. Sound effects and music should help establish the mood of the story, not overpower the story.

Anthony Magnacce/Merrill

Books and book-related media build on children's social nature.

Check also for authenticity. If there is a dialect, it should be spoken accurately. If the story has a specific setting, it should be realistically portrayed. Note whether a film, video or DVD based on a children's book has the original artwork. If it does not, you must judge the quality of the art as well as the technical quality of the filming.

Creating a Positive Environment

When you order nonprint materials, note the type of equipment that is needed to share them. When selecting CD-ROMs, note the system requirements. If possible, set up the equipment either before the children arrive or while they are engaged in other activities. They can become restless as they wait for a program to load or a video to be set at the desired starting place. It is also more difficult to concentrate on equipment if you must simultaneously attend to 25 children.

Let the children get settled before beginning a video or DVD. You can ask them to be sure they can see the screen before the lights are turned out. You may want to tell them a little about what they are going to see to set the mood or ask them to watch for specific happenings.

Think about the length of the presentation in relation to the attention span of the children who will be experiencing it. Weston Woods Studios has made a motion picture and a video of *The Snowman* (1980), a wordless picture book by Raymond Briggs. It is exquisitely produced, with smooth animation and a beautiful orchestral score. The story is easier to follow in this format than in the original because only one scene appears on the screen at a time, rather than the progression of small scenes that appear on a single page in the book. The video has few omitted scenes and several added sequences. It is a superb production, yet it runs for 26 minutes—a long time for preschool or primary children, particularly because the film is rather slow paced. To retain the attention of young children, you may want to show the movie in two segments. Decide where to make the break during your preview session.

Adapting a story to a new medium does not necessarily change the level of difficulty of comprehension. If 5-year-olds are baffled by the four parallel stories that comprise David Macaulay's *Black and White* (1990), it is likely that they will have the same difficulty whether they encounter the story as a picture book, a video, or a CD. If the content or presentation is too sophisticated for your group, make another selection, even though the work itself and the translation into audiovisual format may be outstanding.

Think also about the children's reactions to the presentation. If children might perceive a movie as scary, then tell them it is a scary movie before showing it so they are prepared. This sort of preparation could make the difference between children's enjoyment of a film and their dislike of a film they find frightening.

Helping Children Construct Meaning

Children are very accustomed to taking in information visually. They see advertisements, Web TV, videos, and animated cartoons. Flood and Lapp noted, "From a very early age, children see and respond to images shifting approximately every 7 seconds on the television screen with the background 'noise' of musical and verbal messages" (1998, p. 343). Although they may not understand all these messages, they do come to expect many of the accompanying features. Teachers and child-care providers can help children make sense of what they are seeing and hearing by encouraging them to talk about the meaning they are getting and how they have arrived at it. There may be elements to which they are responding but that they have never identified. For example, musical background while a title and credits are showing often sets the mood of a video or film.

Narrative Structure   A pivotal element that sets interactive media apart from books or videos is that it is often nonlinear in construction. That is, the viewer can move back and forth in a retelling or can decide to take a side trip, as it were. Things are happening simultaneously. They are not in the neat, sequentially organized, planned recounting of events. The author has less control in the construction of meaning and the reader/viewer has more than in books. The author no longer determines the sequence in which children will experience a story. This may be "good news/bad news" for the viewer. The good news is the opportunities it opens, such as the possibility of finding new meanings by clicking on an icon and new ways of understanding how a story is put together. The bad news is that the side trips may block out the main path, with children remembering the animation but having no idea of the actual story line.

Visual Literacy   It is helpful to have children explain orally what they are seeing or have seen and how they have interpreted visual action and symbols. Media can be played and replayed so that children can check on their observations. Teachers have also found that with media, as with books, it is important to set, or have the children set, purposes for viewing and listening.

The ways in which meaning is created visually can be explored by children using programs, such as Hyperstudio, with which they are manipulating the visual elements in combination with text to create meaning themselves. And viewing a video or DVD or listening to a cassette or CD several times encourages more attention to detail and form.

Teachers have a wide selection of literature they may share with children and ways in which to share it. Guided by their purposes, their knowledge of children, and their evaluation of the literature itself, they can bring children and books together in ways that will make the relationship a lasting one.

HELPING OTHERS SHARE LITERATURE

It is likely that you will have either professional or volunteer aides at least part of the time to assist you in your classroom or center work. Some child-care centers have a regular schedule of "grandparents" who come once a week to work with the children. Some actually are the grandparents of the children in the program, but many others are older community residents who enjoy being with children and want to contribute their time and skills to a meaningful activity.

Having these people share literature with children is an excellent use of their time. They can read to one or two youngsters, letting them select their favorite stories. It is important that children hear some stories over and over, because this helps them gain the concept that print holds a story constant and that whoever reads the story will use the same words. The words are in the book, not in the adult's head. The story that one child wants to hear again, however, may not be the favorite of others. Thus individual and small-group sharing of literature is vital.

In addition, when reading to only one or two children, the adult can allow the child to point to objects and to discuss the book in the midst of the reading. This practice can become distracting when done with a large group, for as one child discusses, others may become confused about the story line or lose interest in hearing the book. The adult can focus on left-to-right progression of words, point to certain words and tell what they say, have the child find words that he or she can recognize, and, in general, engage in practices that set the stage for the child to learn to read. Those children who can read already might read every other page themselves or perhaps even read the whole story with the adult as the listener.

When the adult reads to just one child, he or she can emphasize certain aspects of the story, talk with the child about their reaction to the story, or let the child retell the story, either from memory or by looking at the illustrations. It is an ideal time for communication and for maximum involvement of the child regardless of the age.

You may need to be very direct in suggesting to the aide which behaviors contribute to effective oral reading. Often, when we compare the oral reading skills of teachers with those of aides, we find that the aides are not as effective as teachers in oral reading. Even aides who indicated that they read regularly to their own children at home may not necessarily be skilled readers. Be certain that aides know what is expected of them. They should practice so that they read with expression, using appropriate volume and speed. They should show the illustrations, involve children with the reading, and maintain eye contact as much as possible.

If you have an aide who is skilled as a storyteller, by all means make use of him or her in this capacity. Find out if your aide speaks and reads in the language or languages spoken by your bilingual students. This opens up more possibilities for the sharing of literature, because many public libraries have sections of children's books in other languages. Train your aides in the skills they need to work effectively, and build on the unique skills they bring to the center or classroom.

SUMMARY

To involve children with literature, whether by reading, telling, or using audiovisual materials, it is necessary to prepare carefully. One way of thinking about this is to focus first on finding the right book to read, story to tell, or media version to experience.

During the selection process, you find the literature you may share, using selection guides when necessary. Apply the standards of good literature to any story or poem under consideration, with added criteria applied to stories for telling or in audiovisual format. Make the selection with a specific group of children in mind.

The next step is to create a positive classroom atmosphere for enjoying literature. Decide how you will share the literature and how you will involve the children. Plan so that distractions are kept at a minimum. A regular time and procedure for sharing literature help establish a pattern and demonstrate that you consider literature an important activity. Know how you are going to introduce the literature, perhaps by having children describe what they think the story may be about as they look at the book cover and hear the title or by setting the stage by working with a hand puppet. Know also what concluding statements, questions, or activities will follow the actual sharing of the literature.

Read aloud the stories and poems you plan to share; make cards to help you recall the sequence of action in a story you plan to tell; stack the figures for a felt or flannel board story in the order in which you will use them; and preview audiovisual materials both for the content and to make certain you know how to use the equipment.

If you have aides to assist you, have them read to one or two children at a time. Teach them to read skillfully. Careful preparation by you and your aides will help bring children and books together not only for the 15 minutes it takes to read a story, but also for the rest of their lives.

Extending Your Learning

1. Make a tape recording of yourself reading a book for children and evaluate your oral reading skill in relation to speed and volume, enunciation, and expression.

2. Develop a plan for introducing three different picture books to a group of children.

3. Read five folktales that are in picture-book format. For each, assess whether it would be good for telling as well as reading.

4. Make felt-board characters and use them to tell a story. You may want to use the list of cumulative stories recommended in this chapter to assist you in finding an appropriate book.

5. Read a folktale or predictable story and divide it into units of action for telling.

6. Preview a video or DVD based on a children's book. Assess the quality of the production and describe a potential audience for the material.

7. Preview a CD-ROM based on a children's book. Describe the interactive features and assess their merit in terms of developing literary understanding.

REFERENCES

Professional References Cited

Bank Street Bookstore, 610 West 112th Street, New York, NY, 10025. http://www.bankstreetbooks.com

Bowker's complete video directory. (2007). New Providence, NJ: Bowker. http://www.bowker.com

Briggs, N., & Wagner, J. (1979). *Children's literature through storytelling and drama.* Dubuque, IA: Brown.

Children's catalog. (2006). New York: Wilson. (Annual softcover supplements. Also available as online database.)

Church, E. B. (2002). Flannel board fun. *Scholastic Early Childhood Today, 16*(4), 52-53.

Coalition of Quality Children's Media. http://www.kidsfirst.org

Flood, J., & Lapp, D. (1998). Conceptualizations of literacy: The visual and communicative arts. *The Reading Teacher 51*(4), 342-44.

Honig, Alice. (2004). Sharing books with babies. *Scholastic Early Childhood Today 18*(4), 25-27.

The Horn Book Guide. Published spring and fall by The Horn Book, Inc., 56 Roland Street, Suite 200, Boston, MA 02129.

The Horn Book Guide Online. (2002). Published by The Horn Book, Inc., 56 Roland Street, Suite 200, Boston, MA 02129. http://www.hbook.com

Huck, C., Keifer, B., Hepler, S., & Hickman, J. (2006). *Children's literature in the elementary school* (9th ed.). Boston: McGraw-Hill.

Live Oak Media. http://www.liveoakmedia.com

Reading Rainbow. http://pbskids.org/readingrainbow

Sipe, L. (1998). The construction of literary understanding by first and second graders in response to picture storybook read-alouds. *Reading Research Quarterly 33*(4), 376-78.

Spoken Arts. http://www.spokenartsmedia.com

Stewig, J. (1992). Reading pictures, reading texts: Some similarities. *The New Advocate 5*(1), 11-22.

Subject guide to children's books in print. (2008). New Providence, NJ: R. R. Bowker (annual).

Weston Woods. http://teacher.scholastic.com/products/westonwoods/index.htm

Children's Literature Cited

Aylesworth, Jim. (2003). *Goldilocks and the Three Bears.* Ill. Barbara McClintock. New York: Scholastic.

Barton, Byron. (1993). *The Little Red Hen.* New York: HarperCollins.

Brett, Jan. (1987). *Goldilocks and the Three Bears.* New York: Dodd.

Briggs, Raymond. (1980). *The Snowman* (video) Weston, CT: Weston Woods.

Buehner, Carolyn. (2007). *Goldilocks and the Three Bears.* Ill. Mark Buehner. New York: Dial.

Carle, Eric. (1981). *The Very Hungry Caterpillar.* New York: Philomel.

Galdone, Paul. (1976). *The Little Red Hen.* New York: Scholastic.

Macaulay, David. (1990). *Black and White.* Boston: Houghton Mifflin.

Neitzel, Shirley. (1989). *The Jacket I Wear in the Snow.* Ill. Nancy Winslow Parker. New York: Greenwillow.

Numeroff, Laura Joffe. (1985). *If You Give a Mouse a Cookie.* Ill. Felicia Bond. New York: HarperCollins.

Pinkney, Jerry. (2006). *The Little Red Hen.* New York: Dial.

Rosen, Michael. (1989). *We're Going on a Bear Hunt.* Ill. Helen Oxenbury. New York: Simon & Schuster.

Stellaluna. CD-Rom. The Learning Company, 2006.

Turkle, Brinton. (1976). *Deep in the Forest.* New York: Dutton.

CHAPTER FOUR

JARRED, Age 6
"Leaves to the Sky" inspired by Books to
the Ceiling from *Good Books, Good Times*
by Lee Bennett Hopkins

Jarred's (age 6) poem inspired by "Books to the Ceiling" by
Arnold Lobel in *Good Books, Good Times*! selected by
Lee Bennett Hopkins (1990).

The Literature Curriculum

The kindergarten teacher looked around her classroom after the children had gone home. She visualized the house the four youngsters had constructed in the block corner; she smiled at her remembrance of the dramatic play in the housekeeping corner and "mother" Darice's insistence that the "children" take a nap; she looked at the four paintings still drying on the easels and decided to display them on the wall above the bookshelves.

The teacher was actively engaged in using her imagination. She was forming mental images, some based on events that had happened, others based on projections of ideas. The children, too, had been using their imaginations as they created pictures and buildings and as they took the roles of other people in dramatic play.

DEVELOPING THE IMAGINATION

Imagination is central to the competent functioning of independent individuals and of free societies. The ability to construct mental images allows individuals to weigh evidence and explore the possible consequences of particular actions. It allows them to create and to evaluate new ideas. Northrop Frye (1964) wrote, "The fundamental job of the imagination in ordinary life is to produce, out of the society we have to live in, a vision of the society we want to live in" (p. 140). Without an educated imagination, we can only adjust to society as it is. With an educated imagination, we can evaluate and attempt to change society and exercise what Frye sees as free speech, the capability of using language effectively, and having thoughts of our own to express with that language.

Literature contributes to the development of our imaginations. Participating in the literary experience is itself an imaginative endeavor because readers are projecting themselves into a story. Often they are seeing worlds that they could not—or would not choose to—experience themselves. The confrontation with lives both better and worse than their own and with experiences quite different from their own refines their sensibilities and broadens their perspectives.

Literature exposes for readers the basic wants and needs of other people, the problems they have, and the values and attitudes that underlie their decision making. Readers are forced to look at their own values—and their own prejudices—more objectively. Frye (1964) wrote that as readers experience literature, they gain a kind of detachment in viewing others and themselves. This detachment leads to an ability to accept the existence of differing beliefs and to the development of tolerance.

Literature presents readers with a more structured picture of life than does real experience. Authors select for presentation those events that have the most relevance to characters' actions and those feelings that most epitomize the characters' personalities. They impose an order or mode of presentation designed to help the reader grasp the significance of the total happening. Literature aids readers in their ability to interpret experiences by narrowing the range of events discussed.

The development of the imagination through literature is particularly vital for children. In *Introducing Books to Children*, Aiden Chambers wrote

> All of these different ways in which literature functions have enormous value for children, as for adults. Children are forming attitudes, finding points of reference, building concepts, forming images to think with, all of which interact to form a basis for decision-making judgment, for understanding, for sympathy with the human condition. Literary experience feeds the imagination, that faculty by which we come to grips with the astonishing amount of data which assails our everyday lives, and find patterns of meaning in it. *(1983, p. 28)*

Glenna Davis Sloan, author of *The Child as Critic,* concurs.

> The structures of literature are self-contained; the reality they present is an imaginative reality. Contemplating these structures critically and reflectively can help us to develop the capacity to view with detachment other verbal structures that surround us. A well-developed imagination, educated on literature, is protection against social mythology in all its forms: entertainment, advertising, propaganda, the language of cliché and stereotype, the abstractions of jargon and gobbledegook. In an irrational world the trained reason is important, but an educated imagination is fundamental to the survival of a same society. *(2003, p. 14)*

A basic goal of a literature curriculum is the education of children's imaginations. By listening to a broad spectrum of literature, children participate in the imaginative experiences of many authors and illustrators and begin to see that all literature is part of a body of interrelated works. Child-care professionals and teachers of young children contribute to this basic goal by involving children with literature in ways that establish positive attitudes toward it and by grouping books and structuring presentations so that children begin to perceive the interrelatedness of literature.

PROMOTING POSITIVE ATTITUDES

Because literature is experienced more than taught, if children are to become deeply involved with it, they must choose to do so. This will happen if literature is a satisfying experience for them. You can assist children in becoming involved and developing positive attitudes toward literature through regular reading and careful selection of stories and poetry and through involving children in activities that extend books in a pleasurable manner.

Regular Sharing of Literature

Obviously, for prereaders to experience literature it must be read to them or presented through dramatic or audiovisual means. Even after children have begun to read themselves, the teacher, caregiver and parents should continue to share literature orally on a daily basis. Many books and poems that are appropriate for young children are still too difficult for them to read themselves. Most are more enjoyable when presented by a skilled reader than when deciphered on a word-by-word basis. An adult has the opportunity to show children how effectively language can be used and what enjoyment it can bring.

Literature Selection

As suggested in chapter 1, you need to know children and their backgrounds as you select books to read to them. Most young children like humor, with slapstick being very popular and the verbal humor of puns and riddles becoming more and more appreciated. Young children respond to exaggeration in words and illustrations and enjoy being in on pranks and jokes that are played on fictional characters. Humorous books should be a basic part of your literature curriculum. So, too, should books whose contents appeal to many young children: books about everyday events, animals, and the world of "once upon a time."

In a study examining poetry preferences of young children, Kutiper and Wilson (1993) found that "readers do not like poetry in which figurative language interferes with the instant understanding that most young readers desire" (p. 32). Children like narrative poetry best, with free verse, lyric poetry, and haiku the least popular forms; they like rhymed, metered poetry, but they often dislike poetry that is heavily dependent on metaphorical language. They like poems about familiar experiences involving children and animals, but they almost always like humorous poetry the best. Children also tend to like poems they have heard before, so it's important to revisit poetry that might have been enjoyed previously.

Keeping in mind the general preferences of young children, you will also need to assess the difficulty of the poem or book you are considering. Children (and adults, too) often dislike what they do not understand. If the literature is beyond the children's comprehension, you are likely to be wasting both your time and theirs by reading it.

There are no hard-and-fast rules for determining *exactly* which book is appropriate for exactly which child, nor for saying exactly how much of a book a child should understand for the literary experience to be a legitimate one. Still, you will get an idea of the difficulty of a book if you assess the style of writing, the approach to the content, and the complexity of the theme.

Style of writing includes, among other aspects, the choice of vocabulary and the sentence length and structure. Reading and listening comprehension are related to these items. Following are excerpts from two picture books. The first is from *Best Best Friends* (Chodos-Irvine, 2006), a story about two young girls who are best friends.

> Clare and Mary are best friends.
> Every day, when they get to preschool, they give each other big hugs.
> They sit together at storytime.
> When they go outside to play, they always hold hands. *(n.p.)*

The second passage is from *Freedom Summer* (Wiles, 2001), the story of two boys living in the South during the early 1960s. Joe and John Henry are a lot alike, except for the color of their skin. When a new law is passed that forbids segregation,

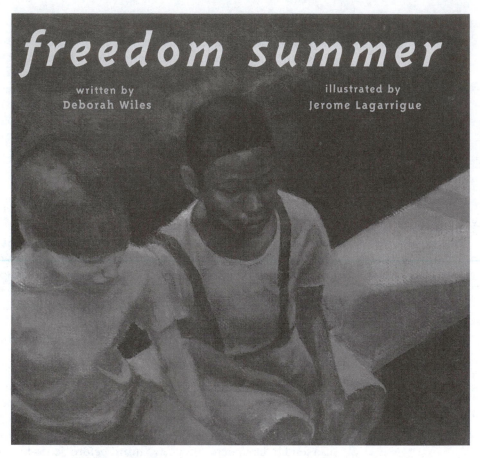

written by
Deborah Wiles

illustrated by
Jerome Lagarrigue

Set in Mississippi during the summer of 1964, Wiles's story focuses on two boys—one white and the other African-American—having to deal with the bittersweet aftermath of the passage of the Civil Rights Act.
(Reprinted with the permission of Atheneum Books for Young Readers, an imprint of Simon & Schuster Children's Publishing Division from FREEDOM SUMMER by Deborah Wiles, illustrated by Jerome Lagarrigue. Illustrations copyright © 2001 Jerome Lagarrigue.)

the boys eagerly await their opportunity to swim in the town pool together. The next morning, the boys race to the pool only to find

> County dump trucks are here. They grind and back up to the empty pool.
>
> Workers rake steaming asphalt into the hole where sparkling clean water used to be.
>
> One of them is John Henry's big brother, Will Rogers. We start to call to him, "What happened?" but he sees us first and points back on down the road—it means "Git on home!"
>
> But our feet feel stuck, we can't budge.
>
> So we hunker in the tall weeds and watch all morning until the pool is filled with hot, spongy tar. *(n.p.)*

The vocabulary in the second passage is more advanced than that of the first. Words such as *asphalt* and *hunker*, for example, are used, but there are also idiomatic expressions, such as Git on home! Neither passage has inordinately complex sentence structures, which would make comprehension difficult for young children.

Both books are about friendship as well as conflict. In *Best Best Friends*, the girls are inseparable until Mary has a birthday and receives special queen-for-a-day treatment from the teacher and her classmates. Clare becomes jealous and starts an argument with Mary. But soon, all is forgiven and they are once again best friends. This is a familiar situation that many children have experienced and will understand. The story will prompt preschoolers to share their own best friend stories.

Joe and John Henry in *Freedom Summer* are facing both a racial and legal issue that—it is hoped—children today will not encounter. They enjoy swimming in Fiddler's Creek, but John Henry's desire and, later, disappointment at not being able to do everything that Joe can do is vividly expressed through Wiles's poignant text and Jerome Lagarrigue's riveting impressionistic paintings. Joe wants to see the town through John Henry's eyes, and they begin doing so by walking together into a once-segregated store to purchase an ice pop.

Both books share the theme of friendship; one through feelings of resentment and envy, the other through awareness and sensitivity. Clare and Mary characterize typical preschoolers who are learning about socialization, empathy, and loyalty. These themes are also present in *Freedom Summer*. The boys also recognize that bravery doesn't mean not being afraid and that friendship and caring do not depend on skin color.

Writing style, approach to content, and theme all make *Freedom Summer* a book appropriate for children age 6 or older, whereas *Best Best Friends* can be shared with children as young as 2 or 3. There are, however, books that are enjoyed by both age groups. Use your judgment about the difficulty of a book; then watch the children's reactions as you read and listen to their comments. Use their responses to determine how well you are matching their level of comprehension.

Strategies and Activities for Responding to Books

In addition to careful selection, you can maintain and enhance positive attitudes toward literature by suggesting strategies and activities for extending the books that are enjoyable and satisfying for children. You can utilize strategies such as creating a timeline, sketching the meaning of a story, or comparing and contrasting books in all areas of the curriculum; they serve to extend the child's response to a story. Activities may be more limited if you focus on an aspect of the story to enhance the response. Strategies and activities should encourage further involvement with literature. If second-graders must fill in book report forms for each book they complete, they may decide to stop reading. If they are asked to draw their favorite part of *every* book they hear, they may begin to dread story time. If, however, they are engaged in a variety of creative responses, as suggested in chapters 4 through 9, and have the opportunity to work both with others and by themselves and make choices about how they respond, they are likely to want to hear and read more literature.

Strategies and activities serve many purposes. They help children explore the structure of literature. They encourage comparisons of stories, leading to a concept of what a story is. They support growth in many areas of development. They give teachers a measure of their students' comprehension.

Glenna Sloan writes

> The child's response to the literature is a central aspect of criticism. The response may come in the form of a question or comment; it may involve sharing a favorite poem or retelling a familiar story; it may be an original composition in words, a drawing, a dramatization, a puppet play, a dance drama, or the story board for a film or a video. . . . Response is both free and guided, the teacher building upon initial response to guide young critics to a greater insight and appreciation of literary works and literature as a whole. *(2003, pp. 39–40)*

Here, criticism means the study of literature in which children learn the verbal trappings for talking about prose and poetry. They learn these in a context in which the terms arise naturally, and they build a foundation for a later, more formal analysis of literature. It is one more reason for encouraging creative responses to literature.

GROUPING BOOKS FOR INSTRUCTION

You should guide children to perceive literature as a body of work rather than as separate and unrelated stories and poems. If you group books for presentation, you set the stage for children to see the relationships among books and, to notice the recurring structural patterns of literature. You give children a database from which they can make their own generalizations about literature.

In a research study that has relevance still today, Arthur Applebee (1978) analyzed the patterns children used in telling stories and the responses they gave when asked about fiction and fictional characters to determine the concept of story held by children ages 2 through 17. He assumed that young children, who might not say directly what they expected to find in a story, would reveal their expectations in the stories they told. He found that even 2-year-olds distinguished some conventions of a story. They told stories having formal openings or titles:

> "Once upon a time . . ."; having formal closings: ". . . and they lived happily ever after" or "the end"; and which were consistently in the past tense. Seventy percent of the 2-year-olds included at least one of these conventions in the stories they told. The use of the three devices rose with age until by age 5, 93% of the children used at least one of them and 47% used all three. *(pp. 36–38)*

Applebee noted that many of the stories read to young children are based on the oral tradition and employ these conventions. The data also showed that as the children matured, they told stories that became more and more removed from the immediate setting of home and family. They also used the conventions of story to explore behaviors unacceptable in terms of general social norms. As the unacceptable behaviors were included, the use of realistic settings dropped. The threat of exploring bad actions was lessened by the distance from reality.

Young children often see stories more as histories than as fictions. At age 6, nearly three fourths of the children studied were still uncertain about whether stories were real, but by age 9, all the children classified stories as make-believe. This interview with Joseph, age 6 years and 3 months, shows a process that occurs often. Children combine the events of the story with the rest of their knowledge about the world.

> Is Cinderella a real person? No
> Was she ever a real person? Nope, she died.
> Did she used to be alive? Yes.
> When did she live? A long time ago, when I was one years old.
> Are stories always about things that really happened? Yes.
> When did the things in Little Red Riding Hood happen? A long time ago when I was a baby, they happened. There was witches and that, a long time ago. So when they started witch . . . they say two good people and they made some more good people, so did the more horrible people. And they made more good people and the bad people got drowned.
> Are there still people like that? Nope, they were all killed, the police got them.
>
> *(Applebee, 1978, p. 44)*

Joseph's knowledge of police is combined with characters from folktales and with the biblical story of Noah and the flood. Applebee reasons,

> It is only after the story has emerged as a fiction that it can begin a new journey toward a role in the exploration of the world not as it is but as it might be, a world which poses alternatives rather than declares certainties.   *(p. 41).*

One role of the preschool and primary-grade teacher is to guide this emerging realization that fiction presents possible alternatives, which is of the imaginative world. Children develop a sense of story as they mature intellectually. Realizing that the world of literature is not factual but is an imaginative way of learning and knowing is a gradual process. Applebee found that many children of age 6 said that stories in general did not have to be about real happenings, but they nonetheless contended that certain fictional characters special to them were real. Stories might be make-believe, but yes, they could visit Snow White if only she did not live so far away.

As you share books with children, tell them the names of the authors and illustrators. This gives them the information that stories were created by people, information that will take on meaning for them when they are ready to fit it into their schemata for organizing their world. Present examples of many types of stories, with diverse settings and varied characters, so that children have the data to generalize broadly about the conventions of story. Group stories to help children see that certain events, images, or story shapes occur repeatedly. They can observe how two stories, with differing characters, settings, and plots, may still offer the same theme. They can see that one animal character and one human character may occupy the same role in different stories as each leaves home for an adventure, is successful, and returns home. There are many ways of grouping books. During any one school year, you should vary your approach to grouping. At times you may group only two books for comparison, whereas at other times you may use either the unit or the web approach to larger groupings.

Book Comparisons

Questions in any discussion about books usually focus attention on only a few of the many responses to literature. Some questions help children identify with the characters; others stimulate creative thought. Still others guide children in their literary understandings. It is particularly useful to discuss more than one book at a time if the goal of the discussion is sharpening children's awareness of the interrelatedness of literature. Book comparisons demonstrate that certain patterns, themes, and types of characters appear in many stories. They show that the elements of literature work together in any one story and that these same elements are the core of all literature.

Suppose you read *Duck and Goose*, written and illustrated by Tad Hills (2006), to a group of first-graders. When a young duck and a little goose encounter a big spotted sphere, they quickly decide that it is an egg (which, it is hoped, shrewd kindergarteners or first-graders will quickly realize closely resembles a soccer ball). "I saw it first," says the yellow duck. "I touched it first," exclaims the white-feathered goose as he raises one webbed foot and plants it firmly on the ball. They both envision encircling the "egg" with a fence and plenty of signs—for duck the signs read, "No geese allowed," and "No honking $5 fine." The goose has his own signage: "If you are a duck, keep walking," and "Absolutely no quacking in this area." Both are unyielding in their desire for the egg and express all the hopes and dreams any expectant parent might have for a happy child that is an extension of themselves. Finally, when a bird inquires, "Can I play, too?" the two finally realize that this egg is never going to hatch. But they still deem it a "keeper," and the two decide to hold onto the ball and to their friendship.

The themes of getting along, sharing, and set-tling one's differences come across loud and clear in Hills's humorous story.

An important initial understanding of the story is that what the duck and goose are fighting over is not an egg but a ball. This is an instance where you need to pause in the reading to determine if children clearly understand this aspect of the story. Once listeners have that insight, then the verbal exchange between the two earnest fowls becomes both ridiculous and humorous. To assist children in developing literary understandings, you do need to ask questions or suggest activities that focus on the events and structure of the story. These should be questions that explore the relationship of one part of the story to another or describe how the author and illustrator create mood or tone. Some additional questions that could be asked for discussion of *Duck and Goose* could include the following:

1. Why did duck and goose believe that the ball was an egg?

2. How does the illustrator show us what duck and goose are thinking?

3. How do you know that duck and goose have sat on the egg for a long time?

4. At what point in the story do you think duck and goose became friends? How did they learn to become friends? Why do you think that?

5. If this story was about you and you were waiting for the egg to hatch, how would the sentence "I would teach this baby bird to . . ." be completed?

6. What do you think they will do with the ball at the end of the story? Will they remain friends?

7. How would the story be different if it really were an egg instead of a ball? What would happen then?

Patrick White/Merrill

Books provide a model and inspiration for writing.

When children tell how a story might be different if one thing were changed, whether it is a happening, a character, or a setting, they are seeing how that element fits into the total story and the impact it has on every other part. When they tell what one of the major characters "learned," they frequently are identifying the theme of the story. When they tell whether they were surprised by an event, they are demonstrating their expectations about the story—expectations founded on characterizations and plot development. And when they tell why a character may have acted as he or she did, they are looking at motivation and characterization.

Questions should be phrased so that they allow children to explain, in their own words, their understanding of the story. If children answer with only yes or no, they miss the opportunity to develop their own ideas, and the adult and the other children miss the opportunity to see how the child is reasoning. If a child has difficulty with a question, it can be rephrased so that the response requires less information or fewer inferences but still allows the child to explain fully. And sometimes a question, such as question 4, can be broken down into two or more questions so that children aren't overwhelmed with having to remember numerous things that are being asked at once.

To extend the story of *Duck and Goose* further, children could draw or write about something they have shared with a friend. A closer inspection of Tad Hills's cartoon-style illustrations to determine how he expresses emotion is another way to extend the book. The book also lends itself to dramatization for students to retell the story or even to perform a readers' theater of the book.

Reading a second book on a similar theme, about a similar situation, or of the same genre or contrasting a second book sharply with the first provides more information for children to process—information about how literature works. After reading *Duck and Goose,* you could share *Don't Let the Pigeon Drive the Bus* (Willems, 2003), another book that presents the idea of negotiation to gain what is desired. It describes a very persistent pigeon that begs, pleads, cajoles and eventually throws a tantrum to get what he wants—which is to drive the bus. Although there isn't another voice that provides a response to the pigeon, it is evident that he isn't going to get his way, so he continues to try another approach. Willems has also used cartoon-style illustrations,

but they are very different from those of Hills. Both books would be considered fantasy that portrays feathered fowls in absurd situations. Some of the questions that could be asked of young listeners might be these:

1. Why would the pigeon want to drive the bus?

2. The pigeon is expressing different emotions. How do you know what he is feeling and how he would say it?

3. If you were answering the pigeon, what would you tell him? "You can't drive the bus because . . ."

4. At the end of the story, the pigeon sees a red tractor trailer truck and says, "Hey . . ." What do you think he is going to ask or do?

5. How are the stories of *Duck and Goose* and *Don't Let the Pigeon Drive the Bus* alike? How are they different?

In response to *Don't Let the Pigeon Drive the Bus* and as a way to extend the story, children can share stories about what they have wanted and how they tried to get it. They can also create their own versions of a "pigeon" story, such as Don't Let the Pigeon Drive the Taxi or Don't Let the Pigeon Drive the Truck, which 4-year-old Bethany did. Her story is shared in chapter 10.

Having compared books under your guidance, children can then begin to compare them on their own, working within a framework that includes literary comparisons. They can also discover the sequels of *Duck, Duck, Goose* (Hills, 2006) and *Don't Let the Pigeon Stay Up Late* (Willems, 2006) and compare those to the books that were read as well as to the others.

Units of Study

You can group books with common characteristics into units of study that focus on a single item, describe similar content, or represent literature of a particular genre or by a particular author or illustrator. When you plan a unit of study, consider a variety of titles, but narrow the selection to those books that best fit your purposes and include only those that you actually plan to use. You usually plan the sequence of books and strategies and activities in advance, although modifications may be made based on children's reactions or new information.

Suppose you are working with 5- or 6-year-olds. You think about how their interests and needs are covered in the literature you know. You might do a unit of study on making friends, being afraid, or stories about animals that talk. You decide to do a unit of study on books in which the characters use their imaginations in ways that are understandable to young children. You want the children to recognize that people use their imaginations in a variety of ways and for a variety of purposes. You hope to engage the children in response strategies and activities that stimulate their imaginations and that enable them to discern techniques used by authors and illustrators to indicate the imaginative life of the characters.

You list books with which you are familiar and use the book-selection guides available in the library to make a general list. Then you decide on five or six classic and contemporary stories to share with the children. You choose the following:

Burningham, John. (1977). *Come Away from the Water, Shirley.* New York: Crowell.

> Shirley and her parents go to the beach, where her parents set up their beach chairs and get comfortable. Shirley stands at the water's edge. While her parents, shown on the left page throughout the book, make comments to her about not petting the dog and being careful not to get tar on her shoes, Shirley imagines all sorts of adventures for herself, all shown on the right-hand pages.

Lawson, Janet. (2002). *Audrey and Barbara.* New York: Atheneum.

> Audrey, a diminutive, yet determined, pony-tailed girl, reads a book about India and decides that she and her orange cat, Barbara, will travel there to ride an elephant. Barbara reluctantly assists Audrey, even though her preference is napping on a pillow. Audrey converts a bathtub into a sailboat, using a quilt as a sail. When the young girl realizes that they could get stuck in the ocean, Barbara finally captures the spirit of imagination and suggests they "could ask a whale for a tow." Humorous watercolor illustrations and a brief text convey a story of true friendship.

McCarty, Peter. (2006). *Moon Plane.* New York: Holt.

> A small boy sees a plane flying through the sky and imagines riding in it—traveling faster than a car, soaring past a train, and bursting into space where he lands on the moon. There, he experiences weightlessness as he jumps on the moon's surface and flies like an airplane. When he returns home, his mother tucks him into bed and he dreams of airplanes. McCarty's soft-edged, silver-tone artwork along with brief soothing text will spark imagination in young children.

Portis, Antoinette. (2006). *Not a Box.* New York: HarperCollins

> With a cover that resembles a plain brown cardboard box, this streamlined book visualizes a child's imagined games. An unknown person asks a small rabbit why he is sitting in a box. The rabbit, who appears next to a simple, black-lined square, replies, "It's not a box." The next page presents text on a bold red background, and the opposite page

in red and yellow shows the rabbit in a speeding roadster. In the following spreads, the questioner continues to ask about the rabbit's plans while the little voice continues to answer, "It's not a box." The spare design and the rabbit's vivid imagination are engaging.

Sendak, Maurice. (1963). *Where the Wild Things Are.* New York: Harper & Row.

 Max, wearing his wolf suit and making mischief, is called a wild thing and sent to bed without his supper. He fantasizes a forest in his room and sails to where the wild things are. They make him king and at his command take part in the "rumpus," and although they beg Max to stay, he sails home. He wants to be where someone cares for him, and when he returns his supper is waiting for him.

Sis, Peter. (2002). *Madlenka's Dog.* New York: Farrar, Straus & Giroux.

 Precocious Madlenka's persistent requests for a dog are denied. So she decides to take matters into her own hands by walking her imaginary dog around the city block. As she meets neighbors and friends, they share their own memories of dogs past, which are cleverly displayed under lift-the-flaps. Finally, Madlenka and her friend Cleopatra, who just happens to have an imaginary horse, go off on further adventures accompanied by both dog and horse.

To determine the sequence of presentation, look for ways the books relate to one another and for natural progressions. Plan discussion questions and activities that will help children explore the relationships among the books and support their growth in other areas.

You want to begin the unit with the children's experience, so engage them in guided fantasy. They sit comfortably in a group and you tell them that they will have the chance to play an imagination game. They are to close their eyes and make a picture in their minds of what you tell them. Your description goes something like this: "Picture yourself traveling to another place. What kind of transportation would you use? Who would you take with you on your travels? What would you pack? Imagine yourself arriving. As you look around, what do you see? What will you do now that you have arrived?"

You ask each child to describe a trip they are imagining. After the children have finished sharing their thoughts and ideas, you introduce *Moon Plane* by telling them that this is a story about a boy who used his imagination. *Moon Plane* contains simple text with much of the story conveyed through the monochromatic illustrations. When you have finished reading the book, ask if this really happened and why. You place the book on a special table, and on the wall behind it you post a large sheet of paper for the children to draw their own pictures of arriving at their imaginary destinations— what they are wearing, who has traveled with them, and their type of transportation.

The next day you continue with the idea of imagination and imaginative activities by reading *Audrey and Barbara.* This book encompasses ingenuity and inseparable friends with imagination and provides a perfect way to build from the storyline presented in *Moon Plane.* Instead of just one child being immersed in imaginative play, there is a second character that gets caught up in the adventure of traveling to a new place. At the book's conclusion, you ask the children to tell what is real and what is imagined in this story.

The third day you read *Come Away from the Water, Shirley.* The children have heard two stories in which the characters use their imaginations. In the discussion that follows your reading, you concentrate on the artist's technique for differentiating the fantasy from the realism of the story.

1. If Shirley's parents told about their day at the beach, what might they say? (Show the illustrations again here.)

2. If Shirley told about her day, what might she say? (Again, show the pictures.)

3. Do Shirley's parents know what she is doing? What makes you think this?

4. How does the artist let you know what is going on?

5. Would you rather have Shirley's day or her parent's day? Why?

Call the children's attention to the fact that Shirley figures prominently in the stories she imagines. She rows herself out to the pirate ship, engages in battle with the pirates, and discovers buried treasure. Then let two or three children tell an adventure with themselves in the key positions, recording their stories for transcription later. You can put the stories with the books and the wall drawings. Encourage the other children to dictate stories to you or classroom aides about themselves in an adventure or to write it themselves, so that the collection grows and each child has the opportunity to tell a story.

Now read *Where the Wild Things Are*. You lead a brief discussion, asking questions designed to stimulate the children to think about Max's feelings as related to his fantasy and to see the illustrator's use of increasingly larger pictures to build a climax. You ask these questions:

1. How did a forest grow in Max's room?

2. Why do you think Max went to visit the wild things?

3. Do you think the wild things are scary? Why or why not?

4. Watch as I show the pictures again. What do you notice about them? Why do you think the illustrator made them that way?

5. How do you think Max was feeling at the end of the story? What made him feel this way?

You and the children look again at the wild rumpus scenes. The children try to imagine the sounds the wild things are making. Then you ask, "What kind of music could the wild things hear as they danced?" Using rhythm instruments, the children develop music for the rumpus. Once the rhythm is established, other children dance to it, having their own "rumpus."

You conclude the unit with *Madlenka's Dog*. You have all six books handy for the discussion that follows the reading, first asking a few questions about the book just completed:

1. As you look at the title page and the page opposite it, what do you think the small squares and the squares on the opposite circle are?

2. Why does the picture of the dog under the flap look different from the person who said he or she owned it?

3. What do the dots mean on the small black-and-white drawing in the left-hand corner of each page?

4. What type of animal would you imagine that you owned, and why would that animal be a good pet?

Then guide the children in a comparison of the books, holding up the books as you mention them. Begin by asking the children what they remember about each book. Call on several children to respond to each question.

1. As I hold up each book, tell me one thing you remember about it.

2. In what ways are these books like each other?

3. What are some of the ways characters in these books used their imaginations? Why did they use their imaginations?

With the children dictating, make a chart that lists all the ways they use their imaginations.

You place the books, chart, drawings, and dictations in the same area. You listen to the children's comments during the week, and after a few days, you ask the children to select one of the books for you to reread. Moving the books back to the regular bookshelves, you inform the children of what you are doing as you prepare the space for a new display and new work.

When the unit of study has been completed, look at your purposes to evaluate whether they have been fulfilled. Did the children recognize that imagination was being used for differing reasons, sometimes for the enjoyment of it and other times for escaping fear, boredom, or frustration? Were the children stimulated to use their own imaginations? Did they participate in the guided fantasy, tell a story in which they had fantastic adventures, create and move to a "wild thing" rhythm, and contribute to a listing of ways the imagination can be used? Did they notice how the illustrator showed fantasy within a story, using techniques such as placing the fantasy within a frame, or placing reality on one page and fantasy on another? Your purposes should be sufficiently clear for you to assess the effectiveness of specific lessons.

If you are working with 2-, 3-, or 4-year-olds, the literature you select will, of course, be simpler than that you would choose for 6- and 7-year-olds. You will plan to involve the children in the language, content, and feelings of the stories, but you will spend less time analyzing the literature itself. You will, however, be aware yourself of the types of literature you are choosing and will plan to expose children to a variety of genres.

Suppose you are working with 2-, 3-, or 4-year-olds in a childcare center or preschool. You decide that you will select books about a topic of interest that they have expressed. You begin by looking at stories about cars, trucks and other vehicles. Because the children have enjoyed the humorous, rhyming tale in *My Truck is Stuck* (Lewis, 2002), you decide to select books about various types of trucks. When you begin to search for books, you realize that there are many books for very young children about trucks, both real and fictional. Some are counting books, which enable you to work on basic skills, whereas others including a rhyming text that invites children to participate in the storytelling. They also contain colorful illustrations that are easy for a group of children to see. You select the following five books as the core of your unit.

Carter, Don. (2002). *Get to Work Trucks.* New Milford, CT: Roaring Brook.

> From dawn to dusk, a road crew works with a variety of machines as they construct a bridge over a pond. When the supervisor yells, "Stop!" the construction workers must wait until a turtle passes by. An exploration of colors and numbers is presented within the simple text, whereas the acrylic paintings offer the numerous construction vehicles needed to complete the job.

Hunter, Jana Novotny. (2006). *When Daddy's Truck Picks Me Up.* Ill. Carol Thompson. Morton Grove, IL: Whitman.

> A preschooler knows that this is the day his trucker daddy will be picking him up from school in a tanker truck. All day the boy thinks about his father as he waits and waits, until finally his dad arrives and the two set off for the open road. Some illustrations depict the father's activities with childlike, crayon drawings that present the boy's perspective. The bouncy rhyme and colorful watercolor illustrations present a story that most children can relate to—waiting for parents to pick them up.

Lyon, George Ella. (2007). *Trucks Roll.* Ill. Craig Frazier. New York: Atheneum.

      Everyday, trucks bring ice cream, blocks, books, bulldozers, dolls, and socks. They roll through mountains and flatlands, and past deserts and towns. Lyon's rhyming text and Frazier's bold illustrations provide children with a glimpse into the life of truckers and the things that they haul.

Maass, Robert. (2007). *Little Trucks with Big Jobs.* New York: Holt.

      Big trucks are impressive and powerful, but little trucks are important, too. A tow truck, ambulance, forklift, and plane tug are just a few of the little trucks that have big jobs. Size doesn't matter when it comes to getting the job done. It's all in a day's work for these mighty trucks. Colorful photographs assist in the naming process for each truck.

McMullan, Kate. (2006). *I'm Dirty.* Ill. Jim McMullan. New York: Holt

      Counting down from 10 to 1, the dirt-loving backhoe removes the alliterative trash from 10 torn-up truck tires to 1 wonky washing machine. Finally, he pulls out a tree stump, takes a mud bath, and drags his bucket over the dirt. Throughout the story, the backhoe becomes progressively dirtier. The text flies about the pages, changing size and shape. The dynamic cartoon illustrations complement the humorous text.

With these five books you expose children to fiction written in rhyming and narrative styles as well as to informational books. They will hear several types of plot construction. *I'm Dirty* and *When Daddy's Truck Picks Me Up* have progressive plots that advance toward a single climax. *Get to Work Trucks!* and *Trucks Roll* have cumulative plots with a repetitive phrase. *Little Trucks with Big Jobs* is expository text that provides information.

    You begin the unit with *Get to Work Trucks!* because the brief text is engaging and will pique children's interest in trucks. After the children listen to the story and see the pictures, you go back through the story and discuss the different types of trucks that were featured in the text and illustrations. Start a word wall with the words loader, dump truck, digger, bulldozer, cement mixer, tow truck, and crane.

    Next you share *Little Trucks with Big Jobs.* This is written in a different style from *Get to Work Trucks!* and some words, such as tow truck, are repeated. There is also information about what each truck is used for. You add these truck words to the word wall as well. As you brainstorm other types of trucks that the children are familiar with, begin recording questions that the children raise about trucks and their purposes.

    The third book you use in this unit is *Trucks Roll!* As you read the story, have the children join in while reading the repetitive phrase, "trucks roll." Talk about the items that each truck hauls. Also discuss the different types of trucks that are needed to carry ice cream, books, or trees. Ask if they have seen trucks on the road and what types of things they thought the trucks were carrying. Start another chart to list this brainstorming.

    I'm Dirty is written in short, choppy sentences and, at times, the text flies around the page. This is also a humorous story that is a departure from the books that provide information through rhyme and expository text. Once you finish reading the story, go back and engage in the counting of each item. Linger over the cartoon illustrations and allow children time to discuss them. This would be a good time to talk about other books that Kate McMullen has written that are similar to *I'm Dirty,* such as *I Stink* (2002) and *I'm Mighty* (2003).

    As you prepare to read the last book, *When Daddy's Truck Picks Me Up,* ask the children to tell you what they think will happen in the story and why. What kind of truck does the boy's father drive? Why is he picking him up in that particular truck? Do you think the boy is excited to see his father and why? Then have the children look at the covers of the other books about trucks that you have read and decide if each is make-believe or could really happen.

You then put all the books together on a "Books about Trucks" shelf. You also create book bags for two of the books and begin circulating them. Children bring in books they have about trucks and other vehicles and you add these to the shelf as well. You notice that the children are looking at these books regularly, and you hear one little girl saying, "Trucks roll!" From these responses, you know that your literature presentation has been successful.

Webs

A web is a diagram that charts either the potential within a single book or the possible ways of developing a single topic through literature. Webs differ from units in that they show far more ideas than will be actually used, and they do not show sequence. They are a form of brainstorming. Think of all the possible extensions of a book or all the aspects of a topic. Jot them down around the main heading, categorizing as you go. When you have finished, you will have many ideas you might pursue with children. Webs can help you remain flexible in your use of books because they encourage an exploration of many facets of a book or topic. You may then emphasize one aspect of the book or topic with one group of children and another aspect with a second group.

Figure 4–1 shows a web on the topic of school. Stories, poems, and activities are grouped around topics related to school experiences. If you were using this web, you would select those items from it that seemed appropriate for your group of children, developing the ideas more fully before you presented them.

For example, if you were talking about the first day of school, you might use all the books and the activity under that heading. Later in the school year, you might explore the topic of bullies. Also, you could explore the first 100 days of school using the literature cited in chapter 1. You can use webs to provide a spectrum of books and activities that can be accessed over a period of time rather than to concentrate on a single aspect of a topic. You would be most likely to use the web by selecting one or two books, poems, or activities from each heading.

USING LITERATURE ACROSS THE CURRICULUM

You can integrate literature and other curricular areas in a variety of patterns. You can often combine literature with other sources of knowledge to broaden the study of a topic in science or social studies, mathematics or the arts, or the language arts. Select trade books because they include up-to-date information, give a broader view of a topic, and provide for the interests and capabilities of a diverse group of children. The key concepts come from the subject area.

For example, you might read the *The Doorbell Rang* (Hutchins, 1986) as part of a study of division. In this book, Ma places a plate of cookies between Victoria and Sam and tells them they can share. Sam quickly figures that they will each get six. Then the doorbell rings and Tom and Hannah drop by, and when they are to share the cookies, the number for each child is down to three. The doorbell keeps ringing, more children keep arriving, and the number of cookies per person keeps dropping. When they each have only one cookie and the doorbell rings, there is hesitation about answering it. But it is grandma, with a big plate of cookies. You might engage children

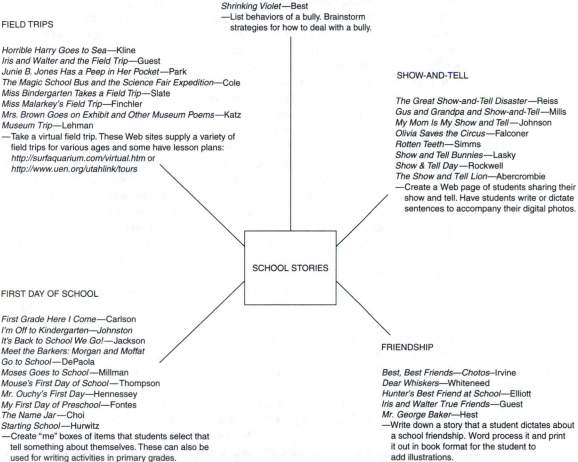

BULLIES

Bootsic Barker Bites—Bottner
Enemy Pie—Munson
Hooway for Wodney Wat—Lester
How to Lose All your Friends—Carlson
Jake Drake, Bully Buster—Clements
Plantzilla Goes to Camp—Nolen
The Recess Queen—O'Neill
Shrinking Violet—Best
—List behaviors of a bully. Brainstorm
    strategies for how to deal with a bully.

FIELD TRIPS

Horrible Harry Goes to Sea—Kline
Iris and Walter and the Field Trip—Guest
Junie B. Jones Has a Peep in Her Pocket—Park
The Magic School Bus and the Science Fair Expedition—Cole
Miss Bindergarten Takes a Field Trip—Slate
Miss Malarkey's Field Trip—Finchler
Mrs. Brown Goes on Exhibit and Other Museum Poems—Katz
Museum Trip—Lehman
—Take a virtual field trip. These Web sites supply a variety of
    field trips for various ages and some have lesson plans:
    http://surfaquarium.com/virtual.htm or
    http://www.uen.org/utahlink/tours

SHOW-AND-TELL

The Great Show-and-Tell Disaster—Reiss
Gus and Grandpa and Show-and-Tell—Mills
My Mom Is My Show and Tell—Johnson
Olivia Saves the Circus—Falconer
Rotten Teeth—Simms
Show and Tell Bunnies—Lasky
Show & Tell Day—Rockwell
The Show and Tell Lion—Abercrombie
—Create a Web page of students sharing their
    show and tell. Have students write or dictate
    sentences to accompany their digital photos.

SCHOOL STORIES

FIRST DAY OF SCHOOL

First Grade Here I Come—Carlson
I'm Off to Kindergarten—Johnston
It's Back to School We Go!—Jackson
*Meet the Barkers: Morgan and Moffat
Go to School*—DePaola
Moses Goes to School—Millman
Mouse's First Day of School—Thompson
Mr. Ouchy's First Day—Hennessey
My First Day of Preschool—Fontes
The Name Jar—Choi
Starting School—Hurwitz
—Create "me" boxes of items that students select that
    tell something about themselves. These can also be
    used for writing activities in primary grades.

FRIENDSHIP

Best, Best Friends—Chotos–Irvine
Dear Whiskers—Whiteneed
Hunter's Best Friend at School—Elliott
Iris and Walter True Friends—Guest
Mr. George Baker—Hest
—Write down a story that a student dictates about
    a school friendship. Word process it and print
    it out in book format for the student to
    add illustrations.

Figure 4–1

in dramatization with cookies (or manipulatives to represent the cookies) that they would try to distribute evenly, perhaps changing the number of cookies and the number of children. You might have children respond to the story, perhaps by sharing how they would feel in the same situation or by comparing the book to other stories with repetitive patterns.

The books you select should match the topic at hand and the understanding level of the children. *One Grain of Rice* (Demi, 1997) might be shared with slightly older children. It is a folktale set in India. The raja refuses to give rice to his people in a time of famine, even though he collected it from them with the promise that it would be used to see that no one went hungry. A small village girl returns some spilled rice to him, and he says he will give her anything she wants. She wants only one grain of rice the first day, but for the next 29 days the raja is to give her double the rice given her the day before. The raja readily agrees, realizing too late the effect of the mathematical progression. On day 30, she gets 536,870,912 grains of rice. Children can do further activity with the mathematics involved as well as discuss the raja's development into a fair and wise ruler.

Another pattern for integrating literature and other content areas is that of the literature-based curriculum, in which the literature is the focal point for the study of all other content areas. *One Grain of Rice* might be the focal point for a study of folktales in language arts, of India in social studies, of the concept of fairness and of the rights and responsibilities of rulers in social studies, of style of painting and the use of objects drawn partly outside the borders of a picture in art, or of the need for water and the causes of drought in science. Other books might be combined with it for each of the topics.

In this textbook the organizing principle is how books can stimulate and support children's growth in five different areas of development. These areas cut across the infant, toddler, preschool and primary years and are important in themselves. However, some of these goals correlate with the goals of particular academic areas. For example, observing and classifying as part of intellectual development are goals of science and of art education. Learning to see from the viewpoint of another, a goal for social and moral development, is also a goal of many social studies programs. And, certainly, language development addresses the goals of many areas of the language arts. If you are working with preschool children, you will focus on the goals as stated. If you are working with primary-grade children, you may want to think of the goals as both developmental for the child and as a way of looking at curriculum goals.

SUMMARY

A basic goal of a literature curriculum is the education of children's imaginations. Teachers of young children and childcare professionals contribute to this goal by involving children with literature in ways that establish positive attitudes toward it and by grouping books and structuring presentations so that children begin to perceive the interrelatedness of literature.

You can develop positive attitudes through the regular sharing of literature, careful selection of high-quality literature so that it matches children's interests and understandings, and activities that allow children to respond to books in a stimulating and satisfying manner.

Children begin to perceive the interrelatedness of literature when books are grouped, either in pairs for comparison or in units of study or webs. When books are paired, questions should focus on the structure of the stories so that children see how each is like or different from the other. You may also group books into units of study that focus on a single theme, describe similar content, or represent the literature of a particular genre or by a particular author or illustrator. Generally, you plan the books, the sequence in which you present them, and the accompanying activities in advance, although you may make modifications.

A web is a diagram that charts either the potential within a single book or the possible ways of developing a single topic through literature. Webs differ from units in that they show far more ideas than will be actually used, and they do not show sequence. Both units and webs present literature so that children see the relationships among several works.

Literature is a basic part of the curriculum in itself, but it can also be used across the curriculum in conjunction with other content areas. Sometimes the literature is the core around which the content area concepts are developed, and at other times it serves as a source of information, supplementing other approaches to content area instruction. The growth in children that literature supports, as explored in chapters 5 through 9, often relates to processes and skills utilized in the study of various content areas.

Extending Your Learning

1. Interview a child between the ages of 3 and 5 to determine his or her attitudes about reading or books.

2. Read any two books that are similar in content or theme. Respond to the books yourself using the phrases I think, I feel, I wonder.

3. Develop a unit using books on a single topic or theme or by a particular author or illustrator.

4. Develop a web on a topic of interest to toddlers, preschoolers, or primary age children.

5. Look at two or three of the bibliographies listed in the recommended references. Describe the criteria that were used for selecting the books and how this might influence your use of the list.

REFERENCES

Unit of Study Web Books

Friendship

Chodos-Irvine, Margaret. (2006). *Best Best Friends.* San Diego, CA: Harcourt. (preschool picture book)

Elliott, Laura Malone. (2002). *Hunter's Best Friend at School.* Ill. Lynn Munsinger. New York: Harper Collins. (picture book)

Guest, Elissa Haden. (2001). *Iris and Walter, True Friends.* Ill. Christine Davenier. New York: Gulliver. (beginning-to-read chapter book)

Hest, Amy. (2004). *Mr. George Baker.* Ill. Jon J. Muth. Cambridge, MA: Candlewick. (picture book)

Whitehead, Ann Nagda. (2000). *Dear Whiskers.* Ill. Stephanie Roth. New York: Holiday House. (chapter book)

Bullies

Best, Cari. (2001). *Shrinking Violet.* Ill. Giselle Potter. New York: Farrar, Straus & Giroux. (picture book)

Bottner, Barbara. (1992). *Bootsie Barker Bites.* Ill. Peggy Rathmann. New York: Putnam. (picture book)

Carlson, Nancy. (1994). *How to Lose All Your Friends.* New York: Viking. (picture book)

Caseley, Judith. (2001). *Bully.* New York: Greenwillow. (picture book)

Clements, Andrew. (2001). *Jake Drake, Bully Buster.* New York: Simon & Schuster. (chapter book)

Lester, Helen. (1999). *Hooway for Wodney Wat.* Ill. Lynn Munsinger. Boston: Houghton Mifflin. (picture book)

Munson, Derek. (2000). *Enemy Pie.* Ill. Tara Calahan King. San Francisco: Chronicle. (picture book)

Nolen, Jerdine. (2006). *Plantzilla Goes to Camp.* Ill. David Catrow. New York: Simon & Schuster. (picture book)

O'Neill, Alexis. (2002). *The Recess Queen.* Ill. Laura Huliska-Beith. New York: Scholastic. (picture book)

First Day of School

Carlson, Nancy. (2006). *First Grade, Here I Come.* New York: Viking. (picture book)

Choi, Yangsook. (2001). *The Name Jar.* New York: Knopf. (picture book)

DePaola, Tomie. (2001). *Meet the Barkers: Morgan and Moffat Go to School.* New York: Putnam. (picture book)

Fontes, Justine. (2006). *My First Day of Preschool.* Ill. Matt Novak. New York: Little Simon. (board book)

Hennessey, B. G. (2006). *Mr. Ouchy's First Day.* Ill. Paul Meisel. New York: Putnam. (picture book)

Hurwitz, Johanna. (1998). *Starting School.* Ill. Karen Dugan. New York: Morrow. (chapter book)

Jackson, Ellen. (2003). *It's Back to School We Go! First Day Stories From Around the World.* Ill. Jan Davey Ellis. Brookfield, CT: Millbrook. (picture book)

Millman, Isaac. (2000). *Moses Goes to School.* New York: Farrar, Straus & Giroux. (picture book)

Johnston, Tony. (2007). *I'm Off to Kindergarten.* Ill. Melissa Sweet. New York: Cartwheel. (picture book)

Thompson, Lauren. (2003). *Mouse's First Day of School.* Ill. Buket Erdogan. New York: Simon & Schuster. (picture book)

Field Trips

Cole, Joanna. (2007). *The Magic School Bus and the Science Fair Expedition.* Ill. Bruce Degen. New York: Scholastic. (picture book)

Finchler, Judy. (2004). *Miss Malarkey's Field Trip.* Ill. Kevin O'Malley. New York: Walker (picture book)

Guest, Elissa Haden. (2005). *Iris and Walter and the Field Trip.* Ill. Christine Davenier. New York: Gulliver. (beginning-to-read chapter book)

Katz, Susan. (2002). *Mrs. Brown on Exhibit and Other Museum Poems.* Ill. R. W. Alley. New York: Simon & Schuster. (poetry)

Kline, Suzy. (2001). *Horrible Harry Goes to Sea.* Ill. Frank Remkiewicz. New York: Viking. (chapter book)

Lehman, Barbara. (2006). *Museum Trip.* Boston: Houghton Mifflin. (picture book)

Park, Barbara. (2000). *Junie B. Jones Has a Peep in Her Pocket.* Ill. Denise Brunkus. New York: Random House. (chapter book)

Slate, Joseph. (2001). *Miss Bindergarten Takes a Field Trip.* Ill. Ashley Wolff. New York: Dutton. (rhyming alphabet book)

Show and Tell

Abercrombie, Barbara. (2006). *The Show-and-Tell Lion.* Ill. Lynne Avril Cravath. New York: McElderry. (picture book)

Falconer, Ian. (2001). *Olivia Saves the Circus.* New York: Simon & Schuster. (picture book)

Johnson, Dolores. (1999). *My Mom Is My Show and Tell.* New York: Marshall Cavendish. (picture book)

Lasky, Kathryn. (1998). *Show and Tell Bunnies.* Ill. Marylin Hafner. Cambridge, MA: Candlewick. (picture book)

Mills, Claudia. (2000). *Gus and Grandpa and Show-and-Tell.* Ill. Catherine Stock. New York: Farrar, Straus & Giroux. (beginning-to-read chapter book)

Reiss, Mike. (2001). *The Great Show-and-Tell Disaster.* Ill. Mike Cressy. New York: Penguin. (picture book)

Rockwell, Anne. (1997). *Show & Tell Day.* Ill. Lizzy Rockwell. New York: HarperCollins. (early picture book)

Simms, Laura. (1998). *Rotten Teeth.* Ill. David Catrow. Boston: Houghton Mifflin. (picture book)

Professional References Cited

Applebee, A. (1978). *The child's concept of story.* Chicago: University of Chicago Press.

Chambers, A. (1983). *Introducing books to children.* Boston: The Horn Book.

Frye, N. (1964). *The educated imagination.* Bloomington: Indiana University Press.

Kutiper, K. & Wilson, P. (1993). Updating poetry preferences: A look at the poetry children really like. *The Reading Teacher* 47(1), 28–36.

Sloan, G. (2003). *The child as critic* (4th ed.). New York: Teachers College Press.

Children's Literature Cited

Chodos-Irvine, Margaret. (2006). *Best Best Friends.* San Diego, CA: Harcourt.

Demi. (1997). *One Grain of Rice.* New York: Scholastic.

Hills, Tad. (2006). *Duck and Goose.* New York: Schwartz & Wade.

Hills, Tad. (2007). *Duck Duck Goose.* New York: Schwartz & Wade.

Hutchins, Pat. (1986). *The Doorbell Rang.* New York: Scholastic.

Lewis, Kevin. (2002). *My Truck is Stuck.* Ill. Daniel Kirk. New York: Hyperion.

McMullen, Kate. (2002). *I Stink.* Ill. Jim McMullen. New York: HarperCollins.

McMullen, Kate. (2003). *I'm Mighty.* Ill. Jim McMullen. New York: HarperCollins.

Wiles, Deborah. (2001). *Freedom Summer.* New York: Atheneum.

Willems, Mo. (2003). *Don't Let the Pigeon Drive the Bus.* New York: Hyperion.

Willems, Mo. (2006). *Don't Let the Pigeon Stay Up Late.* New York: Hyperion.

CHAPTER FIVE

CHRISTIAN, Age 6
"Interesting words" from literature

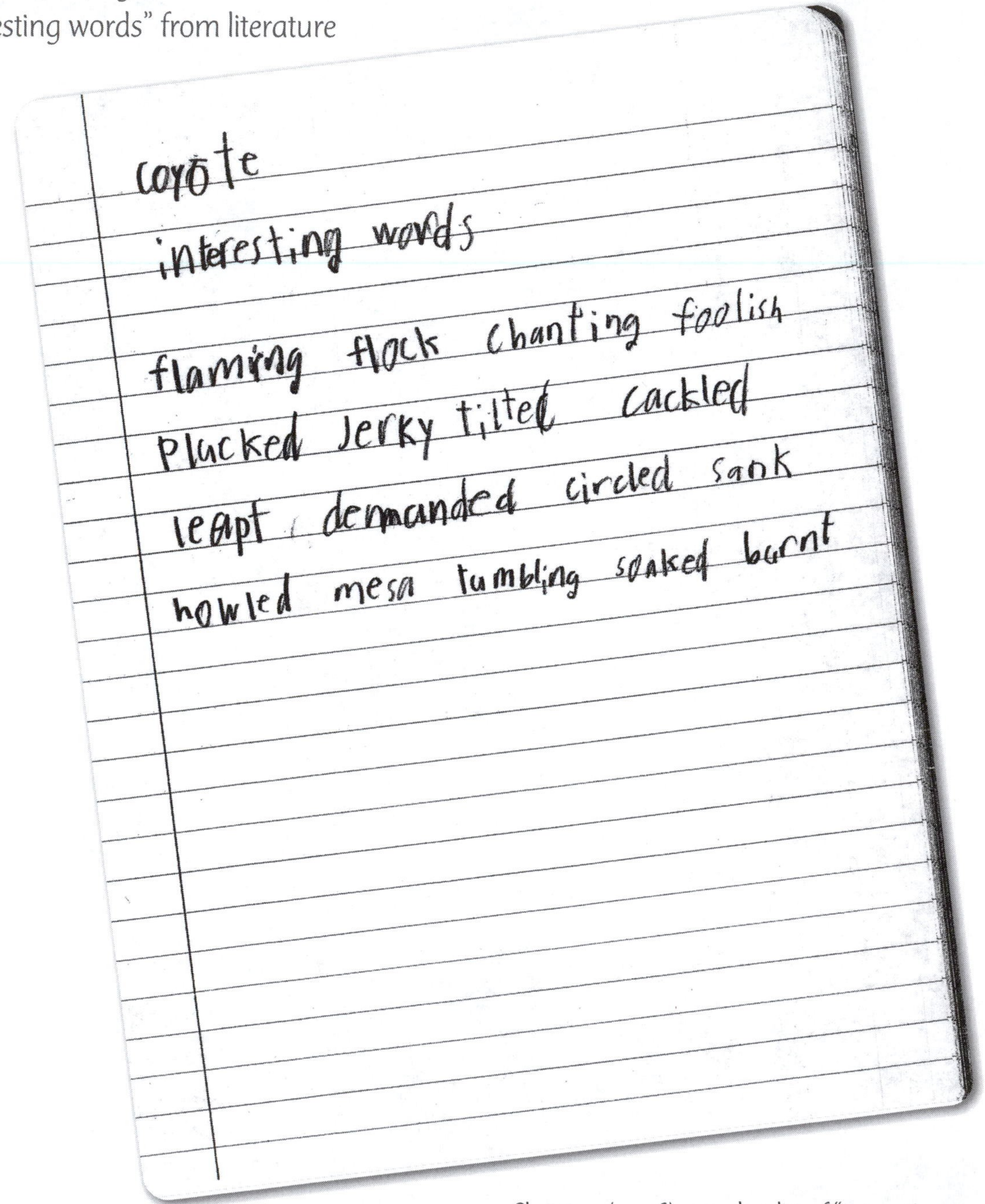
coyote
interesting words
flaming flock chanting foolish
plucked jerky tilted cackled
leapt demanded circled sank
howled mesa tumbling soaked burnt

Christian (age 6) records a list of "interesting words" that he discovers in the books that he reads.

Supporting Children's Language Development

Linguists have listened to the utterances of children as eagerly as new parents awaiting the first *Da Da* or *Mama*. They have identified certain patterns in children's development of language and attempted to explain just what is happening.

Although linguists do not agree on all aspects of language acquisition, there is a consensus that children are born with a natural capacity for oral language and that youngsters are influenced by the language environment in which they find themselves. Children also go through predictable stages in acquiring the phonology, or sound system, and the syntax, or word order, of their native tongues. Their semantic knowledge increases as they both learn new words and clarify and refine their concepts of words already familiar to them. In a similar manner, their knowledge of the meaning and function of print grows from their experiences with it.

LANGUAGE DEVELOPMENT IN YOUNG CHILDREN

How Children Learn Language

The process by which children learn language is one in which they construct for themselves the grammar, or rules, of the language they are hearing. This construction of the rules is not a conscious effort, however; a 4-year-old cannot state the rule for making a verb past tense. Yet the same 4-year-old can use the rule to tell about yesterday's trip to the dentist: "I played in the waiting room until it was time to go in. I looked at all the things on the tray. Dr. Carroll cleaned my teeth." It is because she knows the rules subconsciously that she is able to create new sentences and not simply repeat the exact sentences she has heard someone else say. It is because she is using rules that she will over generalize on occasion, applying the rule when the example at hand is irregular and does not follow the rule. She may say, "I runned all the way home," or "That one's yours and this one's mines." As she matures, she will include the exceptions as well as the rule-based word formations in her language repertoire.

How Children Become Literate

Marilyn Cochran-Smith, in *The Making of a Reader* (1984), looked at the way adults help children understand and develop the ability to read and write. The process by which children figure out how print works grows out of their experiences with adults in print-related situations. Cochran-Smith describes these literacy events as being with "contextualized print," such as street signs or labels, where much of the meaning can be derived from the context in which it occurs, and "decontextualized print," such as books, where the meaning of the language is independent of the environmental context. Children in the nursery school she observed had many opportunities to interact with print in the environment, learning in social situations where adults acted as "intermediaries" between the children and the print, performing tasks children were unable to do themselves. The children also had wide experiences with story reading, learning how to use their own knowledge of the world to make sense of the text and illustration in books.

Reading with infants and young children is a powerful way to enhance early language development. Through picture-book sharing, caregivers boost prereading skills, attention spans, word comprehension, and pleasure with books (Honig, 2001). Babies learn to "recognize different two-dimensional objects in picture books as related to toys, animals, and objects in the three-dimensional world" (p. 193).

An adult sharing books with a toddler can see the child's growing concept of print as the child listener no longer covers the words with his or her hand and stops turning pages rapidly when there is print but no picture. These actions show that the child knows it is the print that is carrying the message. The child may engage in "readinglike" behavior, providing some of the text of stories he or she has heard before or repeating a phrase immediately after it has been read. Many toddlers absorb a story so thoroughly that they can "read" the book by looking at the illustrations, often maintaining most of the story language but at times using their own language while retaining the meaning. As children begin to associate the print with the exact words, they go through a time when the number of words appearing on a page does not match the number of words they are using, particularly if they think of each syllable as a word. Knowing a story by heart allows them to go back again and again to a page, work on the problem, and teach themselves that long words have more than one syllable.

Careful observation of and conversations with young children have demonstrated to a series of researchers that children know more about writing than had once been assumed. Harste, Woodward, and Burke (1984) contend that adults often confuse product with process and thus overlook what children know. They point out that if children's writing doesn't look like adult writing, this does not mean that the children do not know about writing. If their spelling differs from standard spelling, that does not mean that the children do not know about spelling. These researchers noted that the children they observed could produce writing when asked to and could tell what their writing said, even though it might appear to be a scribble to the adult observer.

> We have found that by the age of 3 all children in our study could, under certain conditions, distinguish art from writing. Their decisions in writing, as in art, are systematic and organized. We found further that all 3-year-olds have developed a marking, which to them symbolized their name. This marking acted as any symbol acts, serving to placehold meaning during writing, and to reconstruct that meaning during reading.
> *(p. 18)*

Children refine their writing over time, learning to make the letters in standard form. However, their initial understanding of what print is and how writing functions comes from their experiences with print and with writing in their everyday lives. Living in a literate society, they expect that reading and writing will be part of their lives.

There are two basic ways in which adults can nurture the language learning of young children. The first is to provide rich, varied, and abundant samples of both oral and written language. The second is to give children regular opportunities to use their language.

The Need to Hear Rich Language

Babies start out with a remarkable facility for learning language. A 4-month-old infant can discriminate among sounds used in all languages (Odean, 2003). For this reason as others, it is important that children hear rich samples of language, for this is the database from which they generalize rules for how the language works. It is also their source of vocabulary items. Adults are of more help to children's language growth if they use mature syntax than if they limit their speech to what they perceive to be the child's level and if they respond to the content of children's telegraphic speech with mature language of their own (Cazden, 1972). Other researchers have reached the same conclusion, finding that adults are most effective in aiding children's language development if they respond with new information or if they encourage the child to add to his or her previous comments (Genishi, 1984).

Literature provides another source of mature and expressive language. Children listening to stories read aloud are being exposed to language that is often more complex than what they hear in ordinary conversation. They hear new sentence patterns and new words. Chomsky (1972) found that there was a positive correlation between the linguistic development of the children in her study and the average complexity level of the books each had encountered, the number of books each named as familiar, and the numerical score each received based on factors such as having been read to during the early years. This positive relationship between linguistic development and exposure to literature was true for prereaders who had listened to books as well as for older children who had read the books themselves. The prereaders in the high linguistic stages had heard more books each week, were read to by more people, and had heard more books at higher complexity levels than had those children at lower linguistic stages.

Hearing books read aloud increased children's competence in other areas of language as well. Sipe (2002) studied first- and second-graders' responses during read-alouds of picture books to determine that children were developing literary understanding. He found that children engaged in text and visual analysis, formed links with other texts, connected text with their own lives, and playfully manipulated the story for their own creative purposes. Sipe's study also indicated that it was important for children to talk during the read-aloud, at least on occasion, because waiting until the end of the story could result in the loss of their responses.

These studies demonstrate the positive results of presenting children with examples of effective language. Note that in all these studies, the language was used in context. Adults responded to children in light of the situation and with regard to the children's comments. The books described experiences or thoughts as wholes, giving vocabulary and sentence patterns within the total story setting. It is essential that language be tied to experience and that it be presented in context if it is to have optimal meaning for children.

The Need to Use Language

In addition to presenting abundant samples of language, adults can nurture children's language growth by providing opportunities for them to use language. Children form hypotheses about grammar and must then test them. This testing by using language themselves provides direct feedback. Children can judge whether or not they have communicated effectively. They may also refine their definitions of particular words as they gather more information about the concept named by the word. For example, they no longer use car for any four-wheeled vehicle but applied it only to one type of vehicle.

It seems logical that correcting children's speech would accelerate their grasp of adult language patterns. This is not the case, however. Only when children are ready to assimilate a new pattern will it have meaning for them. McNeill (1966) cites the following example of a conversation between a parent and child. Even though this study appeared several decades ago, you will see that language hasn't changed, nor have conversations between children and parents.

> **CHILD:** Nobody don't like me.
>
> **PARENT:** No, say "Nobody likes me."
>
> **CHILD:** Nobody don't like me.
>
> **PARENT:** No, "Nobody likes me."
>
> **CHILD:** Nobody don't like me. (seven more repetitions of this)
>
> **PARENT:** No! Now listen carefully. Say "Nobody likes me."
>
> **CHILD:** Oh! Nobody don't likes me.   *(p. 69)*

The form the parent is attempting to teach is not within the child's current rule system; therefore, the child is not able to assimilate this new information. You, as a child-care professional or teacher, should give children opportunities to use their language in conversations, discussions, spontaneous dramatics, and writing. Efforts to encourage extensive use of language will prove far more productive than attempts to correct children's grammar or their handwriting and spelling. Overcorrecting a child's grammar may result in that child's refusal to talk, the exact opposite of the desired behavior. Overcorrecting the mechanical aspects of writing may result in the child's avoidance of composition. Jane Hansen (2001), in discussing writing conferences with children, says

> Adults respond to the messages young children try to communicate, not to the errors they make in their attempts. Toddlers' early words confuse us, but we concentrate on trying to figure out their intent as we listen to their tone and watch their body language. We respond to what we think they are trying to tell us. If we respond to children in an encouraging way, they try again. The more supportive we are, the more likely it is that they will want to experiment with language, both oral and written. The bottom line in the writing conference is, "The writer wants to write again."
>
> *(p. 13)*

Structure your program so that children become more skilled in all areas of language. Work in one area is likely to have a strong influence on other areas. Children who are experimenting with writing are also learning about reading. Comprehension taught through listening is an aid to comprehension in reading. In addition, children who have been exposed to literature are familiar with the patterns of written language—patterns they will encounter when they read by themselves.

Morrow, Strickland, and Woo (1998), in their application of research findings to the design of effective kindergarten literacy programs, concluded the following:

> Research also suggests the concurrent learning of reading, writing, oral language, and listening in a meaningful way through the integration of these skills into play and into content-area teaching such as art, music, math, science, and social studies. This integration can be done through the use of themes that bring meaning and purpose to learning and provide a reason to read, write, listen and speak. Children's literature should be a major source of these themes. *(pp. 69–70)*

Immersion in literature, which helps children make sense of written language, also helps create a positive attitude toward learning to read. Reading becomes desirable because there are things to be learned and tales to be enjoyed in books. Children are also intrigued by the sounds of language, from its poetic beauty to its lighthearted nonsense. Three-year-olds will often repeat pairs of rhymed words and enjoy playing games with repetition and rhyme. Literature builds on and expands this fascination with language.

Children should be encouraged to experiment individually with print. The child who has used scribbles symbolically, knowing how writing functions if not how letters are formed, moves into more standard writing while maintaining the view of writing as a purposeful activity. Regular writing times in the primary grades, where children know that they will write and that they will usually choose the topic themselves, lets them know that writing is a personal and effective way of communicating.

To summarize, children's language develops best in an environment in which mature language is heard, where children have many opportunities to communicate with others, and where language is presented in context.

GOALS FOR TEACHING

Teaching goals for language growth can be categorized into long-term developmental goals, into general goals for each grade or age level, and into specific goals for individual children. Long-term goals describe behaviors or competencies that are developed over time and are thought of as desired patterns of behavior. One long-term goal for language development is that children will enjoy the creative and aesthetic use of language. They will become lifelong readers and appreciators of literature.

General goals for each grade level are often listed in curriculum guides. At other times they are developed by the teacher or child-care professional as he or she plans an outline for the year's learning. A general goal for the preschool level is that children will listen attentively and follow simple directions.

Goals for specific children are more individualized. Teachers develop these as they come to know each child. A specific goal for a second grader might be, Roberta will read one book by herself and tell her classmates one incident from the story. The goal reflects Roberta's need, a need that may not be shared by other members of the class. Goals of this type are referred to as objectives in some planning schemes.

Your use of books can aid in the achievement of many types of goals and standards. This chapter focuses on long-term developmental goals common to the toddler, preschool, and primary years. Literature offers opportunities for you to assist children in acquiring competency of the following goals for language development:

Children will understand and use the mature syntax of their language.

Children will expand their vocabularies.

Children will enjoy the creative and aesthetic use of language.

(continues)

Children will become skilled listeners.

Children will learn to read.

Children will communicate effectively in oral, written, and visual formats.

As with other areas, these goals can be correlated with national and regional standards. For example, the goal that children will communicate effectively in oral, written, and visual formats correlates with Standard 4 of the International Reading Association/National Council of Teachers of English *Standards for the English Language Arts*. That standard states that "Students adjust their use of spoken, written, and visual language (e.g., conventions, style, vocabulary) to communicate effectively with a variety of audiences and for different purposes" (1996, p. 25). As you look at national standards or those for your region or school district, look for ways in which these goals and the specific standards mesh.

OPPORTUNITIES BOOKS OFFER

Exposing Children to Mature Language

Children should hear many examples of mature language if they are to develop an understanding of the more complex syntactic structures of the language and if they are to become users of those structures themselves. Read to children every day, perhaps twice each day. Encourage parents and guardians to share literature with their children at home. Become aware of the kind of language being used in a book.

Listening to Varied Syntax   Language varies. This is one of the reasons that literature is so beguiling. Some authors present material in a direct manner, yet use more compound and complex sentences. This passage is from *Enemy Pie* (Munson, 2000):

> It was all good until Jeremy Ross moved into the neighborhood, right next door to my best friend Stanley. I did not like Jeremy Ross. He laughed at me when he struck me out in a baseball game. He had a party on his trampoline and I wasn't even invited. But my best friend Stanley was.
> Jeremy Ross was the one and only person on my enemy list. I never even had a enemy list until he moved into the neighborhood. But as soon as he came along, I needed one. *(n.p.)* (From *Enemy Pie* © 2000 by Derek Munson. Used with permission of Chronicle Books LLC, San Francisco. Visit ChronicleBooks.com.)

Children hearing this passage are being given data about standard word order in English and about ways that several pieces of information can be combined into a single sentence.

Other authors may use whimsical rhyming verse to encourage imagination. In *Mud Is Cake* (2002), author Pam Muñoz Ryan begins

> Mud is cake
>
> if you pretend
>
> and don't really take a bite.
>
> And juice is tea
>
> with a fairy queen
>
> if you act it out just right.

(n.p.) (From *Mud Is Cake* by Pam Muñoz Ryan. Text copyright © 2002 by Pam Muñoz: Ryan. Illustrations copyright © 2002 by David McPhail. Reprinted by permission of Hyperion Books for Children. All Rights Reserved.)

With the assistance of watercolor illustrations by David McPhail, children gain an understanding that you can pretend that one thing is something else. The text and illustrations demonstrate how imagination can turn the ordinary into the fanciful or the fantastic. There is also a pattern to Ryan's rhymes that children quickly identify. Hearing patterns that occur far more frequently in writing than in speech prepares children to cope with written language when they begin reading themselves.

Enjoying Figurative Language   Authors often use expressive language, with carefully chosen words and figurative language fitting naturally into the text. In *Come on, Rain* (Hesse, 1999), Tess is hoping for a few raindrops to cool off a sweltering summer day. Finally, the rain begins to fall:

> "Come on rain!" we shout.
>
> It streams through our hair and down our back.
>
> It freckles our feet, glazes our toes.
>
> We turn in circles,
>
> glistening in our rain skin.
>
> Our mouths wide,
>
> we gulp down the rain.
>
> *(n.p.)* (Excerpt from *Come On, Rain* by Karen Hesse. Text copyright © 1999 by Karen Hesse. Reprinted by permission of Scholastic Inc.)

Listening to this story, children are exposed to the flexibility of language and its creative possibilities. If a face can have freckles, how could rain freckle our feet? And how does it look when rain glistens on our skin?

Listening to *Cooper's Lesson* (Shin, 2004), children can appreciate that figurative language describes feelings. Cooper is tired of being referred to as "half and half," and he resents Mr. Lee, the owner of the neighborhood grocery store, who always speaks in Korean. Author Sun Yung Shin uses figurative language such as, "his tongue lay as heavy and still in his mouth as a dead fish" (p. 10), and "The Korean writing on the cans and boxes seemed to dance off the labels" (p. 12), along with "Cooper felt hot prickles under his skin" (p. 12). Children can discuss what these phrases mean and how it helps them to understand how Cooper is feeling.*

Children need to hear the language of books such as that contained in these stories. They can also discuss it when the books that are being shared are appropriate for them. Your task as a caregiver or teacher is to select books that the children will enjoy and that will, in the process, give them exposure to the mature and effective use of language.

Hearing Different Dialects   You will find that books give you the opportunity to let children hear a variety of different dialects. Some may give a feel for the language but not follow all the rules of the specific dialect.

Candace Fleming effectively uses Creole cadence, demonstrates playfulness with words, and incorporates good ol' out-smartin' flavor in her tasty bayou story *Gator Gumbo* (2004), a variant of the story of the Little Red Hen. When Monsieur Gator becomes too old, too gray, and too slow to catch any of his tasty fellow bayou creatures to eat, he asks possum, skunk, and otter to help him make some gumbo.

> GUMBO! "I'm gonna cook up some gumbo just like Maman used to make!" he cried.
> So Monsieur Gator, he builds a fire.

*Reprinted with permission of the publisher, Children's Book Press, San Francisco, CA, www. childrensbookpress.org. Cooper's Lesson. Text © 2004 by Sun Yung Shin.

GATOR GUMBO

CANDACE FLEMING   Pictures by SALLY ANNE LAMBERT

Poor Monsieur Gator is too old to catch his dinner. When he decides to cook up some gumbo he ponders who will help him boil, catch, sprinkle and chop in this delightful retelling of The Little Red Hen.
(Jacket design and excerpt from GATOR GUMBO by Candace Fleming, pictures by Sally Anne Lambert. Text copyright © 2004 by Candace Fleming. Pictures copyright © 2004 by Sally Anne Lambert. Reprinted by permission of Farrar, Straus and Giroux, LLC.)

He sets a big pot over the flames.
He calls out to them slap-laughing critters, "Who's gonna fill this pot with water so I can cook up some gumbo?"
"I ain't," snickers Mademoiselle Possum.
"I ain't," snickers Monsieur Otter.
"I ain't," snickers Madame Skunk.
"Then I'll be doin' it myself," says Monsieur Gator. *(n.p.)* (Jacket design and excerpt from GATOR GUMBO by Candace Fleming, pictures by Sally Anne Lambert. Text copyright © 2004 by Candace Fleming. Pictures copyright © 2004 by Sally Anne Lambert. Reprinted by permission of Farrar, Straus and Giroux, LLC.)

Of course, as the story unfolds, the three contemptuous characters refuse to help but finally get a well-deserved comeuppance. Both the story and the watercolor illustrations are well executed. Listeners have the opportunity to hear this language, discuss the use of words like ain't, and begin to build an appreciation for the variety of speech patterns within the English language.

Because of Winn-Dixie, by Kate DiCamillo (2000), tells the story of lonely, 10-year-old Opal Buloni, who befriends a big, mangy, yet happy dog. This chapter book for third-grade students is set in Naomi, Florida. DiCamillo skillfully weaves Southern dialect into this compassionate story told in the voice of a likable girl as she relates her day-to-day experiences in making new friends with the assistance of her adopted pet, Winn-Dixie. The use of Southern expressions and the well-crafted realistic story line will promote discussions through a class read-aloud or in small literature-discussion groups.

In general, the books currently available in dialects other than standard English are for children of school age. Books for 3- and 4-year-olds are direct, simple, and in standard English. *Gator Gumbo* would be more appropriate for children in first or second grade than for toddlers. Five- and 6-year-olds recognize when a dialect differs from their own, although they may not be able to tell how it differs. Let children begin early to hear various dialects and to appreciate the many ways in which English is spoken and written.

Introducing New Vocabulary in Context

Vocabulary expands as children learn new concepts and the words that denote them and as new words are presented for concepts already known. When new words are presented in context, children often can determine the meanings themselves. If they do, they are less likely to forget the word than they would be if its meaning has been explained to them in isolation. Thus, teachers of young children introduce new words as they arise in the course of ongoing activities.

Presenting New Words   Literature presents new words to children in the context of a complete story or poem. When you call attention to a particular word, look carefully at the section where it appears to determine if the context needed is the entire story, one or two paragraphs, or just one sentence. For example, in the book *The Storytellers* (Lewin, 1998), Abdul and his grandfather are walking through a town in Morocco on their way to work. At one point the text describes the noise at the copper and brass *souk;* two pages later Abdul and his grandfather pass through the date souk. The following page begins, "The souks go on and on—streets of spice sellers and chicken vendors and saddle makers." Later they pass the carpet souk.

In this story, *souk* is explained in the text that follows its initial appearance (as well as in a glossary of Arab words). After reading the entire story, you could return to several of the pages that refer to a souk. Show the illustrations, read the references again, and then ask the children what they think a souk is. Let them tell you what they think and how they know. They might rely on the several examples that are given, or they might key into the page that incorporates the definition into the text. It is important to read the story through so that the children have the full context and to reread the sections under discussion so that they are fresh in the children's memories.

Sometimes the explanation for a word is developed through many examples. *Hurty Feelings* (Lester, 2004) tells the story of Fragility, a hippopotamus whose feelings are easily hurt. Fragility takes offense at everything, including compliments. After hearing her constant whining and wailing of, "You hurt my *feelings!*" her friends begin to avoid her. When Fragility is confronted by a bully elephant, she finally stands up for herself and gains confidence and a bit of perspective. Although the word fragility is never defined directly, children will be able to determine the meaning of it through both the words and actions of this high-strung hippo.

If you plan to ask children to use context to hypothesize about the meaning of a word, make certain that there is indeed context that is explanatory. *Delicious* (Cooper, 2007) is a companion book to *Pumpkin Soup* (1999) and *A Pipkin of Pepper* (2005) and features the characters of Cat, Duck, and Squirrel. Disaster has struck the pumpkin patch, and there are no pumpkins for the animal's favorite dish. So, the animals decide to make something new to eat. Duck, however, is unwilling to try fish soup, mushroom soup, or beet soup (which is tinted pink). Cat tries to fool Duck by mixing a combination of the vegetables and other ingredients that results in a broth that is exactly the color of pumpkin soup. Duck sips it and declares it is "Delicious!" Children will quickly ascertain the meaning of "scrumptious," in opposition to "yuck." One kindergartener even proclaimed her lunch as "scrumptious" a few days later.

There are opportunities to evaluate and to reinforce children's comprehension of words that may be new to them. You can ask them to tell what happened in the story or use phrases from the story to elicit personal responses from the children. There are five short stories in *George and Martha Round and Round* (Marshall, 1998). This is the beginning of the story titled "The Artist."

> George was painting in oils.
> "That ocean doesn't look right," said Martha.
> "Add some more blue.
> And that sand looks all wrong. Add a bit more yellow."
> "Please," said George.
> "Artists don't like interference."
> But Martha just couldn't help herself.
> "Those palm trees look funny," she said. *(n.p.)* (Excerpt from "The Artist", from GEORGE AND MARTHA ROUND AND ROUND by James Marshall. Copyright © 1988 by James Marshall. Reprinted by permission of Houghton Mifflin Company. All rights reserved.)

George goes off in a huff, telling Martha to see if she can do any better. She notes that some artists are "touchy" and then makes "improvements" in the painting. When George returns, he thinks she has ruined the picture. Martha just says she is sorry he feels that way, but that she likes it. She is not a touchy artist.

Children might be asked to tell the class about or draw pictures of times when they interfered with someone else or when someone interfered with what they were doing. They could list things that others might be "touchy" about. After the children have been introduced to words in one context, activities such as these help them apply those words to other contexts.

Unless you are certain the story will be misunderstood without fully discussing the meaning of a word or phrase, wait until the book is completed before talking with children about the word or give only a brief explanation and continue reading. If it is necessary to explain a number of words for the children to make sense of the selection, the book is probably too difficult for that group of children and should not be shared with them until they are older.

Sharing Books That Emphasize Word Meanings   Most books present the vocabulary as part of the story, as a tool needed to convey the content. Some books, however, work directly with vocabulary. An example is *I See* by Helen Oxenbury (1995). This board book shows a drawing on the left page, with a caption identifying the object and then

Martha begins her "interference" with George's painting.
(From George and Martha Round and Round by *James Marshall.*
Copyright © 1988 by James Marshall. Reprinted by permission of
Houghton Miffin Company.)

a toddler interacting with the object or person on the facing page. The books *Daddy and Me* (Ricklen, 1997a) and *Mommy and Me* (Ricklen, 1997b) label everyday activities of parent and child.

Sometimes the books are concept books, exploring the qualities of the concept as well as the word that names it. *Hands Can* (Hudson, 2003) utilizes clear, colorful photographs and simple text that holds great appeal for toddlers and preschoolers. Children use their hands in many ways—for waving, catching, throwing, clapping, and playing peek-a-boo. It is quickly understood what action each child in the photograph is doing, which makes reading the text so much easier.

Involving Children with New Vocabulary   Whether you are working with vocabulary within a story or as part of a book emphasizing new words, involve children as actively as possible with the meanings of the words. You may do this by having them act out the meanings. Suppose you read "Jump or Jiggle" by Evelyn Beyer.

> Frogs jump
>
> Caterpillars hump
>
> Worms wiggle
>
> Bugs jiggle
>
> Rabbits hop
>
> Horses clop

Snakes slide

Sea gulls glide

Mice creep

Deer leap

Puppies bounce

Kittens pounce

Lions stalk—

But—

I walk!

Beyer, in Poetry Place Anthology (p. 131) (From *Poetry Place Anthology*. Copyright © 1983 by Edgell Communications, Inc. Reprinted by permission of Scholastic Inc.)

Children can listen to the poem; then on the second reading they can show how each animal moves. Children enjoy the fun of the movement and the rhyming language, and some learn new words.

You might involve them by having them tell about experiences they have had that are similar to those you are reading about. In *Adele & Simon* (McClintock, 2006), a young girl implores her little brother, Simon, not to lose anything on their walk home from school. As the children take a leisurely stroll they visit friends, a street market, a park, and two museums. At each stop, Simon loses something, whether it's a drawing he had made, his books, or one of his gloves. Even though this book is set in Paris during the early 20th century, the theme of losing something is universal and timeless. There is also vocabulary throughout the story that will provide children with new words to use in describing their misfortunes. McClintock uses pen-and-ink and watercolor illustrations that provide a retro look and includes a map of Adele and Simon's route on the endpapers. Children might describe a time when they went for a leisurely stroll and what they saw. They could also tell about when they have lost something and whether or not they were able to find it again. Using vocabulary written in the context of the story, children will be able to describe their own experiences thus making it part of their repertoire.

Several Books on a Single Topic   You can reinforce vocabulary by reading several books on the same topic. If you had been discussing baby animals with a small group of 2- or 3-year-olds, you might want to read *Whose Baby Am I?* (Butler, 2001), a story that begins by asking the title question and then revealing the answer on the next page. The adorable illustrations are done in acrylics and colored pencils on a soft pastel background. You might then introduce other books by John Butler, including *Can You Cuddle Like a Koala* (2005), which depicts a variety of cuddly animals in action, or *Whose Nose and Toes?* (2004), which introduces different baby animals and their noses and feet. Both *Whose Baby Am I?* and *Whose Nose and Toes?* are interactive by presenting the information in a guessing game format. Next, you could share Eve Bunting's *Hurry! Hurry!* (2006), which has all the animals in the barnyard rushing to greet the newest member of their community. *Five Little Chicks* (Tafuri, 2007) also provides an opportunity to interact with the story as the chicks repeatedly ask, "What can we eat?" All these books introduce and/or reinforce vocabulary within the context of enjoyable stories that children will easily comprehend. Infants and toddlers will enjoy *Zoo Animals* (Barton, 1995) and *Who Says Woof?* (Butler, 2003) that also name animals and identify their sounds.

Encouraging Language Play and Demonstrating How Others Have Used Language Creatively

If you listen to young children as they play, you will find that they seem to have a natural enjoyment of language. They repeat nonsense words just for the fun of listening to the sounds; they use jump rope rhymes and other chants in their games; they tell riddles. Literature that exudes this same delight in language appeals to them, and often their favorite books are those that capitalize on the sound of language.

Playing with Language   Using literature that demonstrates how others have played with language has several benefits for children. First, of course, they enjoy it and thus develop positive attitudes toward literature. It sets the stage for continued enjoyment of poetry, with its reliance on the rhythm, rhyme, and patterns in language. It shows them that the tone and feeling of a word contribute to its meaning—that words connote as well as denote. It stimulates them to reflect on the language itself, not just the message being conveyed. Linguists refer to this ability to attend to the forms of language as metalinguistic awareness and suggest that it may be critically important in both reading and writing (Lightsey, 2004).

Language play takes on a variety of forms. It may center on the sound of the language, on the patterns within the language, on the appearance of written language, or on the meanings of words or phrases. Children's books can stimulate children to engage in word play themselves.

One nursery school teacher suggested to her group of 3- and 4-year-olds that they make their own goodnight poem after listening to *Goodnight Moon*. The children followed the book's short couplet format naturally. Here is their poem:

> Goodnight toys,
> Goodnight boys,
> Goodnight book,
> And goodnight hook.
> Goodnight fire,
> And goodnight tire.
> Goodnight flowers,
> And goodnight powers.
> Goodnight rocks,
> And goodnight box.
> Goodnight cradle,
> Goodnight dreydl.
> Goodnight dolls,
> And goodnight balls.
> Goodnight berries,
> Goodnight cherries.
> Goodnight koala bear,
> Goodnight little chair.
> Goodnight Daddy,
> Goodnight Matty.

Goodnight Mummy,

Goodnight tummy.

Goodnight bee,

Goodnight flea.

Goodnight everything,

And goodnight me.

(Kaplan, n.d.)

The children explained as they dictated that the "powers" in line 8 were space heroes. They also changed the position of the last two lines from the middle to the end after hearing their poem reread.

Recommended Poetry

Demarest, Chris L. (2002). *I Invited a Dragon to Dinner and Other Poems to Make You Laugh Out Loud.* New York: Philomel.

Dotlich, Rebecca Kai. (2006). *What is Science?* Ill. Sachiko Yoshikawa. New York: Holt.

Florian, Douglas. (2003). *Bow Wow Meow Meow.* San Diego, CA: Harcourt.

George, Kristine O'Connell. (2002). *Little Dog and Duncan.* Ill. June Otani. New York: Clarion.

Hoberman, Mary Ann. (1998). *The Llama Who Had No Pajama: 100 Favorite Poems.* Ill. Betty Fraser. San Diego, CA: Harcourt.

Hopkins, Lee Bennett. (2000). *School Supplies: A Book of Poems.* Ill. Renee Flower. New York: Aladdin.

Katz, Alan. (2001). *Take Me Out of the Bathtub and Other Silly Dilly Songs.* Ill. David Catrow. New York: McElderry.

Lewis, J. Patrick. (2007). *Big is Big (and little, little): A Book of Contrasts.* Ill. Bob Barner. New York: Holiday House.

Prelutsky, Jack. (2004). *If Not for the Cat.* Ill. Ted Rand. New York: Greenwillow.

Yolen, Jane. (2007). *Shape Me a Rhyme.* Photos. Jason Stemple. Honesdale, PA: Boyds Mills.

Playing with the Sounds of Language Playing with the sounds of language may take many forms, but those appearing most frequently in books for children are rhythm, rhyme, alliteration, and onomatopoeia. Infants and toddlers often bounce to the rhythms of a Mother Goose nursery rhyme. Preschoolers respond to the toe-tapping rhythm and rhyme of *Chicken Soup with Rice* (Sendak, 1962). By the time the narrator has told of the joys of chicken soup in each month of the year, the listener is ready to join in extolling its virtues. The rollicking rhythm and rhyme in *Chicka Chicka Boom Boom* (Martin and Archambault, 1989) capture children's interest as they see the letters of the alphabet race to the top of the coconut tree, only to weigh it down so much that they all tumble to the ground.

A contrasting rhythm, "I Like," in *You Read to Me, I'll Read to You* (Hoberman, 2001) presents different perspectives:

I like soda.

   I like milk.

I like satin.

   I like silk.

I like puppies.

   I like kittens.

I like gloves.

And I like mittens. *(n.p.)*

This unique book in two voices invites young children to read along with an adult. Through both text format and color, the reader understands when the different voice is heard. As the poem continues:

I like apples.

I like pears.

I like tigers.

I like bears.

I like to slide.

I like to swing.

We don't agree

On anything. *(n.p.)*

Some authors write narratives in rhyme. Their work may be lighthearted and humorous or of a serious and thoughtful mood. If you are working with children in the toddler, preschool, or kindergarten years, look for the books of Sandra Boynton, Rosemary Wells, Denise Fleming, and Margaret Wise Brown. If you are working with primary-grade children, look for the works of Theodor Geisel (Dr. Seuss), Mary Ann Hoberman, Nancy Shaw, and Judy Sierra. These will give you a standard of good writing by which you can measure other poetic narratives for children.

Look also at the works of poets J. Patrick Lewis, Douglas Florian, and Eve Merriam. All three have written poems that play with the language in various ways. You will need to select poems from their collections that are appropriate for the age of your students.

Alliteration is a technique of writing in which initial consonant sounds are repeated at close intervals. *Walter was Worried* (Seeger, 2005) combines word art and simple text to relate the story of reacting to a storm. The characters' emotions are literally spelled out on their faces as Seeger tells us that Priscilla was puzzled, Shirley was shocked, and Frederick was frightened. With one sentence per page, accompanied by a delightful illustration, there is time to linger over the alliteration and discuss the character and the word on their face. This book can be used with preschoolers and primary-grade students alike.

Tongue twisters are often based on alliteration and may be written in rhyme. They intrigue children all through the preschool and primary years. Read aloud the Dr. Seuss classic, *Fox in Socks* (1963, 1995). After reading it to the children, ask them to make up their own tongue-twisting sentences. Kindergartners can work as a group, dictating their twisters for the teacher to write down. Primary children can work individually, spelling words using their best guesses based on the sounds they hear. All can try saying the tongue twisters and then repeating them as fast as they can.

They might also illustrate their twister. *Giggle Fit: Tricky Tongue Twisters* (Atwell, 2001), presents common tongue twisters, such as "Sally sells sea shells at the seashore" as well as "Ike ships ice chips." There are many ways to bring unity to a class book of tongue twisters. One group of third graders made their own counting book, with each child responsible for providing their own tongue twister and illustration for one numeral. Their book went to 22. The class favorite was the illustration that accompanied "Fifteen frisbees flying forward," showing members of the class engaged in a frisbee-throwing contest.

Preschoolers enjoy the slapstick action and the wordplay in *Thump and Plunk* (Udry, 1981, 2001), about two duckling siblings and their frog dolls, Thumpit and Plunk, who manage to "thump" and "plunk" their way through an entire story. The repetition of sounds delights the young listener.

Onomatopoeia, the use of words whose sound suggests their meaning, is another element of writing that is popular with children. Janet S. Wong's *Buzz* (2000) is built on a technique of using words so that they make the sound of the buzzing of the alarm clock or of the gardener mowing the grass. Denise Fleming's short rhymes *In the Tall, Tall Grass* (1991) captures animal sounds, as in the "ritch, ratch" as moles scratch. In *Umbrella* (Yashima, 1958), Moma listens to the sound of the raindrops on her umbrella.

Bon polo

bon polo

ponpolo ponpolo

ponpolo ponpolo

bolo bolo ponpolo

bolo bolo ponpolo

boto boto ponpolo

boto boto

ponpolo *(n.p.)*

Children hear how others have used language to describe sounds. They can listen to sounds on the playground, in the lunchroom, or in their own classroom. What word could they make up for each sound? Try having children listen to machines in their homes or in the neighborhood and then make their own words for those sounds. What sound does a vacuum cleaner make? A washing machine? A hair dryer?

As children play with the sounds of the language, they can appreciate when a book character has trouble with those sounds. *The Surprise Party* (1969, 1991) by Pat Hutchins opens with Rabbit whispering to Owl that he is having a party. Owl repeats the news to Squirrel, explaining that Rabbit is going to be hoeing the parsley. Squirrel repeats it as Rabbit going to sea, and the message continues to be garbled as it passes from animal to animal. The game of Telephone, where each child whispers a message to the next person, saying it only once, would be a natural follow-up to this book. For primary grades, Chris Raschka's *Ring! Yo?* (2000) relates half of a phone conversation and encourages students to invent the other portion.

Playing with the Patterns of Language

Authors may play with the pattern of language as well as with the sound. *The Little Engine That Could* (Piper, 1930) has remained a favorite with children for more than 70 years. Some of its popularity may be attributed to the story itself—that of getting the toys to the children on the other side of the mountain—but equally important is the author's use of onomatopoeia in the sounds of the engine and the patterning of the language. The engine's pep talk to herself, where she keeps repeating, "I think I can," sounds like the rotation of the train wheels, getting faster and faster as she picks up speed. The pattern is established on the way up the mountain and continues after she has made it to the top and started down. The refrain is then, "I thought I could."

The use of refrains invites children to join in with the teacher as the story is being read. The little old man and little old woman in *Millions of Cats* (Gag, 1996), who must contend with

Hundreds of cats

Thousands of cats

Millions and billions and trillions of cats *(n.p.)*

in order to find the one cat to be their own, are remembered both for their plight and for the language that tells about it.

Cumulative tales have a patterning of language that is part of the story. As each new event or character is added, all the earlier ones are repeated. *There Was an Old Lady Who Swallowed a Fly* (Taback, 1997) can be read or sung and intrigues children as the old lady, who first swallowed a fly, keeps swallowing larger and larger animals in order to catch the animal before. All the while the spider, which she swallowed to catch the fly, just keeps wiggling and jiggling and tickling inside her. After they have experienced this song, they will particularly enjoy *I Know an Old Lady Who Swallowed a Pie* (Jackson, 1997), a clever take-off in which an old lady swallows an entire Thanksgiving meal. These versions can be shared along with others for comparing and contrasting.

Versions and Variants of *There Was An Old Lady Who Swallowed a Fly*

Bonne, Rose, and Mills, Alan. (1994). *I Know an Old Lady*. Ill. G. Brian Karas. New York: Scholastic.

Garriel, Barbara S. (2004). *I Know a Shy Fellow Who Swallowed a Cello*. Ill. John O'Brien. Honesdale, PA: Boyds Mills.

Harper, Charise Mericle. (2002). *There Was a Bold Lady Who Wanted a Star*. Boston: Little, Brown.

Hoberman, Mary Ann. (2003). *I Know an Old Lady Who Swallowed a Fly*. Ill. Nadine Bernard Westcott. Boston: Little, Brown.

Rounds, Glen. (1991). *I Know an Old Lady Who Swallowed a Fly*. New York: Holiday House.

Sloat, Teri. (1998). *There Was An Old Lady Who Swallowed a Trout!* Ill. Reynold Ruffins. New York: Holt.

Ward, Jennifer. (2007). *There Was a Coyote Who Swallowed a Flea*. Ill. Steve Gray. Flagstaff, AZ: Rising Moon.

The patterning may consist of positive versus negative, real versus imaginative, or other opposites. In *Fortunately* (Charlip, 1993), first something good happens, fortunately, and then something bad, unfortunately. Children in the primary grades generally see the pattern after four or five pages and are then thoroughly captivated by the humor. In the story, Ned has been invited to a surprise party, but has to get from New York to Florida. What ensues is a series of mishaps in which the airplane motor explodes, there is a hole in the parachute and Ned encounters a shark. Fortunately, he arrives in time to attend his surprise birthday party.

Ask the children what they notice about the pages to see if they recognize the use of color on the "fortunately" pages and black and white on the "unfortunately" pages. Let them do short sequences themselves, perhaps giving them the opening statement. This is the sort of composing that could be made into a roll story, where each phrase and a picture illustrating it is drawn on a roll of shelf paper, so that the story unwinds as the paper unwinds. *Fortunately* also prompts students to write their own "fortunately/unfortunately" stories.

Playing with the Appearance of Language   Authors can play visual games with language. Rebus writing is one such game. It is a combination of words and pictures in sentence form. To read it, one must name the object in the order in which it appears and read the words or parts of words attached to it. *I'm Not Feeling Well Today* (Neitzel, 2001) is a cumulative rebus story that presents the written word in context of the story and then incorporates it into a sentence as a rebus picture. Children can return to previous pages to identify the word and then return to the rebus pictures to connect the two. This format allows prereaders to participate and to increase their sight word vocabulary. Kes Gray's *Eat Your Peas* (2006) tells the story of a mother who will do anything to get her daughter Daisy to eat peas. As the desperate woman continues to beg and negotiate, a small picture of the items she offers appears on the page. This book is more appropriate for children who are reading because there is more text than the previous book. In Kate Banks's *The Turtle and the Hippopotamus* (2002), turtle will not swim across the river because she is afraid of the hippopotamus standing in the middle of it. She asks a bird, a grasshopper, some ants, and a possum for advice, but she cannot find the courage to cross to eat the delicious reeds on the other side—until she makes a new friend. The pictures are incorporated into the text, with a key to them printed at the bottom of each page. Banks's text assists emergent readers through her rebus story that also introduces new vocabulary.

Another visual game with language is to print the word in a way that signifies its meaning. In *Barnyard Lullaby* (Asch, 1998), the farmer is trying to sleep but keeps hearing the sounds of the animals. The cow, for example, is "moo, moo, mooing." The intensity of the noise is shown as the letters get larger and the color of the words gets stronger. In *So Say the Little Monkeys* (Van Laan, 1998), the words curve around, mirroring the actions of the monkeys. Children need to see the illustrations closely to appreciate what is happening with the print.

Playing with the Meanings of Language   One last broad area of language play is based on the meaning of words. This includes puns, riddles, nonsense words that sound as though they have meaning, idioms, and figurative language. The books about Amelia Bedelia look at the literal interpretation of idioms. Amelia is a maid who believes in interpreting language literally. In the first of the series, *Amelia Bedelia* (Parish, 1963), she does what Mrs. Rogers has told her to do in a list of instructions. When the list says to dust the furniture, she sprinkles dusting powder all over the sofas and tables. When it says to change the towels, she does so by cutting them into a different shape. Amelia is not totally unknowing, however. When Mrs. Rogers returns to find all the mistakes and is about to fire Amelia, she gets a taste of the lemon meringue pie that Amelia has baked, even without instructions to do so. The job is saved, and Mrs. Rogers learns to say things such as "undust" the furniture. Primary-grade children delight in Amelia's interpretation of idioms they understand, and they often can think of other examples.

There are many Amelia Bedelia books, including the last of the original series by Peggy Parish, which is *Amelia Bedelia's Family Album* (1988). Amelia shows pictures in the album and tells the occupation of each family member, but once again, the terms are used literally. Aunt Mary, a bank teller, does not work with money—she tells everyone in the bank where to go.

A similar approach to language play is used by actor/author Fred Gwynne in his books, *A Little Pigeon Toad* (1988) and *A Chocolate Moose for Dinner* (1976). These books have been reissued due to their popularity. In the latter, a little girl repeats some of the things her parents have said, with her interpretation of the meaning shown by the illustrations. Some are idioms, such as her father playing the piano by ear. He is shown banging away on the keys with—yes—his ear. Others are plays on homophones, such as the title picture, which shows a brown moose sitting at the table with a napkin tied carefully around its neck. This is the "chocolate moose" they had for dinner. The spellings given are for the words as interpreted by the girl. If the book is to be enjoyed by children, they must understand the correct meaning for the phrases. Seeing men in seashells rowing with oars is not funny unless they know what is really meant by rowing in shells. This book and others like it are most appropriate for second- and third-graders and even older children. They might even make up full stories based on one of the homophones, seeing how the author of *Truman's Ant Farm* (Rattigan, 1994) plays on the difference between *ant* and *aunt*. Truman gets hundreds of "aunts," all ready to be kind and attentive to their new nephew. Younger children will enjoy *The Aunts Go Marching* (Manning, 2003), which provides a clever twist on the popular song. Author Brian P. Cleary (2005) offers a humorous, but effective introduction to grammar in his books about the parts of speech including *How Much Can a Bare Bear Bear: What are Homonyms and Homophones?*

Children of all ages delight in riddles. There is a vast supply of available books with riddles. *Guess Again! Riddle Poems* by Lillian Morrison (2006) is a collection of 23 original poems accompanied by an illustration that provides a clue to the answer. *Pig Giggles and Rabbit Rhymes: A Book of Animal Riddles* (Downs, 2002) uses rhyming word pairs as a response to the question asked. "What would a mallard drive around town? A duck truck!" Select one or two riddles from these or other books and let children guess the answers. Then let them tell what they think makes a good riddle. They can make up their own to try on their classmates. Having them tell you several riddles themselves will give you some insight on how complex the riddles should be in books you select for them. Here are riddles several children offered when asked simply, Can you tell me a riddle? You may remember some of these from your own childhood.

Three-year-old: Why did the bunny cross the road?
To get to the other side.
Four-year-old: What has two eyes and a sheet over it?
A ghost.
Four-year-old: Knock, knock.
Who's there?
Lettuce.
Lettuce who?
Lettuce in, it's cold out here.
Six-year-old: What is black and white, black and white, black and white and green?
Two skunks fighting over a pickle.
Six-year-old: What time is it when an elephant sits on a fence?
Time to get a new fence.
Eight-year-old: What can jump higher than a house?
Anything—houses can't jump.
Eight-year-old: What is a vampire's favorite holiday?
Fangsgiving.

Understanding Figurative Language   Riddles are similar to figurative language in that new meanings are often attached to words, and differences and similarities are emphasized. Young children sometimes have difficulty understanding the figurative language that others use, even though they may use metaphors that seem very inventive themselves. To see the similarity between a psychological state and a physical entity, as in phrases such as "heart of stone," requires a high level of abstract thinking.

Fisher and Natarella (1979), in their study of primary children's poetry preferences, found that none of the children's favorite poems contain metaphors, whereas the least preferred poems were heavily dependent on metaphorical language. They concluded that it may be because the children did not understand the poems with metaphors or because the poems with metaphors tended to be descriptive rather than narrative. They note, however, that every poem in the study was given the top rating by some pupils.

It would seem that figurative language can best be presented in a context that provides other clues to the meaning and should not be singled out for study. If children are to hear the full range of language, they must be exposed to the use of metaphor. It is central to much literature, both poetry and prose.

Effective use of metaphor gives the reader insight into ideas being expressed, as well as new ways of looking at old ideas. Yet it is illogical to stress the discussion of topics that do not appear to be compatible with the developmental level of young children. The inclusion of well-written stories in a literature curriculum will ensure that children hear metaphorical language. Children hearing Lyle's reaction to a birthday party for Joshua in *Lyle and The Birthday Party* will identify with his feelings and will at the same time hear figurative language such as, "Suddenly, like storm clouds coming down upon a lovely day, Lyle was jealous . . ." (Waber, 1966, p. 6).

Enjoying Mother Goose Rhymes   For encouraging language play, the key source of material for young children is Mother Goose. The verses are catchy, are often humorous, and display the range of play with language. For those children who have heard the rhymes at home, hearing you read them provides a link between home and school that fosters a feeling of security. For the increasing number of children who are not read to at home and are not familiar with Mother Goose, it brings to them a part of their literary heritage that nearly all enjoy. Here is just a quick sampling of the kinds of language that appear in Mother Goose.

Rhythm and rhyme

> Tom, Tom, the piper's son,
>
> stole a pig, and away he run.
>
> The pig was eat, and Tom was beat,
>
> and Tom went roaring down the street.
>
> Pease-porridge hot,
>
> pease-porridge cold.
>
> Pease-porridge in the pot,
>
> nine days old.
>
> Some like it hot,
>
> some like it cold.
>
> Some like it in the pot,
>
> nine days old.

Alliteration

> Peter Piper picked a peck of pickled peppers,
>
> A peck of pickled peppers Peter Piper picked;
>
> If Peter Piper picked a peck of pickled peppers,
>
> Where's the peck of pickled peppers Peter Piper picked?

Onomatopoeia

This is the way the ladies ride,

Tri, tre, tre, tree,

Tri, tre, tre, tree;

This is the way the ladies ride,

Tri, tre, tre, tre, tri-tre-tre-tree!

This is the way the gentlemen ride,

Gallop-a-trot,

Gallop-a-trot;

This is the way the gentlemen ride,

Gallop-a-gallop-a-trot!

This is the way the farmers ride,

Hobbledy-hoy,

Hobbledy-hoy;

This is the way the farmers ride,

Hobbledy hobbledy-hoy!

Patterning of language

There was a crooked man, and he went a crooked mile,

He found a crooked sixpence against a crooked stile;

He bought a crooked cat, which caught a crooked mouse,

And they all lived together in a little crooked house.

Nonsense

Hey diddle diddle,

The cat and the fiddle,

The cow jumped over the moon;

The little dog laughed

to see such sport,

and the dish ran away with the spoon.

Riddles

Humpty Dumpty sat on a wall;

Humpty Dumpty had a great fall.

All the king's horses and all the king's men

Couldn't put Humpty Dumpty together again.

"A Candle"

Little Nanny Etticoat

In a white petticoat,

And a red nose;

The longer she stands

The shorter she grows.

Look through collections of Mother Goose. Plan to read the verses to children on a regular basis. Look also for ways that children can be involved with the rhymes. Which ones lend themselves to dramatization? Which have games that accompany them? Which could children clap to, sway to, move to? Which have refrains that could be repeated? Which can be sung? Look for and build on the strengths of these rhymes, which have enthralled children for generations.

Select rhymes from various cultures. *Diez Deditos: Ten Little Fingers and Other Play Rhymes and Action Songs from Latin America* (Orozco, 1997), *iPío Peep: Traditional Spanish Nursery Rhymes* (Ada, Campoy, & Schertle, 2003), and *Cada Niño/Every Child: A Bilingual Songbook for Kids* (Hinojosa, 2002) give the music, the motions, and the text in both Spanish and English for more than 30 rhymes. *Dragon Kites and Dragonflies* (Demi, 1986) gives many short Chinese nursery rhymes. The illustrations in the books depict a style of art frequently used in the culture.

Exploring Other Languages

The increasing number of bilingual books being published and of familiar stories translated into languages other than English give teachers and child-care providers a wide selection of literature from which to choose. Many of these books introduce children to aspects of a culture in which the language is spoken, although not all do.

Vocabulary items from other languages may be introduced in context, either with or without explanation. In *Mice and Beans* (Ryan, 2001), the meaning is given in apposition, exclaiming "iQue boba soy! Silly me . . . !" or " iCielos!" she said. "Heavens! . . . " In *The Day Gogo Went to Vote* (Sisulu, 1996), the reader must ascertain on his or her own that "gogo" means grandmother, because in the text Thembi talks about her gogo, and the illustrations picture the old woman, but no specific information is given within the story. A glossary, however, does explain that "gogo" is "grandmother" in both Xhosa and Zulu.

Other books work vocabulary from other languages into English text. *I Live in Tokyo* (Takabayashi, 2001) takes children through a year of festivals, activities, food and a family's daily routine. The name of each month is written along the left border in phonetic Japanese, English, and Kanji (Chinese characters used in Japanese writing). Other words are incorporated into the story line, such as "shodo" or calligraphy or "bento box" for lunchbox. The meaning of the Japanese words is defined within the context of the story or through the illustrations.

Still other books will give the complete text in both English and another language. Spanish is the most common language for bilingual books at present. With short text, as in Pat Mora's poetic text *Listen to the Desert/Oye al desierto* (1994), children can repeat the phrases after you, and it is very easy for them to compare the writing in the two languages. In more complex books, such as *A Gift for Abuelita/Un regalo para Abuelita* (Luenn, 1998), you might want to have children just listen as you read first in one language and then another or as you and a reader of the other language take turns reading the text. You might also want to ask a native speaker of the language to make a tape of himself or herself reading so that you can use it several times.

Using such books introduces your English-speaking students to the concept of the many languages that are spoken around the world and supports the native language of your students for whom English is their second language. Just as for many children, hearing stories or rhymes in school that they have heard at home helps ease the transition into a new environment, so hearing their native language can help make students feel at home in school and feel pride in their heritage.

Giving Children Practice in Attentive, Critical, and Appreciative Listening Skills

Educators use a variety of terms to describe and categorize types of listening skills. One such system classifies listening as marginal, attentive, critical, or appreciative. The sort of listening that occurs when a child is not really paying attention but does respond if his or her name is called or if a sound such as a siren intrudes is often termed *marginal,* or *passive,* listening. Sharing literature with children is seldom concerned with this type of listening.

Building Attentive Listening Skills   Attentive listening occurs when the listener can decipher the literal meaning of what he or she hears, recall sequence, and follow directions. It requires that the listener attend to what you are presented and understand the meaning directly conveyed by the words. One way in which literature can build skills in attentive listening is for the teacher to involve the children with the story during the reading. This can be done if you have children repeat refrains in cumulative stories. They must listen to the story and be ready when it is time to say "Hundreds of cats, millions of cats . . ." or "I think I can."

You can give children special parts in the telling of a story so that they must listen for their time to participate. You could read a story such as *Good-Night, Owl!* (Hutchins, 1972), in which the owl is trying to sleep but all the other animals are alert and noisy. The pattern of the book is such that as each animal is named, the sound it makes follows. Thus, the bees "buzz, buzz," and the jays scream "ark, ark." Read it through once so that the children see the pattern. Then have two or three children take the part of each animal. When you read that the bees buzzed, the two or three will respond "buzz, buzz." The story reading becomes a joint project in which the children provide the sound effects. There is the possibility of expanding on this, perhaps having all the children make the sounds together to hear what owl heard as he tried to sleep. Many teachers find it useful to have a hand signal that the children recognize when sound effects or musical instruments are being used. For example, teach the children that when you lift your hand in the air, the sound is to begin, and when you lower it to the top of the book, the sound is to end. The higher your hand, the louder the sound; the lower your hand, the softer the sound. This allows you to orchestrate the effects and lets you and the children work together rather than having to stop their continued buzzing and barking in a voice that rings of reprimand.

A second technique for helping children become attentive listeners is to give them or have them decide on a specific purpose for listening. Most people listen more carefully when they need or want to know the information being given. Before reading an informational book, ask children to listen for the answer to specific questions or for what they hope to find out or to listen for one new bit of information. Second- and third-graders can dictate to the teacher what they already know about the topic or what they would like to find out. This helps focus their listening. Sometimes teachers will give each child a different question to answer. Sometimes they will ask children to raise their hands when they hear a specific piece of information. All these set a purpose for listening.

Building Critical Listening Skills   The kinds of questions you ask about a book determine the kind of listening children are likely to do. If you ask only questions that require direct recall, then children are going to form the habit of listening for detail only. To encourage critical listening, you will need to develop a pattern of asking questions and providing activities that go beyond memory. Critical listening, sometimes called analytical listening, requires the listener to go beyond the data as stated directly. The listener interprets facts, makes generalizations and inferences, and evaluates the material. The listener engages in critical thinking about what has been heard.

Responding to *Good-Night, Owl!* with sounds is an activity that promotes attentive listening. If, following the reading, you were to ask, What did the woodpecker do? or What did owl want to do? you would reinforce habits of attentive listening. To encourage critical listening, you need to plan activities and questions that require thinking that goes beyond the memory level. You might ask questions such as, Do you think the other animals will behave any differently toward owl in the future? Why or why not? or How do you think owl felt about the other animals? What makes you think this? You could have children draw a picture showing one solution to owl's problem of not being able to get his daytime sleep.

In general, memory-type questions and activities do not lead children to explore the more important aspects of literature. Thus, you should go beyond this level and engage children in critical listening and thinking. Chapter 6 provides a more detailed discussion of questioning and types of activities that encourage children to interpret, compare, and evaluate literature.

Building Appreciative Listening Skills   The fourth type of listening, appreciative, is listening that leads to aesthetic enjoyment. This is the sort of listening you engage in when attending a symphony or concert, hearing poetry, or enjoying the humor in a story. You can encourage appreciative listening by showing that you value it. This means that you listen to a poet read several of her poems on a recording as the children listen and do not succumb to the temptation to fill out the attendance chart while the children are listening.

You can encourage the children to make mental images as they listen. How did they picture the dog in the poem? Did they imagine themselves when they had an ice-cream cone melt in their hands? They might later transfer some of their mental images to paper.

For all types of listening, you can help children develop skills by occasionally rereading a story after a discussion. Children can check their own impressions as they hear once again what the author said.

Leading Naturally into Reading

The best preparation for reading is no doubt the desire to read. Literature shared orally helps instill this desire because children learn that books give interesting information and contain enjoyable stories and poems. In addition, those who have listened to a variety of stories have been introduced to many new words and sentence patterns that they will encounter when they read themselves.

Observing the Reading Process   The oral sharing of literature can be structured in such a way that it helps children understand the process of reading. Simply from watching the adult look at the page, turn the pages, and "tell" a story from it, children begin to realize that the print on the page carries a message. When they hear the same story several times, they learn that somehow the book keeps the story constant. If they watch the print as the adult reads, they begin to associate certain segments of print with segments of speech. At first this may be the entire sentence or phrase; later it will be separate words and eventually will be the correspondence between letters and sounds.

To help children gain these understandings, it is essential that you provide ways for children to hear a story more than once. This may be accomplished by reading it to a group when many of them request it again, but more often it should be a reread-ing for the individual who requests it. Have parents who are willing to help or class-room aides set up an area for reading, where a child can come to have his or her spe-cial book read again and again. It is through this repetition that children can begin to generalize about print and speech. The adult can point to words as they are read, rein-force the left-to-right progression that you have demonstrated in your reading to the entire class, let the child read any words that he or she knows, let the child turn the page, and talk about ideas or words with the child.

Big books, published in a format large enough for children to see the print clearly when they are sitting in a group, serve this purpose well. Children watch as the print is read, and because so many of these books have predictable story and lan-guage patterns, children can begin to read a book with the teacher, often after hear-ing only part of the story.

Some teachers invite fifth- and sixth-graders to their kindergarten and primary classes to read to individual children. This can be a valuable experience for the older as well as the younger children. Older children have a chance to improve their own oral reading skills, get feedback on how well they are doing, and build self-confidence. Younger ones get attention and individual help with reading. It may be necessary, however, for you to provide some instruction on oral reading, not only for older chil-dren but for parents and aides as well. This is especially true if you want them to involve children in the story through discussion and pointing out words and phrases.

Set up a listening or computer center where children can listen to tapes or CDs or view CD-ROMs of stories and poems. Place the books in the listening center so that children can follow the story as they hear it, seeing the illustrations and the print as well. Several companies, including Scholastic/Weston Woods, Spoken Arts, and Random House/Listening Library, sell media packages that include a copy of the book and an audio of the text. For children who are not yet reading or are just beginning to read, a bell or beep on the soundtrack that indicates a page is to be turned helps them follow accurately. If you are making the tape yourself, consider using a sound to tell children to turn the page, or simply say "Turn the page." When children are viewing CD-ROM versions of stories, encourage them to go through the story at least once, watching as the print is bolded to show the words being read. A listening or computer center can be a regular option for children as they make work choices or as you assign tasks.

Sharing Familiar Texts in Writing   Let children see in writing the rhymes, chants, or poems that they know. If they can repeat "Mary Had a Little Lamb," make a wall chart of that rhyme and point to the words as they say or "read" it. You can make copies of the rhyme and let them create the illustration. If you do this for several rhymes, they can make a booklet. Your regular sharing of Mother Goose and other nursery rhymes should ensure that the children will have a repertoire of rhymes, even those children who did not know any when they first came to preschool or school. Select and dis-play for the children's perusal several books of Mother Goose rhymes that have only one rhyme per page and have illustrations that will help children identify the rhyme. Two good editions by Iona Opie and Rosemary Wells are *My Very First Mother Goose* (1996) and *Mother Goose's Little Treasures* (Opie, 2007).

All these procedures are designed to help children move into reading naturally by letting them observe for themselves the uses of written language. The process is one in which they see enough examples to begin making generalizations for themselves.

Give children opportunities to read words they see regularly in their environment. Two books by Tana Hoban, *I Read Signs* (1983a) and *I Read Symbols* (1983b), have clear and colorful photographs of common signs and symbols. There is no text. Children will readily recognize and read words such as stop, exit, and don't walk. Because the books show photographs, children see the print exactly as it appears, which helps in recognition and demonstrates that there are many different styles of print.

Providing Time for Reading   Depending on whether you are working in a child-care center, a kindergarten, or the primary grades, you will have different expectations for the children, and the day may be structured in other ways. You should provide time on a regular basis for the children to read and to look at books. This may be done through a period of sustained silent reading, as a work choice for the children, or while others are working in small groups with the teacher.

Children should select some books themselves. Begin early to help them become responsible for their own choices, and let them know that reading is also for personal enjoyment. They need not read every story aloud nor discuss every story with an adult. Particularly in sustained silent reading, children choose books independently and are not responsible for reporting on their reading. Children who are not yet reading text also need the opportunity to look at books, enjoy and "read" the illustrations, and think of themselves as "book people" and "readers" right from the start.

Encouraging Children to Respond to Books Orally

Activities frequently involve more than one aspect of language development, even though only one may be emphasized. While some children are speaking, others are listening. What one child writes, another reads. Oral activities for children can help both the speakers and the listeners: speakers to become more fluent and lucid and listeners to become more attentive and analytical. For example, a child opens a picture book and describes one of the illustrations without showing it to other members of the class. Then give the closed book to another child and ask the child to find the illustration just described. The speaker needs to be detailed in describing the illustration; the listener needs to be attentive so that the description can be compared with each picture until a match is found. Most oral activities either naturally involve listening activities, or you can structure them so that they do. The discussion that follows focuses on oral presentation, but there is a listening component as well.

Dramatizing a Story   Literature offers many opportunities for creative dramatics, both interpreting and improvising. Children interpret a story when they dramatize it following the plot closely; they are improvising when they create their own plot. A story that has long been a favorite with young children is *Caps for Sale* (Slobodkina, 1940). In this story, a peddler who sells caps walks along with his merchandise stacked on his head. After a morning of calling out "Caps for sale" and having made no sales, he walks out into the country and sits beneath a tree to take a nap, still carefully balancing the caps. When he awakens, he finds only his own hat on his head. Looking up, he discovers that the tree is filled with monkeys, and on the head of each monkey is one of his caps. He shakes his finger at them and demands that they return his caps. They shake their fingers back at him. With each action emphasizing his pleas to return his caps, the monkeys only mimic him. In disgust, he throws his hat on the ground—and all the monkeys follow suit. Picking up his caps, the peddler returns to the village to try once again to sell his wares.

Children in Megan Sloan's primary grade classroom acting out the story In the Small Small Pond *by Denise Fleming (1993).*

Another approach is for you to narrate parts of the story, having the children speak the dialogue. You tell about the peddler; then the "peddler" calls out his pitch of caps for sale. As you prepare for this, children can take turns saying the peddler's words and trying to make their voices the way they think his would sound. They do not memorize lines, but rather they say what fits with the progression of the story. The "monkeys" could work to make their voices reflect a teasing mood.

You might have the children dramatize the story, providing all the dialogue themselves and adding words or phrases that would help move the story along. The peddler, for instance, might mutter to himself about feeling hungry or make some exclamation on discovering that his hats were gone. The monkeys could talk among themselves as they picked up the hats from the head of the sleeping peddler.

For any of these three approaches you could use simple props, such as hats for the peddler, or you could have children pantomime. You should not get involved in the extensive use of props, which is more appropriate to a production than to a classroom story interpretation.

Role-Playing and Improvising   Literature can provide a stimulus for drama that does not follow the content of the story but builds on themes, characters, or ideas within it. Role-play and improvisation both fit into this category. In role-play, the child takes on the role of one of the characters and then reacts to a new situation as he or she thinks the character would respond. A child role-playing the peddler might be told that it is the next day, and the peddler is once more at the tree where he had rested previously. He must decide what to do. Will he take off the caps to protect them? Will he keep going? The monkeys also must decide what to do. Will they follow the peddler? Will they grab for the caps even if the peddler does not go to sleep?

Role-play involves being able to understand the viewpoint of another. For this reason, it is more appropriate for children who are in the primary grades than for toddlers or preschoolers. Often children will be themselves in the situation, giving their own reactions and not those that they think the character might have. Even so, role-play encourages children to listen to others and express ideas clearly in speech.

Improvisation builds an entirely new story but may use the characters or a problem from literature as its source. Using an idea from *Caps for Sale,* children could be asked to pretend that they are in the painting area and then go out for recess or stop for snack time. When they go back to finish their painting, the paints and paper are gone. The improvisation begins at the point where they go back to the painting area. They discover their paints missing and must decide what to do. When the improvisation is completed, children talk about what happened and how they felt. They can often repeat role-plays or improvisations, exploring different actions and solutions to problems.

Using Masks and Puppets   Children who are somewhat reticent to speak are sometimes more verbal if they use a mask or puppets in the interpretation of literature. It becomes less them and more the characters who are speaking. Children can make masks to represent characters and hold them in front of their faces as they speak. Some have a space cut out for the child's face; some have just the eyes cut out. Picture-book author and illustrator Jan Brett provides masks on her Web site (*www.janbrett.com*) that can be printed out for children to use. Puppets, too, can be constructed from various objects that are then attached to a stick or dowel of some kind and manipulated by moving the rod. Paper plates, pictures cut from magazines and mounted on heavy cardboard, figures drawn on heavy paper, and paper cups are all commonly used as puppet heads or bodies. The important thing to remember in helping children make puppets is that the youngsters should be able to manipulate them easily. The children can then concentrate on the action and dialogue of the puppets and the interaction among the characters.

Talking About and Telling Stories   In addition to leading to dramatization, books can also lead to other oral activities. Children can tell parts of stories they liked to classmates, with a period in which they can be asked questions. They can record their opinions on particular books and put the tapes in the book area for other children to hear. These same tapes can be played for the speakers to listen to, not to evaluate but to hear how they sound. They can retell a story using the felt board. They can engage in book discussions. They can explain art activities based on books as they share their creations.

Wordless picture books offer many opportunities for children to tell a story. First-graders looking at *Pancakes for Breakfast* (dePaola, 1978) can add to the text by looking at the pictures and giving a sentence or two for each illustration. They can describe the woman who awoke thinking of pancakes, got out her recipe book, began gathering the ingredients for the pancakes, and, after collecting eggs from the hen-house and milking the cow, still needed maple syrup. They can describe how she returned home with the syrup to discover that her cat and dog had knocked over the batter and ruined her breakfast plans. Finally, they can end by telling how she smelled pancakes from the house next door, went over, and ate her neighbor's breakfast.

They might tell the story by passing the book around a group of four children, each telling about a page when it was his or her turn. One child might tell the story by making a recording of it and seeing if other children could understand the book from the tape or CD alone. They might tell the story as if they were the old woman, beginning with "When I woke up . . ." instead of narrating it in third person. As you listen to the descriptions children give, you will learn about their understanding of the story itself and gain some insight into their language development.

As you preview books and poems, look for those that lend themselves to choral speaking. Books with refrains, such as *Move Over, Rover* (Beaumont, 2006), or with sounds, such as *Good-Night, Owl!* (Hutchins, 1972), invite class participation. Short poems can be spoken in unison or divided so that groups within the class say different lines. All might recite "Jack Be Nimble" as they act out the rhyme and jump over an imaginary candlestick. "Jack Sprat" is easily divided. The first line is said by one group: "Jack Sprat could eat no fat"; the second, by a second group: "His wife could eat no lean"; and the last two by the entire group: "And so between them, they licked the platter clean." Find opportunities where you can lead children in echo reading, where you say the phrase first, with them repeating it. *Bears Snores On* (Wilson, 2002) allows the teacher to model—and have children follow—volume, speed, and phrasing as each animal occupies the den as the bear snores on.

Finally, give children the opportunity to talk with one another as they work on projects that are book related. This informal conversation provides language practice in a natural situation and gives many children the opportunity to speak if they are working in pairs or small groups. Their turn to talk comes often, and they actively engage in listening.

If two or three children work on the same project, then their conversation can be focused. They must also use group-interaction skills. The children can hear and repeat the brief poems in *Poetry in Motion* (Lillegard, 2006) a book that highlights the unique personalities of things that go. Children may brainstorm things that go and create a class big book using the text but creating their own illustrations. In groups of three, children can select which page they wish to illustrate. Then they can present their ideas to one another and plan just how the illustration would be drawn. When completed, each illustration can be shared with the other groups and then combined into a single book for repeated reading.

Engaging Children in a Variety of Writing Activities

In a discussion of writing activities, it is necessary to remember that there is a strong connection between reading and writing. Oral and written aspects of language develop simultaneously and are linked in that both engage the child in actively making meaning of the world (Johnson and Giorgis, 2007; Fletcher, 1993). Talking about their topic, both before they write and while they write, helps some children to write in a more focused manner. They may share their writing while the piece is in progress, getting feedback from an audience of their peers.

Children select their own topics to write about and may record thoughts and feelings in a daily response journal. There are times, however, when you may want to provide an idea, or prompt, for their writing. Sometimes books seem to lead directly into writing activities. *The Friend* (Stewart, 2004), for instance, alternates between pages having text and those with illustration only. The text tells of a little girl named Annabelle Bernadette Clementine Dodd, who was a good little girl, though "decidedly odd." She is cared for by the housekeeper, Bea, and they form a remarkable bond. Then the rhyming text is followed by a double-page spread that extends the storyline. Children can create a piece of descriptive writing by looking at the illustration and adding the text for what Belle and Bea are doing.

Doreen Cronin's *Diary of a Worm* (2003), *Diary of a Spider* (2005), and *Diary of a Fly* (2007) provide humorous diary entries that share the typical events in the

By Doreen Cronin • Pictures by Harry Bliss

DIARY OF A FLY

FROM THE #1 *NEW YORK TIMES* BESTSELLING TEAM

Fly records her daily happenings through humorous diary entries which involves trying to escape her 327 brothers and sisters who are driving her crazy!

(Text copyright © 2007 Doreen Cronin. Used by permission of HarperCollins Publishers.)

life of a worm, spider, and fly, respectively. These humorous and lively stories introduce children to what diary entries are and what they might include. They can select their own animal or insect to research. Then they can present those findings in a diary format, using Cronin's books as models. For assessment, ask children what they included in their diary or what the diary could tell someone who read it. Children might offer what they can or do write in a diary about the events in their lives, their feelings about what is happening, what they plan to do tomorrow, and their dreams for the future.

At times, both the content of a book and its format will suggest writing activities. *Letters from a Desperate Dog* (Christelow, 2006) shares the feelings of Emma the dog, who believes she is misunderstood and unappreciated by her owners. *Amelia's*

Notebook (Moss, 1999) and the subsequent books in the series provide a perspective from a young girl who writes about her life. Both books serve as models for children to write about the happenings in their daily life.

Yuck! (Stevenson, 1984) is told in cartoon format, with characters' dialogue appearing above them in balloons. This is a format many children know from looking at comics in newspapers and one they can manipulate to tell stories in a combination of art and writing. The story itself appeals to children both for the terrible sounding—and smelling—potions that the witches Emma and Lavinia brew and for the poetic justice as the little witch, Emma, outwits these two after they have refused to let her help. The book encourages children to play with language, perhaps making their own recipes for potions, and to explore storywriting in cartoon format.

Stringbean's Trip to the Shining Sea (Williams, 1988) is about a boy's trip from Kansas to the Pacific Ocean with his older brother, told through the postcards he sends home. His messages reveal his feelings and his relationship with his brother as well as the experience he has. Children could explore the whole world of postcards—the messages, pictures, descriptions, and special stamps—first explored through this book.

Ann Whitehead Nagda incorporates letters into the chapter book *Dear Whiskers* (2000) as fourth-grader Jenny must pretend she is a mouse for a school project. Jenny is assigned to write to a second-grader, Sameera, who has just moved to the United States and is not fluent in English. Nagda provides a purpose for writing and the frustration of not receiving a reply.

Recommended Literature to Support Children's Writing

Ahlberg, Janet & Allan. (1995). *The Jolly Pocket Postman.* Boston: Little, Brown.

Conrad, Pam. (1991). *Pedro's Journal: A Voyage with Christopher Columbus August 3, 1492–February 14, 1493.* New York: Scholastic.

Cronin, Doreen. (2007). *Diary of a Fly.* Ill. Harry Bliss. New York: Cotler/HarperCollins.

Holabird, Katharine. (2003). *Angelina Ballerina's Invitation to the Ballet.* Ill. Helen Craig. Middleton, WI: Pleasant Company.

Leedy, Loreen. (2006). *Messages from Mars.* Ill. Andrew Schuerger. New York: Holiday House.

Nolen, Jerdine. (2002). *Plantzilla.* Ill. David Catrow. San Diego, CA: Harcourt.

Pak, Soyung. (1999). *Dear Juno.* Ill. Susan Kathleen Hartung. New York: Viking.

Stewart, Sarah. (1997). *The Gardener.* Ill. David Small. New York: Farrar, Straus & Giroux.

Teague, Mark. (2002). *Dear Mrs. LaRue: Letters from Obedience School.* New York: Scholastic.

Turner, Ann. (1997). *Mississippi Mud: Three Prairie Journals.* Ill. Robert J. Blake. New York: HarperCollins.

Building Ideas from Types of Writing

At other times, it may be helpful to use a category system as a stimulus to find writing activities that will extend children's responses to literature. One such category system is based on the type of writing: narrative, expository, persuasive, or descriptive. Narrative writing tells a story and has a plot. Children can listen to the first part of a story and then write an ending for it, or they can listen to the actual ending first and then write a new one. They can use a character from a book—Curious George, for instance—and create a new adventure for him. They might look at the structure of a specific kind of narrative, such as a folktale with wise and foolish beasts, and write a story in that mode.

Expository writing explains how something is done. Children who have heard how the characters in a book spend their holidays can then write how their own family celebrates or how they decide where to go on vacation. They might try writing their own recipe for stone soup after hearing how the soldiers in the book of that title made soup with the help of the villagers.

Persuasive writing is designed to influence people, to be convincing. Children can write commercials for their favorite books, using language that highlights all the good points of the book and makes it sound appealing to others. They might write a letter in a defense of a book character.

Descriptive writing portrays a character or situation. It describes how an object appears to the senses, how someone feels, or what a scene was like. Children can write descriptions of book characters without including the names of the characters. The descriptions can be put on a bulletin board as part of a riddle game. Children read the descriptions and try to guess who the characters are.

After reading *Stellaluna* (Cannon, 1993) orally, one second-grade teacher brought in a Stellaluna puppet and let a different child take it home each week, along with Stellaluna's diary. During the week, the child, as Stellaluna, wrote entries, from a bat's perspective, telling what she had seen and done. Children were eager to take Stellaluna home and equally eager to share her diary the following week.

Being Flexible in Amount of Writing   A second way of thinking about writing is to consider the quantity of writing. Some responses to books may take the form of lists or one-word answers. Children might be asked to list four places they think a cricket could hide in their classroom or, after reading *If You Give a Mouse a Cookie* (Numeroff, 1985), to list other food items the mouse might be interested in eating. Often the written response may be just one sentence. First-graders answered the question at the end of *Clifford's Halloween* (Bridwell, 1986)—"What would Clifford be for Halloween?"—with these responses: He could be Santa Claus; He could be a big red bird; He could be a red witch; He could be Superman. Because Clifford is a huge red dog, disguising him is somewhat of a problem. The children drew pictures to accompany their answers. Both the pictures and the sentences kept the bigness and the redness of Clifford in mind. Only one of the students used a suggestion that had appeared in the book.

Children may write a paragraph or more, developing an idea fully. A special writing corner, a writer's club, and access to a computer for word processing often encourage children to write. Also, having an adult who can write down children's ideas or stories is also motivating when those children can then read the stories they created without having to perform the physical task of writing it. So, too, will writing and illustrating their own books, which can be sewn together and bound in cardboard covered with cloth. These are placed in the classroom library where other children may read them. Several companies are now producing books with cloth covers and blank pages. You might suggest these books to parents as a way of encouraging their children to write at home.

Helping Children Write Well   As you plan writing activities related to literature, you will want to do all that you can to make the writing experience a successful one for the children. Generally, this means that you should engage children in a discussion period before they begin writing. During this time, children exchange ideas and think through their own responses so that when they begin to compose, they have some notion of what they want to say. In a good writing program, children write daily, taking responsibility for choosing most of their own topics and having regular conferences with the teacher during the writing process. These procedures will carry over when children write about literature.

According to recent research, children's approaches to writing change as they mature. Children of ages 5 or 6 put thoughts on paper with little preplanning. Writing is like play in that the children put on paper whatever comes to mind and are not concerned with the product or potential readers. They develop a sense of audience gradually. Children become aware of others' reactions to their stories and the need for the conventions of punctuation, capitalization, and correct spelling. By the end of first grade, many children are able to postpone the immediate task of writing to do preliminary tasks such as checking the spelling of a word.

Once children begin to plan, they frequently go through a period of overplanning, wanting everything decided before they begin so that there will be no "mistakes." The period of spontaneity has given way to a period of deliberateness. Before children begin composing as a professional writer does, they must rediscover the playful aspects of writing (Calkins, 1994). They must combine initial personal response with their awareness of audience, compose, and then edit.

Your task as a primary-grade teacher is to encourage and support the concept of planning and to work with children as they write, helping them clarify thoughts and consider whether they are writing for an audience or just for themselves. You will introduce the ideas of proofreading and editing, both in stories dictated by a group and in the writing of individuals. In this way, children learn that the first draft may or may not say exactly what they want, and that changes and corrections are not only permissible but also desirable. If you are working with preschoolers, your task is to encourage the children to tell stories, to engage in oral composition, and to experiment with print, writing their stories and telling you what each says.

Try to vary the writing activities that you suggest to children. This will help maintain their interest in writing and will give breadth to their concept of content and style. Structure writing activities so that they are challenging but not overwhelming, allowing the children to see growth in their own skill.

Incorporating Visual Literacy

Visual literacy, the ability to discriminate and interpret images, has taken on new importance as children both view and create images on computer programs, and as more information and entertainment are presented through visual means. Just as you help children become more knowledgeable and more skilled in their use of verbal communication, so, too, you can help them gain skill in using and understanding visual images. Illustrator studies, in which children compare several works of a single artist, allow children to explore the techniques that person uses and to show that there are choices being made. An artist often thinks of the book's audience, just as a writer does.

Because books capture selected events within a story, children can describe what else might have been shown and think about why the artist chose to illustrate particular portions of a story. Comparing the book format with an animated format of the same story can enhance this strategy. The books, CDs, and television programs based on the Arthur stories of Marc Brown are numerous and easily purchased and so make an easy place to start.

Ann Morris's *Families* (2000) clearly shows how people use visual images to learn about other cultures. Morris shows that all children are part of families and that they come in different sizes, nationalities, and configurations. The photographs depict families from around the world, including the United Kingdom, Brazil, Vietnam, and Saudi Arabia. Children can look at photographs from many books, both fiction and nonfiction, and tell what they learn from the visual elements.

SUMMARY

Children learn language by constructing for themselves the grammar of the language they hear. To develop mature syntax and vocabulary, they need to be exposed to rich, varied, and abundant samples of language, for this is the database from which they generalize. They should hear stories and see print in their daily environments. They also need the opportunity to use their language for a variety of purposes and in a variety of settings.

The following long-term developmental goals are appropriate for the language growth of young children:

Children will understand and use the mature syntax of their language.

Children will expand their vocabularies.

Children will enjoy the creative and aesthetic use of language.

Children will become skilled listeners.

Children will learn to read.

Children will communicate effectively in oral, written, and visual formats.

Books offer opportunities for helping children achieve these goals. Teacher Feature 5.1 (pp. 130–133) suggests appropriate teaching strategies. Children can be exposed to mature language in literature, hearing varied and complex syntactical structures, figurative language, and a variety of English dialects. They can be introduced to new vocabulary in context, sometimes as part of a story and at other times in concept books that focus on language. Children should be involved in using the new words they are learning.

Children can be encouraged to enjoy the ways others use language and to play with it themselves. Some "play" is with the sound of language, rhythm, rhyme, and repetition; some is with patterns, refrains in books, and songs. Still other play involves both the visual aspect of language and the meaning. As children listen to and recite Mother Goose rhymes, they are introduced to the flexibility and fun of language.

As they listen to literature, children can practice attentive, critical, and appreciative listening skills. They can be guided to think analytically about what they have heard through carefully structured questions and activities. They also develop a concept of the reading process as they observe how adults use the printed page and how verses they recite orally can be preserved in print.

Finally, literature provides myriad opportunities for children to engage in oral, written, and visual language. Story interpretations and improvisations, role-playing, the use of masks and puppets, written responses to books, character studies, diaries, making one's own book, and comparing a story in several different formats all enhance children's appreciation of literature and strengthen children's communication skills.

Extending Your Learning

1. Have a child retell a story after you have read it orally, first without the book and then looking at the illustrations. Describe and analyze the retellings.

2. Assess the language strengths of any three of the recommended children's books listed in this chapter.

3. Begin a collection of riddles children tell. Classify them by the age of the teller. See if you identify any patterns.

4. Look through a collection of Mother Goose rhymes and find ones that lend themselves to dramatization, movement, singing, or game playing.

5. Select a book that you feel has potential for use in a dramatic activity. Suggest three different approaches for its use.

6. Have children add narration or dialogue to a wordless picture book. You might want to do the narration twice, once in first person and once in third person.

7. Suggest two writing activities that vary in difficulty but are based on the same book.

Teacher Feature 5.1   Supporting Children's Language Development

Developmental Goals	Teaching Suggestions
Children will understand and use the mature syntax of their language.	• Provide rich and varied samples of mature language. • Respond to the content of children's telegraphic speech with mature language. • Read regularly to children. • Encourage primary caregivers to read to the children. • Encourage children to read on their own. • Expose children to a variety of writing styles and dialects.
Children will expand their vocabularies.	• Introduce new words in the context of a story. Let children explain the meaning from the context. • Let children retell a story in their own words. • Use phrases from a story to elicit personal responses from children. • Share concept books that present vocabulary items. Have children create sentences or stories from the words and pictures given. • Let children respond physically to words in a story or poem. • Read several books on the same topic to reinforce vocabulary. • Have children use accurate vocabulary to tell personal experiences similar to ones presented in literature. • Guide children to dramatize stories so they will use the vocabulary they have heard.
Children will enjoy the creative and aesthetic use of language.	• Read literature that emphasizes language play and follow up by engaging children in wordplay themselves. • Read poetry regularly to the children. • Let children listen to and write tongue twisters. • Encourage children to say refrains in books with you as you read. • Share literature in which there is a patterning of language. Let children create short sequences themselves. • Present cumulative folktales. • Show visual games with language such as rebus writing. • Encourage riddles and other play on the meanings of words. • Read or recite a wide selection of Mother Goose rhymes.
Children will become skilled listeners.	• Give children a specific purpose for listening. • Have children participate in telling a story. • Set a pattern of asking questions that require critical thinking. • Model appropriate listening behavior. • Suggest that children create mental images as they listen. • Reread stories occasionally for children to check their original impression.

Recommended Literature

Ages 2–5		Ages 5–8	
Hesse	*Come on, Rain*	DiCamillo	*Because of Winn-Dixie*
Ryan	*Mud Is Cake*	Fleming	*Gator Gumbo*
		Munson	*Enemy Pie*
		Shin	*Cooper's Lesson*

Ages 0–2		Ages 5–8	
Butler	*Whose Baby Am I?*	Cooper	*Delicious*
Butler	*Whose Nose and Toes?*	Lester	*Hurty Feelings*
Oxenbury	*I See*	Lewin	*The Storytellers*
Ricklen	*Daddy and Me*	McClintock	*Adele & Simon*
Ricklen	*Mommy and Me*		
Tafuri	*Five Little Chicks*		

Ages 2–5	
Beyer	*"Jump or Jiggle"*
Bunting	*Hurry! Hurry!*
Butler	*Can You Cuddle Like a Koala?*
Hudson	*Hands Can*
Marshall	*George and Martha Round and Round*

Ages 2–5		Ages 5–8	
Beaumont	*Move Over, Rover*	Atwell	*Giggle Fit: Tricky Tongue Twisters*
Emberley	*Drummer Hoff*	Banks	*The Turtle and the Hippopotamus*
Fleming	*In the Tall, Tall Grass*	Charlip	*Fortunately*
Gag	*Millions of Cats*	Gwynne	*A Chocolate Moose for Dinner*
Hutchins	*The Surprise Party*	Gwynne	*A Little Pigeon Toad*
Manning	*The Aunts Go Marching*	Hoberman	*You Read to Me, I'll Read to You*
Martin	*Chicka Chicka Boom Boom*	Luenn	*A Gift for Abuelita*
Mora	*Listen to the Desert*	Parish	*Amelia Bedelia*
Morrison	*Guess Again: Riddle Poems*	Parish	*Amelia Bedelia's Family Album*
Piper	*The Little Engine That Could*	Raschka	*Ring! yo?*
Sendak	*Chicken Soup with Rice*	Rattigan	*Truman's Ant Farm*
Taback	*There Was an Old Lady Who Swallowed a Fly*	Seeger	*Walter was Worried*
Takabayashi	*I Live in Tokyo*	Seuss	*Fox in Socks*
Udry	*Thump and Plunk*		
Van Laan	*So Say the Little Monkeys*		
Wilson	*Bear Snores On*		
Yashima	*Umbrella*		

Ages 2–5	
Hutchins	*Good-night, Owl!*

(continued)

Teacher Feature 5.1 Supporting Children's Language Development (*continued*)

Developmental Goals	Teaching Suggestions
Children will learn to read.	• Share literature so that children hear language patterns that occur more frequently in writing than in speech. • Present whole stories, giving children a broad context for comprehending meaning. • Hold books so that children observe the process of reading—looking at print, turning pages. • Use "big books." • Reread children's favorite stories and poems. • Plan for an aide or parent to read to children individually. • Reinforce left-to-right progression in reading. • Present books in such a way that reading becomes desirable. • Set up listening centers where children can hear a story while looking at the book. • Make charts or individual booklets of rhymes children know. • Display books that contain rhymes children know. • Provide time for reading.
Children will communicate effectively in oral, written, and visual formats.	• Transcribe stories that children dictate. • Let children tell about stories they like. • Have children retell a story using a felt board. • Let children interpret stories dramatically. • Encourage use of masks and puppets for dramatization. • Have children provide the text for wordless picture books. • Tape-record children telling plot of wordless books. • Engage children in choral speaking. • Pair children for a game in which one describes a picture in a book and the other tries to locate it. • Allow informal conversation as children work on projects. • Suggest activities that require group interaction and discussion. • Conference with children as they write. • Encourage varied types of writing.

Recommended Literature

Ages 0–2

Chorao	*The Baby's Lap Book*
dePaola	*Tomie dePaola's Mother Goose Favorites*

Ages 2–5

Hoban	*I Read Signs*
Hoban	*I Read Symbols*

Ages 2–5

Bridwell	*Clifford's Halloween*
Gag	*Millions of Cats*
Lillegard	*Poetry in Motion*
Morris	*Families*
Slobodkina	*Caps for Sale*

Ages 5–8

Christelow	*Letters from a Desperate Dog*
Cronin	*Diary of a Worm*
dePaola	*Pancakes for Breakfast*
Nagda	*Dear Whiskers*
Stewart	The Friend
Stevenson	*Yuck!*
Williams	*Stringbean's Trip to the Shining Sea*

REFERENCES

Professional References Cited

Calkins, L. (1994). *The art of teaching writing.* Portsmouth, NH: Heinemann.

Cazden, C. (1972). *Child language and education.* New York: Holt.

Chomsky, C. (1972). Stages in language development and reading exposure. *Harvard Educational Review, 42,* 124–28.

Cochran-Smith, M. (1984). *The making of a reader.* Norwood, NJ: Ablex.

Fisher, C., & Natarella, M. (1979). Of cabbages and kings: On what kind of poetry young children like. *Language Arts, 56,* 380–85.

Fletcher, R. (1993). Roots and wings: Literature and children's writing. In B. Cullinan (Ed.), *Pen in hand: Children become writers.* Newark, DE: International Reading Association.

Genishi, C., & Dyson, A. (1984). *Language assessment in the early years.* Norwood, NJ: Ablex.

Hansen, J. (2001). *When writers read.* Portsmouth, NH: Heinemann.

Harste, J., Woodward, V., & Burke, C. (1984). *Language stories and literacy lessons.* Portsmouth, NH: Heinemann.

Honig, A. (2001). Reading aloud with infants and toddlers in child care settings: An observational study. *Early Childhood Education Journal 28*(3), 193–197.

Johnson, Nancy J. and Giorgis, Cyndi. (2007). *The wonder of it all: When literature and literacy intersect.* Portsmouth, NH: Heinemann.

Kaplan, N. (n.d.) Nursery school teacher at Jewish Community Center, Providence, RI.

Lightsey, G. E., & Frye, Barbara. (2004). Teaching Metalinguistic Skills to Enhance Early Reading Instruction. *Reading Horizons, 45*(1), 27–37.

McNeill, D. (1966). Developmental psycholinguistics. In F. Smith & G. Miller (Eds.), *The genesis of language: A psycholinguistic approach.* Cambridge: Massachusetts Institute of Technology Press.

Morrow, L., Strickland, D., & Woo, D. (1998). *Literacy instruction in half- and whole-day kindergarten: Research to practice.* Newark, DE: International Reading Association.

Sipe, L. (2002). Talking back and taking over: Young children's expressive engagement during storybook read-alouds. *The Reading Teacher 55*(5), 476–83.

International Reading Association. (1996). *Standards for the English language arts.* Newark, DE: Author.

Children's Literature Cited

Ada, Alma Flor, Campoy, Isabel, & Schertle, Alice. (2003). *¡Pío Peep: Traditional Spanish Nursery Rhymes.* Ill. Vivi Escriva. New York: Rayo.

Asch, Frank. (1998). *Barnyard Lullaby.* New York: Simon.

Atwell, Mike. (2001). *Giggle Fit: Tricky Tongue Twisters.* Ill. Steve Harpster. New York: Sterling.

Banks, Kate. (2002). *The Turtle and the Hippopotamus.* Ill. Tomek Bogacki. New York: Farrar, Straus & Giroux.

Barton, Byron. (1995). *Zoo Animals.* New York: Harper.

Beaumont, Karen. (2006). *Move Over, Rover!* Ill. Jane Dyer. San Diego, CA: Harcourt.

Beyer, Evelyn. (1983). "Jump or Jiggle." *Poetry Place Anthology.* NY: Scholastic, p. 131.

Bridwell, Norman. (1986). *Clifford's Halloween.* New York: Scholastic.

Bunting, Eve. (2006). *Hurry! Hurry!* Ill. Jeff Mack. San Diego, CA: Harcourt.

Butler, John. (2001). *Whose Baby Am I?* New York: Viking.

Butler, John. (2004). *Whose Nose and Toes?* New York: Viking.

Butler, John. (2003). *Who Says Woof?* New York: Viking.

Butler, John. (2005). *Can You Cuddle Like a Koala?* Atlanta, GA: Peachtree.

Cannon, Janell. (1993). *Stellaluna.* San Diego: Harcourt Brace.

Charlip, Remy. (1993, 1964). *Fortunately.* New York: Aladdin.

Chorao, Kay. (2004). *The Baby's Lap Book*. New York: Dutton.

Christelow, Eileen. (2006). *Letters from a Desperate Dog.* New York: Clarion.

Cleary, Brian P. (2005). *How Much Can a Bare Bear Bear: What are Homonyms and Homophones?* Minneapolis, MN: Millbrook Press.

Cooper, Helen. (1999). *Pumpkin Soup.* New York: Farrar, Straus & Giroux.

Cooper, Helen. (2005). *A Pipkin of Pepper.* New York: Farrar, Straus & Giroux.

Cooper, Helen. (2007). *Delicious.* New York: Farrar, Straus & Giroux.

Cronin, Doreen. (2003). *Diary of a Worm.* Ill. Harry Bliss. New York: HarperCollins.

Cronin, Doreen. (2005). *Diary of a Spider.* Ill. Harry Bliss. New York: HarperCollins.

Cronin, Doreen. (2007). *Diary of a Fly.* Ill. Harry Bliss. New York: HarperCollins.

Demi. (1986). *Dragon Kites and Dragonflies.* San Diego, CA: Harcourt.

dePaola, Tomie. (2000). *Tomie dePaola's Mother Goose Favorites*. New York: Tandem.

dePaola, Tomie. (1978). *Pancakes for Breakfast.* San Diego, CA: Harcourt.

DiCamillo, Kate. (2000). *Because of Winn-Dixie*. Cambridge, MA: Candlewick.

Downs, Mike. (2002). *Pig Giggles and Rabbit Rhymes: A Book of Animal Riddles.* Ill. David Sheldon. San Francisco: Chronicle.

Emberley, Barbara. (1967). *Drummer Hoff.* Ill. Ed Emberley. New York: Prentice Hall.

Fleming, Candace. (2004). *Gator Gumbo.* Ill. Sally Anne Lambert. New York: Simon & Schuster.

Fleming, Denise. (1991). *In the Tall, Tall Grass.* New York: Holt.

Gag, Wanda. (Reissue 1996). *Millions of Cats.* New York: Coward-McCann.

Gray, Kes. (2006). *Eat Your Peas.* Ill. Nick Sharratt. New York: Abrams.

Gwynne, Fred. (1976). *A Chocolate Moose for Dinner.* New York: Dutton.

Gwynne, Fred. (1988). *A Little Pigeon Toad.* New York: Simon.

Hesse, Karen. (1999). *Come on, Rain.* New York: Scholastic.

Hinojosa, Tish. (2002). *Cada Niño/Every Child: A Bilingual Songbook for Kids*. New York: Cinco Puntos Press.

Hoban, Tana. (1983a). *I Read Signs.* New York: Greenwillow.

Hoban, Tana. (1983b). *I Read Symbols.* New York: Greenwillow.

Hoberman, Mary Ann. (2001). *You Read to Me, I'll Read to You.* Boston: Little Brown.

Hudson, Cheryl Willis. (2003). *Hands Can.* Photos. John-Francis Bourke. Cambridge, MA: Candlewick.

Hutchins, Pat. (1969, 1991). *The Surprise Party.* New York: Macmillan.

Hutchins, Pat. (1972). *Good-Night Owl!* New York: Macmillan.

Jackson, Alison. (1997). *I Know an Old Lady Who Swallowed a Pie.* Ill. Judith Schachner. New York: Dutton.

Lester, Helen. (2004). *Hurty Feelings.* Ill. Lynn Munsinger. Boston: Houghton Mifflin.

Lewin, Ted. (1998). *The Storytellers.* New York: Lothrop.

Lillegard, Dee. (2006). *Poetry in Motion.* Ill. Valeri Gorbachev. New York: Knopf.

Luenn, Nancy. (1998). *A Gift for Abuelita/Un regalo para Abuelita.* Ill. Robert Chapman. Phoenix, AZ: Rising Moon.

Manning, Maurie J. (2003). *The Aunts Go Marching.* Honesdale, PA: Boyds Mills.

Marshall, James. (1988). *George and Martha Round and Round.* Boston: Houghton Mifflin.

Martin, Bill, and Archambault, John. (1989). *Chicka Chicka Boom Boom.* Ill. Lois Ehlert. New York: Simon.

McClintock, Barbara. (2006). *Adele & Simon.* New York: Farrar, Straus & Giroux.

Mora, Pat. (1994). *Listen to the Desert/Oye al desierto.* Ill. Francisco Mora. New York: Clarion.

Morris, Ann. (2000). *Families.* New York: HarperCollins.

Morrison, Lillian. (2006). *Guess Again: Riddle Poems.* Atlanta, GA: August House.

Moss, Marissa. (1999). *Amelia's Notebook.* Middleton, WI: Pleasant Company.

Munson, Derek. (2000). *Enemy Pie.* Ill. Tara Calahan King. San Francisco: Chronicle.

Nagda, Ann Whitehead. (2000). *Dear Whiskers.* Ill. Stephanie Roth. New York: Holiday House.

Neitzel, Shirley. (2001). *I'm Not Feeling Well Today.* Ill. Nancy Winslow Parker. New York: Greenwillow.

Numeroff, Laura Joffe. (1985). *If You Give a Mouse a Cookie.* Ill. Felicia Bond. New York: HarperCollins.

Opie, Iona Archibald (Ed.). (1996). *My Very First Mother Goose.* Ill. Rosemary Wells. Cambridge, MA: Candlewick.

Opie, Iona Archibald (Ed.). (2007). *Mother Goose's Little Treasures.* Ill. Rosemary Wells. Cambridge, MA: Candlewick.

Orozco, Jose-Luis. (1997). *Diez Deditos: Ten Little Fingers and Other Play Rhymes and Action Songs from Latin America.* Ill. Elisa Kleven. New York: Dutton.

Oxenbury, Helen. (1995). *I See.* Cambridge, MA: Candlewick.

Parish, Peggy. (1963). *Amelia Bedelia.* Ill. Fritz Siebel. New York: Harper & Row.

Parish, Peggy. (1988). *Amelia Bedelia's Family Album.* Ill. Lynn Sweat. New York: Greenwillow.

Piper, Watty. (1930). *The Little Engine That Could.* Ill. George and Doris Hauman. New York: Platt & Munk.

Poetry Place Anthology. (1983). New York: Scholastic.

Raschka, Chris. (2000). *Ring! Yo?* New York: DK Publishers.

Rattigan, Jama Kim. (1994). *Truman's Ant Farm.* Ill. G. Brian Karas. Boston: Houghton Mifflin.

Ricklen, Neil. (1997a). *Daddy and Me.* New York: Simon & Schuster.

Ricklen, Neil. (1997b). *Mommy and Me.* New York: Simon & Schuster.

Ryan, Pam Muñoz. (2001). *Mice and Beans.* Ill. Joe Cepeda. New York: Scholastic.

Ryan, Pam Muñoz. (2002). *Mud Is Cake.* Ill. David McPhail. New York: Hyperion.

Seeger, Laura Vaccaro. (2005). *Walter was Worried.* New Milford, CT: Roaring Brook.

Sendak, Maurice. (1962, 1991). *Chicken Soup with Rice.* New York: HarperCollins.

Seuss, Dr. (1963, 1995). *Fox in Socks.* New York: Random House.

Shin, Sun Yung. (2004). *Cooper's Lesson.* Ill. Kim Cogan. San Francisco: Children's Book Press.

Sisulu, Elinor Batezat. (1996). *The Day Gogo Went to Vote.* Ill. Sharon Wilson. Boston: Little Brown.

Slobodkina, Esphyr. (1940). *Caps for Sale.* Reading, MA: Addison-Wesley.

Stevenson, James. (1984). *Yuck!* New York: Greenwillow.

Stewart, Sarah. (2004). *The Friend.* Ill. David Small. New York: Farrar, Straus & Giroux.

Taback, Simms. (1997). *There Was an Old Lady Who Swallowed a Fly*. New York: Viking.

Tafuri, Nancy. (2006). *Five Little Chicks.* New York: Simon & Schuster.

Takabayashi, Mari. (2001). *I Live in Tokyo.* Boston: Houghton Mifflin.

Udry, Janice. (1981, 2001). *Thump and Plunk.* Ill. Geoffrey Hayes. New York: Harper.

Van Laan, Nancy. (1998). *So Say the Little Monkeys.* Ill. Yumi Heo. New York: Atheneum.

Waber, Bernard. (1966). *Lyle and the Birthday Party.* Boston: Houghton Mifflin.

Williams, Vera. (1988). *Stringbean's Trip to the Shining Sea.* New York: Greenwillow.

Wilson, Karma. (2002). *Bear Snores On.* Ill Jane Chapman. New York: McElderry.

Wong, Janet S. (2000). *Buzz*. Ill. Margaret Chodos-Irvine. San Diego, CA: Harcourt.

Yashima, Taro. (1958). *Umbrella.* New York: Viking.

CHAPTER SIX

DEVEN, Age 8

Response to Diary of a Wimpy Kid by Jeff Kinney

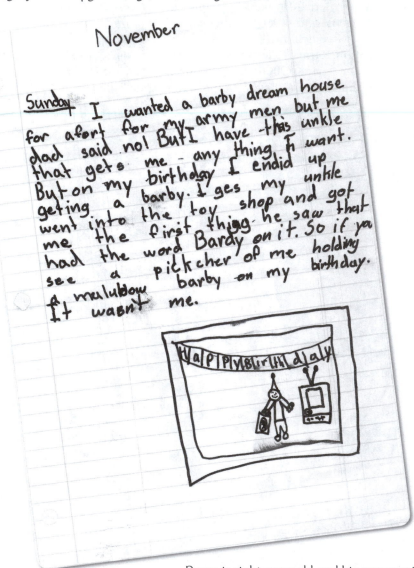

November

Sunday I wanted a barby dream house
for afort for my army men but me
dad said no! But I have this unkle
that gets me - any thing I want.
But on my birthday I endid up
geting a barby. I ges my unkle
went into the toy shop and got
me the first thing he saw that
had the word Bardy on it. So if you
see a pickcher of me holding
A maluubou barby on my birthday.
It wasnt me.

Deven is eight years old and his response is a diary entry based
on *Diary of a Wimpy Kid*. He was inspired by the humor in
the book which is apparent in his response. He chose to write
a diary entry as he loved the format of the book and wanted
to imitate it. This book is particularly superb for boys,
especially those who are a bit mischievous.

Supporting Children's Intellectual Development

Young children come to school with a wealth of information. They are attempting to organize that information, make sense of their world, and integrate their experiences. They are beginning to form concepts from isolated pieces of knowledge.

INTELLECTUAL DEVELOPMENT IN YOUNG CHILDREN

A concept is an idea that represents a class of objects or events (Coon, 2006). It embodies many images and memories that blend to make a meaningful whole. The advantage of developing a system of concepts is that it allows us to process new information by fitting it into an existing framework. Each impression, object, or event need not be assessed and remembered separately. When children have seen several round objects and have been told that each is a ball, they generalize so that new examples fit into their concept of ball. When they hear the term *heavy* used to describe a box that is difficult to lift, a desk their father cannot move, or a large animal such as an elephant, they begin to develop a concept of heavy. This learning of concepts is termed concept formation and refers to the discernment of the properties common to a class of objects or ideas (Solso, MacLin and MacLin, 2008).

Adults are often more aware of young children's ability to conceptualize when they are inaccurate than when they conform to expected perspectives. A 4-year-old was told that her grandfather was in the hospital. She asked each day when he would be coming home. After nearly two weeks of frustration, she announced that she wished he could get out of the hospital soon because "I want to see the baby." This child's experiences with hospitals had been limited to expectant mothers making the trip. Her concept of hospital was that of a place where people went to have babies. If Grandpa had gone there, he should be returning with a baby. The problem with the generalization is not with the reasoning but that it was made on the basis of insufficient examples. When the parent explained that Grandpa was in the hospital because he was sick and that doctors there were trying to help him get well, the child's concept of hospital was enlarged. The changing and enlarging of concepts as new events are experienced and new insights are gained is a continual process.

One task of the child-care professional or teacher is to assist young children to form accurate concepts. Teachers supply materials for the children to manipulate, bring information to the classroom or center, take children on trips, and encourage children to discuss what they have seen. In other words, they provide the raw data from which the children can construct their own concepts. Through questioning, teachers guide children to think about and order what they have experienced.

Simply telling children the concepts you would like them to acquire is seldom effective. It may result in rote learning, but not in real understanding. "Concepts are constructions that must be made by each person for herself. Words, of course, can be given to others" (1983, p. 34), writes Helen Robison, a specialist in early childhood education. Thus, the adult may provide the conventional name, but the child must build the concept.

Young children engage in thinking processes that are fundamental in concept formation. They associate ideas, classify, generalize, and reach logical conclusions (Papalia, Olds, & Felman, 2006). Until they are 7 or 8 years of age, however, children rely more on sensory data than on logic to reach conclusions regarding physical objects. Almost all 4-year-olds will look at two short, wide glasses of water equally filled and report that both glasses have the same amount of water. After watching the water from one of these glasses being poured into a tall, narrow container, the children will report that the tall glass has more water than the short one, or vice versa. The logic that no water has been added or taken away is secondary to the sensory data that after the water is poured from one glass into a taller container, it looks as if the amounts are different. Around the age of 7, children begin to rely on the logic of the situation and will report that the quantities of water remain equal. At this time, they are also able to keep more than one attribute in mind, looking at both the height and the width of the containers.

After the age of 7, children are also more likely to use the standard forms of logical reasoning. They will use deductive reasoning, which goes from the general to the particular. All collies are dogs. This is a collie. Therefore it is a dog. They will also use inductive reasoning, which goes from the particular to the general. Collies, spaniels, boxers, beagles, and terriers all have hair, four legs, and make a barking sound. They are dogs. It is likely that all dogs have hair, four legs, and make a barking sound.

Four- and five-year-olds sometimes use what is termed transductive reasoning (Papalia, Olds, & Felman, 2006). They go from particular to particular, without any reference to the general. This often results in faulty conclusions. The child may connect two events in a cause-and-effect relationship simply because they occur together. The dog ran away. My Daddy was late getting home from work. The dog ran away because Daddy was late.

One 4-year-old, reasoning from particular to particular, was not concerned that Santa Claus appeared in three department stores she and her mother went into, nor that he was also stationed in the center of the shopping mall. It did not occur to her that there might be more than one. For her 7-year-old brother, however, the generalization that a man cannot be in two places at the same time led to a questioning of the ever-present Santa and the conclusion that there had to be more than one.

The Swiss psychologist Piaget has concluded that the order in which children's thinking matures is the same for all children, but that the pace varies from child to child (Piaget & Inhelder, 1969). Particularly if you are teaching 7- and 8-year-olds, who are in a period of transition from one stage of intellectual development to another, you may find great variety in the logic children use as they explain what they observe.

Young children engage in intuitive and associative as well as rational thought. An essential aspect of cognitive development is the development of the imagination. Many young children have imaginary playmates. They talk to them, play with them, and reserve space for them at the table. The fantasy world may seem real to 4- and 5-year-olds, and at times they may have difficulty distinguishing between fantasy and reality. The teacher or child-care professional helps them as they develop the ability to differentiate but at the same time encourages them to use their imaginations.

Children develop their cognitive abilities through interactions with other people. Lev Vygotsky, a Russian psychologist, looked at tasks children could perform independently and at tasks they could perform with assistance but not on their own. He described what he called the zone of proximal development (Vygotsky, 1978), the range beyond the independent level but within the child's potential. Working with guidance from others helps children reach this potential. Teachers provide support, or scaffolding, for children to encourage intellectual growth.

GOALS FOR TEACHING

As in other areas, teaching goals for intellectual growth can be categorized as long-term developmental goals, general goals for an age or grade level, and specific goals for individual children. The long-term goals are those behaviors or competencies that are developed over time and are considered desired patterns of behavior. A long-term goal for intellectual development is that children will continue to acquire new concepts and to refine old ones. Teachers and child-care professionals will help children attain this goal throughout the preschool and primary years.

General goals for each grade level are often listed in curriculum guides. At other times they are developed by the teacher as he or she plans an outline for the year's learning. A general goal for the first-grade level is that children will verbalize the criteria they use to classify various sets of objects.

At times you will have specific goals for individual children. An example for a 3-year-old might be: Katanya will place the scissors and crayons in the appropriate boxes when she is finished using them. It is an intellectual goal because it requires classification, putting scissors with scissors and crayons with crayons. Although most of the children may be doing this, it is a goal for Katanya because she is not yet cognizant of the categorization system being used.

Literature contributes to the achievement of all three types of goals. This chapter focuses on selected long-term developmental goals common to the preschool and primary years. Literature offers opportunities for you to assist children to grow toward the following goals for intellectual development.

Children will continue to acquire new concepts and to refine concepts already held.

Children will develop skill in a variety of thinking processes.

Children will expand their powers of logical reasoning.

Children will utilize critical-thinking skills.

Children will engage successfully in problem solving.

As with other areas, these goals can be correlated with national and regional standards. For example, the goal that children will develop skill in a variety of thinking processes is addressed in the Geometry Standard for Grade PreK–2 (National Council of Teachers of Mathematics, 2000). That standard addresses geometry and spatial sense and suggests that in grades K–2, the expectation should be such that students can recognize, name, build, draw, compare, and sort two- and three-dimensional shapes. Classifying is one of the thinking skills within that goal, and many concept books for children focus on identifying and classifying shapes. As you look at standards, look at how these goals and the specific standards mesh.

OPPORTUNITIES BOOKS OFFER

Assisting in the Acquisition and Refinement of Concepts

Young children have many concrete experiences that aid them in the process of developing and refining concepts. Books, both fiction and nonfiction, are another source of information from which children gather data necessary for generalizing and through which they assess the accuracy of concepts already held.

Giving Information   Literature often provides information that children could not discover through their own manipulations and observations of the environment. Some are in the form of naming what they have observed. Children may know that there are three different kinds of fish in the aquarium, but no amount of watching will teach them what those fish are called. You may want to read books to children that will provide this information, or you may want to leave the books for them to use themselves. If the children are learning about different types of bears, *Polar Bears* by Gail Gibbons (2001) will prove to be useful. Children will obtain information about polar bears, such as their size, what they hunt and eat, and ways they adapt to their environment and will also be able to identify other Arctic animals through well-labeled illustrations.

Books may also explain a process. *Look at My Book* (Leedy, 2004) focuses on the creation of a book from start to finish. Leedy details the process of making a book from brainstorming ideas, conducting research, creating characters and setting, generating a rough draft, choosing a title, and revising what has been written. Then it's time to select a format for the book, along with the layout of the pages. Finally, the process involves drawing the illustrations and binding the finished product. Each page contains tips, ideas, captioned illustrations, and thought bubbles from the characters. The book concludes with a list of resources for teachers and parents of aspiring writers.

Many times books will give information about a topic that is familiar to children but will present new facets of that topic. *Dogs and Cats* (Jenkins, 2007) isn't just another book about pets; rather, it presents information and facts about people's best friends. And the way the information is presented is just as fascinating—once you read about dogs, flip the oversized book over and there is a similar format about cats. The two—cat and dog—meet in the center of the book in a double-page spread. Children learn about the history of cats and dogs, where they first came from, their physical characteristics, and their behaviors. There are also amazing facts about each as well as answers to questions such as, Why do dogs eat grass? or Why do cats chase their tails? The cut-and-torn paper collage illustrations have an almost 3-D effect, encouraging children—and adults—to reach out and pet the animals.

When books about familiar topics are shared with children, they can compare the information in the book to their own knowledge. It is always interesting to hear what children "know" about pets based on their own observation or what others have told them. As a class or individually, additional research can be done to determine if what they know is fact or fiction. A book about dogs and cats can be created with information and illustrations and placed in the book area for future reading.

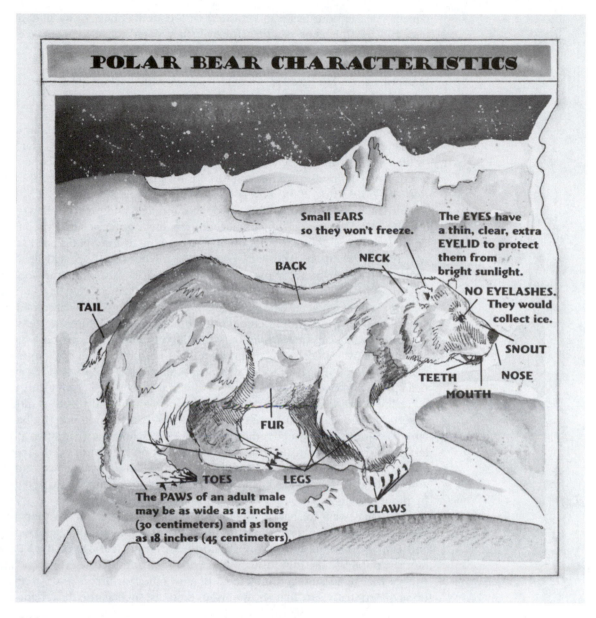

Gibbons conducts extensive research into her topics to ensure that her books present facts accurately.
(Illustration copyright by Gail Gibbons. Used by permission of Holiday House.)

With other books, you can present ideas about people, places, and events far removed from the children's own situations. Young children have ideas about different peoples and places from television and from the conversation of the adults around them. Even though their concept of distance is vague, they can learn about different places and people. There should, however, be some point of reference between the children's experiences and those presented in the book. Often this reference point is in the characters' emotions. Most American children listening to *How Much? Visiting Markets Around the World* (Lewin, 2006) have never been to Bangkok, Peru, Cairo, or maybe even New Jersey. They would not have purchased a llama wool poncho, or a banana fried in flour paste and covered with coconut sugar, or a camel that could be used to carry things or as a pet. However, they could relate to going to a flea market such as the one pictured on the remaining pages of the book. And then they could talk about the different types of markets they have shopped, such as quick mart down the block or a street fair held last summer. Teachers and childcare professionals presenting this book should talk with children about the differences in the ways people live but stress the similarities of needs and feelings.

As you choose books about different peoples, look for those that consider the characters' emotions and motivations. Books that emphasize only "strange" customs or lifestyles may influence children to have negative reactions to people who are different from themselves, rather than to appreciate cultural diversity. The little girl in *Bee-bim Bop!* (Park, 2005) is very excited about what her family will be having for dinner. This bouncy, rhyming text introduces toddlers and preschoolers to the Korean dish bee-bim bop. The girl helps her mother select groceries and prepare the meal. There is a feeling of frenzied shopping and cooking in anticipation of a favorite meal, which many children can relate to. A recipe for bee-bim bop, with instructions for "you" and a "grown-up," closes this engaging story. Although the food might be unknown to children listening to the book, they will all cetainly have a favorite meal that they enjoy or even help to prepare. A chart listing those meals could be made to show the similiarites and differences of food choices of children in the same group.

Past events can be introduced, with emphasis being placed on what happened and why it was interesting or important. As children listen to *Apples to Oregon* (Hopkinson, 2004), a story about a pioneer family that attempts to bring apple, peach, pear, plum, and cherry trees (as well as children) across the plains, they can imagine what life was like for the early settlers as they attempted to cross mountains and deserts on the way from Iowa to Oregon. They can learn about the hailstones the family endured, the droughts that left them thirsty, and the rivers that posed a challenge to cross. They can also learn that the first apple trees really did come to Oregon in wagons. Children can learn about history through enjoyable text and illustration and discover that many fruits and vegetables were introduced into geographic areas by pioneers.

You may want to share with children books that represent a variety of American settings. As a beginning step, look at the books of Robert McCloskey, Donald Carrick, and Donald Hall for settings on the northeast coast; at those of Byrd Baylor or Pat Mora or publications from Rising Moon Press for a Southwest setting; and at the work of Ezra Jack Keats, Lucille Clifton, and Bryan Collier for urban settings or the illustrations of Arthur Geisert that show various settings, such as the desert and the prairie.

Using Books as Teaching Aids   Some books have qualities that make them visual aids in themselves. This is true of many alphabet, counting, and concept books. *A Pig Is Big* (Florian, 2000) provides the concept of size through both rhyming text and cartoonlike illustrations by indicating that a pig is bigger than a hat. Then it goes on to ask what can be bigger than a pig? A cow is bigger than a pig, and a car is bigger than a cow, but what could compare to the size of the universe? The rhyming text is engaging, and the illustrations add humor as children explore the concept of relative size. *Big and Little* (Berger, 1999) is appropriate for infants and toddlers as it shows comparison using colorful photographs.

Often a group of books can be used. Suppose you are working on color names with a small group of children. You could begin by showing *Lemons Are Not Red* (Seeger, 2004). This creatively designed book combines an introduction to colors along with a story. Simple repetitive text provides the names of the items and colors. For example, "lemons are not/RED." The word red appears on a bright yellow page beneath the die-cut shape of a lemon with a red background showing through. When the page is turned, the die-cut shape is now seen on the correct yellow background with the words, "lemons are YELLOW" underneath. Children will quickly catch on to the rhyming game and want to join in. Once you complete the book, you can read it again and ask children to identify the objects and the color being featured. They could do a variety of classification activities: objects by color, objects by shape, objects that move, or objects that are alive. There are opportunities to describe the pictures and to make up stories about them. You might use the book for classifying colors with one group and for language experience in storytelling with another.

Some teachers help children with color names by having them cut pictures of a certain color from magazines; some have them draw pictures using different shades of the same color; some have days when everyone wears something of a certain color or when the snack is food of that color; some reinforce color concepts by daily reminders, such as calling children to a table by the colors they are wearing.

If you use some of these ideas, you might then want to use another book that includes color concepts, *Freight Train* (Crews, 1978). This book, available as a picture book, as a board book, and in Spanish, shows a train with each car a different color. The print matches the color of the car. Reading almost like a poem, the story names the cars and then shows the train traveling. The last illustration shows only smoke. There are strong possibilities for vocabulary development and for information about trains as well as about color. If you were using the book for the color aspects, you might read it several times. After they had heard it once, the children could supply the name of each color as it appeared. Then they could say as much as they remembered while you read. Finally, you could have them repeat the phrases in choral speaking, capturing the rhythm of a train. You reinforce the color aspect while at the same time giving enjoyment in the sound of language.

You might further involve children with books and with color by sharing books that play with and build on the concept. *My Box of Color* (Siomades, 1998) asks in rhyme if particular objects and animals would either act or be considered differently if their color were changed. Would spiders still be scary if they were bright colors? The illustrations show the changed colors. The book concludes with a page of inchworms of many different colors and asks if "I" were not the color I am, would "you" still be my friend? If you find several books on the same topic, you will have more opportunities for approaching that subject from many perspectives and for involving children in a variety of ways.

Look at books for ways in which they can be used by the children themselves. Alphabet books can be shared by two children learning to recognize letter sounds. They can take turns opening the book, seeing the letter, naming its sound or sounds, and naming the objects pictured. Counting books can be used by having a child open the book randomly, see the numeral, select that many counters, and then place one counter on each object to see if he or she counted correctly. Cathryn Falwell's *Turtle Splash! Countdown at the Pond* (2001) is a combination counting book and nature tale as 10 timid turtles sit on a log in the pond. Each time a new creature enters the habitat, one turtle jumps off the log, until only one is left. The rhyming text, with vivid, descriptive words, will encourage preschoolers to count along.

You do not need to use books in their entirety. Select those portions that fit your goals. The preceding section mentioned a book for exploring comparative size. If you had used it and were observing items in the classroom, you might share one page of

ABC: A Child's First Alphabet Book (Jay, 2003). This imaginative alphabet book contains familiar (and a few exotic) objects for each letter. A child could try naming the objects while listening for the sounds the letters make. You could focus on one page for a period of time or explore additional pages. Children will enjoy observing one large object beginning with a letter sound and other items dotting the landscape behind it.

Sharing Books That Stimulate Projects   You can use books as direct models for further work. Two books of poetry by Jane Yolen, *Color Me a Rhyme* (2003) and *Shape Me a Rhyme* (2007), both contain well-crafted poems and stunning photographs of things in nature. Selected poems could be shared with children, depending upon the age group. Then children can go outside and observe colors and shapes as they tour the school grounds, making notes and sketches of what they observe. At the end of the day, they can read what they have said and see what they have noticed. This gives an opportunity for them to summarize what they learned through their own observation. Primary-grade students could write their own poetry and accompany it with a drawing or digital photo of what inspired their poem.

Another project could be modeled after *Harriet, You'll Drive Me Wild!* (Fox, 2000). Harriet Harris doesn't mean to be pesky, but she sometimes is just that—prompting her mother to yell. But even when children and mothers do things they wish they hadn't, they still love each other. Children can talk about times they have been a little pesky. Later, they can dictate or write short descriptive passages or show through illustration what occurred and the outcome.

You may choose books to introduce an area of study or a new learning center. Stories about the beach are often popular with young children, whether they live by the ocean or not. Start by asking children, What is the beach? Where is it located? Then introduce a chart with the five sensory headings: see, hear, touch, taste, and smell. As students share what they know about the beach, write down their descriptive words and under the sensory headings. Have students help you to decide which category the words should go under. Next, read aloud *Hello Ocean* (Ryan, 2001). Then ask children to think of new words or concepts from the book and add these to the sensory lists. These words could also generate a word wall as children discover new words and phrases from other books about the beach, such as *All You Need for a Beach* (Schertle, 2004), *Beach* (Cooper, 2006), *Beach Day* (Roosa, 2001), *Sally Goes to the Beach* (Huneck, 2000), and *Sand Castle* (Yee, 1999). In addition to generating lists of words, children can compare and contrast the way the beach is shown in each book. They can, as a class or individually, create a rhyme about going to the beach and list the items they would take, using a familiar pattern like *The House that Jack Built*. The key to stimulating projects from books is to select a topic that interests children and is something they can relate to in some way.

Sometimes a book will catch children's attention even if you have not planned it as an introduction to further work. Be open to children's responses so that you can take advantage of what some have termed the *teachable moment*, that unplanned yet perfect opportunity to extend children's knowledge and thinking skills. Some of these naturally emerging topics for study may generate curriculum that is worth pursuing. Remember also that fiction can be as effective as nonfiction in providing a stimulus for study.

Reinforcing Concepts   Just as some books can be used to introduce ideas, others serve to reinforce concepts or to add further information to a topic children have already explored through direct experience. The concept book *So Many Circles, So Many*

Squares (Hoban, 1998) is excellent for reinforcing children's understanding of shapes. This wordless picture book shows appealing photographs of various images that contain circles and squares, from dishwashers to musical instruments to street signs. The photographs will spark both conversation and imaginative thinking. Students can engage in a walk inside and outside the school to locate objects and items that contain circles, squares, or other shapes. A class book can be created using children's drawings of their found shapes or by their creative writing about them that is placed alongside a photograph.

Reinforcement of a concept may occur by simply reading a book. If you read *Rosie's Walk* (Hutchins, 1968), you reinforce the concepts of *in, on, under,* and *through* because they are used to describe Rosie's walk around the barnyard. You may choose to read the book with no further work, knowing that children are hearing the terms used in context.

You can use books to answer questions that have been raised or to give further information. If the children are fascinated by dinosaurs, you might want to extend their knowledge by bringing in books that show how scientists piece together information to learn about topics they cannot observe directly. *Digging Up Dinosaurs* (Aliki, 1981) and *Dinosaur Bones* (Aliki, 1988) both show how paleontologists discover, retrieve, and analyze fossils. They show the mistakes as well as the successes as the scientists attempt to make sense of what has been found. You might share *Big Old Bones: A Dinosaur Tale* (Carrick, 1989), a fiction story in which Professor Potts attempts to reconstruct a dinosaur from the bones he has found, with some astonishingly inaccurate results. Students will also enjoy learning about Mary Anning in *Rare Treasure: Mary Anning and Her Remarkable Discoveries* (Don Brown, 1999) and her childhood discovery of a complete ichthyosaur fossil.

Often you will find books that describe experiences similar to those children in your group have had. Read some of these so the children can see how others have reacted and compare their feelings and their knowledge with those of characters in books. *The New Baby at Your House* (Cole, 1998) has a warm and loving tone as it welcomes a new baby and describes both positive and negative feelings of older siblings. This is an appropriate book if one or more of the children have new brothers or sisters. Children can describe what they have noticed about the baby in their family and how it compares to what the book says.

Recommended Concept Books

Bruel, Nick. (2005). *Bad Kitty.* Brookfield, CT: Roaring Brook.

Carle, Eric. (1977). *The Grouchy Ladybug.* New York: Crowell.

Carlstrom, Nancy White. (1992). *How Do You Say It Today, Jesse Bear?* Ill. Bruce Degen. New York: Simon & Schuster.

Ehlert, Lois. (1989). *Color Zoo.* New York: HarperCollins.

Florian, Douglas. (2000). *A Pig Is Big.* New York: Greenwillow.

Harper, Dan. (1998). *Telling Time with Big Mama Cat.* Ill. Barry Moser. New York: Harper.

Hoban, Tana. (1998). *So Many Circles, So Many Squares.* New York: Greenwillow.

Lionni, Leo. (2006). *A Color of His Own.* New York: Knopf.

McNamara, Margaret. (2007). *How Many Seeds in a Pumpkin?* Ill. G. Brian Karas. New York: Schwartz & Wade.

Schwartz, David. (2003). *Millions to Measure.* Ill. Steven Kellogg. New York: HarperCollins.

Tafuri, Nancy. (1997). *What the Sun Sees/What the Moon Sees.* New York: Greenwillow.

Walsh, Ellen Stoll. (2007). *Mouse Shapes.* San Diego, CA: Harcourt.

Clarifying Misconceptions   One of the ways people learn is by expressing their ideas to others and listening to the comments and reactions that result. Teachers who listen to what children are saying will find that children's talk often reveals misconceptions they may have. The teacher is then in a position to help children clarify their thinking.

There are times when books are very helpful in this endeavor. There are other times when direct experience makes far more sense. One first-grader commented to her teacher, "Mr. Gaddis and Mrs. Crabtree sure are good singers." The teacher was puzzled at first over the child's assessment of the musical abilities of the principal and the school secretary. Her pause was filled by further comment from the child: "I like the way they sing those songs at noon." Then she understood: As a special project, music was being played on the intercom system during the lunch hour. The only voices that the child had heard on the intercom were those of the principal and the secretary. Therefore, if there was singing at noon, they must be the ones doing it. This was one of those times when direct experience was far better than a book. The teacher explained that the singing was coming from the office, but that the secretary was playing a tape, not singing herself. Then that afternoon, the teacher and several of the children went to the office to see just how it was done.

At other times, however, a book may be a better aid for clarifying concepts. A 5-year-old came to school telling about an old movie he had seen on television. The cars were funny, he said, and nobody dressed like that. Earlier the class had been talking about *real* and *make-believe* stories. He gave his judgment of the film, saying it had to be make-believe.

There are several concepts involved in his statement. There is the distinction between realism and fantasy. He was including in realism only that which he had experienced himself and knew to be possible. Everything else was fantasy. The teacher needs to help him define other criteria for deciding the differences between realism and fantasy, perhaps emphasizing the aspect of impossibility within fantasy. Also involved in his statement was a lack of realization that changes are occurring continually, in cars, in clothing, in people, and in himself.

Both of these involve more than a single experience, and both can be explored through books. In the regular period for literature, the teacher might read a book of historical fiction, perhaps a book by historical fiction author Verla Kay or Ann Turner. The teacher could introduce it by saying, "This story is about people who lived long ago." After comparing their lives and feelings with those of the characters, the children could be asked if they thought there was anything make-believe about the story.

On another day, the teacher could look for a book that deals specifically how children change over time. Sometimes children are not sure or have misconceptions about when they were able to walk or when they said their first word. One such book about growth is Margaret Wise Brown's *Another Important Book* (1999), illustrated by Chris Raschka. This wonderful rhyming picture book highlights what is the most important things about being 1, 2, 3, 4, 5, and 6 years old. "The most important thing about being four/is that you are bigger than you were before. Now at four you can open the door . . . You can blink and think quick as a wink." Children enjoy hearing about each year's growth, success, and characteristics. Raschka's energetic watercolors feature babies, toddlers and kids growing up as well as numbers cleverly woven into the background, such as a five-point start behind the 5-year-old.

Children can be encouraged to talk with their parents and grandparents about what they have done at each year of their life so far. Another project might be for the children to bring in pictures of themselves as babies and as toddlers, seeing how they have changed already. Many classrooms keep charts of children's growth during the year. This could be a time for seeing what growth had occurred thus far in the year.

When you hear children making comments that indicate misconceptions, you will have several decisions to make. First, you will need to decide whether to approach the misconception directly, such as the teacher did with the singing on the intercom, or to make notes to provide experiences at a later time, as suggested for the comments about the old movie. You will also have to decide how to go about giving the child some feedback. Generally speaking, it is better if you can provide firsthand experience for the children. Not all concepts, however, lend themselves to this approach. Sometimes, you will need preparation time to do a good job. Literature can be particularly useful for giving information and for providing a starting point for discussions and projects.

If you are just beginning to work with young children, books that are written for them may give you some help in gearing your expectations to the children's level of understanding. *Another Important Book* illustrates how people change over. This is in keeping with young children's concept of time, which is not clearly developed. Look at several books on the same topic, plan your presentation to be on what seems a reasonable level in terms of the books and what you know of your class, and then listen carefully to the children's reactions.

Developing Skill in a Variety of Thinking Processes

Books provide the opportunity for children to engage in many thinking processes. Obviously, almost any picture book you select could be used to help children improve in their observational skills. Some, however, are better than others.

Observing   If you want children to become aware of detail, you might select a wordless book that relies upon the reader to look carefully at the illustrations in order to interpret the story. *Once Upon a Banana* (Armstrong, 2006) contains 18 everyday signs that serve as captions for the story of what happens after a monkey tries to toss a banana peel into a garbage can and misses. David Small's detailed illustrations begin on the endpapers, where a rambunctious monkey scurries away from his juggler and snatches a banana from a shopkeeper's display. Once he eats the banana, the monkey throws the peel on the sidewalk rather than in the garbage can that says, Please put litter in its place. After a motorcyclist slips on the peel, one mishap after another occurs. Slowing down and lingering over each illustration is a must because there is a lot going on for children to discover. The book also contains various perspectives, such as a bird's eye view, to add to the merriment. The final endpapers present an aerial map of the city block and a key to identify where each calamity happened. Ask the children if they can find any repeating characters on the pages. What connections can they make between the signs and what is happening in the illustrations? What happens at the conclusion of the story? Children can look at the story once and then go back and pick out the details.

The color illustrations in *What Color Is Camouflage?* (Otto, 1996) stimulate attention to detail in a different way. The text describes the protective coloration and strategies of both prey and predators. Children looking at the photos will enjoy both finding the animal and identifying the protective device.

If you are using books such as these, be certain that the children can easily see the illustrations. This will mean working with a few children at a time or using a device that projects images onto a screen. This way you can show a particular illustration to more students.

Some books are observational guessing games. For children ages 4 to 6, *Each Peach Pear Plum* (Ahlberg and Ahlberg, 2004) challenges them to find a storybook or nursery rhyme character hidden in each illustration. A couplet tells about one character and then says "I spy" another one. Children can look for Bo Peep, Mother Hubbard, Jack and Jill, and others. If you have shared the book with one child, you might then ask the child to choose a friend and play the game again, with the friend doing the guessing. The "I spy" technique can be applied to other books. One child can look at an illustration and tell something he or she spies in the picture, and another can then find the object. This and similar guessing games can be played with *1 Hunter* (Hutchins, 1982), the counting book in which a lone hunter walks through the jungle, unaware of the many partially hidden animals, and *Pigs in Hiding* (Dubanevich, 1983), a story of trickery in which the hidden pigs are found only when food lures them into the open.

Children often enjoy the challenge of picture riddle books that involve finding hidden objects within a scene. Jean Marzollo and Walter Wick have published numerous *I Spy* books that require children to use the unique and detailed photographs to find the items that are described in the riddles. *I Spy: Year Round Challenger* (2005) follows the holidays and months of the year by asking children to spy beach balls, shovels, and a "surfin fella" on the sand in June and exclamation points, a Q, erasers, and a yellow 3 on a classroom chalkboard in September. There are *I Spy* books published in a picture-book size as well as beginning-to-read- formats. Books such as *I Spy* may motivate children to create their own riddles and set of objects to photograph and share with others.

Another book that requires careful observation and involves guessing is *Look Book* (Hoban, 1997). Readers open the book to find that they are seeing part of something through a square hole that has been cut from a black page covering a photograph. They try to guess what they are seeing. When they turn the white page, the whole photograph shows, and they can see how accurate their guesses were. Seven- and 8-year-olds, as well as intermediate-grade children, can play the game. They might tell why they guess what they do before they turn the page. Some might want to make their own *Look Books*, cutting pictures from magazines and making cover sheets with windows showing only a portion of each picture.

Another book that uses the technique of a hole in one page for viewing the pages before and after it is *Peek-A-Boo!* (Ahlberg and Ahlberg, 1997), appropriate for toddlers and preschoolers. It adds the element of perspective—for example, a left page shows a baby, with what the baby sees showing through the hole in the page on the right. When the page with the hole is turned, the viewer is now the character on the right, and it is the baby being seen.

Children who enjoy this will also enjoy *Look Closer!* (Ziebel, 1989), where they can see the close-up photograph of an everyday object. A question about the object provides a clue to its identity. Thus the book asks children about what keeps their teeth clean as they see the photograph of the bristles on a toothbrush. A turn of the page answers the question and presents a new one.

Perspective plays a role in *Round Trip* (Jonas, 1983) and in *Looking Down* (Jenkins, 1995). In *Round Trip*, the black-and-white illustrations show a trip from a small town, through the country, to the city. When reversed and read backwards, the story is of the trip home. The now upside-down illustrations reverse foreground and background to create new images. *Looking Down* is a wordless book in which readers first see Earth as the astronauts do. As the point of view moves gradually closer, children see continents and oceans, then the East Coast of the United States, and then a town, until finally they see the close-up of a ladybug through a magnifying glass. Both books are intriguing and encourage careful and flexible observation.

You may want children to observe the action in a story or the reactions of characters. As with *Looking Down*, wordless picture books are excellent for this purpose, because the entire story is told through illustrations. Children can describe what is happening. In books such as *A Boy, a Dog, a Frog, and a Friend* (Mayer and Mayer, 1971), in which facial expressions play a prominent part, children can tell how a character feels. Children can explain the body language of a finger in front of a closed mouth or the boy's reaction when he falls in the water.

Keep in mind the maturity level and the experience of the children as you select books for practice in observing. The 3-year-old needs less complex books with clearer illustrations than does the 7-year-old. Alphabet and counting books can be used with very young children just to enjoy the objects pictured. Books such as *Anno's Spain* (Anno, 2004), with more detail and a somewhat unfamiliar setting, are better used with slightly older children. Detailed pen-and-ink drawings and watercolors provide an aerial tour of Spanish landscapes and townscapes. There are also scenes of 15th-century ships at sea, olive harvesting, country fairs, and the running of the bulls at Pamplona. As usual, there is a lot going on in Anno's illustrations, some of which may be discovered by children; others, only adults will find.

Hypothesizing   Children can be guided to hypothesize about any book you are sharing with them. They can look at the cover or listen to the title and make reasonable guesses about the book's possible content. They can take a "picture walk" through the book first before reading it and telling what they think a character will do or what might happen next. Teach children that hypothesizing means taking into account the information one already has in order to make predictions, and encourage them to give reasons for their conjectures. Teach them that hypothesizing is a logical process and is not simply telling what one would like to happen or what one thinks would be interesting. Their guesses may prove to be exactly what the author has done with plot, but it may turn out to be quite different though still reasonable. The object is to suggest logical possibilities, not to match exactly the author's choice.

Some books have plots that naturally invite hypothesizing, especially when the story is about a beloved character with which they are familiar. *Lilly's Big Day* (Henkes, 2006) features everyone's favorite mouse, Lilly, making a huge assumption about Mr. Slinger's upcoming wedding—that she is going to be a flower girl. Lilly's teacher has announced to the class that he is getting married to Ms. Shotwell, the school nurse. At home, Lilly begins practicing being a flower girl and when questioned by her parents if she has been asked, she tells them, "not yet." When Mr. Slinger breaks the news to Lilly that his niece Ginger is going to be the flower girl, Lilly is devastated. However, she does agree to be Ginger's assistant and in her usual Lilly way, makes the best of a unique situation. There are several points in the story where hypothesizing could be done. What do they think will happen next? How will Lilly react knowing how much she wants to be a flower girl? Will Ginger be Lilly's flower girl some day? It might be helpful for children to be familiar with Lilly by reading *Lilly's Purple Plastic Purse* (1996) so that they clearly understand her behavior as well as her relationship with Mr. Slinger.

Other books have such strong characterization that this becomes the basis for children's hypotheses about what will happen next. They see the character's feelings and reactions and use these, as well as their own understanding of the emotions, for anticipating actions. After hearing any one of the *George and Martha* books by James

Marshall (1997), children will know that neither George nor Martha will knowingly do anything that might hurt the other and that both are tolerant of the other's foibles.

Still other books have an identifiable pattern to the actions within them. Folktales such as *The Gingerbread Boy* or *The House that Jack Built* often have cumulative or repetitive plots. Children may use the generalizations they make about the literary form itself to suggest what will happen.

Comparing   Literature offers the opportunity for children to engage in structured comparisons. When you group books in pairs, units, or webs, you set the stage for the children to compare and contrast one work of literature with another.

Fairy tales offer an opportunity to compare and contrast stories. Often we make the assumption that children are familiar with different fairy tales, but sadly that may not be the case. One second-grade student thought Walt Disney wrote *Cinderella* and *Snow White* because the only fairy tales to which she had been exposed were the movies produced by Disney. Although those present one version, there are so many more that can be shared with young children.

Begin by reading traditional versions of *The Three Little Pigs* by James Marshall (1989) and Steven Kellogg (1997). Choose one illustration from each book depicting a similar action or event and have students compare and contrast them. Initially, it is better to begin with one illustration rather than overwhelming the children with comparing and contrasting the entire story. When working with second-language learners, take the time to discuss the illustration and name objects that appear in each. A good strategy is to write the naming word on a sticky note and place it in the book next to the object. Children can then revisit the book and use the sticky note as a reminder of the word. After another reading of the stories, compare and contrast the entire stories using a Venn diagram. If children struggle to remember events in the story, then it might be too soon to use this strategy.

Once the children are familiar with the traditional story of *The Three Little Pigs*, introduce them to different versions and variants. One popular story is *The True Story of the Three Little Pigs* (Scieszka, 1989), which is told from the viewpoint of A. Wolf, who claims he was framed in being accused of huffing and puffing and blowing the pigs' houses down. Compare this version with those by Marshall and Kellogg to determine the differences. Ask which story they liked better and why. Do they believe the wolf when he says he was just trying to borrow a cup of sugar and didn't mean to sneeze? Are there clues in Lane Smith's illustrations that would support the wolf's arguments?

Read other variants, such as *The Three Javelinas* (Lowell, 1992), set in the Southwest United States and depicting wild pigs as the main characters, and *Wait! No Paint!* (Whatley, 2001), which begins using the familiar story but then changes as a cup of juice spills just as the wolf is blowing down the straw house. These stories should be discussed and compared following the reading of the traditional stories or later in the year. Comparing and contrasting builds on and strengthens skills in observing. These books and experiences encourage the development of both. They are also stories that easily lend themselves to dramatization.

Classifying   Some books, such as *The Elves and the Shoemaker* (Grimm, 2003), readily lend themselves to experiences in classification. This traditional tale stimulates a number of related sorting and graphing activities. Children can discuss attributes, such as color, style, or material, that could be used to classify the shoes worn by members of the class. Have the children remove their shoes, sort them, and then represent the results in table and in graph form. The response to the story can utilize real-life

The Elves and the Shoemaker *by the Brothers Grimm presents a variety of activities related to sorting and graphing.*
(From *The Elves and the Shoemaker* © 2003 by Jim Lamarche. Used with permission of Chronicle Books LLC, San Francisco. Visit ChronicleBooks.com)

analysis through skills related to observing, questioning, classifying, graphing, and interpreting data.

Other books have the potential if the teacher sees it. One teacher had read *Frog and Toad Are Friends* (Lobel, 1970) to her kindergarten class. At one point in the book Toad and Frog return home from a walk, and Toad discovers that he has lost a button off his jacket. He and Frog go back over all the places they have walked in an attempt to find it. Frog and several other animals find buttons, but none matches the one Toad lost. They find a black one, but his was white. They find one with two holes, but his had four. Attribute by attribute, it is narrowed to a white, four-holed, big, round, thick button. They cannot find it, and an angry Toad returns home to find the button on the floor of his living room. Concerned about the trouble he has caused his friend, he sews on the button and also sews on all the other buttons that they have found. The next day he gives his button-covered jacket to Frog.

After the children had heard the story, the teacher produced a large box of buttons. Each child decided what kind of button he or she would look for. They used the classifications Toad used, such as thick or white, but chose others as well. They tried to see how many they could find that would fit their classification and then compared their collections of buttons. Later some of the children made pictures of Frog wearing Toad's jacket. They used fabric from the scrap box to make jackets and then pasted buttons all over the jackets for decoration. The children enjoyed the experience, in part because of the story and in part because the teacher selected a classification activity that was challenging but not overwhelming for the children. They pasted the buttons on their pictures because the teacher knew that attempting to sew small buttons onto cloth would have been frustrating for them.

Children might be asked to classify some of the stories they have heard. If the categories are not given, children can begin to develop their own. They might divide stories into those they liked and those they did not like; they might divide them into stories that could happen and stories that were make-believe or stories about animals and stories about people. The teacher guides the children to think about the content of the stories, and perhaps the format, and talks about how to find a variety of ways of classifying them.

Organizing Another thinking skill is that of organizing. Young children can be helped to organize by learning to sequence events. Cumulative folktales, as well as many contemporary stories, are a rich source of material. Reconstructing the sequence of events in some tales, however, is a difficult task because knowing the order of events is a matter of straight recall. For example, in *If You Give a Mouse a Cookie* (Numeroff, 1985) he will certainly need a glass of milk to wash down the cookie. And you can't expect him to drink the milk without a straw. And then he'll need a napkin. This cumulative tale builds from each object until it comes full circle. There is a cause-and-effect relationship related to the objects that makes the organization of them necessary. Subsequent titles by Laura Joffe Numeroff and illustrator Felicia Bond also would work well for organizing and sequencing a story.

Other tales have a patterned order to the events. The goats in *The Three Billy Goats Gruff* (Rounds, 1993) get progressively larger, until the third and largest is able to crush the ugly troll. The poor villager whose house is too small with his mother, his wife, and his six children follows the rabbi's advice in *It Could Always Be Worse* (Zemach, 1976). He brings larger and larger animals into the house with them, from chickens to the cow. When the largest has been there for a week and the man can stand it no longer, the rabbi advises him to put all the animals out. Suddenly the house is larger and quieter, and life is sweeter. Again, a pattern of increase in size makes the sequence of events easier to remember.

Sometimes the pattern is that of chronological order. In *Charlie Needs a Cloak* (dePaola, 1973), Charlie first shears his sheep and then washes the wool and cards it. From spring to fall Charlie proceeds with the preparation of his cloak: dyeing the yarn, weaving the cloth, and sewing the pieces of fabric. When winter comes, he has completed his new cloak. In *The Little Red Hen* (Galdone, 1973), the hen gets no help from the cat, the dog, or the mouse from the time she finds the grains of wheat until she has planted them, harvested them, had them ground into flour, and used the flour to bake a cake. The others are willing to help her eat the cake, but having done all the work by herself, the hen decides to eat the cake by herself. The sequence in these books reflects the way something is made. Children repeating the sequence can infer as well as recall what comes next.

Children can be given the need to sequence the events in a story by making plans to interpret it dramatically. After talking about the characters in the story, they can review what happened first, second, and so on. They may tell how they know when each event in the story happened. For primary-grade children, use a variation of a familiar story such as *The Little Red Hen Makes a Pizza* (Sturges, 1999) to encourage their ongoing acquisition of sequencing skills.

You might encourage children to work with sequencing by telling the story on a felt board and then letting children retell it. Put all the figures in random order on a table beside the felt board. Children can take turns selecting the piece that should go up next and telling that part of the story.

Another technique to engage children in sequencing is to have the children draw a picture of one thing that happened in the story. Working with only three or four children, ask each to tell what is happening in his or her picture. Then ask them which of the pictures would come first in the story, which next, and so on, until all are ordered. Work with small groups, in part because the more pictures there are, the more complex the task becomes, and in part because children tire of listening to many children describing their pictures.

Sequencing should allow the children to be active participants, doing something that requires them to use the sequence, not just answering the question, Then what happened?

Applying Books that describe "how to do it" can be used to give children the opportunity to apply what they are hearing or reading. The directions need to be clear and the project within the capabilities of the children. Roche's *Loo-Loo, Boo, and Art You Can Do* (1996) gives clear and careful directions for a variety of art projects, including face masks, potato prints, and collages. The materials are easily available. Directions are accompanied by paintings of the bespectacled Loo-Loo and her dog Boo. A teacher might read one project from this already clear book to a small group of first- or second-graders and then give the book to them to follow the directions for a different project. They should be able to make the projects on their own.

A kindergarten teacher might read the directions and then work with the children, reading each direction again as the children complete each step. A book such as this might also be used as a model for children to dictate or write their own directions for making something. Can they describe the procedure clearly enough for another child to follow the directions? They can find out by trying it.

Loreen Leedy's *Look at My Book: How Kids Can Write and Illustrate Terrific Books* (2004) is also an excellent example of a book that provides information and instructions for how to create something. These books also assist students in following a process in order to achieve a desired goal.

Expanding the Ability to Reason Logically

For young children, basic experiences with logical thinking involve working with *if . . . then* propositions. If it rains, then we will stay inside all day. If she forgets to return the permission slip, then she cannot go on the picnic. Certainly much literature involves such cause-and-effect relationships. Letting children predict what will happen next in a story is one technique for encouraging them to think about causality and to determine when connections between events appear reasonable.

David Macaulay's *Why the Chicken Crossed the Road* (1987) takes the cause and effect to delightful extremes. It opens by stating that one day a chicken ran across the road, but in doing so startled some cows, which then ran across a bridge, which collapsed onto a train. The series of events comes full circle eventually to answer the question, with the final two pages showing the same illustrations as the first two—the chicken is crossing the road and the cows are stampeding across the bridge. A hilarious book to pair with Macaulay's is *Why Did the Chicken Cross the Road?* (Agee, 2006), in which various children's book illustrators provide a visual response to this age-old question.

There are also books for children that center on errors in logical reasoning, on trickery, or on the humor of exaggeration. Reading them gives children a chance to feel superior to the book characters because they know what is going on. They recognize the absurdity and enjoy their own mastery of the situation. Young children know that it is an alligator that has hatched, not a chicken, in Lionni's *An Extraordinary Egg* (1994), even though the confident frog Marilyn insists that she knows what it is because there are some things you "just know."

Then there is Mr. Higgins in *Clocks and More Clocks* (Hutchins, 1970). When he finds a clock in the attic, he wants to know if it tells the correct time. He buys another clock to check, but when he walks from clock to clock, he notices that they always read about 1 minute different. After buying several more clocks and having the problem continue, Mr. Higgins invites the Clockmaker to check the clocks. As the Clockmaker goes from clock to clock and compares their time to that on his watch, he finds that they are all correct. Mr. Higgins is so impressed that he buys the watch.

Some books depend on the illustrations to show the absurdity of what the characters are saying. *Dear Mrs. LaRue: Letters from Obedience School* (Teague, 2002), finds Ike LaRue, the cat-chasing, chicken-pie-eating pooch, banished to the Brotweiler Canine Academy by his "cruel" owner, Mrs. LaRue. Desperate to come home, Ike begins a letter-writing campaign to convince Mrs. LaRue of the grim circumstances and intolerable hardships he is facing at the academy. Teague splits each double-page spread between what is really happening, done in full color (waiters in white coats serving academy dogs gourmet meals and frozen drinks), with Ike's imagining and exaggerating to Mrs. LaRue (his striped prison garb and ball and chain). The humorous illustrations clearly show that Ike isn't being honest in his assessment of the situation.

Some books show cleverness in the form of trickery. The Haitian tale *Bouki Dances the Kokioko* (Wolkstein, 1997) shows first the king's plan to enjoy dancing, free of any expense, every evening by announcing that anyone who can dance the Kokioko will be given five thousand gourdes. Only the king knows the steps to this dance he has invented, but many come to try. Then Malice, the gardener, sees the king dancing, learns the steps, and goes to his friend Bouki with a proposition. He will teach Bouki the steps, and Bouki can win the prize. The plan works, even though Bouki has never trusted Malice. As he returns home with the sack full of money, Bouki meets Malice, who teaches him another dance, this one to words that say if he had no sense, he will put his sack down and dance. Not listening to the words, Bouki puts the sack down, closes his eyes, and performs the new steps, allowing Malice's wife to slip quietly away with the sack. Malice assures Bouki that he tried to warn him not to put the sack down.

In Istvan Banyai's *Zoom* (1995b), children can "read" this wordless book from front to back or back to front. The illustrations zoom out as though the reader has backed away from each. Second- or third-graders might look at the illustrations and try to verbalize the shifting perspectives. They will also enjoy *Re-Zoom* (1995a) which employs the same technique.

For each of these books, the children's responses during the reading may give you an indication of whether they understand the twists of logic that the authors employ. You may want to ask children, "If you could tell Mrs. LaRue (or another character) one thing that you think would help her, what would it be?" Children can then demonstrate their command of the situation.

Encouraging Critical Thinking

The term *critical thinking* is used in this text to indicate thought that involves seeing relationships between events, inferring what is not stated directly, analyzing events within a story, synthesizing evidence, and evaluating both the content and the quality of literature. It is thinking that goes beyond the literal level. Two strategies for encouraging children to think critically are the asking of higher level questions and the planning of questions and activities that will elicit divergent responses.

Asking Higher Level Questions   One widely used system for categorizing questions is that of Sanders (1966). Based on the work of Benjamin Bloom (1956), this system categorizes questions by the kind of thinking required to answer them. Thus a question that asks for information directly stated in a reading is a *memory* question because it requires recall, or memory, to answer.

The other types of questions described by Sanders and applied to literature are as follows.

> TRANSLATION—These questions ask children to translate an idea in a book into a different form, such as telling part of the plot in their own words or drawing a picture of a scene that has been described.
>
> INTERPRETATION—These questions ask children to draw inferences, explain cause-and-effect relationships, or compare facts. Children must process the information presented in a book.
>
> APPLICATION—These questions ask children to apply ideas from literature to new situations.
>
> ANALYSIS—These questions ask children to respond based on a knowledge of logical reasoning processes or knowledge of literary forms.
>
> SYNTHESIS—These questions ask children to combine pieces of information in a new way.
>
> EVALUATION—These questions ask children to both develop and apply standards for judging a work.

Thinking about questions in this way is useful because it helps a teacher provide variety in the kinds of thinking he or she asks children to do and because it emphasizes forms of critical thinking.

To plan a series of questions for a discussion with young children, decide first on the focus of your questions. Then devise questions that will develop this focus and that will engage children in such processes as interpretation or synthesis or evaluation. For each of your higher level questions, think of what memory level of information it encompasses. You may need to ask several memory questions to establish the children's base of literal understanding before progressing with your key questions.

Comstock/Superstock Royalty Free

Children of all ages can engage in a discussion about a story heard or read.

Suppose you read *Dog and Bear: Two Friends, Three Stories* (Seeger, 2007) to a group of preschoolers or kindergarteners. This colorful picture book contains three stories about a dachshund and a multicolored teddy bear. These stories are excellent to share with young children because they are brief yet provide opportunities to ask the types of questions listed earlier. In the first story, "Bear in the Chair," Dog wants to go outside but Bear is sitting on a very tall chair. Bear doesn't know how he is going to get down from the chair, but Dog comes up with an ingenious idea—Bear can slide down the long back of the dachshund. Unfortunately, Bear forgets to bring his scarf with him and so the two decide to just stay inside. In the second story, Dog really wants to play and brings out numerous toys. Bear just wants to read and tells his friend that sometimes people (and bears apparently) need some time to themselves. Finally, Bear succumbs to Dog's pleading to "Play with me!" When asked what he wants to do, Dog replies, "Read to me." In the third story, dog decides to change his name. Bear's visions of Dog as Spot, Champ, or Skippy, just don't seem to suit the long-bodied pooch. Bear thinks of a name that Dog likes ("My Best Friend Dog"), but the dachshund decides to shorten it to just Dog.

Friendship is the central theme of *Dog and Bear*. Although they seem a somewhat unlikely pair to be friends, they do encourage, support, and—at times—endure the other. Young children will easily be able to grasp the storylines, and the choice of a teddy bear and dachshund will certainly grab their attention. The following will assist the children in responding to higher level questions. The questions can be asked for each story or for the book overall.

1. What was Dog and Bear's problem in the first story? The second? The third?
2. What did they do to resolve the problem in each story?
3. Do you think the way they solved the problem in each story was a good solution?
4. Why do you think Bear was sitting on the tall chair (first story)? Why didn't Bear want to play with Dog (second story)? Why would Dog want to change his name (third story)?

Dog and Bear
TWO FRIENDS · THREE STORIES

Laura Vaccaro Seeger

Seeger's three stories about two endearing characters will appeal to young children.
(Cover illustration copyright Laura Vaccaro Seeger from *Dog and Bear*: *Two Friends, Three Stories*. Used with permission of Roaring Book Press.)

5. Have you ever had problems getting down from something tall (first story)? Have you ever wanted to be by yourself for awhile (second story)? Have you ever wanted to change your name (third story)?

6. Why do you think Dog and Bear are friends?

With younger children, it is better to start with a few questions rather than to overwhelm them with a series of questions for each chapter. However, by asking these questions, you will have asked them to remember details from the story (1, 2), interpret (6), apply (5), analyze (4), and evaluate (3). When we ask younger children different types of questions such as these, they will begin thinking on a higher level.

A book appropriate for the primary grades is Eve Bunting's *The Memory String* (2000). In the story, Laura has a memory string filled with buttons, each of which represents a piece of her family history. The buttons that Laura cherishes most are those that belonged to her mother—a button from her prom dress, a white button from her wedding dress, and one small button from the nightgown Laura's mother was wearing when she died. When the cat lunges at the string, it breaks, and buttons are scattered everywhere. Laura's father and stepmother, Jane, help the distraught girl to locate the buttons, but one remains lost. Jane tries to help, but it isn't the same because she isn't Mom. When Jane locates the last button, she decides that it should be left by a good fairy. Laura finally realizes that her stepmother is a part of her family and new memories can be made.

As you think about a focus for your discussion, consider the idea of memories, the topic of acceptance, and the theme of family. You decide to use the topic of acceptance because it is so central to the story and because young children will be able to identify with that emotion of old and new memories. You decide to begin with two memory questions to establish the children's grasp of the facts of the story and then proceed to questions requiring other thinking skills. You plan to ask the following questions.

1. Why was Laura so resentful of her stepmother?
2. Why was the memory string so important to her?
3. Do you think the idea of memory string was a good idea? Why or why not?
4. What could Jane have done for Laura to accept her?
5. Why do you think the cat jumped at the string and later hissed at Laura? (Show illustrations of those two pages.)
6. Tell us about a time when you would not accept someone. What did you do? Did anyone help you?
7. When do you think it might be good to be afraid?
8. Do you think that Laura will add one of Jane's buttons to her memory string? What makes you think this?
9. What type of memories do you think Laura and Jane could create? What type of button would be a reminder of that event?

You will have guided children in a discussion about their own emotions, starting and ending with the story itself and making your final question one that concludes the unit. In the process, children will have been asked memory (1, 2, 6), interpretation (8, 9), analysis (5), synthesis (4), and evaluation (3, 7) questions. After you have led several similar discussions, categorize the kinds of questions you have been asking. If there are types that you never seem to use naturally, work in a conscious manner to develop your questioning skills in the appropriate areas.

Try to state your questions as concisely as possible so that young children don't lose the thread of meaning or answer one part before you finish the entire question. Pace yourself to wait for answers. If the question requires thought, then you must give children time to think. Silence makes some teachers and child-care professionals nervous, so they answer the question themselves or ask another question to fill the space. You can remind yourself to give children time to think. Some teachers count to themselves until they establish the habit of allowing the children time to respond.

Not every book should be followed by questions. Discussion is only one means of exploring a book's ideas more fully. You need a balance among discussion, activities, and no follow-up at all.

Planning for Divergent Responses   Another way of classifying questions and activities is to assess the number of *correct* responses that may be offered. Convergent questions have only one best, or right, answer. Divergent questions have more than one acceptable response. The question, What did Jane do to help Laura? is a convergent one because the book clearly shows what Jane did, and so there is only one correct answer. The question, Why it is important to accept someone? is a divergent one because both the answer given and the rationale behind it would vary from child to child. Sometimes a question is convergent because it is on a literal level, but at other times it may be a higher level question for which the evidence is so strong that there appears to be only one reasonable answer.

Activities, like questions, may call for either convergent or divergent responses. The book *Jumanji* (1981) by Chris Van Allsburg captures children's imaginations and lends itself to many divergent activities. It is the story of Judy and Peter, who are left home alone for the afternoon and get bored. They decide to take a walk in the park, where they find a game titled *Jumanji: A Jungle Adventure Game*, with a notation on the box in what appears to be a child's handwriting that the game is free and that the instructions should be read carefully. They take the game home, discovering during play that the events described on the game board really do happen. The lion actually does appear in their house and attack, the monkeys steal food, and the monsoon season arrives. When Judy finally reaches the Golden City, thus winning the game, the house is cleared of all its jungle inhabitants and order is restored. The children take the game back to the park, leaving it just where they found it. The book closes with two other children picking up the box.

Children might write a new set of directions for the game, perhaps suggesting a different method of ending the game. (In the book the game could be ended only by someone winning.) They might create a story about a time when one of their board games became like *Jumanji* or one about who would pick up the game next and what would happen. They might construct a board game using only events that they would like to see happen for each of the squares, or they might role-play Judy and Peter explaining to their parents what was going on, as though the parents had returned in the middle of the game. All these activities would encourage a variety of responses.

Divergent questions and activities stimulate children to consider a broad range of possibilities, both as they think through responses themselves and as they listen to the ideas and opinions of others. Many of the activities suggested throughout this book call for divergent responses. Look particularly at the section in chapter 9 entitled "Stimulating Creativity in Art, Music, and Movement."

Engaging in Problem Solving

You will be helping children to regularly define and solve their problems. How can Jason get a turn at jump rope? What can Rachel do to keep Megan from teasing her? What could the class make as gifts for their parents?

Literature presents ample opportunities for children to define and suggest possible solutions to problems book characters have. Their solutions may not be the one or ones chosen by the book characters. It is important to help children realize that there may be many solutions to a problem and that solutions may be evaluated according to their consequences. Some may be problems much like those the children themselves have; others may be totally in the realm of fantasy.

Preschoolers can listen to *D.W.'s Lost Blankie* (Brown, 1998), which focuses on the popular Marc Brown characters of Arthur and D.W. When D.W. loses her blankie, the family looks everywhere—at the playground, at the library, and even at the car wash—but it is nowhere to be found. Mother saves the day and returns D.W.'s clean blankie to her, even though it doesn't seem to smell or look the same. Children can tell about any toy or object that they usually take to bed with them. Then present two problems for them to solve. First, if you could not find your blanket or toy at bedtime, where would you look? And second, if you did not find it, what could you do?

Five-year-olds could find another blanket problem more challenging. *Owen* (Henkes, 1993) has owned and loved his yellow blanket Fuzzy since he was a baby. Urged on by the rather nosey neighbor, Mrs. Tweezers, Owen's parents try several strategies to get rid of it, but Owen outsmarts them. The blanket fairy, for example, cannot take the blanket and leave something in its place because Owen stuffs the blanket into his pajamas when he goes to bed. When Owen must go to school, Owen's parents take a firm stand—Owen cannot take it with him. Owen's mother thinks of a solution—she cuts the blanket into many squares and hems the edges. Now Owen has many handkerchiefs that he can take with him wherever he goes.

Children can be asked to brainstorm ideas for what might be done about a comfort object they may not want to leave at home. In brainstorming, they try to think of as many ideas as they can, not stopping to evaluate any of the ideas. The teacher lists their suggestions on the board or on chart paper. Once all their ideas are listed, the teacher leads a discussion in which they look at each suggestion and tell what might happen if it were done. As a group, they decide on which solution they think has the most merit and discuss it further.

Recommended Literature to Support Problem Solving

Bang-Campbell, Monika. (2002). *Little Rat Sets Sail*. Ill. Molly Bang. San Diego, CA: Harcourt.

Clark, Emma Chichester. (2003). *What Shall We Do, Blue Kangaroo?* New York: Doubleday.

Cronin, Doreen. (2000). *Click, Clack Moo: Cows That Type*. Ill. Betsy Lewin. New York: Simon & Schuster.

Duke, Kate. (2007). *The Tale of Pip and Squeak*. New York: Dutton.

Edwards, Pamela Duncan. (2002). *Rude Mule*. Ill. Barbara Nascimbeni. New York: Holt.

Fleming, Candace. (2002). *Muncha! Muncha! Muncha!* Ill. G. Brian Karas. New York: Atheneum.

Root, Phyllis. (1998). *One Duck Stuck*. Ill. Jane Chapman. Cambridge, MA: Candlewick.

Rylant, Cynthia. (2001). *The Great Gracie Chase*. Ill. Mark Teague. New York: Scholastic.

Simms, Laura. (1998). *Rotten Teeth*. Ill. David Catrow. Boston: Houghton Mifflin.

Weeks, Sarah. (2007). *Ella, Of Course!* Ill. Doug Cushman. San Diego, CA: Harcourt.

Because most stories involve some problem that must be solved, it is possible to stop in almost any book and ask children what the problem is and what solutions they might have for it. Doing this on a regular basis, however, is likely to lessen their enjoyment of the literature. Select only one or two books each month to use for problem solving. Look for ones where the problem is fairly clear.

Thinking of solutions to problems of book characters can be like a game. The idea is to present alternatives, not to guess what happened in the book. For this reason, you might well ask some of your problem-solving questions after a book has been completed. You can then ask what a character might have done other than what he or she actually did do.

SUMMARY

Young children come to school with a wealth of information. They are attempting to organize that information, to make sense of their world, and to integrate their experiences. They are actively constructing concepts and engaging in the thought processes that are fundamental in concept formation. Until they are 6 or 7 years of age, children tend to rely more on sensory data than on logic to reach conclusions regarding physical objects. They may also engage in reasoning, going from particular to particular without reference to the general, resulting in faulty conclusions. They engage in intuitive and associative thought, as well as the rational, and find enjoyment in imaginative thought and play.

The following long-term goals are appropriate for the intellectual growth of young children:

Children will continue to acquire new concepts and to refine those already held.

Children will develop skill in a variety of thinking processes.

Children will expand their powers of logical reasoning.

Children will utilize critical-thinking skills.

Children will engage successfully in problem solving.

Books offer opportunities to help children in the acquisition and refinement of concepts. Teacher Feature 6.1 (pp. 164–165) suggests appropriate teaching strategies. Often information that children could not discover on their own is presented in books. Other books, particularly concept books, are in themselves teaching aids because they organize information logically and present it with illustrations that add to children's understanding. Literature can both stimulate children to explore a topic and provide reinforcement for knowledge they have acquired through direct experience.

Literature furnishes an opportunity for children to engage in many thinking processes. They may observe carefully as they look at the illustrations in picture books; they may make predictions about what will happen in a book; they may compare two books on similar topics or themes; they may classify objects portrayed in books or classify the stories themselves; they may organize, using sequence as the organizing factor; and they may apply the information given in books, following directions that they have read themselves or that the teacher has read to them.

Much literature involves cause-and-effect relationships. Because of this, children are able to gain experience in predicting outcomes using an if . . . then approach to logic. There are also books that center on errors in logical reasoning or on trickery that give children the chance to show their grasp of the absurdity described.

Children can be encouraged to think critically and to engage in problem solving through carefully planned questions and activities. After establishing a firm base of literal understanding, the teacher guides the children to use higher levels of thinking, making inferences and judgments. He or she plans questions and activities that elicit divergent rather than convergent responses, praising children for new and thoughtful ideas.

Extending Your Learning

1. With two or three children, share one of the books mentioned in chapter 5 that requires the children to observe closely. Compare their responses to the book.

2. Select a picture book appropriate for first-, second-, or third-graders. Develop a set of open-ended questions to use when discussing it. The majority of questions should be above the memory level and all should be sequenced logically.

3. For a single picture book, describe two activities that would evoke divergent responses.

4. Select three books of children's literature that you have discovered and believe are high quality. Tell how each of these might support a child's intellectual growth.

5. Explore a variety of basic concepts books. How do the books contribute to a children's acquisition of the concepts.

Teacher Feature 6.1   Supporting Children's Language Development

Developmental Goals	Teaching Suggestions
Children will continue to acquire new concepts and to refine those already held.	• Share concept and informational books. • Have children compare experiential knowledge with information from books. • Use books as visual teaching aids. • Read several books on the same topic to provide more than one perspective. • Let children use books themselves to reinforce concepts. • Use books as a stimulus for further exploration. • Present books that reinforce concepts already being acquired. • Read books that may help clarify misconceptions.
Children will develop skill in a variety of thinking processes.	• Have children observe and describe detail in illustrations. • Have children play observational guessing games with book illustrations. • Let children tell the story in wordless picture books. • Encourage children to make predictions. • Engage children in structural comparisons of books. • Compare changes in illustrations within a single book. • Share books that classify objects. • Build classification activities based on books. • Dramatize stories so that children must organize by sequencing events. • Let children apply the information in "how-to-do-it" books.
Children will expand their powers of logical reasoning.	• Let children predict what will happen next in a story. • Have children discover errors in reasoning in books or trickery or humor.
Children will utilize critical-thinking skills.	• Ask questions about literature that is above the literal level. • Plan questions and activities that will elicit divergent responses.
Children will engage successfully in problem solving.	• Let children define problems book characters have. • Have children brainstorm possible solutions to problems. • Encourage children to evaluate possible solutions in terms of consequences. • Let children engage in imaginative and humorous problem solving.

Recommended Literature

	Ages 0–2		Ages 5–8
Berger	Big and Little	Aliki	Digging Up Dinosaurs
Crews	Freight Train	Aliki	Dinosaur Bones
		Brown	Rare Treasure
	Ages 2–5	Carrick	Big Old Bones: A Dinosaur's Tale
Brown	Another Important Book	Cooper	Beach
Cole	The New Baby at Your House	Hopkinson	Apples to Oregon
Falwell	Turtle Splash!	Jay	ABC: A Child's First Alphabet Book
Florian	A Pig Is Big	Jenkins	Dogs and Cats
Hoban	So Many Circles, So Many Squares	Leedy	Look at My Book
Park	Bee-bim Bop	Lewin	How Much? Visiting Markets Around the World
Seeger	Lemons Are Not Red	Ryan	Hello Ocean
Siomades	My Box of Color	Yee	Sand Castle
		Yolen	Color Me a Rhyme
		Yolen	Shape Me a Rhyme

	Ages 0–2		Ages 5–8
Ahlberg & Ahlberg	Peek-a-Boo!	Anno	Anno's Spain
		Armstrong	Once Upon a Banana
	Ages 2–5	dePaola	Charlie Needs a Cloak
Ahlberg & Ahlberg	Each Peach Pear Plum	Grimm	The Elves and the Shoemaker
Dubanevic	Pigs in Hiding	Henkes	Lilly's Big Day
Galdone	The Little Red Hen	Hoban	Look Book
Hutchins	1 Hunter	Jenkins	Looking Down
Lobel	Frog and Toad Are Friends	Jonas	Round Trip
Marshall	The Three Little Pigs	Marzollo	I Spy: Year Round Challenger
Rounds	The Three Billy Goats Gruff	Mayer & Mayer	A Boy, a Dog, a Frog, and a Friend
Zemach	It Could Always Be Worse	Roche	Loo-Loo, Boo, and Art You Can Do
		Sturges	Little Red Hen Makes a Pizza
		Ziebel	Look Closer

	Ages 2–5		Ages 5–8
Lionni	An Extraordinary Egg	Hutchins	Clocks and More Clocks
Numeroff	If You Give a Mouse a Cookie	Macaulay	Why the Chicken Crossed the Road
		Teague	Dear Mrs. LaRue: Letters from Obedience School
		Wolkstein	Bouki Dances the Kokioki

			Ages 5–8
		Bunting	The Memory String
		Van Allsburg	Jumanji

	Ages 2–5
Brown	D.W.'s Lost Blankie
Henkes	Owen
Seeger	Dog and Bear

REFERENCES

Professional References Cited

Bloom, B. (1956). *Taxonomy of educational objectives.* New York: Longman.
Coon, D. (2006). *Introduction to psychology* (11th ed.). St. Paul, MN: Wadsworth.
National Council of Teachers of Mathematics. (2000). Principles and Standards for School Mathematics. Reston, VA: Author.
Papalia, D., Olds, S., and Felman, R. (2006). *Human development* (10th Ed.). Boston: McGraw-Hill.
Piaget, J., and Inhelder, B. (1969). *The psychology of the child.* New York: Basic Books.
Robison, H. (1983). *Exploring teaching in early childhood education.* Boston: Allyn & Bacon.
Sanders, N. (1966). *Classroom questions: What kinds?* New York: Harper & Row.
Solso, R. L., MacLin, K. M., and MacLin, O. H. (2008). *Cognitive Psychology* (8th ed.). Boston: Allyn & Bacon.
Vygotsky, L. (1978). *Mind in society: The development of higher psychological processes.* Cambridge, MA: Harvard University Press.

Children's Literature Cited

Agee, Jon, (2006). *Why Did the Chicken Cross the Road?* New York: Dial.
Ahlberg, Janet, and Ahlberg, Allan. (1997). *Peek-A-Boo!* New York: Viking.
Ahlberg, Janet, and Ahlberg, Allan. (2004). *Each Peach Pear Plum.* New York: Viking.
Aliki. (1981). *Digging Up Dinosaurs.* New York: Crowell.
Aliki. (1988). *Dinosaur Bones.* New York: Crowell.
Anno, Mitsumasa. (2004). *Anno's Journey.* New York: Philomel.
Armstrong, Jennifer. (2006). *Once Upon a Banana.* Ill. David Small. New York: Simon & Schuster.
Banyai, Istvan. (1995a). *Re-Zoom.* New York: Viking.
Banyai, Istvan. (1995b). *Zoom.* New York: Viking.
Berger, Samantha. (1999). *Big and Little.* New York: Scholastic.
Brown, Don. (1999). *Rare Treasure: Mary Anning and her Remarkable Discoveries.* Boston: Houghton Mifflin.
Brown, Marc. (1998). *D.W.'s Lost Blankie.* Boston: Little, Brown.
Brown, Margaret Wise. (1999). *Another Important Book.* Ill. Chris Raschka. New York: Cotler/HarperCollins.
Bunting, Eve. (2000). *The Memory String.* Ill. Ted Rand. New York: Clarion.
Carrick, Carol. (1989). *Big Old Bones: A Dinosaur Tale.* Ill. Donald Carrick. New York: Clarion.
Cole, Joanna. (1998). *The New Baby at Your House.* Ill. Margaret Miller. New York: Morrow.
Cooper, Elisha. (2006). *Beach.* New York: Orchard.
Crews, Donald. (1978). *Freight Train.* New York: Greenwillow.
dePaola, Tomie. (1973). *Charlie Needs a Cloak.* Englewood Cliffs, NJ: Prentice Hall.
Dubanevich, Arlene. (1983). *Pigs in Hiding.* New York: Four Winds.

Falwell, Cathryn. (2001). *Turtle Splash! Countdown at the Pond.* New York: Greenwillow.

Florian, Douglas. (2000). *A Pig Is Big.* New York: Greenwillow.

Fox, Mem. (2000). *Harriet, You'll Drive Me Wild!* Ill. Marla Frazee. San Diego, CA: Harcourt.

Galdone, Paul. (1973). *The Little Red Hen.* New York: Seabury.

Gibbons, Gail. (2001). *Polar Bears.* New York: Holiday House.

Grimm, Jacob. (2003). *The Elves and the Shoemaker.* Ill. Jim LaMarche. San Francisco: Chronicle.

Henkes, Kevin. (1993). *Owen.* New York: Greenwillow.

Henkes, Kevin. (1996). *Lilly's Purple Plastic Purse.* New York: Greenwillow.

Henkes, Kevin. (2006). *Lilly's Big Day.* New York: Greenwillow.

Hoban, Tana. (1997). *Look Book.* New York: Harper Collins.

Hoban, Tana. (1998). *So Many Circles, So Many Squares.* New York: Greenwillow.

Hopkinson, Deborah. (2004). *Apples to Oregon.* Ill. Nancy Carpenter. New York: Atheneum.

Huneck, Stephen. (2000). *Sally Goes to the Beach.* New York: Abrams.

Hutchins, Pat. (1968). *Rosie's Walk.* New York: Macmillan.

Hutchins, Pat. (1970). *Clocks and More Clocks.* New York: Macmillan.

Hutchins, Pat. (1982). *I Hunter.* New York: Greenwillow.

Jay, Alison. (2003). *ABC: A Child's First Alphabet Book.* New York: Dutton.

Jenkins, Steve. (1995). *Looking Down.* Boston: Houghton Mifflin.

Jenkins, Steve. (2007). *Dogs and Cats.* Boston: Houghton Mifflin.

Jonas, Ann. (1983). *Round Trip.* New York: Greenwillow.

Kellogg, Steven. (1997). *The Three Little Pigs.* New York: HarperCollins.

Leedy, Loreen. (2004). *Look at My Book. How Kids Can Write and Illustrate Terrific Books.* New York: Holiday House.

Lewin, Ted. (2006). *How Much? Visiting Markets Around the World.* New York: HarperCollins.

Lionni, Leo. (1994). *An Extraordinary Egg.* New York: Knopf.

Lobel, Arnold. (1970). *Frog and Toad Are Friends.* New York: Harper & Row.

Lowell, Susan. (1992). *The Three Little Javelinas.* Ill. Jim Harris. Flagstaff, AZ: Rising Moon.

Macaulay, David. (1987). *Why the Chicken Crossed the Road.* Boston: Houghton Mifflin.

Marshall, James. (1997). *George and Martha: The Complete Stories of Two Best Friends.* Boston: Houghton Mifflin.

Marshall, James. (1989). *The Three Little Pigs.* New York: Dial.

Marzollo, Jean. (2005). *I Spy: Year Round Challenger.* Photos. Walter Wick. New York: Scholastic.

Mayer, Mercer, and Mayer, Marianna. (1971). *A Boy, a Dog, a Frog, and a Friend.* New York: Dial.

Numeroff, Laura Joffe. (1985). *If You Give a Mouse a Cookie.* Ill. Felicia Bond. New York: HarperCollins.

Otto, Carolyn. (1996). *What Color Is Camouflage?* Ill. Megan Lloyd. New York: Harper.

Park, Linda Sue. (2005). *Bee-bim Bop!* Ill. Ho Baek Lee. New York: Clarion.

Roche, Denis. (1996). *Loo-Loo, Boo, and Art You Can Do.* Boston: Houghton Mifflin.

Roosa, Karen. (2001). *Beach Day.* Ill. Maggie Smith. New York: Clarion.

Rounds, Glen. (1993). *The Three Billy Goats Gruff.* New York: Holiday.

Ryan, Pam Munoz. (2001). *Hello Ocean.* Ill. Mark Astrella. Watertown, MA: Charlesbridge.

Schertle, Alice. (2004). *All You Need for a Beach.* Ill. Barbara Lavallee. San Diego, CA: Harcourt.

Scieszka, Jon. (1989). *The True Story of the Three Little Pigs.* Ill. Lane Smith. New York: Viking.

Seeger, Laura Vaccaro. (2004). *Lemons Are Not Red.* Brookfield, CT: Roaring Brook.

Seeger, Laura Vaccaro. (2007). *Dog and Bear: Two Friends, Three Stories.* New Milford, CT: Roaring Brook.

Siomades, Lorianne. (1998). *My Box of Color.* Honesdale, PA: Boyds Mills Press.

Sturges, Philemon. (1999). *The Little Red Hen Makes a Pizza.* Ill. Amy Walrod. New York: Dutton.

Teague, Mark. (2002). *Dear Mrs. LaRue: Letters from Obedience School.* New York: Scholastic.

Van Allsburg, Chris. (1981). *Jumanji.* Boston: Houghton Mifflin.

Whatley, Bruce. (2001). *Wait! No Paint.* New York: HarperCollins.

Wolkstein, Diane. (1997). *Bouki Dances the Kokioko.* Ill. Jesse Sweetwater. San Diego: Harcourt.

Yee, Brenda Shannon. (1999). *Sand Castle.* Ill. Thea Kliros. New York: Greenwillow.

Yolen, Jane. (2003). *Color Me a Rhyme.* Photos Jason Stemple. Honesdale, PA: Boyds Mills.

Yolen, Jane. (2007). *Shape Me a Rhyme.* Photos Jason Stemple. Honesdale, PA: Boyds Mills.

Zemach, Margot. (1976). *It Could Always Be Worse.* New York: Farrar, Straus & Giroux.

Ziebel, Peter. (1989). *Look Closer!* New York: Clarion.

CHAPTER SEVEN

JOELLE, Age 6
The Story of Ruby Bridges

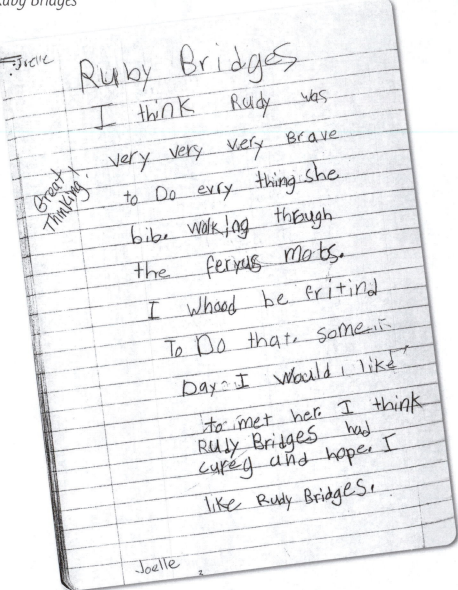

Ruby Bridges

I think Rudy was

very very very brave

Great Thinking!

to Do evry thing she

bibe walking through

the feryus mobs.

I whood be fritind

To Do that. some

Day I would like

to met her. I think

Rudy Bridges had

cureg and hope. I

like Rudy Bridges.

Joelle

Joelle (age 6) is responding to Robert Coles *The Story of Ruby Bridges* (1990), an account of the sole African American child who must attend a New Orleans elementary school after court-ordered desegregation in 1960. Federal marshals escorted the 6-year-old past angry crowds of white protestors.

Supporting Children's Personality Development

Emotions, values, ways of perceiving, and feelings about self are all a part of personality. Papalia, Olds, and Felman (2006) define personality as encompassing a person's overall pattern of character, behavioral, temperamental, emotional, and mental traits. Some aspects of personality are genetically influenced. For example, children who are physically attractive often find others reacting to them in positive ways, and this helps them to think positively about themselves. The social environment, however, plays a greater role in the development of personality than does the biological inheritance of an individual. A child raised in a society that stresses competition is more likely to become competitive than is a child raised in a society that emphasizes sharing and cooperation.

PERSONALITY DEVELOPMENT IN YOUNG CHILDREN

Erikson (1986) seeks to explain personality growth by describing how human beings respond to potential conflicts at specific periods in their lives. He posits eight stages in a total life span, of which the first four are most applicable for young children. The first stage, the first year of life, is critical in that it is during this period that children develop trust, which leads to later feelings of security. The conflict is between trust and mistrust. Trust develops when the primary caregiver responds warmly and lovingly to the child.

During the ages of 2 and 3, children struggle for autonomy. The conflict is between autonomy and doubt. Children want to explore, to do things for themselves, and to be in control. Sometimes children at the age of 2 or 3 have difficulty sharing toys and often cannot remember rules. Children who have been encouraged by their parents to be independent at this age are more highly motivated to achieve when they reach school than are children who were not rewarded for such behavior.

At ages 4 and 5, children have a conflict between initiative, wanting to carry out activities on their own, and guilt over what they would like to do. For preschool and kindergarten teachers, this is a time when children can be encouraged to make choices and to take action on their own.

From ages 6 to 11, children struggle with industry versus inferiority. Productivity becomes important. They want to complete tasks, to learn what is expected of them, and to gain recognition for their efforts. These are crucial years in the development of self-concept and self-esteem.

Self-concept refers to individuals' ideas of their own capabilities—what they see themselves as being able to do. *Self-esteem* is the value individuals put on themselves, or how worthy they feel themselves to be. Both self-concept and self-esteem are influenced strongly by the way in which others react to and treat the individual. Children who know that the important people in their lives value them think more highly of themselves. They become more confident, and this confidence leads them to attempt difficult tasks and to anticipate success. Teachers and childcare professionals can aid the development of positive self-concepts in children by suggesting tasks that are challenging, yet attainable. They can also show that they value and support each child's efforts.

The development of self-concept begins early at home. So, too, does another learning based on children's interactions with their parents. This is the process of identification, in which an individual accepts the characteristics and beliefs of another as his or her own. A boy may walk just like his father, or a girl may use the mannerisms and voice inflection of her mother. This early identification with the parent of the same sex leads to sex typing, the adoption of the sex roles considered appropriate in a particular culture (Brewer, 2006). As sex roles become far less restricted, childcare professionals and teachers need to provide children with ways of identifying their own sexuality while remaining free from sex-role stereotypes.

Identification is a lifelong process. As children encounter a larger social world, they begin to identify with models other than their parents. Teachers, friends, and characters from books, movies, and television may all be emulated. Children thus acquire a complex system of beliefs and behaviors.

Children just coming to school are learning about themselves and their emotions as well as about their physical and social environments. One may learn that his temper tantrum, which effectively provided attention at home, is ignored at school. Katz and McClellan note that "children's ability to regulate their emotions is a major contributor to the development of both peer status and friendships" (1997, p. 4). Another child may find that many of her classmates, like her, are afraid of the dark and fear being left alone. As children begin to learn ways of expressing and managing their feelings, they learn what acceptable behavior in a particular situation is and what is not. In seeking to help children, the adult must provide experiences that will enhance each child's self-concept, that will help him or her function as independently as possible, and that will assist in dealing successfully with his or her emotions.

GOALS FOR TEACHING

Teaching goals for personality development can be categorized into long-term developmental goals, into general goals for each grade or age level, and into specific goals for individual children. Long-term goals describe behaviors or competencies that are developed over time and that are thought of as desired patterns of behavior. The long-term goal that children will attempt new tasks willingly is reflective of personality development because the willingness to attempt something new is related both to self-concept and to the need to achieve.

General goals for each grade level are often listed in curriculum guides. Personality goals and social goals may be combined under the heading of *affective goals*, distinguishing them from the *cognitive*, or intellectual, goals. One such goal for kindergarten is that children will function independently in several work areas within the classroom. It is more specific than a long-term goal and is keyed to the needs and abilities of children of this age. All, or nearly all, the children in the group will be expected to reach this general goal.

Goals for individual children are even more specific. You will develop these goals as you work with a group and come to know each child. "Steven will overcome his fear of the coatroom and go in by himself to get his coat" is an individual goal, one developed by a teacher who saw Steven's need, a need that was not shared by other children in the classroom.

There are times when your use of books will help to achieve all three types of goals. This chapter focuses on long-term developmental goals, those common to the toddler, preschool and primary years. Books offer opportunities for you to help children grow toward the following goals for personality development.

Children will weigh evidence and make appropriate choices.

Children will set tasks for themselves and will complete tasks they begin.

Children will develop positive and realistic self-concepts.

Children will develop feelings of self-worth and self-esteem.

Children will begin to recognize their own values and to choose from among values.

Children will understand their emotions and will express them in socially acceptable ways.

As with other areas, these goals can be correlated with national and regional standards. For example, the goal that children will develop positive and realistic self-concepts relates to Theme IV, Individual Development and Identity, in the 10 themes that provide the organizational framework for the social studies standards developed by the National Council for the Social Studies (1997). That standard focuses on the idea that "personal identity is shaped by one's culture, by groups, and by institutional influences" (1997, p. 25). It is suggested that in the early grades, activities such as observing brothers and sisters and older adults and engaging in "remembering past achievements and projecting oneself into the future" are useful because "young learners develop their personal identities in the context of families, peers, schools, and communities." As you look at national standards or those for your region or school district, look for ways in which these goals and the specific standards mesh.

OPPORTUNITIES BOOKS OFFER

Involving Children in Making Choices

Would you like to hear a story? is more often a rhetorical than a real question in a classroom or center. You are not asking children for their preferences; you are telling them that it is story time and the adult is going to read to them. Listen to your own way of telling children about planned activities. If they have no choice, try to introduce the activity in statement rather than question form. "Today I am going to read a story about Henry and Mudge," or "Please get ready for story time. I think you'll be surprised at how this story ends."

Presenting Options   Begin to think of ways that children can be encouraged to make choices. If you present children with a choice, you must be willing to accept their decision. This means that you should not present objectionable options. As you share literature with children, there are many opportunities for them to make choices and ways for you to structure the choice-making so that all the alternatives are acceptable. Some are very simple ones. You may ask children which story or poem they would like to hear read or reread. Narrow the choices to two or three, and have all available. Poetry especially lends itself to this sort of choice-making because poems become better liked as they become more familiar. One preschool school teacher constructed a poster board titled *poetry rabbit*. In its basket the rabbit had a collection of paper eggs of different sizes, colors, and designs. On each egg was a poem about spring. The 3- and 4-year-olds could select an egg, and the teacher would read the poem on it. After several days, the children knew which egg had the poem they particularly liked. Rereading poems helps children find poetry pleasurable and gives them a chance to choose.

Sometimes the choice will be one of sequence—of what will be done first. Would they like to hear the story before or after snack time? Would they like to have art first, or story time first? These choices are group ones, where each child's opinion counts, but which are decided by what the majority prefers. Many others can be individual choices, where one child makes the choice and where the decision involves only the child's behavior.

One area for choice is whether the child wants to listen to a story or not. It may be in the form of announcing that all who are ready for a story should come to the story circle or should go to the corner where an aide is sitting with the book to be read. The principal of one elementary school reads to children during the lunch period each day. She announces as they come into the lunchroom what the book for that day will be. Children who wish to hear it go with her to another room, listening to the story as they eat their lunches. She reports that the number of listeners fluctuates and that different children attend. The choice is theirs, each day, whether they would like to hear that story or whether they would like to eat in the lunchroom, visiting with friends as they eat. They are responsible for their choices. Once made, they cannot change rooms that day. However, they are not asked to make a long commitment. In a classroom or child-care facility, children can be given a choice of listening or not by having a listening center set up in the room. Those who want to hear a story or poem may go to the center; those who do not can engage in other quiet activities.

Encouraging Book Selection   Young children can select which book they would like to take with them from the library to their room or perhaps from the classroom or center to their homes. Some classes have periods for *Sustained Silent Reading* (SSR) or *Drop Everything and Read* (DEAR), a period when everyone, including the teacher, reads the book of his or her choice. The purpose for sustained silent reading is to show that recreational and independent reading is valued by the school as well as to give each child the opportunity to read in a quiet setting. In preschool and primary classes, where some children are reading and some are not, this might be a brief period of looking at books following a trip to the library. Their choices of books become important because the children know there is a special time for looking at them.

In schools or centers where book clubs are permitted or in those that have book fairs, children can select books not just to borrow, but to keep. In these cases, they can purchase paperback books at moderate prices. The Reading Is Fundamental (RIF) program also provides children with books of their own.

Planning Several Activities   If you have planned to have an activity following the reading of a book, think about having two or three independent activities and allowing each child to choose one of them. Suppose you have read *Officer Buckle and Gloria* (Rathmann, 1995) to a class of kindergarten children. In this story, Officer Buckle visits schools, giving talks on safety to the children. When he brings his dog Gloria with him, he notices that the children really pay attention, and he is asked to give these talks quite often. What the children see is Gloria standing behind Officer Buckle and imitating him or enacting the rule he is stating. When he says that the children should not leave a thumbtack where someone might sit on it, Gloria is jumping high into the air with her paw on her bottom. Whenever Officer Buckle looks around, Gloria is sitting at attention. It is only when one of his talks is taped and shown on television that Officer Buckle learns the source of his popularity.

One activity might be for children to illustrate one of Officer Buckle's safety rules, or one of their own, by showing what Gloria might do onstage to dramatize it. They might write the safety tip under their drawing or perhaps put the tip and the illustration on a star, as is done on the endpapers of the book.

Another activity might be for children to make a card for Officer Buckle to make him feel better after he has learned that it is Gloria whom the children enjoy. What could they say that would encourage him to continue his school safety presentations?

Children could choose one of the two activities or devise one of their own. The teacher's time would be spent talking with children as they work and perhaps transcribing their invented spelling into standard orthography. All the children would be engaged in discussions of their reactions to the story and to the illustrations.

Varying the Types of Choices   You can vary the sorts of choices you provide. The choice might be variety in art media; it might be variety in oral versus written work; it might be variety in level of difficulty of the activities. In a third-grade class, one activity might involve writing a paragraph. Another might be making a list. Both would engage the children in thinking about the literature that had been shared, but one would require more skill in composition than the other. This would allow children at differing skill levels to select an activity in which they could be successful.

Children can be encouraged to work together on projects for both the social and the language growth such cooperation promotes. For many children, working together makes a task more enjoyable. There are times, however, when children prefer to work alone. Some activities based on literature may be phrased so that children choose to "work with a friend or by yourself." Two children might easily work together on an album of drawings or making a chart. They might make felt-board stories and tell them to their class or other classes. Given two activities, one group and one individual, children may choose on the basis of the type of activity or on the basis of the number of people participating in it.

Children can decide whether or not they wish to share literature activities they have completed. They can display their work or describe their activities. They may tell the entire class or just a few children what they have done. Giving them the opportunity to show their work demonstrates that you value it; giving the option of not sharing shows that you respect their feelings.

Helping Children Make Responsible Choices   As you encourage children to make choices, try to make certain that they have the information necessary to make satisfactory choices. If they are to select their own book from the library, do they know where the picture book section is? Where they can find the poetry? How do they get a librarian to help them if they cannot find what they want? Do readers know to open the book and try reading a page or two to see how difficult the reading is? Do prereaders know to look at some of the pictures as well as the cover before taking a book?

Once they have made their choices, encourage children to stay with the books long enough to give them a good try. Although it is unreasonable to force children to keep looking at books they are tired of or to prohibit children from sharing their projects if they have had to hear three other children before getting the courage to speak, it is equally unproductive to allow children to change their choices capriciously. A part of learning to make choices is learning to accept responsibility for them. If children have made poor choices, this is the time for discussing the selection process they used and how it could be modified for better results.

Finally, keep notes on the activities and the types of books children choose, noting if any of your students are in a pattern that is limiting to their growth. You can then counteract their choices through planned activities. A child who always chooses to work alone can be assigned group experiences in other classroom or center projects. You may require another who never chooses a writing activity to write at other times or be given a choice between two writing activities. It is possible to balance children's choices with your perception of their needs by making all options you offer valid learning experiences and by structuring other activities to compensate for areas of neglect in those they may choose.

Encouraging Children to Set and Complete Tasks

Children in the primary grades can set tasks for themselves with some guidance from teachers and other adults. For example, a group sharing special toys from home becomes curious about teddy bears and panda bears. Are there really animals that look like that?

Defining a Task   A teacher helps children define a task so that the action they need to take to answer their question is clear. Two children from the group go to the library

Scott Cunningham/Merrill

Children can learn to make book selections carefully, looking at the illustrations and reading a page or two.

or to classroom references, if they are available, to look in dictionaries and encyclopedias under *teddy bear* and *panda*. If they have not used these references before, this is an ideal time to demonstrate their use. The children return quickly, reporting that there is indeed an animal called a giant panda but that there is no listing under teddy bear.

At this point the teacher asks the group how they could find more about the panda and where else they might look to find out about teddy bears. Some of the children suggest library books, but not all know how to use the online catalogue. One child who does know how to search for books online goes to the library with two others to see what they can find on pandas. As they look, two of the three children will be learning ways of using the library.

Three other children are to look under the listing for teddy bear, to look in several dictionaries, and to ask the librarian for help. When the first group returns, they have found a book titled *Giant Pandas* by Gail Gibbons (2002) and another titled *The Giant Pandas* by Lynn M. Stone (2003). The other group has found that teddy bears are modeled after koalas and returns with *I Lost my Bear* by Jules Feiffer (1998) and *The Life Cycle of a Koala* by Bobbie Kalman (2001).

Keeping Children Task Oriented   The children then list, and the teacher records on chart paper, what they would like to know about these bears. Where do they live? What do they eat? How big are they? Do they have lots of babies? When the questions have been listed, the teacher asks for volunteers to listen especially for the answers to particular questions. One by one the questions are assigned. The teacher reads the book about pandas. Children go down the list and tell what they have learned about these bears. The question the teacher adds at the end, What did you think was especially interesting about pandas?, allows children to tell other information they have gleaned. They can even eat splinters without hurting their stomachs, and they get new teeth just like we do. There are also new questions as a result of the information they have heard. What is a takin? and Are pandas found in other places besides China?

In this case, the children found appropriate books that are also excellent nonfiction. In the book by Gibbons, the transparent watercolor illustrations amplify the information about this gentle giant. Children look at the pictures and read the brief informative text to learn that pandas have pink skin under their white fur, the average panda consumes 27 pounds of bamboo a day, and that a mother panda weighs 900 times more than her tiny baby. The Stone book features clear photographs by Keren Su that pique children's interest about pandas and their habitat.

Helping Children Assess Their Efforts   Sometimes children find books that are not appropriate to the questions being asked. This is a time for teaching children to listen critically to the content and to make judgments themselves about its value for them. They can be guided to look at the content of a book in depth in the classroom and to check content briefly as they are selecting the book.

The teacher notes that two of the books the second group found about koalas are nonfiction and one is fiction. She reads the nonfiction books first, with children listening for specific information, as they did for pandas. When she has finished *The Life Cycle of a Koala*, the children answer their own questions. Again, more questions are raised. What's special about eucalyptus leaves that koalas need them to eat? Where did the name *teddy bear* come from? Why call it a teddy *bear* when it isn't a bear? There are plans for further investigation.

She then reads *I Lost My Bear* to the class. "How is this book different from the other ones about koalas?" she asks. The children answer that it is a story about a toy teddy bear rather than a real animal. "Which book is better for learning about real koalas?" she asks. Then she continues by asking what they liked about each of the books.

As you talk with children about the appropriateness of particular books, try to make it clear that appropriateness is related to purpose. Rather than books being *good* or *bad*, there are some that answer their needs and others that do not. Be careful also not to over generalize. It is tempting to guide children to the conclusion that informational books give facts and that these are the books to read when information is needed. Many fiction books include accurate informational content and are a prime source for information about how people act and feel. The insight gained from reading fiction should not be made to sound insignificant in comparison to the factual knowledge gained from nonfiction. Nor should the categories be labeled so that nonfiction becomes associated only with work, whereas fiction fits under fun. This contradicts the feelings of many readers who choose nonfiction for recreational reading. It also can make fiction appear less important than nonfiction.

Judging the Appropriateness of Tasks   You will need to judge the maturity and capabilities of your students as you help them set tasks. Some can go to the library themselves. Others may need your guidance. Some may be able to listen for answers to an entire list of questions, but others can concentrate on only one.

Both fiction and nonfiction offer opportunities for children to set tasks. The books may be needed in the completion of the task or may be the forerunner to the task of describing a response to literature. Children who have had experience in sharing their reactions to books can decide for themselves how they would like to present their thoughts and feelings. They could tell two friends how the story begins, trying to make it interesting enough that the friends will read the book. They could create a painting that they think the main character in a book would like. Then they could tell their classmates about their painting and its appeal to the book character. They could make clay models of characters from the book. Second- and third-graders may want to write comments about the book for display in the book corner.

Primary-grade children may find that a chart in the room that lists suggestions for sharing a book can help them set their own tasks. They may use the ideas as stated or may build on the ideas to develop a new idea. Both preschool and primary children can set tasks in consultation with the teacher.

Whether children set the task or chose it from a series of alternatives, you can urge that it be completed. Successfully finishing a project makes children feel competent and enhances their self-concept. You can make this completion more likely to occur by ensuring the following:

1. The task is on an appropriate level for the child.
2. The standards for successful completion are reasonable.
3. The materials needed are readily available.
4. The project is feasible in terms of teacher time; that is, it will not require an inordinate amount of explanation in relation to the time the project itself takes.
5. There is a classroom pattern of giving attention to completed projects.

Suppose that you were the teacher of the class learning about pandas and koalas. After reading the books discussed earlier, you decide to read the classic story *Corduroy* (Freeman, 1968), a picture book about a teddy bear living in a department store. Corduroy overhears Lisa say that he is the bear she has always wanted. He also hears her mother say that they have spent too much money already and that the bear is missing a button on the strap of his overalls. That night, after the shoppers have gone, Corduroy begins searching for his lost button. He wanders around the store, finally discovering the bedding department. As he is pulling a button off a mattress, it gives way and he falls backward, knocking over a lamp. The watchman who hears the noise finds Corduroy and takes him back to his shelf in the toy department. The next morning Lisa is the first customer in the store. She has counted the money in her piggy bank and has come to buy Corduroy. When she gets him home, she sews a button on the strap and gives him a big hug.

You have decided to read this book because it goes back to the children's initial interest in their own toys and because it is good literature. You introduce it by saying, "Remember the story we heard about the little girl who couldn't find her bear?" After the children have responded to this question, you continue, "This is another story about a teddy bear, and it is called *Corduroy*." After reading the story, you ask the children to get their own toys and come back to the reading circle. Then you have them close their eyes and imagine what their toys might like to do in their houses at night, when everyone is asleep. They imagine what their toys like and what they might say if they could talk. Children then choose one of two activities. They can create a picture that shows what their toy might do at night, or they can use their toy as a puppet and have a conversation with another toy. Those who choose to draw should be able to get the paper and crayons or paint and chalk for themselves and begin. Those who choose the conversation may work in pairs simultaneously or may listen as pairs take turns with the dialogue. This would depend on their experience with the use of puppets in spontaneous drama and their ability to work together on their own.

You suggest the tasks knowing that the children can do them. You might need to give help midway, perhaps joining a conversation with a toy yourself, but children will feel good about what they have done. You look at the thought that went into the pictures and conversations, not expecting mature artists or master puppeteers. You have planned so that the children think about the ideas before they begin to work. When they get the materials, they begin quickly. You show your interest in their tasks by talking with the children as they work and by allowing them to share their work with their classmates if they wish. Your planning and follow-up are strong motivators for children to establish the habit of completing their work.

Building Self-Concept

Literature can help children develop positive self-concepts through content and theme and also through activities, which may follow the sharing of a book. One aspect of self-concept is recognizing one's strengths and weaknesses.

Recognizing Capabilities   Some books for young children emphasize the many capabilities that they have. *Jamaica Louise James*, in the book of that name (Hest, 1996), uses the paints she is given for her eighth birthday to paint a series of pictures. Then, on her grandmother's birthday, Jamaica and her mother go to the subway station where Grammy sells tokens and post the pictures on the walls as a surprise for Grammy. It was Jamaica's idea, and it works. It even makes the harried and grouchy subway riders smile. Children not only have good ideas, they can make those ideas reality.

Beginning with a wave to say hello, *Hands Can* (Hudson, 2003) shows the different things that hands can do—catching, throwing, clapping, and playing peek-a-boo. This book is perfect for toddlers and preschoolers because it has a rhyming text

Hudson presents rich, full-color photographs that illustrate the variety of fine and gross motor activities in which little hands become engaged.
(Text © Copyright 2003 Cheryl Willis Hudson. Photographs Copyright © 2003 John-Francis Bourke. Reproduced by permission of the publisher, Candlewick Press, Inc., Cambridge, MA.)

that directly ties to the clear, colorful photographs. Children listening to the story might take turns telling one thing they can do or perhaps demonstrate or pantomime the skill. They might play follow the leader using their hands for each action to be imitated. Both content and activities reinforce the concept that children are capable.

Another book appropriate for toddlers, *Can You Growl Like a Bear?* (Butler, 2007) asks children to growl like a bear, croak like a tree frog, roar like a leopard, and howl like a wolf. The one-line text on each double-page spread presents the sound in large font and the animal that makes it. Children listening to the book can demonstrate the sounds that animals make as well as their own sounds, such as laughing, crying, and talking.

In *The Dot* (Reynolds, 2003), Vashti is convinced that she cannot draw. "Just make a mark and see where it takes you," encourages her teacher. Once Vashti makes the first dot, she realizes that she can also draw a yellow dot, a green dot, a red dot, and a blue dot. By mixing red and blue, she can make a purple dot. And by splashing colors with a bigger brush, Vashti can even make giant dots. Through self-expression, experimentation, and success, Vashti recognizes her true capabilities. Children who have also stated that they cannot draw will be inspired.

In Stephen Krensky's short chapter book, *Louise, Soccer Star?* (2000), Louise is confident that she will be the star of her team this year. When a flashy new player arrives with all the tricky moves, Louise must realize that what she is able to offer to the team in relation to sports ability and friendship is just as valuable.

Seeing Oneself Realistically   Literature can help children see themselves realistically, yet with a focus on their strong points. In *Ready, Set, Skip!* (O'Connor, 2007), a little girl laments that she can't skip like other kids. She can do lots of things, such as leaping, creeping, twirling, and skating. She is even a soda-straw slurper and a champion burper. But she just can't skip. Her mother asks if she can hop. If she can hop, then skipping is just hopping on one foot and then the other. Then making sure no one is watching, she begins to skip down the street as her feet feel the beat. The rhyming text makes this a good choice for reading aloud to preschoolers and will inspire them to get up and skip.

As children come to see themselves in relation to others and to compare themselves with others, both in characteristics and in physical appearance, books can help them make realistic yet positive judgments.

At times, children might think that they are ready to experience other aspects of life, even though age and ability may not allow them to do so. Such is the case in *Little Brown Bear Won't Go to School!* (Dyer, 2002). Little Brown Bear doesn't want to go to school and instead sets off to find a job—just like Mama Bear and Papa Bear. Little Brown Bear's first job is at Miss Flo's Diner as a waiter. When Little Brown Bear has to write down the order, he explains that he doesn't know how to write. With each subsequent job, Little Brown Bear realizes that he doesn't have the knowledge to do the job, so he decides to go to school. Discuss with children things they think they are old enough to do and why that may or may not be a possibility.

Viewing oneself realistically is explored in a humorous way in *Loretta, Ace Pinky Scout* (Graves, 2002). Loretta, an unrelenting perfectionist, is devastated when she cannot master the art of toasting marshmallows and fails to earn her Golden Marshmallow Badge. When her grandmother's portrait speaks to her, Loretta learns that everyone "stinks" at something. Loretta presents an example of being realistic about doing your best while sometimes not being able to feel successful in everything.

Recognizing Growth and Change   These books lead into another aspect of self-concept, the realization that one is continually growing and changing. *It's Going to Be Perfect* by Carlson (1998) shows a mother describing how she thought her daughter's life would be from birth through kindergarten and contrasting that with how things really turned out—not quite as orderly as expected, but certainly loving. In *Birthday Presents* (Rylant, 1987), appropriate for primary-grade children, the parents recall, with love and affection, each of their children's birthdays. They tell what happened and the child's reaction, beginning with the day she was born—when they told her they loved her and she screamed. The pattern continues until the year the child is 6. Then she makes cards for her parents' birthdays and tells them that she loves them. *Another Important Book* (Brown, 2004) tells what the most important things about being 1, 2, 3, 4, 5, and 6 years old.

After hearing either of them, children could ask their parents to tell them what they were like as a baby or at age 2 or 3. They could also collect photographs of themselves at various ages and use these to tell how they have changed. You might even develop your own book of photographs to share with the children, showing how you have changed.

Many children will enjoy and identify with the title character in *You'll Soon Grow Into Them, Titch* (Hutchins, 1983) because they have worn hand-me-down clothes, which older children in the family have outgrown and which may not be a perfect fit for the next in line. Titch inherits pants from his older brother, a sweater from his sister, and socks from both of them. All are too large, but his brother and sister assure him that he will soon grow into them. Titch's parents, however, decide that he should have some new clothes. Once he is outfitted, Titch presents his old clothes to the new baby; after all, he'll soon grow into them.

Children might also dictate a list of skills that they have acquired only recently to demonstrate that changes aren't related solely to physical appearance. They could create poems using one in the form suggested by Kenneth Koch (2000). Children begin every odd line with "I used to _____," and every even line with "But now _____," resulting in a poem that tells about the changes in their lives. They might tell stories about times when they learned to do something special: cross the street by themselves, ride a bicycle, or get out their own milk and cereal in the morning. They might even draw pictures in which they show what they hope to be able to do next year. After such sharing of experiences, try reading poems such as Mary Ann Hoberman's classic—yet still relevant—verse, "A Year Later."

> *A Year Later*
>
> Last summer I couldn't swim at all
>
> I couldn't even float!
>
> I had to use a rubber tube
>
> Or hang on to a boat;
>
> I had to sit on shore
>
> While everybody swam
>
> But now it's this summer
>
> And I can!   *(1959)*

The poem relates the good feeling that comes from mastering a new skill, and both show that the skill did not come automatically. Growth takes time; not all skills are acquired the moment one wants.

Some children may relate to the feelings of growing up that can be intensified when a new sibling arrives. Benny's new brother does nothing but scream and scream in *Benny and the Binky* (Lindgren, 2002). Finally mother gives the baby a binky. Benny wants one too, but his mother tells him he is too old for one. So Benny takes his brother outside, steals the binky, and then runs away. He passes by a childcare center where the children shout, "You're too old for a binky," but Benny just keeps running. When he encounters three tough pigs with soccer shoes who punch him in the snout, Benny decides that maybe the binky really does belong to his brother. In the Martha Alexander's (2006) reissued book *When the New Baby Comes, I'm Moving Out,* Oliver is upset when his mother begins to fix up his old things in preparation for the new baby. Fortunately, his mother recognizes the impending rivalry and offers some new options. Those children with siblings may connect with the changes that occurred in their own homes when a new baby arrived.

Becoming Confident   You can help children see themselves as generally capable and as having within themselves the resources that will help them to meet difficult or unexpected demands. Of the different forms of literature, two—comedy and romance—show how the protagonist overcomes problems and goes on to achieve fulfillment and success. The mood is one of hope. Most of the stories you share with children offer a picture of a book character that succeeds. These books show children, or even an animal, able to cope with problems.

Stanley is thrilled when his turn to be *Star of the Week* (Saltzberg, 2006) finally arrives. He is going to share his favorite food, his favorite toy, and his favorite activity with the class. Unfortunately, no one shares his enthusiasm for tofu bologna, cream cheese, jelly, and pickles on pumpernickel. The toy he brings is his decrepit toy robot. On the third day of his special week, he freezes while drawing on the blackboard. However, he gains the admiration of his classmates with his imaginative drawings and, in turn, a level of self-confidence.

Buster: The Very Shy Dog (Bechtold, 1999) hides when guests come to the house, is intimidated by bossy dogs, and scurries away from children. Even Phoebe, who Buster thinks is an amazing dog, isn't able to help the timid canine. However, when Buster listens with his good ears, he is able to catch the garbage bandits that have remained elusive for several nights. In this short chapter book, Buster gains his confidence by recognizing his talent for listening. To illustrate that all children have abilities and something special to offer, develop a class chart with input from all the children that records the talents of each child in the class.

Identifying with One's Heritage   Self-concept involves identification with one's heritage. There are books for young children that address this theme directly. *I Lost My Tooth in Africa* (Diakite, 2006) is a first-person account of a little girl who relates her

Diakite wrote this story when she was eight years old about her connection between her home in Oregon and her extended family in Africa.

(Cover illustration from I LOST MY TOOTH IN AFRICA, illustrated by Baba Wague Diakite. Illustration copyright © 2006 by Baba Wague Diakite. Reprinted by permission of Scholastic Inc.)

excitement about flying from America to visit her father's family in Mali. One of her teeth is loose, and her dad tells her that if she loses her tooth in Africa and places it under a gourd, she will get a chicken from the African Tooth Fairy. The girl waits and waits, and when her patience runs out she returns to the gourd to retrieve her tooth, but then a chicken and a rooster emerge. The final page shows the girl, minus one tooth, holding a speckled hen. The daily life of the community and the warmth of the African extended family are highlighted as the young girl celebrates her African heritage. A glossary and a recipe for African onion sauce are included.

Cynthia Leitich Smith's *Jingle Dancer* (2000) is a contemporary story about a young Native American girl, Jenna, who longs to be a jingle dancer like Grandma Wolfe. Unfortunately, her dress doesn't have enough of the tin jingles to make it "sing." Jenna borrows a row of jingles from Great-aunt Sis, another from Mrs. Scott who sells fry bread, one from Cousin Elizabeth who cannot attend the powwow, and finally a row from Grandma. She carefully sews the jingles to her dress and prepares for the big day. Jenna knows that she will be representing the four women as she engages in the traditional dance performed by many generations.

Many children's books feature grandparents as the link to understanding heritage. Jennifer, a Korean American, is concerned that her grandmother, visiting from Korea, will embarrass her on Grandparents' Day. Jennifer's grandmother doesn't speak English and wears traditional Korean clothing. *Halmoni's Day* (Bercaw, 2000) celebrates intergenerational relationships by showing that there are many ways to express love, ways that cross barriers of language, time, and place.

Books that present characters of varying ethnic backgrounds are also discussed in chapter 8, on the social development of children. Learning about children who are different from themselves is part of children's social development. The book that for one student presents a model for ethnic identification is for another student an introduction to a new group of people or new customs. Suggested books in chapter 8 emphasize that teachers and childcare professionals should have a variety of peoples represented in the books they choose, no matter what the ethnic makeup of their class. You will want to be certain, however, that you read some books whose major characters represent the ethnic backgrounds of the children in your class.

Developing Sex-Role Expectations

Just as books present models for ethnic identification, so too do they present models for sex-role identification. When you read books to children, be aware that you are showing them one perception of how the world is structured. If you read only books that show female characters as passive and male characters as active, you are saying to them that this is the behavior expected of females and of males.

Many books for children have broken away from sex-role stereotypes. They include more female characters who are active, assertive, and competent. Women in some books are portrayed as career oriented and successful outside the home. Males are permitted to show tenderness and to cry. One second-grade girl, involved in a discussion of appropriate sex-role behaviors, pondered the question of why it had been considered acceptable for girls to cry but not for boys to do so. Her solution was simple: Girls had more to cry about. Those who have seen their horizons expanded in recent years may well agree with her assessment.

As you select books, eliminate those that present stereotyped characters, whether the character is sexist or not. Stereotyping means that all individuals within a group are described as though they were alike. Women work in the home and wear aprons; men work in offices and wear suits. Boys play baseball; girls play with dolls.

Books whose characters are stereotyped are poor literature because the author has not developed the individuality necessary for good characterization. Thus these books should be discarded on literary grounds.

Do not depend on the date of publication to tell you if a stereotype exists. Some recent books present stereotyped characters and many old favorites do not. One could hardly ask for a more active and unique female than Madeline in the books by Ludwig Bemelmans, the first of which was published in 1939. There are many bibliographies available of nonstereotyped books for children, which you may find useful.

A second problem exists, and that is to provide a balance of types of characters in the total body of literature you share with children. To present only books that show women working at exciting careers is to create as imbalanced a picture as to present only books that show women functioning as mothers or homemakers. Assess each book for its literary value; then make a list of role models presented. See if any gaps exist, and if so, look for books to rectify omissions.

There will be opportunities to discuss children's attitudes toward certain behaviors of characters with them. One teacher read *Max* (Isadora, 1976), *Ira Sleeps Over* (Waber, 1972), and *Tough Eddie* (Winthrop, 1985) to his class of first-graders.

In the first book, Max is on his way to a baseball game when he stops in at his sister's ballet lesson. Intrigued by the whole procedure, he joins the line of girls in doing exercises at the barre and particularly enjoys the leaps. He goes to the baseball game, plays well, and decides to warm up for each game with ballet.

Ira, in *Ira Sleeps Over*, is invited to spend the night with his friend Reggie. His sister begins needling him about his teddy bear, asking him if he plans to take it to Reggie's and reminding him that he has never slept without it. His parents reassure him that it is fine to take Tah Tah, but his sister insists that Reggie will laugh. When the time comes, Ira goes next door, leaving his teddy bear behind. As the two boys tell ghost stories in bed, Reggie gets up and gets something from a drawer—his teddy bear, named Foo Foo. Ira goes home to get Tah Tah, this time convinced that Reggie will not laugh.

In *Tough Eddie*, it is again the sister who makes life difficult. This time she tells Eddie's two friends, Andrew and Philip, about the dollhouse Eddie keeps in his closet. They are interested, and although they never show any negative reaction, Eddie assumes one and won't talk to them. He just keeps walking, feeling tough as he always does when he is wearing his cowboy boots and his thick leather belt. When their class takes a trip to the park, Eddie proves his bravery by not panicking when a bee lands on him. And when Philip considers bringing his cricket for show-and-tell, Eddie responds that he might bring his dollhouse.

The teacher talked with one group of eight children. They readily described the toys they slept with. The names ranged from a bear called Fuz to a more elegant stuffed rabbit called Mr. O. Hare. None of the children had ever been to a ballet lesson. All, however, played with dolls or "action figures" of some type, often those related to television cartoons. In the discussions they all agreed that boys did sleep with stuffed animals. They thought that playing with dolls was fine, particularly as they defined dolls. They weren't sure about the dollhouse, although one boy described the play stove and sink he had at home. They could readily understand the concerns of each of the characters, who feared being laughed at by his friends. They did not, however, agree on Max's dancing. Some said that dancing was fun and that anyone could do it. Others said that boys should not take ballet, but that this was okay because Max was preparing for a ball game. And still others said that ballet was for girls, not boys. The teacher did not give an opinion but pointed out that they seemed to have different feelings about it and asked them to think about how they knew what boys did and what girls did. This was a first step in urging children to question conventional stereotypes.

As you assess the role models in books that contribute to children's concept of their own sexual identity, plan to provide a variety of nonstereotyped characters and allow discussion of roles. If children are thinking in stereotypical terms, you may well want to introduce evidence that conflicts with their current beliefs. The teacher who read *Max* could later show news clippings of male dancers or have all the children engage in dancing themselves. Literature allows you to provide a great variety of possible behaviors and to broaden children's conceptions of possibilities for themselves.

Building Self-Esteem

Self-esteem is influenced strongly by the reaction of others to the individual. Children gain an impression of their worth from their perception of the treatment they are given by the important people in their lives. Parents, teachers, and classmates all contribute to the total picture. You, as a teacher, can influence this directly through your relations with the children and indirectly as you model behavior for children to use with others. You also can select curriculum materials and activities that build self-esteem.

Using Content That Reaffirms Self-Worth   Andrea and Brian Pinkney's *Pretty Brown Face* (1997) is a simple board book emphasizing special aspects of a child and is perfect for infants. Look for literature with content that reaffirms self-worth. *Big Sister Tells Me That I'm Black* gives a catchy, cheerleader beat to a poem celebrating proud feelings:

> big sister tells me
> that i'm black
> she says she knows me
> front and back . . .
> hip hip
> hip hooray
> hip hip
> i'm black today
> © Arnold Adoff, 2004. Used by permission of the author.

Emily's Art (Catalanotto, 2001) describes a situation that many primary-grade children encounter. First-grader Emily is an inspired artist whose paintings reflect her unique perceptions. She paints her beloved teacher with golden wings and her dog with exceptionally large ears "because Thor hears everything." When the teacher announces an upcoming art contest, the process of singling out an entry as the best begins. When the judge dismisses Emily's picture of Thor (because she was once bitten by a dog) in favor of a butterfly painted by Emily's best friend (under her guidance), the child's pain is obvious. Throughout the book, Catalanotto expresses the concerns and reactions of children quite convincingly. In a thought-provoking manner, this realistic story explores the dangers of judging and ranking children's work.

Presenting Themes of Individuality   Also look for books with themes of individuality. Children need to both recognize and value their own uniqueness. *Ella Sarah Gets Dressed* (Chodos-Irvine, 2003) in an outfit of her own choosing, despite the advice of her parents and sister, who think her choice is too dressy, too fancy, or too silly. This young girl has a style all her own, which is colorfully displayed through bold, vivid illustrations.

The theme of individuality is presented for preschoolers and kindergartners in *Incredible Me!* (Appelt, 2003) through bouncy rhymes and energetic illustrations. The redheaded protagonist proclaims, "I'm the one, the only, most marvelous me!" She continues on by naming her other traits through real and imaginary experiences. The bright and colorful illustrations add to the buoyant mood and energetic spirit of the girl.

Jack Prelutsky's poem, *Me I Am!* (2007) is repeated three times, each time featuring a different child. First is a girl who would rather roller skate and ride her bike than wear frilly dresses. Next is a boy who loves science and nature. Finally is a budding ballerina who loves being center stage. On the concluding pages, the three children, as well as others, are joined together as they shout, "I am the only me I am!" Prelutsky's poem honors children who are on the road to self-discovery.

For transitional chapter-book readers, author Lois Lowry has created a delightful second-grade character named Gooney Bird Greene. In *Gooney Bird Greene* (2002), the young girl arrives at her classroom door wearing pajamas and cowboy boots and announces she has just arrived from China. Classmates soon realize that Gooney Bird is a fantastic storyteller. The second book in the series, *Gooney Bird and the Room Mother* (2005) finds the second-graders preparing for the Thanksgiving pageant and in desperate need of a room mother. *Gooney the Fabulous* (2007) features the reading and writing of fables. Although Gooney Bird is a bit precocious, Lowry's stories are well written and entertaining while supporting the interests and reading ability of her young audience.

All these books, on different levels of difficulty, present a theme of the value of one's own decisions, one's own special skills, and one's own preferences. You can follow the reading of these books with activities that focus on the individuality of your students. You might try one or more of the following ideas.

1. Have the children make booklets about themselves, describing in words or pictures their special skills, what they might like to learn to do, what they enjoy, and what they dislike.

2. Make a bulletin board that features pictures of each child, labeled with the child's name. The children can dictate a sentence to accompany each picture, a sentence in which they tell one unique feature about themselves. Parents can be encouraged to help their children with this.

Recommended Literature Focusing on Self-Esteem

Beaumont, Karen. (2004). *I Like Myself!* Beau Ill. David Catrow. San Diego, CA: Harcourt.

Casanova, Mary. (2007). *Some Dog!* Ill. Ard Hoyt. New York: Farrar, Straus & Giroux.

Carle, Eric. (1984). *The Mixed-Up Chameleon.* New York: HarperCollins.

Cocca-Leffler, Maryann. (2007). *Jack's Talent.* New York: Farrar, Straus & Giroux.

Harvey, Amanda. (2002). *Dog Eared.* New York: Doubleday.

Henkes, Kevin. (1991). *Chrysanthemum.* New York: Greenwillow.

Hoffman, Mary. (1991). *Amazing Grace.* Ill. Caroline Binch. New York: Dial.

Howe, James. (2002). *Horace and Morris Join the Chorus (but What About Dolores?).* Ill. Amy Walrod. New York: Atheneum.

Lionni, Leo. (2006). *A Color of His Own.* New York: Knopf.

Lovell, Patty. (2001). *Stand Tall, Molly Lou Melon.* Ill. David Catrow. New York: Putnam.

3. Tape-record the children individually as they tell about a pet, their home, or their favorite food. Then play the tape for the group. As the children guess who is speaking, they learn about that child. Each child becomes the center of attention for a brief period of time. All learn that each person has a unique voice, one that others recognize even when they cannot see the speaker.

Sharing Literature That Promotes Feelings of Security   Books can help give a feeling of security to very young children. The infant or toddler held on the lap of an adult associates reading with the warmth of human contact. The preschool child sits beside an aide, and the two share a moment of understanding as they laugh together over a humorous book. Focusing attention on children in this way helps them feel that they are valued. Books such as *When Mama Comes Home Tonight* (Spinelli, 1998), *Mama, Do You Love Me?* (Joosse, 1991), and *Mama's Coming Home* (Banks, 2003) have content that reinforces that feeling. In the first one, Mama comes home after a long day at work and then cuddles and plays with her toddler, gives her a bath, and tucks her snugly into bed. In the second, a young Inuit girl asks a series of questions to assure herself of her mother's love, much as the little bunny in *The Runaway Bunny* (Brown, 1942) did. And in the third, Papa, two boys, a baby, a dog, and a cat eagerly anticipate Mama's return home from work as they scurry around preparing dinner and straightening up the house. The language patterns in all three books invite rereading, and the message that "you are important" helps build the young child's self-esteem.

Older children, particularly those from single-parent families, may gain security from books that show the love of both parents or of extended family, even though the child is not living with those particular individuals. In *Boundless Grace* (Hoffman, 1995), Grace learns to love two families, her mother and grandmother, with whom she lives, and her father, who has gone back to Nigeria, and his new wife and family. *Fred Stays with Me* (Coffelt, 2007) relates the story of a small girl's bond with her dog, which helps her to deal with her parents' divorce as she goes back and forth between the two homes. But wherever she goes, so does Fred. However, the playful pooch causes trouble at both houses, resulting in her parent's suggestion that the dog must go. But the girl reminds them that Fred stays with her because he provides her with stability and comfort as she makes adjustments to the changes in her life.

Suggesting Activities That Encourage Positive Feedback   Your behavior toward each child can show that each is valued. You can also arrange activities in which children will receive positive comments and treatment from their classmates and learn to give praise themselves. Some positive feedback will occur naturally as children take responsibility for care of classroom pets, plants, and materials. Others may be based on books you read. One teacher read *Odd Velvet* (Whitcomb, 1998) to her class of second-graders. When the book opens, it is the first day of school, and already Velvet is different from the other children. They bring the teacher tea and potpourri; Velvet brings rocks and half a sparrow's egg. As the school year continues, the children are polite to Velvet, but they do not choose her as a playmate. Then Velvet wins the school drawing contest, and she does it without fancy paints, using only her box of eight crayons. Little by little, the children come to recognize the unique things about Velvet—and she teaches them to draw. After she read this story, the teacher used the idea of special talents and an apple, the subject of Velvet's winning drawing. She had each child draw and color an apple and put his or her name on it, collected the apples, and then had each child, without looking, pick one of the apples. The child wrote on the back three things that were special about the child who had drawn the apple. The teacher collected the apples again and read the three special talents or qualities as she handed each apple to its owner, emphasizing the idea that each individual has skills and accomplishments.

The children thought about the special attributes of their friends, and each child received praise. The teacher had built in some checks to ensure that the activity went well. She used two children as examples and asked what they did well, what the children liked about them, and what they liked. This modeling assisted the class in understanding the sorts of comments that were expected. Then she collected the apples just before recess, glancing at the writing on each one. Had there been comments that were denigrating, she was in a position to have them changed without hurting a child's feelings and without making it common classroom knowledge. As you plan what is *right* about an activity, plan also for the *wrongs* that might occur. Those extra few minutes of thought may help children to feel a warm satisfaction about themselves.

Recognizing One's Own Values

Values are the belief system one holds about what is important. Children learn values from the people who are central to their lives. For toddlers and preschool children, parents are of primary importance; for the school-age child, teachers and peers, as well as parents, have influence. Children in school are exposed to more than one set of values and are able to think about them in terms other than Mommy is right or Mommy is wrong.

Literature, in its exploration of actions and motivations for actions, presents a panorama of value systems. Books that present value conflicts clearly lend themselves to discussion and to activities by which children can judge their own beliefs. *Leonardo the Terrible Monster* (Willems, 2005) is supposed to be a monster that frightens others, but he isn't very good at it. Leonardo is small with big blue eyes, a blue tongue, and a furry body. In order to prove how terrible he is, Leonardo decides to find the most "scaredy-cat kid" in the world and "scare the tuna salad" out of him. He finds Sam, who appears to be an easy mark and when he sees Leonardo, he immediately bursts into tears. However, it isn't Leonardo that causes the tears but rather Sam's mean big brother, who stole his action figure right out of his hands. Leonardo decides to become a friend rather than a monster. You can ask children if they have ever intentionally been mean (or nice) to someone else. They can share their responses through art, writing, or oral activities. As they explain their answers, you can ask them to tell whether they act that way often. This is one step in discovering what they value and how consistent they are in acting on those values.

Other times you can emphasize the reasons for holding a particular value and the consequences of acting on it. In the book titled *Frederick* (Lionni, 1967), a group of mice are preparing for the winter. All but Frederick are gathering corn, nuts, and wheat and storing them for the winter. Frederick sits alone and explains that he is gathering sun rays for cold winter days, and colors, and words. When winter comes, the mice eat through their store of supplies. Then they call upon Frederick, who alleviates their discomfort by reciting a poem that makes them feel the sun and see the colors of summer.

Children can be asked to write down whether they think Frederick should have been permitted to share in the mice's food because he did not gather any of it. Having them write yes or no on a paper forces them to decide for themselves, not be swayed by what a friend says or by what the majority seem to feel. Those who said yes can be grouped together, as can those who said no. Each group is to list all their reasons for feeling as they do. They could also be asked to select what the group thinks is the best reason.

Then you might lead a discussion in which you ask the groups to apply their beliefs to new situations. Do those children who hold that only people who work should share the food think that children who do not generally hold jobs should share in the family's food? Do those who hold that poets contribute something of value and should not have to work in the way others do also feel that a poetry-writing classmate should be excused from cleanup time to continue writing?

Preschool as well as primary children can identify the values a book character holds if they are asked what is important to that character. They might also be asked if they agree with the character. In *Miss Rumphius* (Cooney, 1982), the story begins with the title character as a small girl telling her artist grandfather about her dreams. She wants to go to distant places and to live in a house by the sea when she grows up. Her grandfather says that she must do a third thing—make the world more beautiful. She agrees but doesn't know how she will do this. The story continues with her travels and her move to a house by the sea. As an old woman, she sees the lovely lupines she had planted in her garden and then others growing where the seeds had spread. She decides she can fulfill her commitment to make the world more beautiful by scattering lupine seeds along the country lanes and walks. The story concludes as Miss Rumphius talks with her great-niece and tells her that she must do something to make the world more beautiful. How could they accomplish this, either now or in the future?

In these examples, children are not told what to believe but are asked only to think about their beliefs. You will find that literature often revolves around questions of values. The strategy of having students take a stand, think through their reasons for it, listen to the reasoning of those who differ, and discuss the consequences of acting on various value systems is one that can apply to many books. It opens the way for children to consider other positions and perhaps make more knowledgeable choices.

Helping Children Understand and Express Their Emotions   Literature highlights the role of emotions in human lives. It shows not only what happens to a character or what a character does but also how that character feels. Part of the reader's response to literature is usually recognition of the emotions being expressed. Much of the discussion of books centers on how characters feel about one another and how their feelings influence their actions. Reading to children every day cannot help but aid their understanding of people and of human emotions.

As you select books, it may be helpful for you to think of these four ways in which literature can contribute to young children's emotional growth. First, literature shows that many of the feelings they experience are experienced by others and are both normal and natural. Second, it explores the feeling from several aspects, giving a fuller picture and providing the base for the naming of that emotion. Third, literature, through the actions of various characters, shows options for ways of dealing with particular emotions. And fourth, literature makes clear that one person experiences many emotions—sometimes conflicting.

Molly Bang's *When Sophie Gets Angry—Really, Really Angry* (1999) depicts Sophie's range of emotions through both text and illustration. Sophie's sister demands a turn at playing with the beloved stuffed gorilla, and mother agrees. Sophie gets so angry that she wants to "smash the world to smithereens." Her anger is shown through the use of orange, red, and yellow illustrations. Sophie runs into the woods, where she begins to calm down, depicted in soothing tones of blue and green. When she returns home, Sophie sees that her sister has lost interest in the gorilla and is now focused on a table game. Bang creates a story that will prompt children to discuss their emotions and also ways to resolve inner conflicts. Todd Parr's *The Feelings Book* (2005), presented in board-book format, will elicit responses from toddlers and preschoolers.

Finding That Others Share Similar Feelings   To show children that others have felt as they do, look for books that describe common childhood experiences. Lola declares, *I Am Too Absolutely Small for School* (Child, 2004) because she is too busy doing important things at home. Her older brother, Charlie, tries to convince her to give school a try. There are equally important things to do at school, he tells her, but more importantly, he would miss her if she weren't there. Many children are nervous about beginning school and leaving the security of home, and it will comfort them to recognize that both book characters and classmates may share the same feelings.

Kevin Henkes explores a similar theme in *Wemberly Worried* (2000). Wemberly is beginning New Morning Nursery School and has many worries. What if her teacher is mean? What if the room smells bad? What if no one is wearing stripes or carrying a doll? Children often have worries not only about making friends but also about the school experience itself.

In *Gettin' Through Thursday* (Cooper, 1998), Andre knows that Thursday, the day before payday, is tight for his family. If they run out of something, be it food or toothpaste or birdseed for the parakeet, they must make do until Friday, when his mother gets paid. When he makes the third-grade honor roll, grade cards are distributed on a Thursday, and he knows that the celebration he was promised cannot be. He is angry and dejected, but he finally succumbs to the family's "pretend" celebration as a rehearsal for the real one—held on Friday. Children who feel the pinch of hard economic times know the disappointment Andre feels. The feelings are treated seriously in this book, a recognition that children care and that their feelings matter.

A second-grader bending down to pick up a crayon bumped his head on his desk as he straightened up. The teacher knew that earlier in the day he had broken his thermos. Seeing the pain on his face, he commiserated by saying, "This is just a bad day for you, Tom." From the depths of his misery Tom answered, "All my days are bad days." The next day the teacher read *Alexander and the Terrible, Horrible, No Good, Very Bad Day* (Viorst, 1972) in which Alexander tells all the horrible, no good things that happened to him. There was no prize in his breakfast cereal, only he had a cavity, there were lima beans for supper, and there was kissing on TV. Tom thoroughly enjoyed the story, as did the rest of the class. It is quite probable, however, that it would not have been so funny to Tom on his bad day. You will need to make a judgment about children's reactions to a book, knowing when they may need time before they are ready to relive or talk about an emotion.

Books for toddlers and preschoolers often concentrate on a single emotion. They understand the distress felt by D.W. when she cannot find her blanket in *D.W.'s Lost Blankie* (Brown, 1998). Or they can share the excitement when *Maisy Goes to School* (Cousins, 1992).

For some books, you may want to discuss with the children times when they have felt the way the character does. At other times, you may want to focus entirely on the literature itself, drawing out how the character felt and how the author let the reader know these feelings.

Exploring Various Aspects of an Emotion   Reading several books in which characters have the same or similar feelings gives children data from which to generalize. It is also an opportunity for putting feelings into words. Suppose you have read two books about the arrival of a new baby, which you chose because several of the children in your group have new brothers or sisters. The two that you read, *A Baby Sister for Frances* (Hoban, 1964) and *Julius, the Baby of the World* (Henkes, 1990), both describe the feelings of jealousy experienced by the older child. To expand on this theme, you choose two more books in which jealousy plays an important role. One, *A Birthday for Frances* (Hoban, 1995) has Frances suffering again—but this time because it is her sister's birthday, not hers. And the other, *Pip and Squeak* (Duke 2007), have nothing in common except their mutual dislike. The children tell what was similar about these feelings. They may relate times when they have felt that way. If none of the children offers the term *jealous*, interject it into the discussion yourself. These children will begin to realize that a single emotion may be produced by many different circumstances and will build a vocabulary for telling others how they feel.

You might then introduce a book in which jealousy is only one of the emotions being experienced and give children the opportunity to describe it in a more complex context. In *Timothy Goes to School* (Wells, 2000), for example, Timothy heads out for his first day at school full of enthusiasm. The teacher seats him next to Claude, who immediately makes fun of the sunsuit Timothy is wearing. The next day Timothy wears a new jacket, and Claude again criticizes his clothes. Timothy hopes that Claude will make mistakes, or fall in a puddle, or have some other mishap, but he never does. Timothy is jealous of Claude's confidence and tries to dress to conform to what appear to be Claude's expectations. At the same time, he dislikes Claude's attitudes and actions. Finally he meets Violet, who has the same feelings toward Grace that Timothy has toward Claude. They become friends and laugh about Claude and Grace as they walk home together. The feelings of the characters are multidimensional. Because all the characters are animals, the ideas, rather than the actual appearance of the characters, are primary.

Recommended Literature that Exhibits and Encourages Imagination

Agee, Jon. (2003). *Z Goes Home*. New York: Hyperion.

Alexander, Martha. (1969, 1999). *The Blackboard Bear*. Cambridge, MA: Candlewick.

Burningham, John. (1987). *John Patrick Norman McHennessy—the Boy Who Was Always Late*. New York: Crown.

Ellery, Amanda. (2006). *If I Had a Dragon*. Ill. Tom Ellery. New York: Simon & Schuster.

Falconer, Ian. (2000). *Olivia*. New York: Atheneum.

Howe, James. (1994). *There's a Dragon in My Sleeping Bag*. Ill. David S. Rose. New York: Atheneum.

Polacco, Patricia. (2005). *Emma and Kate*. New York: Philomel.

Portis, Antoinette. (2006). *Not a Box*. New York: HarperCollins.

Sendak, Maurice. (1963). *Where the Wild Things Are*. New York: Harper.

Van Allsburg, Chris. (1985). *The Polar Express*. Boston: Houghton Mifflin.

Wiesner, David. (2001). *The Three Pigs*. New York: Clarion.

Some teachers have used the form of "Happiness is . . ." to elicit examples of specific emotions. Children complete the sentence in as many ways as they can. The emotion may be whatever the teacher or children select: "Love is . . ." or "Grouchy is . . ." If you begin with this approach, you may want to read literature that approaches the emotion from this perspective. Todd Parr's *The Feel Good Book* (2004) can assist in completing the statement, "I feel good when . . ." *The Happy Book* (Muldrow, 1999) is a boardbook with textures that infants and toddlers can touch as it describes things that make children happy.

Perceiving Options for Managing Emotions   As children see how emotions are expressed by book characters, they are given options for handling their emotions. Some may be methods they already use. Crying may not change the circumstances that produced the disappointment, but it does offer release.

Fantasizing is another way of managing feelings, from anger to longing. Christopher, in *Mommy Go Away* (Jonell, 1997), is tired of his parents telling him what to do, imagines his mother on his toy boat, and tells her to go away as the boat floats in the bathtub. His anger assuaged, he rescues her when the boat capsizes. The title *Next Year I'll Be Special* (Giff, 1993) expresses a little girl's state of mind as she thinks about what school will be like for her next year, when she has the lovely Miss Lark, who never yells, for her second-grade teacher. Unhappiness with "mean Miss Minch" is overshadowed by imaginings of being the best in the class, appreciated by all her classmates, and honored by her teacher. Fantasizing is not offered as a permanent escape but as one way of sorting through feelings and expressing them, if only to oneself. It is also a safe way of previewing possible actions.

Mean Gene hates everyone who's different from him, including the school principal, Mr. Lincoln. Patricia Polacco's *Mr. Lincoln's Way* (2001) depicts a young boy acting out his mistrust of people whom Eugene's father refers to as "not our kind." The African American principal recognizes Eugene's need for acceptance and understanding of others and enlists the help of the boy's grandfather. This story for primary-grade students illustrates that children may act out their frustrations and misunderstandings through inappropriate ways.

Within stories that children are hearing every day, they will encounter characters that hide their feelings, who share them, and who reveal them through their actions. They will see that some characters are misunderstood because they did not explain their feelings. They will experience, with the characters, a full range of feelings.

Exploring the Varied Emotions of a Single Character   Some of the books you read will show the many emotions of a single character. Consider also reading a series of books about one character. The books about Frances by Russell Hoban show this "human" badger in many different situations. David Shannon's semiautobiographical picture books have become favorites with problems and emotions that young children will find familiar. *No, David!* (1998) is a kid who breaks all of his mother's rules. He chews with his mouth open (and full of food), he jumps on the furniture, and he breaks his mother's vase. All this leads to his mother's constant cry of, "No David!" When *David Goes to School* (1999) he discovers his least favorite word, no, is spoken here also. No yelling, no pushing, no running in the halls. *David Gets in Trouble* (2002) in the series' third book and always says, "It's not my fault! I didn't mean to! It was an accident." Whatever the situation, David has a good excuse. But David soon realizes that making excuses makes him feel bad, but saying he's sorry makes him feel better. Babies and toddlers can also meet David through board book format with titles that include, *Oh, David!* (2005b), *Oops!* (2005c), and *David Smells! A Diaper David Book* (2005a).

A series of chapter books for second- and third-grade students features a lively character named Judy Moody created by Megan McDonald. In *Judy Moody* (2000), third-grader Judy is in a bad mood on the first day of school until she gets an assignment to create a collage about herself. *Judy Moody Gets Famous* (2001) when she realizes that she can do something for others without looking for recognition. Judy Moody gets serious about protecting the environment in *Judy Moody Saves the*

World (2002). And finally, the plucky protagonist acquires a mood ring and tries to convince herself and her third-grade classmates that she can make predictions in *Judy Moody Predicts the Future* (2003). Other recent titles in the series include, *Judy Moody, M.D.: The Doctor Is In* (2004), *Judy Moody: Around the World in 8½ Days* (2006), and *Judy Moody Declares Independence* (2007).

Frances, David, and Judy Moody become like familiar friends to readers as you share their adventures. They show that one person may feel a variety of emotions in a manner compatible with young children's ability to comprehend the situations.

Following the reading of books such as these, plan ways for children to verbalize emotions, either their own or those of the book characters. They may add words to wordless picture books, either in dialogue or narrative form. They could dramatize a story, following the plot but giving their own dialogue, thus expressing the feelings in their own words. Older children can role-play a situation. Look for times when the children can use puppets or masks as they engage in dialogue. Children often speak more freely when they are speaking through another personage.

Occasionally you will find books or poems with patterns children can use to express their own feelings. Karla Kuskin (1975) has something to say about her feelings in this poem:

> Okay everybody, listen to this:
>
> I am tired of being smaller
>
> Than you And them
>
> And him
>
> And trees and buildings.
>
> So watch out
>
> All you gorillas and adults
>
> Beginning tomorrow morning
>
> Boy
>
> Am I going to be taller.

What might the children in your group say with an opening line like, "Okay everybody, listen to this"?

Overcoming Unfounded Fears   Common fears of childhood are the themes in some books and common occurrences in others. Characters may be frightened by animals or afraid of the dark. Sometimes children's fears are unfounded in reality, but at other times they are reflective of actual danger. In *Not Afraid of Dogs* (Pitzer, 2006), Daniel declares that he's not afraid of dogs, it's just that he doesn't like them. When Aunt Rose goes on vacation, her dog, Bandit, comes to stay at his house, which results in Daniel retreating to the safety of his bedroom. Daniel soon realizes that even dogs can be afraid, and he becomes the one to comfort Bandit during a thunderstorm. Children talking about their fears and the fears of characters in books are gathering information that will help them determine which fears are useful for providing an awareness of dangerous situations and which inhibit them in areas where the potential danger is minimal. They are also facing their fears, the first step in overcoming them.

Literature can help children cope with fears of the known and unknown by providing knowledge about common objects and events as well as new experiences they are about to undertake. *"Mama! Mama!" Come and see! Creepy Things Are Scaring Me* (Pumphrey, & Pumphrey, 2003). Combining simple rhyme with nighttime bedroom scenes, a child is frightened when the lights go out. He hears a sound under the bed and sees a creepy thing on the ceiling and shadows on the floor. When the boy cries out, mom comes running and helps him see that the sound is his puppy, the creepy thing is really cold air, and the shadow is his teddy bear. When mom turns out the lights again, the boy is suddenly sleepy. For preschoolers, nighttime jitters are very real, and shadows are something to fear.

A child who has never been to a hospital is given valuable information and a large measure of reassurance in Fred Rogers's *Going to the Hospital* (1988). The photographs show just what to expect, and the text is clear. In the section describing X-rays, the child is told that the machine takes pictures of the inside of the body. It also explains that the X-ray table may feel hard and there will be a buzzing sound; that the child will have to stay still and others will have to stay outside the room; and, most importantly, that it does not hurt. This book, like others in this series of books that introduces children to new situations, gives insight into the uneasiness children may feel and arms them against it by making the experience understandable and less strange. As you learn what children in your group are facing, whether it be a trip to the dentist or a move to live with a new set of foster parents, you will be able to share literature with them that will make the experience less frightening.

Literature can give children the opportunity to talk about their fears. If they are responding to a book, they may say how they feel and put the fear in perspective. Children listening to *Something Might Happen* (Lester, 2003), in which Twitchly Fidget must confront his fears or else live his life in a dreary, windowless and doorless hut, will encourage children to talk about their fears—real and imagined. Other tricks of the imagination are humorously but understandingly portrayed in *What's Under My Bed?* (Stevenson, 1983). After laughing at all the terrible things Grandpa describes as having seen and heard when he once stayed with his grandparents long ago, children can talk about the things they imagine lurking in the dark when they are in a strange place. In *Roller Coaster* (Frazee, 2003), a long line of people set aside their fears to ride a roller coaster. One person has never done it before, and her trepidation soon turns into sheer delight as the train goes zipping and zooming on the track.

Young children are often afraid of separation—of being left alone and having no one to care for them. Three- and 4-year-olds listening to the story *Don't Go* (Zalben, 2001) will see that is what Daniel the elephant doesn't want his mother to do as he faces his first day at preschool. He cries and hides behind his mother. She doesn't push him but rather waits patiently for him to work through his feelings while reassuring him that she will always come back. The book concludes with some common-sense preschool adjustment tips from Zalben's editor. Children and parents alike have found comfort and the suggestion of sharing a special "secret" through Audrey Penn's (1993) *The Kissing Hand*. Both books provide an opportunity for children to tell how they feel when their parents leave.

Children between ages 5 and 9 are in a period of realizing that death, the ultimate separation, is permanent. Books about the death of a pet or a grandparent will give them an idea of how others feel when a death occurs. Just as adults have varied beliefs about death, so too is there a range of beliefs presented in literature. Children have a better chance of coping if adults are honest with them, admitting that separation is painful and that people have differing beliefs about death.

Over a year's time you could read several books in which a death occurs, each giving new information about people's responses to it. In *The Forever Dog* (Cochran, 2007), Mike believes that he and his beloved dog, Corky, will be together forever. But when Corky gets sick and dies, the young boy becomes both sad and angry that the dog is gone. *Annie and the Old One* (Miles, 1971) shows that Annie, no matter how much she wishes it, cannot prevent the death of her grandmother. She comes to accept her grandmother's teaching that death is a natural part of life. A young boy questions *Where Is Grandpa?* (Barron, 2000) after his grandfather passes away. As the family reminisces about the times spent with Grandpa, the boy realizes that this influential person remains "in all those places" that they visited and where memories occurred.

To encourage children to talk about their fears and to see ways they might lessen them, read several books that present fears children commonly have. Some of the children may volunteer to talk about fears they have; others may tell about them when asked. You will learn about areas where you may be able to help, and children may give valuable advice to one another.

SUMMARY

Emotions, values, ways of perceiving, and feelings about self are all a part of personality. Erikson seeks to explain personality growth by describing how human beings respond to conflicts at specific periods in their lives. Central to how children resolve such conflicts and to the development of self-esteem and a positive self-concept is the way in which adults and peers respond to them.

The following long-term goals are appropriate for the personality development of young children.

Children will weigh evidence and make appropriate choices.

Children will set tasks for themselves and complete the tasks they begin.

Children will develop positive and realistic self-concepts.

Children will develop feelings of self-worth and self-esteem.

Children will begin to recognize their own values and to choose from among values.

Children will understand their emotions and will express them in socially acceptable ways.

Books offer opportunities for helping children achieve these goals. Teacher Feature 7.1 (pp. 198–199) suggests appropriate teaching strategies. Children can be involved regularly in making choices, deciding which books they would like to hear read, which activity they wish to complete, and which book they will take from the library. They can also learn to be responsible for the choices they make. In many instances teachers can help children set tasks for themselves and assess their own efforts in completing the tasks.

Literature, through content and through activities based on content and theme, can strengthen the development of self-esteem. As children hear literature that shows the skills and abilities of others, they discover that they, too, have many skills and abilities. Comparisons aid in the ability to see oneself realistically and to recognize the process of growth and change. Books present models with which children identify. Thus teachers will want to avoid books that stereotype characters and look for those that present well-developed characters in a variety of roles and settings. Teachers will also share books that promote feelings of security and self-worth.

Because literature explores the actions and motivations of characters, it presents a panorama of value systems and of emotional reactions. Primary-grade children can clarify their own value positions as they assess the actions of book characters. Both primary and preschool children gain experience in recognizing and talking about emotions as they participate in literary experiences. Books provide particular support for helping children overcome unfounded fears, both through giving information about new experiences and through providing a stimulus for the discussion of common fears.

Extending Your Learning

1. Select a picture or chapter book and describe three possible response strategies based upon it.

2. Make a list of five choices children might reasonably be asked to make during one school day or of three choices during a half-day at preschool.

3. Analyze sex-role models presented in 10 picture books. Identify any stereotypes that may be present.

4. Read at least one multicultural book and tell how it might contribute to a child's self-concept and to appreciation of that child's culture by members of other cultures.

5. Identify the values underlying the actions of the main character in five different picture or chapter books.

6. Read several books about the same character, listing the situations and emotions they experience and assessing the range of emotions shown by the character.

Teacher Feature 7.1   Supporting Children's Personality Development

Developmental Goals	Teaching Suggestions
Children will weigh evidence and make appropriate choices.	• Give children real choices and abide by their decisions. • Encourage children to choose their own books for independent perusal. • Provide children with a choice of activities following the reading of a book. • Vary the types of choices offered. • Help children make responsible choices.
Children will set tasks for themselves and will complete tasks they begin.	• Teach children to define the task. • Engage in library projects (7–8 years). • Keep children on task by having them list questions to be answered. • Have children assess their own efforts. • Let children decide how to share a story. • Suggest tasks attainable but challenging for the children.
Children will develop positive and realistic self-concepts.	• Choose books that emphasize capabilities children have. • Choose books that show characters seeing themselves positively and realistically. • Choose literature that shows children growing and changing. • Engage children in activities that demonstrate change. • Read books that show children who can cope with problems. • Choose books that provide models for ethnic and sex role identification. • Discuss children's ideas of appropriate sex-role behaviors.
Children will develop feelings of self-worth and self-esteem.	• Choose literature that reaffirms self-worth. • Choose literature that supports individuality. • Have children make booklets and tapes about themselves. • Read books that give children a feeling of security. • Plan activities that promote children complimenting one another.
Children will begin to recognize their own values and to choose from among values.	• Lead discussions about value conflicts in books. Have children decide which character they agree with when characters express differing values. • Encourage children to evaluate the rationale for particular beliefs.
Children will understand their emotions and express them in socially acceptable ways.	• Share books that show emotions common to young children. • Combine books to explore several facets of a single emotion. • Present children with options for dealing with emotions. • Show one character experiencing many emotions. • Engage children in dialogue that expresses emotion through dramatic activities such as puppetry and role-play. • Let children tell their feelings using the format of a specific book or poem. • Provide children with knowledge about new experiences. • Encourage children to talk about their fears.

Recommended Literature

Ages 2–5

Dyer	*Little Brown Bear Won't Go to School*
Rathmann	*Officer Buckle and Gloria*

Ages 2–5

Feiffer	*I Lost My Bear*
Freeman	*Corduroy*

Ages 5–8

Gibbons	*Giant Pandas*
Kalman	*The Life Cycle of a Koala*
Stone	*The Giant Pandas*

Ages 0–2

Butler	*Can You Growl Like a Bear?*
Hudson	*Hands Can*

Ages 2–5

Bemelmans	*Madeline*
Hoberman	*"A Year Later"*
Hutchins	*You'll Soon Grow into Them, Titch*
O'Connor	*Ready, Set, Skip!*

Ages 5–8

Carlson	*It's Going to be Perfect*
Diakite	*I Lost My Tooth in Africa*
Isadora	*Max*
Lindgren	*Benny and the Binky*
Rylant	*Birthday Presents*
Saltzberg	*Star of the Week*
Waber	*Ira Sleeps Over*
Winthrop	*Tough Eddie*

Ages 0–2

Chodos-Irvine	*Ella Sarah Gets Dressed*
Pinkney	*Pretty Brown Face*

Ages 2–5

Appelt	*Incredible Me!*
Banks	*Mama's Coming Home*
Brown	*The Runaway Bunny*
Joosse	*Mama, Do You Love Me?*
Spinelli	*When Mama Comes Home Tonight*

Ages 5–8

Adoff	*Big Sister Tells Me That I'm Black*
Bechtold	*Buster: The Very Shy Dog*
Graves	*Loretta, Ace Pinky Scout*
Prelutsky	*Me I Am!*
Whitcomb	*Odd Velvet*

Ages 5–8

Cooney	*Miss Rumphius*
Lionni	*Frederick*
Willems	*Leonardo the Terrible Monster*

Ages 0–2

Muldrow	*The Happy Book*
Shannon	*Oh, David!*
Shannon	*Oops!*

Ages 2–5

Child	*I Am Too Absolutely Small for School*
Henkes	*Wemberly Worried*
Hoban	*A Birthday For Frances*
Pumphrey & Pumphrey	*Creepy Things Are Scaring Me*
Shannon	*No, David!*
Stevenson	*What's Under My Bed?*
Wells	*Timothy Goes to School*

Ages 5–8

Bang	*When Sophie Gets Angry—Really, Really Angry*
Barron	*Where Is Grandpa?*
Giff	*Next Year I'll Be Special*
McDonald	*Judy Moody*
Miles	*Annie and the Old One*
Polacco	*Mr. Lincoln's Way*
Viorst	*Alexander and the Terrible, Horrible, No Good, Very Bad Day*

REFERENCES

Professional References Cited

Brewer, J. (2006). *Introduction to early childhood education: Preschool through primary grades* (6th ed.). Boston: Allyn & Bacon.

Erikson, E. (1986). *Childhood and society* (35th anniversary ed.). New York: Norton.

Katz, L., and McClellan, D. (1997). *Fostering children's social competence.* Washington, DC: National Association for the Education of Young Children.

Koch, K. (2000). *Wishes, lies, and dreams.* New York: Perennial.

National Council for the Social Studies. (1997). *Expectations of excellence: Curriculum standards for social studies.* Wilmington, DE: Author.

Papalia, D. E., Olds, S. W., and Felman, R. D. (2006). *Human development* (10th ed.). Boston: McGraw-Hill.

Children's Literature Cited

Adoff, Arnold. (1976). *Big Sister Tells Me That I'm Black.* New York: Holt.

Alexander, Martha G. (2006). *When the New Baby Comes, I'm Moving Out.* Watertown, MA: Charlesbridge.

Appelt, Kathi. (2003). *Incredible Me!* Ill. G. Brian Karas. New York: HarperCollins.

Bang, Molly. (1999). *When Sophie Gets Angry—Really, Really Angry.* New York: Scholastic.

Banks, Kate. (2003). *Mama's Coming Home.* Ill. Tomek Bogacki. New York: Farrar, Straus & Giroux.

Barron, T. A. (2000). *Where Is Grandpa?* Ill. Chris Soentpiet. New York: Philomel.

Bechtold, Lisze. (1999). *Buster: The Very Shy Dog.* Boston: Houghton Mifflin.

Bemelman, Ludwig. (1939). *Madeline.* New York: Viking.

Bercaw, Edna Coe. (2000). *Halmoni's Day.* Ill. Robert Hunt. New York: Dial.

Brown, Marc. (1998). *D.W.'s Lost Blankie.* Boston: Little, Brown.

Brown, Margaret Wise. (1942). *The Runaway Bunny.* Ill. Clement Hurd. New York: Harper.

Brown, Margaret Wise. (2004). *Another Important Book.* Ill. Chris Raschka. New York: HarperCollins.

Butler, John. (2007). *Can You Growl Like a Bear?* Atlanta: Peachtree.

Carlson, Nancy. (1998). *It's Going to Be Perfect.* New York: Viking.

Catalanotto, Peter. (2001). *Emily's Art.* New York: Atheneum.

Child, Lauren. (2004). *I Am Too Absolutely Small for School.* Cambridge, MA: Candlewick.

Chodos-Irvine, Margaret. (2003). *Ella Sarah Gets Dressed.* San Diego, CA: Harcourt.

Cochran, Bill. (2007). *The Forever Dog.* Ill. Dan Andreasen. New York: HarperCollins.

Coffelt, Nancy. (2007). *Fred Stays with Me.* Ill. Tricia Tusa. Boston: Little, Brown.

Cooney, Barbara. (1982). *Miss Rumphius.* New York: Viking.

Cooper, Melrose. (1998). *Gettin' through Thursday.* Ill. Nneka Bennett. New York: Lee & Low.

Cousins, Lucy. (1992). *Maisy Goes to School.* Cambridge, MA: Candlewick.

Diakite, Penda. (2006). *I Lost My Tooth in Africa.* Ill. Baba Wague Diakite. New York: Scholastic.

Duke, Kate. (2007). *Pip and Squeak.* New York: Dutton.

Dyer, Jane. (2002). *Little Brown Bear Won't Go to School.* Boston: Little, Brown.

Feiffer, Jules. (1998). *I Lost My Bear.* New York: Morrow.

Frazee, Marla. (2003). *Roller Coaster.* San Diego, CA: Harcourt.

Freeman, Don. (1968). *Corduroy.* New York: Viking.

Gibbons, Gail. (2002). *Giant Pandas.* New York: Holiday House.

Giff, Patricia Reilly. (1993). *Next Year I'll Be Special.* Ill. Marylin Hafner. New York: Doubleday.

Graves, Keith. (2002). *Loretta, Ace Pinky Scout.* New York: Scholastic.

Henkes, Kevin. (1990). *Julius, the Baby of the World.* New York: Greenwillow.

Henkes, Kevin. (2000). *Wemberly Worried.* New York: Greenwillow.

Hest, Amy. (1996). *Jamaica Louise James.* Ill. Sheila White Samton. Cambridge, MA: Candlewick.

Hoban, Russell. (1964). *A Baby Sister for Frances.* Ill. Lillian Hoban. New York: Harper & Row.

Hoban, Russell. (1995, 1968). *A Birthday for Frances.* Ill. Lillian Hoban. New York: Harper & Row.

Hoberman, Mary Ann. (1959). "A Year Later" in *Hello and Good-By.* Boston: Little, Brown. "A Year Later" reprinted by permission of Russell & Volkening, Inc. as agents for the author. Copyright © by Mary Ann Hoberman.

Hoffman, Mary. (1995). *Boundless Grace.* Ill. Caroline Binch. New York: Dial.

Hudson, Cheryl Willis. (2003). *Hands Can.* Photographs by John-Francis Bourke. Cambridge, MA: Candlewick.

Hutchins, Pat. (1983). *You'll Soon Grow Into Them, Titch.* New York: Greenwillow.

Isadora, Rachel. (1976). *Max.* New York: Macmillan.

Jonell, Lynn. (1997). *Mommy Go Away!* Ill. Petra Mathers. New York: Putnam.

Joosse, Barbara. (1991). *Mama, Do You Love Me?* Ill. Barbara Lavallee. San Francisco: Chronicle.

Kalman, Bobbie. (2001). *The Life Cycle of a Koala.* New York: Crabtree.

Krensky, Stephen. (2000). *Louise, Soccer Star?* Ill. Susanna Natti. New York: Dial.

Kuskin, Karla. (1975). "OK Everybody, Listen to This" in *Near the Window Tree.* New York: Harper. Copyright © by Karla Kuskin. Reprinted by permission of Scott Treimel, New York.

Lester, Helen. (2003). *Something Might Happen.* Ill. Lynn Munsinger. Boston: Houghton Mifflin.

Lindgren, Barbro. (2002). *Benny and the Binky.* Ill. Olof Landstrom. Stockholm: R&S Books.

Lionni, Leo. (1967). *Frederick.* New York: Pantheon.

Lowry, Lois. (2002). *Gooney Bird Greene.* Ill. Middy Thomas. Boston: Houghton Mifflin.

Lowry, Lois. (2005). *Gooney Bird and the Room Mother.* Ill. Middy Thomas. Boston: Houghton Mifflin.

Lowry, Lois. (2007). *Gooney the Fabulous.* Ill. Middy Thomas. Boston: Houghton Mifflin.

McDonald, Megan. (2000). *Judy Moody.* Cambridge, MA: Candlewick.

McDonald, Megan. (2001). *Judy Moody Gets Famous!* Cambridge, MA: Candlewick.

McDonald, Megan. (2002). *Judy Moody Saves the World.* Cambridge, MA: Candlewick.

McDonald, Megan. (2003). *Judy Moody Predicts the Future.* Cambridge, MA: Candlewick.

McDonald, Megan. (2004). *Judy Moody, M.D.: The Doctor Is In.* Cambridge, MA: Candlewick.

McDonald, Megan. (2006). *Judy Moody: Around the World in 8½ Days.* Cambridge, MA: Candlewick.

McDonald, Megan. (2007). *Judy Moody Declares Independence.* Cambridge, MA: Candlewick.

Miles, Miska. (1971). *Annie and the Old One.* Ill. Peter Parnall. Boston: Little, Brown.

Muldrow, Diane. (1999). *The Happy Book.* New York: Scholastic.

O'Connor, Jane. (2007). *Ready, Set, Skip!* Ill. Ann James. New York: Viking.

Parr, Todd. (2004). *The Feel Good Book.* Boston, Little, Brown.

Parr, Todd. (2005). *The Feelings Book.* Boston: Little, Brown.

Penn, Audrey. (1993). *The Kissing Hand.* Washington, D.C.: Child & Family Press.

Pinkey, Andrea and Pinkey, Brian. (1997). *Pretty Brown Face.* San Diego: Harcourt.

Pitzer, Susanna. (2006). *Not Afraid of Dogs.* Ill. Larry Day. New York: Walker.

Polacco, Patricia. (2001). *Mr. Lincoln's Way.* New York: Philomel.

Prelutsky, Jack. (2007). *Me I Am!* Ill. Christine Davenier. New York: Farrar, Straus & Giroux.

Pumphrey, Jerome, and Pumphrey, Jarrett. (2003). *Creepy Things Are Scaring Me.* Ill. Rosanne Litzinger. New York: HarperCollins.

Rathmann, Peggy. (1995). *Officer Buckle and Gloria.* New York: Putnam.

Reynolds, Peter H. (2003). *The Dot.* Cambridge, MA: Candlewick.

Rogers, Fred. (1988). *Going to the Hospital.* Ill. Jim Judkis. New York: Putnam.

Rylant, Cynthia. (1987). *Birthday Presents.* Ill. Sucie Stevenson. New York: Orchard/Watts.

Saltzberg, Barney. (2006). *Star of the Week.* Cambridge, MA: Candlewick.

Shannon, David. (1998). *No, David!* New York: Scholastic.

Shannon, David. (1999). *David Goes to School.* New York: Scholastic.

Shannon, David. (2002). *David Gets in Trouble.* New York: Scholastic.

Shannon, David. (2005a). *David Smells! A Diaper David Book.* New York: Scholastic.

Shannon, David. (2005b). *Oh, David!* New York: Scholastic.

Shannon, David. (2005c). *Oops!* New York: Scholastic.

Smith, Cynthia Leitich. (2000). *Jingle Dancer.* Ill. Cornelius Van Wright. New York: Harper-Collins.

Spinelli, Eileen. (1998). *When Mama Comes Home Tonight.* Ill. Jane Dyer. New York: Simon & Schuster.

Stevenson, James. (1983). *What's Under My Bed?* New York: Greenwillow.

Stone, Lynn M. (2003). *The Giant Pandas.* Ill. Keren Su. Minneapolis, MN: Lerner.

Viorst, Judith. (1972). *Alexander and the Terrible, Horrible, No Good, Very Bad Day.* Ill. Ray Cruz. New York: Atheneum.

Waber, Bernard. (1972). *Ira Sleeps Over.* Boston: Houghton Mifflin.

Wells, Rosemary. (2000). *Timothy Goes to School.* New York: Viking.

Whitcomb, Mary. (1998). *Odd Velvet.* Ill. Tara Calahan King. San Francisco: Chronicle.

Willems, Mo. (2005). *Leonardo the Terrible Monster.* New York: Hyperion.

Winthrop, Elizabeth. (1985). *Tough Eddie.* Ill. Lillian Hoban. New York: Dutton.

Zalben, Jane Breskin. (2001). *Don't Go!* New York: Clarion.

CHAPTER EIGHT

LINNEA, Age 7
What Does Peace Feel Like?

7-20-06 What does Peace Feel Like

Peace looks like friends holding hands on there way back back from resses. Peace tastes like colate chip cookies just coming out of the oven. Peace sounds like leaves cruching from people walking. Peace feels like making snow angels on a

Soft. snow. Peace smells like cupcakes baking in the oven. Peace look like leave spining wind on my way back from resses. Peace looks like people eating a thanksgiving Dinner.

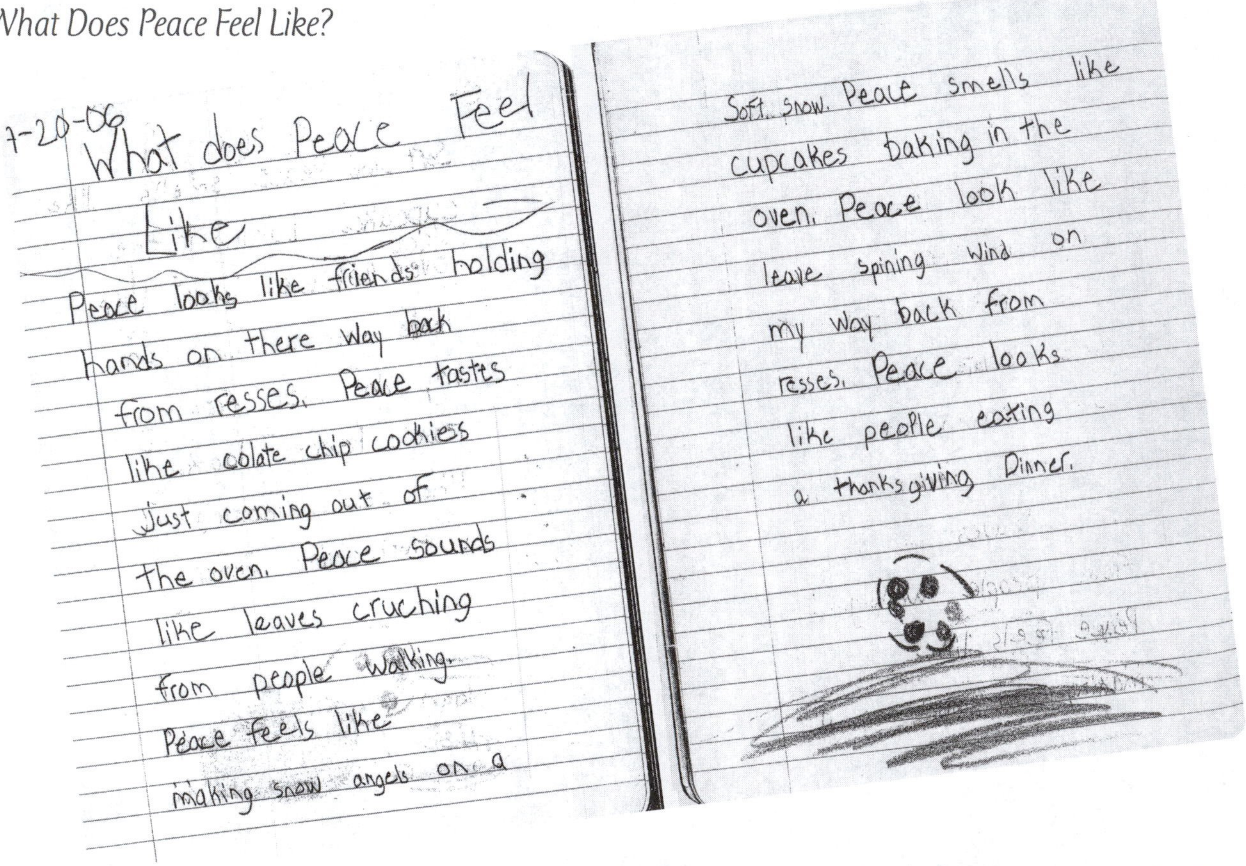

Linnea (age 7) read Vladimir Radunsky's *What Does Peace Feel Like?* (2004). This is the second draft of her response to this colorful picture book that strings together descriptive similes and metaphors to describe the essence of the word "peace."

Supporting Children's Social and Moral Development

Five-year-old Holly came running into the classroom, telling her teacher in indignant tones that Ralph kept chasing her on the playground. The teacher asked Holly what had happened. Holly explained that Ralph was standing near the swings, and that when she approached him, he started after her. "What did you do when he started toward you?" asked the teacher. "I ran away," answered Holly. "What do you suppose might have happened if you had kept walking toward him or perhaps stood still?" probed the teacher. There was a long silence. Then Holly's face showed that she had grasped the idea, and with a decisive "Oh" she turned and walked back to the playground.

Holly was just beginning to learn that her behavior toward others could affect their behavior toward her. It is but one of many social lessons that Holly will learn as she matures.

SOCIAL AND MORAL DEVELOPMENT IN YOUNG CHILDREN

Social Development

Much of children's social development—their ability to relate to other people—is correlated with their ability to see events from the viewpoint of another (Shaffer, 2006). Piaget describes children who are in the preoperational stage of intellectual development, usually from about 2 to about 6 or 7 years of age, as being egocentric. They are unable to consistently put themselves in someone else's place because they consider their own point of view the only possible one. Social workers and child-care professionals are finding that many preschool youngsters whose parents are divorced see themselves as the cause of the separation. They are not able to view the problems from their parents' perspectives or to comprehend that they may not be the center around which all actions revolve. They may also reason from one event to another, adding the element of causation. If Daddy left home and if they had misbehaved, then Daddy must have left because they misbehaved.

The ability to take the perspective of another person increases with age, most likely as a combination of cognitive development and the child's social experience. Thus there will be differences among children in this skill. And as children get older, they become better able to evaluate multiple attributes of a situation. A 3-year-old may look at the situation another child is in and draw a conclusion, valid or not, about the child's feelings from that alone. A 6-year-old will look at the expression on the child's face as well as the situation (Mussen, Conger, Kagan, & Huston, 1990).

Young children often need help recognizing that other people have feelings that matter and that may differ from their own as well as help learning to interpret the emotions of others. Being able to see from another's viewpoint and to interpret another person's response are developments central to the ability to interact success-fully in social relationships.

Hay, Castle, Davies, Demetriou, and Stimson (1999) conducted a study with children at 18, 24, and 30 months to determine whether there was a decline in prosocial behavior throughout childhood. They found that most children shared less as they grew older, but the oldest girls slightly increased their rate of sharing over time. As peer relationships developed, "girls were more likely to share with other girls; boys were more like to show reciprocity in sharing" (p. 905).

Mussen and Eisenberg-Berg (1977) were concerned with conditions under which children exhibited prosocial behavior, actions that were intended to aid another person and for which no rewards were expected. When would a child volunteer to give her toy to someone who did not have one or help a classmate who was injured or crying? After analyzing hundreds of studies, they concluded

> To act in accordance with learned or internalized norms, the child must first per-ceive the other person's needs, interpret them accurately, and recognize that he or she can be helped. In addition, the child must feel competent in this situation, that is, capable of providing what is needed, and the cost or risk entailed in helping must not be prohibitive. Unless these preconditions are met, even the child who knows the norm of social responsibility is not likely to render aid.   *(pp. 5-6)*

Thus it requires more than simply telling children to help others for them actually to provide help when it is needed. The authors write that experiences such as seeing prosocial behavior modeled and having participated in role-playing will enhance prosocial behavior.

The models of behavior that children see are a powerful force in their learning. According to social learning theorists, children observe how behaviors are performed and in what situations. If they see a teacher treating children courteously and kindly, they are likely to adopt this behavior toward one another. They are also influenced by the rewards that follow behaviors, both when the reinforcement comes directly to them and when they observe it being given to someone else. If one child is praised for completing a task, both that child and the observers learn that completing tasks is a behavior that will be rewarded. Likewise, negative reinforcement identifies behav-ior to be avoided.

Children observe a wide variety of models and use these, along with their per-ceptions of the reinforcement given, to determine acceptable behaviors for them-selves. Sometimes they will make mistakes from an adult's perspective. Kelly knew from kindergarten that at snack time each child received an equal share of the food. She listened at home as her parents planned a dinner party, estimating the number of hors d'oeuvres needed for the guests. On the evening of the party, Kelly greeted the guests by explaining, "You each get five shrimp, three little sandwiches, and three meatballs." From her perception, that was acceptable behavior. The reaction of her parents, a look of distress, and that of the guests, amused laughter, indicated to Kelly that the behavior in a kindergarten setting was not appropriate in this setting. Much social learning involves determining when and where behaviors are likely to be condoned, as well as learning the behaviors themselves.

Children are influenced by observing adults interacting with other people of varying ethnic and national backgrounds. Parents and other significant adults who either denigrate those who differ from themselves or totally avoid them contribute to children's distrust of people of different races, religions, or nationalities. Parents and adults who model that they appreciate and value diversity contribute to a more open attitude among children. Including literature that supports a multicultural curriculum can help children see similarities as well as differences among people.

Many behaviors are culturally defined. Children are reared in a cultural context that shows them most aspects of social relationships, and they may take these unwritten rules for granted. They learn when it is appropriate to touch, when not; if one looks directly at an authority figure or keeps one's eyes downcast; whether one competes or cooperates. Then, when they encounter others whose expectations and constraints are different from their own, they may be shocked and uncomfortable. Although teachers and child-care providers cannot know the norms and expectations of all the cultures represented in their group of children, they can work toward understanding and respect for differing backgrounds and model this for children. Katz writes that

> It is likely that teachers who understand and appreciate their own culture and the cultures of others can better help children bridge cultural differences. It is also likely that these teachers will be able to practice and facilitate a broader range of social skills than will teachers who rely solely on their own cultural background.
>
> *(Katz & McClellan, 1997, p. 55)*

Knowledge of children's social development results from both experimental studies and from simply observing children. Observational studies at the Bank Street College of Education have found that toddlers who were together on a consistent basis appeared to learn social skills of interaction earlier than those without that experience (Oppenheim, 1984).

Friendships are important for children for several reasons. First, they provide opportunities for children to learn and practice social skills. Adults will often interpret a child's unclear request or stop conflict the minute it begins; but children engage with one another as equals, which requires that communication be clear to be effective and that techniques of handling conflicts or making requests be learned. Second, friendships give children a context in which they can compare themselves with others. Who is the taller of the two? Who can run faster? This sort of social comparison helps children develop a valid sense of their own identity. Finally, friendships foster a feeling of group belonging, a security that differs from that achieved within the family. However, friendships may have undesirable as well as desirable effects. They may be the cause of jealousy, rejection of others, or antisocial behavior as well as security, self-acceptance, and trust. In writing about children's friendships, Rubin states, "The fact of the matter is that children's closest friendships manifest all of the prominent features of close relationships among adults, including their destructive as well as their constructive elements. Perhaps the biggest difference between children's and adults' interactions is that children tend to be more straight-forward" (Rubin, 1984, p. 11).

Friendships are not the same as popularity. A person can get along with others and have status in a peer group yet not be able to form caring and reciprocal relationships with a few peers. Katz and McClellan note that both aspects of social competence are important, but that "The capacity for friendship most likely has greater significance for long-term development than does popularity" (1997, p. 2).

As children mature, their concept of friendship changes. The 3-year-old is likely to describe a friend in terms of physical attributes. He or she may say, for example, "Carlos is the same size as me." Children at this age often consider those who are playing with them at the moment to be their friends. Two to 3 years later, the description of a friend will include observations about behaviors and physical features, such as "Carlos wears a red coat. He can make people laugh whenever he wants." Friendship is determined by what that person does for the child and is generally tied to specific episodes. By age 8 or 9, children describe the traits they like or dislike and are beginning to see friendship as a relationship that lasts over time. At this stage, a child might say, "Carlos is my friend because we like each other, and he will help me even when he's busy. He's my friend even when he's away visiting his grandmother." Thus the shift is from viewing people as physical entities to seeing them as both physical entities and psychological beings as well and from thinking of friendship as a momentary encounter to seeing it as a lasting relationship.

It is likely that children develop part of their concept of friendship from observing adult friendships. It appears, however, that the major portion of their understanding comes from their own encounters with others and the way they integrate what they have learned. Thus children need to have the experience of working with each other in both large and small groups. Adults must recognize, though, that children vary in their social needs and social styles and must respect these differences.

Moral Development

Moral as well as social development is related to intellectual development. Jean Piaget and Lawrence Kohlberg saw the growth of moral reasoning as developing in stages that coincide with stages of cognitive growth. Piaget (1955) describes two broad stages of moral development. In the first, children have difficulty seeing situations from another's point of view and perceive acts as either totally right or totally wrong. They tend to judge an act on the basis of consequences and not on intention. The child who broke the cookie jar into many pieces trying to dry it is guiltier than the child who only cracked the jar while trying to sneak a cookie. They follow rules set down by adults, not because of a belief in the need for a particular rule, but because the adult who gave it wields authority.

In the second stage, children are more likely to be able to see another's point of view. They are less absolute in their judgments and will assess acts more by intentions than by consequences. They also begin to favor less punishment for wrongdoers. Piaget sees this shift in stages as occurring when the child is around 8 or 9 years old.

Kohlberg (1981) based his studies on Piaget's model of moral development. He describes a total of six stages of development, each keyed to the individual's sense of justice and to the reasoning used to solve moral dilemmas. Children ages 4 to 10 reason at the first two stages, at the *preconventional* level. In stage 1, punishment and obedience orientation, they obey rules in order to avoid punishment. In stage 2, instrumental purpose and exchange, they conform to rules out of self-interest and do things for others in order to get things in return. As they mature, they pass through further stages. Stage 3 is one of doing what "good boys" or "good girls" do, and stage 4 one of respecting the laws as a way of maintaining society. In the last two stages, personally developed moral principles take precedence over concern with authority. Kohlberg believes that most Americans operate at about stage 4.

Children develop their ability in moral reasoning through consideration of moral problems and through contact with the moral reasoning of others. Reasoning just one stage above their own is more meaningful to them than reasoning that is several stages higher. The stage at which children, as well as adults, reason about moral questions is not always a predictor of their actual behavior in a situation involving a moral question.

Kohlberg based his work entirely on the reactions of males. Carol Gilligan (1993), studying the responses of women, found that they based their reasoning on moral dilemmas, on being considerate of others, and on maintaining relationships. They were cognizant of how their actions might affect others. Gilligan notes that women are socialized to consider the effects of their actions on others more than to follow personal principles.

Social learning theorists emphasize the importance of models of moral behavior and the use of rewards and punishment in children's moral development. Children who have internalized the standards of their parents may feel guilty when they do not comply with the standards, even if the parent is not in a position to punish them. The theorists also note that children's responses to moral questions can be changed by their listening to or observing a model that holds the opposite opinion. After being given directions for one set of behaviors and then observing other behaviors being modeled, children are likely to imitate the model. "Do as I say and not as I do" is often ignored.

Although the theories of moral reasoning and social learning have different key elements, they are not contradictory when applied to young children. Children reasoning at Kohlberg's stage 1, that of behaving in a particular way to avoid punishment, will be greatly influenced by rewards and punishments as well as by the behavior they see modeled and the consequences it brings.

But theories are useful in guiding young children's moral development. Piaget and Kohlberg illustrate the need for children to discuss the reasons behind moral decisions and help teachers understand the kinds of reasoning common among young children. Social learning theories remind teachers of the importance of the models of behavior they present, both through their own actions and through vicarious sources introduced into children's learning environments.

GOALS FOR TEACHING

Once again, the goals for teaching can be classified as long-term developmental goals, general goals for a particular age or grade level, and specific goals for individual children. A long-term goal for social and moral development is that children will become sensitive to the feelings and intentions of others. This ability to empathize with others and understand their motivations will help children interact successfully with both peers and adults. Teachers and child-care professionals will be helping children achieve this goal throughout the toddler, preschool, and primary years.

A general social goal for toddlers and preschoolers is that, in a small group, each child will tell about an experience or perhaps share an object and will listen to others tell about their experiences. The children are learning the social skills of taking turns and of listening to others as well as developing their own speaking skills. The amount of waiting time in relation to the amount of action time is kept low by limiting the number of children in the group.

A general social goal for primary grade is that children will work in small groups on specific tasks for 10 to 15 minutes without the teacher's immediate presence and will make progress toward completing the task. It is expected that by the end of the year, nearly all the children in each of these levels will have achieved the general goals set for them.

In addition, there will be goals for individual children that teachers develop as they come to know their classes. A social goal for a third-grader could be that Peter will volunteer to help Robin and Chris with their reading. The teacher knows that Peter is capable of the task but wants him to recognize both his own competence and the needs of others and then engage in prosocial behavior.

Literature can contribute to the achievement of all three types of goals. This chapter focuses on long-term developmental goals. Books offer opportunities for you to help children grow toward the following goals for social and moral development.

Children will make inferences about the feelings and intentions of others.

Children will view a situation from more than one perspective, seeing the viewpoint of another person.

Children will engage in prosocial behavior.

Children will judge the appropriateness of specific behaviors and predict the possible consequences of particular behaviors.

Children will learn about others who differ from themselves and value this diversity.

Children will engage competently in group activities.

Children will evaluate various solutions to moral problems and ethical questions.

As with other areas, these goals can be correlated with national and regional standards. For example, the goal that children will learn about others who differ from themselves and value this diversity fits with Theme 1, Culture, in the 10 themes that provide the organizational framework for the social studies standards developed by the National Council for the Social Studies (1997). That standard states, "Social studies programs should include experiences that provide for the study of culture and cultural diversity" (p. 21). As you look at national standards or those for your region or school district, look for ways in which these goals and the specific standards mesh.

OPPORTUNITIES BOOKS OFFER

Giving Children Experience in Making Inferences About the Feelings and Intentions of Others

Books provide a rich source of data from which children can begin to gain information, make inferences, and check the validity of inferences they make. As stories unfold, characters reveal more and more of their feelings and more and more of their reasons for acting as they do. Children can make hypotheses at several points in a story and, as the story progresses, see if their hypotheses were accurate. The situation is nonthreatening—there is no penalty if their predictions are not what actually happen in the story. Children simply explore whether there was ample evidence to support their guesses or whether they missed some important clues to the feelings of the characters.

Interpreting Nonverbal Language in Illustrations   The illustrations in books give children experience in reading and interpreting body language and facial expressions. Because these illustrations are static, catching a moment in time, they give children a chance to study them and talk about specific aspects. In *The Baby Goes Beep* (O'Connell, 2003) the brightly colored pictures depict a baby excitedly exploring the world around him. The illustrations in *Roller Coaster* (Frazee, 2003) capture the anticipation and excitement of a line of people waiting to ride one of the most popular amusement park attractions. One of those individuals just happens to be riding the roller coaster for the very first time because now she is just tall enough to do so. The faces of the diverse crowd waiting in line are quite expressive as they casually chat with each other. As they near the front of the line, a few folks opt not to get into the cars that are ready to roll. Once the roller coaster jerks forward, the thrill begins with a whoosh, zip, zoom, dips, and dives. The varied facial expressions show those who are happy, terrified, or dizzy. Although Frazee doesn't address any character directly as to how he or she feels about the ride, it is evident from the illustrations whether each one is enjoying it or not.

Wordless picture books are an excellent source of material in which body language and facial expressions are emphasized. From the saucerlike fish eye that stares from the center of the book jacket to the varied faces that appear in color and sepia-toned photographs, *Flotsam* (Wiesner, 2006), the 2007 Caldecott Medal winner, conveys a sense of wonder and excitement through the expressions of both boy and ocean life. After finding a barnacle-crusted camera that has washed up on the beach, a young boy discovers that he isn't the first person to have held the Melville. Once he develops the film, the photographs depict both a surreal undersea world as well as a portrait of a girl, holding a picture of a boy, holding a picture of another boy . . . and so on . . . and so on. The variety of emotions—as well as the changes in emotions—provides much material for drawing inferences. Children can tell the story in their own words, perhaps by one recalling just what happened and the next suggesting how the characters feel. Although *Flotsam* focuses primarily on the emotions of the boy, books with one or multiple characters may entice children to take the parts of the characters and speak in appropriate dialogue. It is useful to give children a card with the name or the picture of their character on it. This avoids confusion about who has which part, and if you want to have different children play the parts, you can help them remember by simply changing the cards. It eliminates arguments about who is to do what.

Wordless picture books vary in difficulty, just as other picture books do. *Flotsam* is more appropriate for children in the primary grades or higher. For kindergarten and younger children, look for books with fairly simple plots in which the action is straightforward. A book such as *Picnic* (McCully, 2003) is appropriate for toddlers and preschoolers because the plot is uncomplicated and easy to follow. The book shows a family of mice heading out for a picnic. As their red truck bounces along the dirt road, one of the nine mouse children falls from the back and is left behind. The pictures then alternately show the lost mouse and the rest of the family. When the family discovers that someone is missing, they begin calling for her; then all get back in the truck and head toward home, searching along the way. The lost mouse hears the truck, runs out to the road, and all are reunited. Before they can continue, however, the rescued one must retrieve her doll, also a mouse, which she had dropped in the excitement of hearing her family returning. Together again, they can at last settle down for the picnic lunch.

Books with text may have illustrations that are as explicit concerning the characters' actions and feelings as those in wordless picture books, but the listeners, or watchers, do not have to make the interpretations themselves. Children can still be given the opportunity to discuss the illustrations. They may be asked to tell what they can about a character from the early illustrations. The book jacket for *Hooway for Wodney Wat* (Lester, 1999) shows the young rodent named Rodney looking very stiff and fearful. On the dedication page, Rodney is not present, but a very large female rat appears to be in charge, and the smaller rats behind her are being knocked down by her elbows. Children can be shown these two pictures before the reading begins and asked to say how they think Rodney and the other rats feel. They should be encouraged to give reasons for their judgments. Then the story can be shared. Rodney Rat cannot pronounce his *r*'s, and his classmates make fun of him. When Rodney is chosen to lead Simon Says, he fears the worst. However, the bully's inability to understand Rodney when he speaks results in her leaving the game and heading west. After the children have heard the story, let them look again at some of the illustrations. Ask the children to tell how Rodney and the other rats feel in selected pictures and how they know. Have the children sit or walk like one of the characters or show with their bodies and faces what the characters were feeling.

In some instances, you may want to ask the children to interpret some of the illustrations and to make predictions about what may happen next as you read a story. At other times, you may want to complete an entire story before engaging the children in any discussion. You can decide how to approach the story and the discussion by remembering that enjoyment and understanding of the story are the central purposes for your reading. If interrupting the narrative would destroy the story, wait until it is completed before talking about illustrations. But if the children seem confused or if discussion throughout the story heightens interest for them, then go ahead with discussions at various points in your reading.

Look for illustrators who are particularly adept at showing facial expressions and body language. Floyd Cooper, Kadir Nelson, Ted Lewin, Pat Cummings, Stephen Gammell, Helen Lester, Jane Dyer, and Chris Soentpiet are just a few whose work almost always captures easily recognizable emotions in physical expressions.

Relating Voice Inflection to Meaning   Children can gain experience in relating voice inflection to meaning and to the feelings of the speaker. The facets of language that linguists call *suprasegmentals* add meaning to speech. These are *pitch,* the high and low tones; *stress,* the emphasis with which a particular word or syllable is said; and *juncture,* the pause between syllables, words, or sentences. Variations in these tell the listener whether the sentence is a question or a statement; whether the phrase is ice cream or I scream; whether the speaker is being sincere or sarcastic.

Children do not need to know the terms or even know how to isolate pitch, stress, and juncture. They do need to hear expressive speech so that they can begin making generalizations for themselves about the speaker's meaning. You can provide many examples through your skillful reading. When Rodney Rat becomes the lead of Simon Says, he tells his classmates to "Wap your paws awound your head." When he looks at the bully to see if she is following his directions, he saw "WHAP! WHAP! WHAPPITY SLAPPITY WAP!" Camilla was whapping her paws around her head so hard she became dizzy . . . and had to sit down." (Lester, n. p.) The font of the text assists the teacher in understanding that those words should be read with expression.

Children can use expression themselves in interpreting the dialogue in *Yo! Yes?* (Raschka, 1993). A more extroverted boy makes friends with a shy youngster, with the entire story told through one- or two-word utterances from each and the illustrations showing the attendant emotions. The text is large enough for a group of children to see as a teacher holds the book. Children can read the dialogue, adding the expression in their voice so that the full meaning of the exchanges is conveyed.

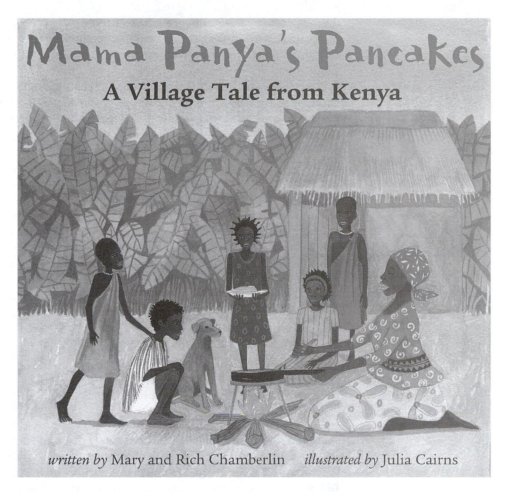

This clever and heartwarming story about Kenyan village life teaches the importance of sharing, even when you have little to give.
(Illustration Copyright © by Julia Cairns. Reprinted with permission from Barefoot Books.)

Going Beyond a Literal Interpretation of Dialogue   Children can be given the opportunity to analyze when dialogue can be accepted at face value and when a meaning other than a literal interpretation of the words is intended. Preschool children can recognize the hidden agenda in Frances's suggestion that perhaps a whole candy bar would be too much for her little sister Gloria to eat in *A Birthday for Frances* (Hoban, 1995). Frances has already put two of the bubble gum balls intended for Gloria into her own mouth without "noticing."

Primary children will comprehend the subtle nuances of the language used by Adika and his mother in *Mama Panya's Pancakes* (Chamberlin, 2005). Mother and son are going to the market to purchase the items needed to make pancakes. When asked how many pancakes she will make, Mama replies, "A little bit and a little bit more." Mama has only a few coins and becomes worried when Adika invites everyone he sees to the pancake dinner. Both appear to be interpreting "a little bit and a little bit more" in different ways. Will there be enough food for all the guests? But there is no reason for concern when everyone arrives, bringing food to accompany the pancakes. This story, set in Kenya, is reminiscent of Stone Soup. The end matter contains a recipe for spicy pancakes, a map, and information about local animals and village life.

Both Lola and Charlie use persuasive language on a trip to the library. In *But Excuse Me That is My Book* (Child, 2005), Lola goes in search of her favorite book, *Beetles, Bugs, and Butterflies,* and is dismayed when she cannot find it. Older brother Charlie tries to distract her by touting other titles, but Lola wants only her beloved book. Charlie tries to explain to Lola that it isn't really *her* book because it belongs to the library, but she still isn't dissuaded. When another girl walks by carrying the sought-after title, Lola reluctantly agrees to try *Cheetahs and Chimpanzees* instead. Ultimately, she proclaims that it is the "most best book in the whole wide world." Author Lauren Child does an excellent job in capturing the way young children think and act. Lola hasn't quite grasped the concept of borrowing. Both children are very persuasive as to what they want and believe—for Lola, it's her book, and for Charlie, it isn't. Children can discuss the arguments made by both characters and the purposes of persuasive language.

No character uses persuasive language more than the short-tempered Pigeon in Mo Willems's delightful picture books. Whether the pigeon is attempting to drive a bus even though the driver has emphatically stated *Don't Let the Pigeon Drive the Bus* (2003), or having the tables turned on him by a wide-eyed duckling in *The Pigeon Finds a Hot Dog!* (2004), or declaring that he is not tired and does not need to go to bed in *Don't Let the Pigeon Stay Up Late* (2006), preschoolers and primary-grade children alike find much to discuss about the protagonists emotional dilemmas.

Following a Sequence of Action   The meaning behind some dialogue is related to an entire sequence of action. Only if the readers know what has happened earlier are they able to interpret the statements of various characters accurately. In *Could Be Worse!* (Stevenson, 1977), Grandpa relates a dream at the breakfast table. He was pulled out of bed by a large bird, had an encounter with an abominable snowman, was chased across the desert by a huge blob of marmalade, met up with a squid and a giant sea turtle, and finally returned to his bed by getting a ride on a piece of toast and an airplane made out of newspaper. The readers know that Grandpa has not lost his mind but is reacting to his grandchildren's comments about him that he had overheard. They think the reason he never says anything interesting is because nothing interesting ever happens to him. Readers who have heard Grandpa respond to all the problems his grandchildren have by saying "Could be worse" are ready and waiting for the response that Grandpa gets when he asks the children what they think of his adventure: "Could be worse!"

Children who have a messy sibling or are a bit messy themselves will relate to Sophie as the *Super-Completely and Totally the Messiest* (Viorst, 2001). There's nobody in the world as messy as Sophie. It's hard to find Sophie in her bedroom because everything is spilling out of the drawers and closet, and the floor and the bed are completely covered with stuff. Even when Sophie is at school or at the beach, she creates a mess. Sophie will never be as neat and tidy as her sister Olivia. But Sophie is kind and smart and definitely her own person, despite being messy.

Bear finds a small empty box and decides that it would be the "greatest thing ever!" for his friend, Mouse. Along the way, Bear meets Monkey, Owl, Fox, Elephant,

Squirrel, and Rabbit, but no one seems to appreciate the box that he has found. Bear begins to doubt whether the box is so great after all. After Mouse explores the box inside and out, he pronounces it the "greatest thing ever!" and curls up inside for a nap. *Thank You, Bear* (Foley, 2007) uses minimal text and simple line and watercolor illustrations, making it a delightful book for toddlers and preschoolers as well as primary-grade children, who will each find something to enjoy about the story.

Following the sequence of action is as helpful for making inferences about characters' feelings and intentions as it is for fully understanding dialogue. Young children develop an understanding of action and reaction in human relationships when they see an entire drama played out in book form.

Observing Patterns of Behavior Some youngsters, like Holly (mentioned earlier), are just beginning to learn that their actions influence the actions of others. It was a new thought that Ralph may have chased her because she had been running herself. Other children, like 6-year-old Rob, have learned how to control the behavior of others in certain situations. "Want to see my mommy get mad?" he asked his uncle and cousins, who were visiting. Before they could answer, he opened a gate to the kitchen and put the cat in where his mother was working. Within seconds the angry words of his mother could be heard. "How did the cat get in here! I told you to keep the gate closed." Rob just grinned.

Children vary in their comprehension of the total situation in which action occurs. To help them see specific behaviors in a broader context, share books in which the action–reaction pattern is fairly clear, and use these books as the basis for dramatization. One such book is *The Quarreling Book* (Zolotow, 1968). When the book opens, Mr. James has just left the house on a rainy morning and has forgotten to kiss his wife good-bye. She is then upset and becomes critical of Jonathan when he comes down for breakfast. He thinks her criticism unfair and so, when Sally appears, he asks why she cannot ever be on time. The pattern continues, with each character having his or her mood spoiled, becoming irritable, and managing to ruin someone else's day in turn. The chain is broken when Eddie shoves his dog off the bed but is licked into better humor by the dog, who has interpreted the action as an invitation to play. Once Eddie feels better, he reacts to his sister's search for her pencil by giving her his best one. The pattern then reverses, with each character cheering another and apologizing for earlier actions. By 5 o'clock the sun has come out, and all is complete when Mr. James returns home and kisses his wife hello.

If children are linked in the order in which the characters appear, they can dramatize this story fairly easily. Each knows that first someone will say something sharp or unkind to them and that, feeling angry, they will then do the same thing to someone else. When the pattern is reversed, the action moves back up the line.

Another story that lends itself to dramatization is *Lilly's Purple Plastic Purse* (Henkes, 1996). Lilly loves everything about school, especially her teacher, Mr. Slinger. One day, Lilly can't wait to show the class her three jingly quarters, her movie-star glasses, and her purple plastic purse "that played a jaunty tune." But when Lilly repeatedly interrupts Mr. Slinger's lessons on types of cheese and words that rhyme with mice, the teacher must resort to confiscating the items. In retaliation, Lilly decides to make a drawing of the "Big Fat Mean Mr. Stealing Teacher." When she discovers a kind note written by Mr. Slinger in her book bag, she feels remorse and wants to find a way to make things right. The actions of Lilly and the reaction of Mr. Slinger are something that children can relate to. They can dramatize the story to assist them in understanding how one person's behavior affected another's.

Character Perspective Chart

Character 1	Character 2
Setting: Where and when does the story take place?	**Setting:** When and where does the story take place?
Problem: What is the character's problem?	**Problem:** What is the character's problem?
Objective: What does the character want?	**Objective:** What does the character want?
Action: What does the character do to solve the problem?	**Action:** What does the character do to solve the problem?
Outcome: What happened as a result of the character's action(s)?	**Outcome:** What happened as a result of the character's action(s)?
Reaction: How does the character feel about the the outcome?	**Reaction:** How does the character feel about outcome?

Chart adapted from Shanahan, Timothy, & Shanahan, Sherrell. (1997). *The Reading Teacher, 50*(8), p. 670.

Empathizing with a Book Character   As children learn to "read" another's feelings, they also become more sensitive to those feelings. You can ask them to empathize with a character by having them think about how they would feel if something similar happened to them. They might each tell about a pet they have (or have had) prior to your reading *Let's Get a Pup! Said Kate* (Graham, 2001). Kate's cat has died, and the family has decided to adopt a new puppy. They find a frisky little pup at the Animal Rescue that is just perfect. However, as they are leaving, they spy an older, sweet-natured dog that tugs at their heart. Kate's parents don't feel they have room for two dogs, but after a sleepless night for the family, they return to the shelter for the other dog. Children who have described their own pets can tell about how they would feel if their pet died or if they adopted a new pet. Others who do not have pets might tell how they would feel if they lost one of their favorite toys. From "How would *you* feel if . . ." to "How do you think Kate felt when . . ." is a transformation from a question that is centered on the child to a question that is centered on the book character, but both ask the child to imagine feelings.

For some discussions, you may want to return to several different places in a book and ask children how they think the character may have been feeling at that time and why they think so. Depending on the story, you may want to do this as you read. For example, if you were sharing *How Smudge Came* (Gregory, 2002), you might first ask how Cindy, a young woman with Down's syndrome, is feeling when she sneaks the puppy she has found past Mrs. Watson and up to her room or as she shows her puppy to one of the patients at Hospice House, where she works. Other points to stop might be when the dog is sent to the SPCA, when Cindy gets help in locating the SPCA from the patients at the hospice, when she goes after the puppy but finds it has been given away, or when she goes to Hospice House and finds that they have retrieved the puppy for her and that she can keep it there.

One step further in the process of identifying and empathizing with a character is for children to be asked to tell about times when they have felt the way they think the character feels. Thus children who have heard *How Smudge Came* might tell about times they have not been allowed to keep something they wanted, have been disappointed, or have had other people be very caring and helpful to them. The emotional contact can help children relate to a person who may be very different from themselves and to gain an appreciation of others. Cindy is a real person with real feelings, real capabilities, and real friends who care about her—not just a person with a disability.

Child-care professionals sometimes encourage self-reporting by young children by supplying incidents that they have observed. Thus the adult might say, "Remember how you felt when you showed your new kitten during sharing time?" as they discuss Cindy's showing the puppy to Jan at Hospice House. Both techniques help children make a connection with another person and increase their awareness of others' feelings.

You might also share literature in which one character shows empathy for another. In *Let's Get a Pup! Said Kate*, the family feels sorry for the older dog, which probably won't be adopted. In *How Smudge Came,* the hospice patients and doctor recognize Cindy's love for Smudge and find a way to both get the puppy back and for Cindy to keep it.

Children can be given the opportunity to empathize with a book character and to see characters within literature empathizing with one another.

Fostering Children's Ability to See from the Viewpoint of Others

When children decenter, that is, recognize that not everyone thinks as they do, they are ready to see from the viewpoint of another. The books and activities that help give children experience in recognizing how others feel provide a base for developing skill in taking various perspectives. Children can talk first about how the character may have felt or how they would have felt under the same circumstances and then begin to take the role of a character: reacting as that character would, telling what that character thinks, and doing what they think that character would do in a new situation.

Sharing Books That Present Several Viewpoints   You can help children recognize different viewpoints by reading to them several books in which different points of view are clearly illustrated. One such book, *The Pain and the Great One* (Blume, 1984), is written in two parts. In one part, a boy of 6 describes life with The Great One, his older sister. In the other part, the sister describes life with her younger brother, The Pain. The same feelings of jealousy are described by both, and the reader sees several incidents told from two different viewpoints.

Children should be familiar with the traditional tale of *The Three Pigs* in order to understand the humor of the story and the different perspective provided by the wolf in *The True Story of the Three Little Pigs* (Scieszka, 1989). The wolf claims that he was only trying to borrow a cup of sugar from his neighbor, the pig, when he sneezed and unfortunately blew the house down. The Big Bad Wolf claims that it was all a misunderstanding and that he is now trying to set the record straight. Children might think about the perspective of other fairy tale characters, such as the stepsisters in *Cinderella* or the grandmother in *Little Red Riding Hood,* and discuss or write about how those characters might have felt or responded.

An example of a book with an omniscient narrator is *The Sweetest Fig* (Van Allsburg, 1993). Bibot is a dentist who is harsh with both his dog and his patients. He doesn't allow the dog to bark at all, and when an old lady, in lieu of a monetary payment, gives him two figs that she says will make his dreams come true, he withholds

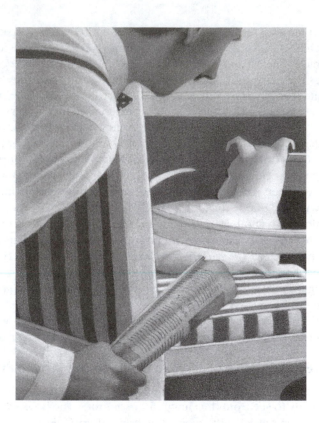

Bibot prepares to teach his dog Marcel to stay off the furniture. (Illustration from *The Sweetest Fig* by Chris Van Allsburg. Copyright © by Chris Van Allsburg. Reprinted by permission of Houghton Mifflin Company. All rights reserved.)

her pain pills. He eats one of the figs, and only when he finds himself in front of a cafe in his underwear and sees the Eiffel Tower drooping, does he recall that this is exactly the dream he had the night before. He vows to make the second fig bring him the dreams he wants. Having prepared himself through self-hypnosis, he places the fig on a dish, but when he turns his back, his dog eats it. He goes to bed angry, awakening in the morning to find himself in his dog's place underneath the bed and facing his own image, an image that reaches down and pulls him out for his morning walk.

Children might list all the specific things Bibot might wish for in his desire to be the richest man in the world and the things the dog would see as useful in changing places with its master. They could role-play the two characters, telling each other why they acted as they did.

Observing Book Characters Whose Perspective Is Limited   In some books, one character's lack of understanding of the viewpoint of another is central to the story. In *The Happy Lion* (Fatio, 1954), the lion does not understand why all the people who greeted him so pleasantly when he was at the zoo run from him as he wanders down the street. After all, on all previous occasions on which they met, the people were polite and friendly.

The fish in *Fish Is Fish* (Lionni, 1970) cannot imagine the land creatures that his friend the frog describes to him. He sees everything as a sort of fish mutation: birds become fish with many-colored wings, two legs, and fins, and cows are fish with udders, horns, four legs, and fins.

The illustrations and the text in Van Allsburg's *Two Bad Ants* (1988) are from an ant's perspective. The ants go through the "woods" (grass) and climb the face of a "mountain" (the bricks on the side of a house). When the other ants take one of the marvelous crystals and head for home, the two bad ants eat until they fall asleep in the sugar bowl. They are awakened in the morning when a "giant silver scoop" lifts them into the air and drops them into a "boiling brown lake." Once children catch on to the point of view, you could read the text before showing the illustrations and let the children guess what the ants are seeing or where they are.

Children could take on the limited perspective of any of these characters, drawing cars, buildings, or various animals as they might appear to the fish, or drawing and describing how a place within the classroom might appear to the ants. After hearing *The Happy Lion,* they could dictate what the lion would write if he kept a diary. In each case, the children develop a broader perspective than the one they have been taking.

Taking the Viewpoint of Another   Children can be asked to take the viewpoint of someone who is far different from themselves if the literature gives some point of contact or if you as the teacher can establish this contact. Young children can imagine what it is like to be much older than they are. They can share with each other what their grandmothers and grandfathers like and dislike or how they behave. They can listen to stories such as *The Piano Man* (Chocolate, 1998), in which a young African American girl describes her grandfather's life as a piano player, first for silent movies, then on Broadway, on to vaudeville, and finally working as a piano tuner. For his 75th birthday, his daughter buys him the old piano that had been stored in the theatre where he played. Now he turns the sound down on the television and accompanies old movies, remembering his days in the silent movie theatres.

One second-grader who had heard this story wrote his own story about his grandfather:

> I know why my grandfather paints. It is because he is old. He paints what he remembers.

Knowing that memories are important to many older people is one step in understanding a different perspective.

Engaging in Role-Play and Puppetry   Children can enjoy and benefit from taking the perspective of first one character and then another. Children who have listened to *Best Best Friends* (Chodos-Irvine, 2006) could dramatize parts of the story when Clare becomes resentful because Mary receives all the attention on her birthday. One child can role-play being Clare and the other Mary; then they can dramatize it again with the roles reversed. In the story, the two girls are friends, who hug when they meet, hold hands while going out to the playground, and sit next to each other during storytime. When jealousy consumes Clare, her bitter outburst, "You are not my friend," results in hurt feelings. But the two girls are able to resolve their problem and become friends once again—without adult intervention. Children could work in pairs, with several pairs dramatizing simultaneously. They could create situations of their own in which one has a new toy and the other comes to play with it. They might conclude by discussing how they felt in each role and times when they have played those roles in real life.

Try using puppets or masks to stimulate children to take different roles. As they change puppets, they change characters. They must switch from one outlook to another, from one set of characteristics to another. You will also see whether children are able to decenter as you listen to their use of puppets. Some may never take the character's role but will only hold the puppet and say what they think. Others may begin as a different character but midway revert to their own outlook, unable to sustain another perspective. This gives you valuable insight into the children's development.

As you plan your literature selections, and especially as you are developing language activities that extend the books, think about ways in which children can be given the opportunity to take the perspective of another person. Role-play and puppets provide natural situations for this to happen. You can also set up special activities. One child may be the book character and the others could be interviewers for a television station. The interviewers ask questions, and the child answers as the character would. What would Bibot say when asked about his dog or the piano man when asked about the role of music in his life?

Or suppose that the book character kept a scrapbook or a photo album. The children can make pages for the book or album and then describe what is in it and why it is important to them as that book character. They might dictate captions for items in the books. What would the lion save as mementos of his trip away from the zoo; or, given snapshots of his stroll through the main street of town, how would he label the reactions of various people upon seeing him? Give children the opportunity to share their books, explaining to classmates what they have included and why it is important.

Providing Models of Prosocial Behavior

Literature that portrays characters engaged in social behavior shows children not only a way of acting but also the ingredients necessary for prosocial behavior to occur. That is, the character is able to recognize that another needs help or that there is something that could be done for him or her, feels confident that he or she can provide that help, and sees the risk as not too great to get involved. When you share stories that include prosocial behavior, you might call attention to these aspects individually as well as looking at the action as a whole.

Reading Books That Demonstrate Prosocial Behavior   Suppose you read *Dumpster Diver* (Wong, 2007) to your class. This story has a different twist about recycling as neighbor Steve enlists a "diving team" of children to assist in finding buried treasure in the apartment dumpster. There are rules to dumpster diving, such as rule number one, "Keep Your Mouth Shut," or rule number two, which states that the person holding the hose must keep the water from going all over the place. A variety of items are made from the recovered lost treasures—a blender becomes a lava lamp or a pair of snow skis becomes a paraskater. When Steve gets hurt from collapsing garbage, the children decide to go door to door to collect useful junk and turn it into a wheelchair for the number-one dumpster diver. Children can talk about what the items they or their parents throw away and how they can recycle them by either turning them into something else or putting them in a proper recycling container. The assumption is that children are capable of getting involved in school and community efforts such as recycling.

After sharing and discussing one book on prosocial behavior, simply read another so that children view various models of such behavior. *Boxes for Katje* (Fleming, 2003) is based on an incident from author Candace Fleming's mother's life. Set during World War II, the people of Olst in Holland are having difficulty in getting necessities such as soap, socks, and warm clothing. When a box arrives from Rosie in Indiana, Katje is thrilled with the contents. She even shares the chocolate bar with her mother and the postman. After Katje writes a thank you note to her new friend in America, another box arrives bearing more gifts. This continues over several months, with the boxes becoming more plentiful in supplies and number. The towns-people in Olst are so thankful for the many gifts being sent to them that they find a way to reciprocate in a very special way. The idea that one person can make a difference is a strong theme from the book.

Manuela wants a new party dress for her birthday, even though times are hard, in *Manuela's Gift* (Estes, 1999). Manuela is very disappointed when she receives an old dress of her mother's. After Papa has hung a piñata and the preparations for the party are in place, Manuela realizes that she has much to celebrate, including the dress that was lovingly cut and stitched to fit her.

Toddlers and preschoolers will identify with Alfie's feelings in *Alfie Gives a Hand* (Hughes, 1987). He attends a backyard birthday party and has to adjust to a rather obstreperous host. He is timid and wants to cling to his blanket. When he must choose between the blanket and giving a comforting hand to another child, however, he is willing—and able—to release the blanket. Helping others may not always be easy, but it is within the capabilities of even the youngest.

Discussing Ways of Providing Help   Once you have read several books that have instances of prosocial behavior, have children tell or role-play what they could do in specific problem situations. Give them the setting and the problem:

> You are walking home by yourself and you see a little boy standing on the side-walk crying. He tells you he is lost. What would you do?

> On the playground a friend of yours tells you that she feels sick. She is holding her stomach. What would you do?

Planning Prosocial Behavior   Also consider grouping books that show social behavior so that children can make some generalizations. One grouping would be to read books in which a character becomes a bully. In *Hooway for Wodney Wat* (Lester, 1999) Camilla Capybera joins Rodney's class and intimidates 11 of the rodents. In *The Recess Queen* (O'Neill, 2002), Mean Jean is the biggest bully on the school playground until a new girl arrives and challenges Jean's status as the Recess Queen. In *Trouble in the Barkers' Class* (dePaola, 2003), the twins, Morgie and Moffie, are excited when a new girl joins their class, but Carole Anne doesn't smile and only causes trouble. After reading two or three of the books, have children think about someone who wasn't very nice to them. Then have them make a catalog of all the good things they could say and do for that person to help them be kinder to others. Have the children think of realistic actions. Another time, have them think about a time when they were not kind to another person. What could they have done differently then and now? By sharing books that provide realistic situations for children, it enables them to see them-selves and others in the story and generates discussion and problem-solving strategies.

Comparing Themes of Helping   Comparing themes could lead into talking about how it feels to help someone without being asked. Children can give examples of their own or refer back to *Boxes for Katje*. Another book to share is *Mrs. Katz and Tush* by Patricia Polacco (1992). Larnel visits Mrs. Katz, an elderly neighbor, with his mother and, seeing how lonely she is, the next day goes to visit on his own. He even talks her into taking a kitten found in the basement of the building. Over the course of many years, Mrs. Katz shares her Jewish heritage with Larnel and he grows to love her. It is a give-and-take relationship.

Children can identify this theme of helping one another by comparing books. A book with a similar theme but very different characters is *Amos & Boris* (Steig, 1971).

In this fantasy, Boris the whale befriends Amos the mouse when Amos falls off his boat. Years later, Boris is washed ashore, and it is Amos who gets two elephants to push him back into the ocean. The language of the book is so evocative that it is likely you will want to concentrate on this aspect of the book. However, asking, "How is this book like *Mrs. Katz and Tush*?" shows children that two very different books may express a common theme and focuses their attention on the idea of helping one another.

A book character is just one model among many to which children are exposed. Some books that you present will show behavior that you would not choose to have children emulate. Often the problem to be solved in the book results from the behavior of one of the characters, behavior that may not reflect values that you condone. However, you would not want to select only those books in which characters exhibit prosocial behavior. This would eliminate excellent literature that may portray humans in some of their very human but not-so-lovable thoughts and actions, and you would be exercising a kind of censorship, a screening of literature based on the values presented. Rather than eliminating these books, add them to the collection of books that show children engaged in prosocial behavior. Help children see that they, too, are capable of aiding others in given situations and that there are internal rewards for such behavior.

Encouraging Children to Judge the Appropriateness of Particular Behaviors

Learning when a behavior is appropriate requires generalizing about types of situations and types of behaviors. A social encounter is not likely to be repeated in exact form. Children can be helped to generalize about the appropriateness of behaviors by seeing many examples of both behaviors and their consequences. Some examples will come from direct observation or participation, but others will come from vicarious experiences such as literature.

Preschoolers and primary-grade children will enjoy reading the antics in *No, David!* (Shannon, 1998). David wreaks havoc in every room of the house. He reaches too far for the cookie jar, tracks in too much dirt, bangs too loudly, and plays with his food at dinner. The text consists mainly of "No, David" or variations of that statement. When a broken chair leads to a time-out and a tear running down his cheek, a motherly hug makes it clear that David is still loved. Because this is a semiautobiographical tale, children will be able to make connections to David's behavior.

Not all situations are as easily assessed, however. Children who hear a story and know the full context of a situation can be asked to make judgments about a character's behavior, noting the circumstances that may have influenced it and the punishment that may follow. In *17 Things I'm Not Allowed to Do Anymore* (Offill, 2006), an incorrigible little girl describes 17 things she is not allowed to do anymore, and children will understand why. Among her "great ideas" are stapling her brother's hair to his pillow (she's not allowed to use the stapler anymore), gluing his slippers to the floor (she's not allowed to use glue anymore), walking backward all the way to school, and dedicating her George Washington report "to all beavers that ever lived." Some of the things that she does are not funny and she is punished for them. She always says she's sorry, which often generates a hug from her mother. This book doesn't condone bad behavior but rather shows the effects and the consequences of thinking outside the box. It will surely provide fuel for discussion with children.

Children can describe what else she could have done and postulate consequences for each of the suggested behaviors. They might relate what their own parents' reaction would be if they behaved as the girl did. Ask questions that will focus children's attention on the relationship between the situation and the behavior. For *17 Things I'm Not Allowed to Do Anymore,* ask, "Do you think that she should have been punished for stapling her brother's hair to the pillow? What type of punishment would it be?"

As children become more accustomed to viewing single incidents within broader contexts and as they become more able to predict the reactions of others, they will be able to assess more accurately the sorts of behaviors that are most likely to be appropriate in any given situation.

Helping Children Learn About and Value Differences Among People

Basic to being open to others is feeling good about oneself. Thus many of the activities designed to enhance the self-concept of young children aid in their acceptance of others. As they explore what they can do, they see also what their classmates can do; as they tell what they like, they hear what their classmates like. Thus they are beginning to see the diversity within their own small group and to value both themselves and their friends. The differences add interest.

Selecting Literature That Values Diversity   Literature can focus attention on how individuals vary and emphasize the value of this variance. In *I Love Saturdays y Domingos* (Ada, 2002), a little girl tells about Saturdays spent with her Euro-American Grandma and Grandpa and Sundays (los domingos) with Abuelito and Abuelita, her Mexican American grandparents. She does different things in each place and goes to different places—the circus, the pier, floating balloons, flying kites. She also hears different stories told that reflect her grandparents' heritage. On the girl's birthday, both sets of grandparents unite in their love of their granddaughter. Spanish words are integrated into the text within a context that makes them easily understood by listeners or readers. Children can compare people they know, telling what is special about each. It may be grandmothers, but it could just as well be neighbors or friends. The discussion can be focused on what children like about each to emphasize positive feelings.

The theme of valuing others different from oneself or from the norm appears in literature at all levels. In *Ballerino Nate* (Bradley, 2006), Nate decides he wants to dance after attending a recital. However, his older brother tells him that boys can't be ballerinas. "They never, ever, ever can." Even though his parents tell him that he can, his big brother's words still haunt him. He also notices that he is the only boy in the ballet class. When he attends a performance by a professional ballet company, he meets one of the male dancers and his concerns disappear. He also decides that he should be called a "ballerino" because he is a boy. A good book to pair with this one is *Oliver Button Is a Sissy* (dePaola, 1979); Oliver is teased when he starts taking tap-dancing lessons and discovers that instead of being called a sissy, he is now called a star. Children might think about what makes their friends "stars," and what their special talents are. Some classrooms in the primary grades have graffiti walls or bulletin boards where youngsters can write messages. A wall such as this could be used to write positive comments about classmates, with the teacher providing several examples and making clear the nature of acceptable comments.

Read books to your students that reflect positive attitudes toward others. Preschool children listening to *Subway Sparrow* (Torres, 1993) see how a child speaking English, a man speaking Spanish, and a woman speaking Polish can work together to capture and then free a sparrow that has flown into a subway car. The book introduces the concept that people may speak different languages but that they are still able to get along with one another and work toward a common goal.

Focusing on Similarities   Share several books that picture a particular people, race, or religion so that one book does not become representative of that group in the minds of the children. You might look over your literature curriculum to see if you could be fostering any misconceptions. If, for instance, all the books you have selected that have African American characters are set in urban settings, you should add several books with African Americans whose settings are suburban or rural areas. You might also select books that have characters with whom children can empathize but that have foreign settings.

To avoid a "we-they" approach, focus on similarities and on individuals within groups rather than on the groups themselves. Thus you could assemble several books by themes or central ideas in which the protagonists represent several different backgrounds and group classifications. You could, for example, read several books that feature a child living in a temporary home. The American father and son in Eve Bunting's *Fly Away Home* (1991) are living in an airport until the father earns enough money for them to rent an apartment. Sami and his family in *Sami and the Time of the Troubles* (Heide & Gilliland, 1992) are living in the basement of his uncle's house in Beirut, emerging only when there is a break in the fighting and gunfire. The boy who describes his life in *The Roses in My Carpets* (Khan, 1998) is living in a refugee camp in Afghanistan.

In each book, the protagonist is a member of a group that could be studied for itself. By grouping the stories according to the circumstances and feelings of the characters, children see the human qualities that they share and that they themselves understand. This helps them to see the similarities among people who may differ from them in some ways but who share common emotions and needs.

Some books demonstrate similarities among cultures directly. *Now We Can Have a Wedding* (Cox, 1998) has neighbors from many different countries contributing to Sallie's wedding banquet, each preparing a dish that is special for weddings in their culture.

Reading Literature from Other Countries   Finally, share literature from other countries with children. Foreign folktales are especially plentiful. When you introduce one, tell the country where it originated. If you are going to read Demi's retelling of *One Grain of Rice* (1997), for example, you might begin by saying, "This story is titled *One Grain of Rice* and it is a tale that was first told in India." Young children have not yet developed clear concepts of distance nor the meaning of country, and learning where India is would add little to their literary experience. However, telling them that the story comes from another country introduces the idea that many countries have literature and that stories from many places can be enjoyed.

The same procedure can be used with books that were first published in another country. Tell children the title of the story and the name of the author, and then tell where the author lives or lived. For example, you might read *A Crash Course for Molly* (Eriksson, 2005) and explain to the children that the author lives in Sweden and has written this and another story about Molly, the piglet. As Molly learns to ride her bike, she is still having difficulty controlling it. As she rides through the park, Molly's grandmother tells her to "Watch out for the pole." Molly watches the pole and smacks right into it. There are other mishaps that follow, but eventually Molly gets the last laugh. This is a story that children can probably relate to based on their own expe-

*Child care centers and schools are natural places for children to develop
social skills.*

riences of learning how to ride a bike. *Horn Book Magazine* often provides a list of
recommended books that have been translated on their website, www.hbook.com.

Some foreign authors whose work is appropriate for young children are
Mitsumasa Anna, Nicola Bayley, Raymond Briggs, Anthony Browne, John Burningham,
Niki Daly, Mem Fox, Shirley Hughes, Pat Hutchins, Barbro Lindgren, Helen Oxenbury,
and Brian Wildsmith. Activities can be based on the literary content of the stories, but
also stress the idea that people of other countries write stories that American children enjoy.

Engaging Children in Group Activities   Children develop social skills only in a context
where they have the opportunity to practice them. Child-care centers, preschools, and
elementary schools are natural places for this to happen. As you plan the presentation
of literature and related activities, capitalize on the opportunities to help children be
a part of the group, such as in activities where all are working together, especially if an
attitude of cooperation permeates the endeavor. This activity may be simply listening
to a story, being quiet so others can hear, or laughing along with others at humorous
passages. It might be a group response to the literature: participating as the book is
read a second time, singing the words to the song illustrated as a picture book, engaging in choral speaking, or doing finger plays. Children enjoy activities such as these
more fully when each child feels secure in his or her own group membership.

As you plan ways of extending books, develop activities that require the children
to work together. For those preschoolers who are working side by side but not *with*
one another, suggest projects where they will need to share materials or space. They
could make a collage of mushroom shapes after hearing *Mushroom in the Rain*
(Ginsburg, 1999). The brightly colored mushrooms used in the book illustrations suggest to children the possibilities for various shapes, colors, and patterns. Paper, fabric,
yarn, foil, magazines, and other materials should be placed in a central location.
Children are grouped around the materials, thus encouraging conversation as they

work. They can comment about each other's work or perhaps tell others about their collages. They become engaged in social interaction because of the way the activity is structured. Other activities that promote the development of social skills are those that require some joint planning. Creative dramatics, puppetry, pantomiming, writing group stories, dancing with partners, and making murals all require children to participate and to listen to the ideas of others to be successful.

Recommended Folktales

Aylesworth, Jim. (1998). *The Gingerbread Man*. Ill. Barbara McClintock. New York: Scholastic. (England)

Brett, Jan. (2007). *The Three Snow Bears*. New York: Putnam. (Inuit)

Demi. (2000). *The Emperor's New Clothes: A Tale Set in China*. New York: McElderry. (China)

dePaola, Tomie. (1975). *Strega Nona*. Upper Saddle River, NJ: Prentice Hall. (Italy)

Farley, Carol. (1997). *Mr. Pak Buys a Story*. Ill. Benrei Huang. Chicago: Whitman. (Korea)

Ho, Minfong, and Ros, Saphan. (1997). *Brother Rabbit: A Cambodian Tale*. New York: Lothrop. (Cambodia)

Hogrogian, Nonny. (1988). *The Cat Who Loved to Sing*. New York: Knopf. (Armenia)

Johnson-Davies, Denys. (2005). *Goha: The Wise Fool*. Ill. Hag Hamdy Mohamed Fattou. New York: Philomel. (Middle East)

Oram, Hiawyn. (1998). *Baba Yaga and the Wise Doll: A Traditional Russian Folktale*. Ill. Ruth Brown. New York: Dutton. (Russia)

Zelinsky, Paul O. (1997). *Rapunzel*. New York: Dutton. (Germany)

Begin with small groups of only two or three children, and enlarge the groups as the children become more adept at handling the situation. Pairs of children could work together to create pictures showing some of Grandpa's adventures in *Could Be Worse!* (Stevenson, 1977). Those children who worked well in pairs could then be put in larger groups for other activities. Four could work together to create a mural showing how the fish in *Fish Is Fish* (Lionni, 1970) might imagine a highway filled with traffic. Vary group membership so that the children learn to cooperate with many different people and so that you can better assess the causes of any difficulty groups may experience. Try to structure the activities and the groups so that the children will not only gain practice in social interaction but also feel successful about their participation.

Stimulating Children to Explore Moral Problems and Ethical Questions

Whether you plan to or not, it is likely that you will read stories to children that represent various levels of moral reasoning on the part of the characters.

Presenting Examples of Moral Reasoning In some books, such as *Arnie and the Stolen Markers* (Carlson, 1987) the character reasons at Kohlberg's stage 1, the avoidance of punishment. Arnie wants markers that he sees in Harvey's Candy and Toy Shop, but he has already spent all his money. He steals the markers, but his mother finds them and makes him return them to the store. Harvey has Arnie work at the store for a week to earn what the markers cost and then gives them to him along with some paper. Arnie had felt guilty about taking the markers and had thought he might be sent to jail. His future behavior will be governed by his fear of punishment.

In *The Hungry Coat* (Demi, 2004) a folktale from Turkey, the character reasons at stage 2, where personal reward determines ethical decisions. Nasrettin Hoca is late arriving at a friend's banquet after helping to catch a villager's frisky goat and putting it back in its' pen. Nasarettin's coat is filthy and tattered, which leads to the host being embarrassed and the guests ignoring him. Nasrettin is not even served any food at the banquet. He quickly goes home, bathes and dresses in his finest clothes, and returns to his friend's house. Everyone greets him warmly and he is served food and drink. Nasrettin begins to stuff the food into his coat. When asked why, Nasrettin replied that everyone shunned him earlier, but when he returned wearing the coat, he realized that it was the coat that was invited to the banquet. This wry tale is an excellent example of moral reasoning at stage 2.

Moral reasoning at stage 3 is widely represented in the decisions that book characters make. At this stage, right is determined by what "good girls" or "good boys" do. For example, Nim in *Nim and the War Effort* (Lee, 1997) is sorry for her actions that have angered her grandfather, but explains that she was trying to bring honor to the family by winning the contest. Her decision was based on trying to be good—she just did not interpret "good" in the same manner as her grandfather.

Children grow in their ability to reason about moral questions as they hear the reasoning of others. In general, they understand the reasoning at their own stage, the stages below their own, and one stage above theirs. Hearing various stages of reasoning expressed by book characters and classmates expands their own reasoning powers and is instrumental in their movement from one stage to another.

Engaging Children in the Reasoning Process   With preschool children, a first step in engaging children in the reading process is to read stories in which characters are faced with a decision to be made and in which there is no clear-cut answer. Read half of the Caldecott Medal book, *Finders Keepers* (Lipkind & Mordvinoff, 1951), and ask the children who should get to keep the bone: Nap, the dog who saw it first, or Winkle, the dog who touched it first. As in many questions of justice, there is reasoning for more than one decision. What makes some ethical decisions so difficult is that the conflict is between two values, both of which seem to represent morality. Should people tell their friends the truth if the truth will be hurtful? Should people lie if in so doing they could save a friend's life? Even young children can be asked to suggest and defend a solution to a problem in which the right answer is debatable.

At other times, ask children to tell about instances when they act in accordance with the reasoning a book character is using. Are there things they would do if they weren't afraid of getting caught and being punished, for instance?

Read some books that present questions about behavior and ask students to decide which behavior they think is right and why. If you read the story about split pea soup in *George and Martha* (Marshall, 1972) you could discuss the theme of the story that friends should always tell each other the truth. Martha has made an enormous quantity of split pea soup, which she serves to George. He does not care for it but does not want to hurt her feelings. When he has eaten all he can, he pours what is left in his bowl into his loafer. Martha sees him from the kitchen and wants to know why he did not tell her that he did not like the soup. When he has explained his reason, Martha responds that friends should always tell each other the truth—and that he will not have to eat split pea soup again.

When Libby is caught in a lie to her mother, she decides that from now on she will only tell *The Honest-to-Goodness Truth* (McKissack, 2000). Libby tells about her friend Ruthie May's hole in her sock, the fact that Thomas didn't have lunch money and need to borrow some from the teacher, and how old Miz Tusselbury's yard looks like a jumble. By telling the truth, nobody wants to talk to Libby anymore. She asks her mother for advice, but only when Libby gets a taste of her own medicine does she understand the difference between telling the truth and being unkind.

Primary-grade children can write their opinions on slips of paper to answer the question of whether friends should *always* tell each other the truth. Have them share their responses and their reasons for agreeing or disagreeing with Martha's position that friends should always tell one another the truth. Ask the group to decide which reasons they think are the best. The emphasis is on the reasoning given, and there is no attempt to reach a consensus on a final yes or no to the question.

Looking at the Same Issue in Several Books   Children might look at a single moral question, such as honesty, through a comparison of several books. After reading *George and Martha,* read *A Bargain for Frances* (Hoban, 1970). When Frances sets out to visit Thelma, her mother tells her to be careful, reminding her that on previous occasions when she played with Thelma, she got the worst of things. Frances says it will be safe because they are just going to have a tea party. Once at Thelma's, Frances explains her plan to buy a new blue china tea set. Thelma convinces her that those sets are not made anymore and offers to sell her red plastic set to Frances. When the deal is completed, Thelma insists on "no backsies." After she returns home, Frances learns from her sister that blue china sets are still made, that they are in the stores, and that Thelma was shown one a day earlier in the candy store. Frances runs to the candy store in time to see Thelma buying a new blue tea set and returns home without being seen. After some thought, Frances puts a penny in the sugar bowl of the set she bought from Thelma and calls her.

> "Remember," said Thelma, "no backsies."
> "I remember," said Frances. "But are you sure you really want no backsies?"
> "Sure I'm sure," said Thelma.
> "You mean I never have to give back the tea set?" said Frances.
> "That's right," said Thelma. "You can keep the tea set."
> "Can I keep what is in the sugar bowl too?" said Frances.
> "What is in the sugar bowl?" said Thelma.
> "Never mind," said Frances. "No backsies. Good-bye."
> Frances hung up. Frances waited for the telephone to ring, and when it rang she said, "Hello."
> "Hello," said Thelma. "This is Thelma."
> "I know," said Frances.
> "I just remembered," said Thelma, "I think I had something in the sugar bowl. I think it was a ring. Did you find a ring?"
> "No," said Frances. "And I don't have to tell you what is in the sugar bowl because you said no backsies."
> "Well," said Thelma, "I just remembered that I put some money in the sugar bowl one time, I think it was some birthday money. I think it was two dollars, or may be it was five dollars. Did you find money?"
> "You said no backsies," said Frances. "So I don't have to tell you. I don't have to say how much money is in the sugar bowl."   *(pp. 41–47)*

With Thelma now eager to make a deal, Frances offers to return the tea set for the money. Thelma must explain that she has purchased another tea set and then offers to trade her new tea set plus a dime for her old one. When the exchange is made and Thelma discovers the penny—and, consequently, the trick—she says it was not nice, and now she will have to be careful when she plays with Frances. The two decide that it is better to be friends than to be careful, and Frances shares the dime with Thelma.

After the children have enjoyed the story, catching on to the trick in time to relish Thelma's entrapment, ask if Frances told a lie to Thelma. Reread parts of the dialogue as the discussion progresses so that the children can listen with this purpose clearly in mind. They might offer opinions about whether deliberately misleading someone is lying. Then ask them if they think it was all right for Frances to trick Thelma. Did she deserve what she got? Did Thelma's behavior justify Frances's?

Next read the Caldecott Medal winner, *Sam, Bangs & Moonshine* (Ness, 1966). Sam makes up tales, "moonshine" her father calls them. Moonshine is not real. But when she tells her friend Thomas, who goes wherever she tells him, that her baby kangaroo is visiting her mermaid mother in a cave behind Blue Rock, her moonshine causes trouble. The tide comes up, covering the road to the Blue Rock. Sam tells her father in time for him to go after Thomas in a boat. When he returns, Sam's father tells her that there is good moonshine and bad moonshine and that she must learn to tell the difference. Children can draw what for them is good moonshine, the use of their imaginations. Then they can explain what the terms *good moonshine* and *bad moonshine* mean to them. Ask whether they think there is any difference between bad moonshine and lying and fibbing.

By reading several books concerning the issue, added dimensions are given. Children begin to look at situations in which the answer to what is right requires them to weigh possible actions themselves and to use their own reasoning power. The purpose is not to recommend specific actions but to encourage children to reason about moral questions.

SUMMARY

Much of children's social development—their ability to relate to other people—is correlated with their ability to see from the viewpoint of another. Realizing how another feels and understanding the intent of another person's response are central to the ability to interact successfully in social relationships. These are also key elements in determining whether children will engage in prosocial behavior.

Children learn socially acceptable behavior through observing a wide variety of models and through positive and negative reinforcement. Children develop their ability to reason about moral questions partially in relation to their stage of intellectual development and partially as a result of rewards and punishment that have been given for particular actions.

The following long-term goals are appropriate for the social and moral development of young children.

Children will make inferences about the feelings and intentions of others.

Children will view a situation from more than one perspective, seeing the viewpoint of another person.

Children will engage in prosocial behavior.

Children will judge the appropriateness of specific behaviors and predict the possible consequences of particular behaviors.

Children will learn about others who differ from themselves and value this diversity.

Children will engage competently in group activities.

Children will evaluate various solutions to moral problems and ethical questions.

Teacher Feature 8.1   Supporting Children's Social and Moral Development

Developmental Goals	Teaching Suggestions
Children will make inferences about the feelings and intentions of others.	• Have children interpret the body language of characters in illustrations. • Let children interpret the meaning of voice inflections in portions of dialogue you have read. • Encourage interpretation of dialogue beyond the literal level. • Help children relate sequences of action of feelings and intentions of book characters. • Encourage children to relate their own feelings to those of book characters.
Children will view a situation from more than one perspective, seeing the viewpoint of another person.	• Read books that present several viewpoints. • Let children analyze the limited perspective of certain characters. • Have children imagine being someone else. • Let children role-play more than one role in a single situation.
Children will engage in prosocial behavior.	• Share books that present models of prosocial behavior. • Discuss the kinds of help children can provide others. • Compare themes of helping.
Children will judge the appropriateness of specific behaviors and predict possible consequences of such behaviors.	• Ask children to evaluate the behaviors of book characters. • Have children suggest other possible behaviors for book characters.
Children will learn about others who differ from themselves and value this diversity.	• Present literature in which diversity among people is valued. • Focus on the similarities rather than the differences among peoples. • Read more than one book about a particular group of people. • Focus on individuals within groups rather than on the groups themselves. • Share literature from other countries.
Children will engage competently in group activities.	• Engage children in choral speaking. • Structure activities so that children must work together. • Begin with groups of two or three, enlarging the membership as children become more adept in group work.
Children will evaluate various solutions to moral problems and ethical questions.	• Read books in which characters engage in various stages of moral reasoning. • Invite children to suggest and defend solutions to moral or ethical problems presented in books. • Have children select the "best" reason for particular solutions to problems. • Let children compare the presentation of a single moral issue in several books.

Recommended Literature

	Ages 0–2		**Ages 5–8**
Foley	*Thank you, Bear*	Chamberlin & Chamberlin	*Mama Panya's Pancakes*
McCully	*Picnic*	Child	*But Excuse Me That is My Book*
O'Connell	*Baby Goes Beep*	Frazee	*Roller Coaster*
	Ages 2–5	Gregory	*How Smudge Came*
		Henkes	*Lilly's Purple Plastic Purse*
Graham	*Let's Get a Pup! Said Kate*	Lester	*Hooway for Wodney Wat*
Hoban	*A Birthday for Frances*	Stevenson	*Could Be Worse!*
Raschka	*Yo! Yes?*	Wiesner	*Flotsam*
Zolotow	*The Quarreling Book*		

	Ages 0–2		**Ages 5–8**
Chodos-Irvine	*Best Best Friends*	Blume	*The Pain and the Great One*
	Ages 2–5	Chocolate	*The Piano Man*
		Van Allsburg	*The Sweetest Fig*
Fatio	*The Happy Lion*	Van Allsburg	*Two Bad Ants*
Lionni	*Fish is Fish*		

	Ages 2–5		**Ages 5–8**
Hughes	*Alfie Gives a Hand*	Estes	*Manuela's Gift*
		O'Neill	*The Recess Queen*
		Polacco	*Mrs. Katz and Tush*
		Steig	*Amos & Boris*
		Wong	*Dumpster Diver*

	Ages 2–5		**Ages 5–8**
Shannon	*No, David!*	Offill	*17 Things I'm Not Allowed to Do Anymore*

	Ages 2–5		**Ages 5–8**
dePaola	*Oliver Button Is a Sissy*	Ada	*I Love Saturdays y Domingos*
		Bunting	*Fly Away Home*
		Cox	*Now We Can Have a Wedding*
		Demi	*One Grain of Rice*
		Heide & Gillihand	*Sami and the Time of the Troubles*
		Khan	*The Roses in My Carpets*

	Ages 2–5		**Ages 5–8**
Ginsburg	*Mushroom in the Rain*	Lionni	*Fish Is Fish*
		Stevenson	*Could Be Worse!*

	Ages 2–5		**Ages 5–8**
Lipkind	*Finders Keepers*	Carlson	*Arnie and the Stolen Markers*
Marshall	*George and Martha*	Demi	*The Hungry Coat*
		Hoban	*A Bargain for Frances*
		Lee	*Nim and the War Effort*
		McKissack	*The Honest-to-Goodness Truth*
		Ness	*Sam, Bangs & Moonshine*

Books offer opportunities to give children experience in making inferences about the feelings and intentions of others. Teacher Feature 8.1 (pp. 230–231) suggests appropriate teaching strategies. Children can interpret nonverbal language as shown in illustrations in picture books; they can relate voice inflection to meaning as they listen to the dialogue from books; they can go beyond a literal interpretation of dialogue, inferring what is really meant; and they can follow sequences of action and observe patterns of behavior in stories.

Literature fosters children's ability to see from the viewpoint of others. Some books will describe an event from several perspectives; others will present a story with a character that has a more limited viewpoint than does the reader. Children can be encouraged to take the perspective of another in discussions and in dramatic activities such as role-play or puppetry. They can begin to assess behavior and the consequences that may follow by discussing what happens to book characters in particular situations. Sometimes that character may provide a model for prosocial behavior, with the children seeing that they, too, would be capable of helping someone else. At other times, the children may generalize about what behaviors are appropriate in specific situations.

Literature provides children with information about people who differ from themselves, and by emphasizing the humanity of individual members of a group, helps children develop positive attitudes toward others and value diversity. Teachers will read books about many ethnic and cultural groups, including folktales from many regions.

Finally, literature can stimulate children to explore moral problems and ethical questions. Characters in books will demonstrate various levels of moral reasoning and will be faced with more dilemmas. Children can reason themselves about the questions facing the characters and may compare how different characters have reacted to the same question.

Extending Your Learning

1. Find specific illustrations in picture books that show a character's feelings. See if your colleagues can identify the emotion from looking at the illustration without knowing the story line.

2. Find a book in which the meaning of the dialogue extends beyond the literal level. Then share the book with a child to see if he or she can interpret the meaning.

3. Read a picture book to a small group of primary children. After you have finished, ask them to retell the story from the viewpoint of a particular character.

4. After reading *Two Bad Ants* (Van Allsburg, 1988), make a chart showing the ants' point of view. Then record what would be the person's point of view of the same objects or items.

5. Select five books that would lend themselves to role-play or puppetry. Tell why each is appropriate for this type of activity.

6. Suppose you had read several books to children in which the characters exhibited prosocial behavior. Write five situations you now could share with the children in which you give a setting and a problem and ask the children what they could or would do to help.

REFERENCES

Professional References Cited

Gilligan, C. (1993). *In a different voice: Psychological theory and women's development*. Cambridge, MA: Harvard University Press.

Hay, D. F., Castle, J., Davies, L., Demetriou, H. & Stimson, C. A. (1999). Prosocial action in very early childhood. *Journal of Child Psychology, 40*(6), 905–916.

Katz, L., & McClellan, D. (1997). *Fostering children's social competence*. Washington, DC: National Association for the Education of Young Children.

Kohlberg, L. (1981). *The philosophy of moral development*. Vol. 1. New York: Harper.

Mussen, P., Conger, J., Kagan, J., & Huston, A. (1990). *Child development and personality* (7th ed.). New York: Harper.

Mussen, P., & Eisenberg-Berg, N. (1977). *Roots of caring, sharing, and helping*. San Francisco: W. H. Freeman.

National Council for the Social Studies. (1997). *Expectations of excellence: Curriculum standards for social studies*. Wilmington, DE: National Council for the Social Studies. http://www.ncss.org

Oppenheim, J. (1984). *Kids and play*. New York: The Bank Street College of Education.

Piaget, J. (1955, 1935). *The moral judgment of the child*. New York: Macmillan.

Rubin, Z. (1984). *Childrens friendships*. Cambridge. MA: Harvard University Press.

Shaffer, D. (2006). *Developmental psychology* (7th ed.). Boston: Wadsworth.

Children's Literature Cited

Ada, Alma Flor. (2002). *I Love Saturdays y Domingos*. Ill. Elivia Savadier. New York: Atheneum.

Blume, Judy. (1984). *The Pain and the Great One*. Ill. Irene Trivas. New York: Bradbury.

Bradley, Kimberly Brubaker. (2006). *Ballerino Nate*. Ill. R. W. Alley. New York: Dial.

Bunting, Eve. (1991). *Fly Away Home*. Ill. Ronald Himler. New York: Clarion.

Carlson, Nancy. (1987). *Arnie and the Stolen Markers*. New York: Viking.

Chamberlin, Mary, and Chamberlin, Rich. (2005). *Mama Panya's Pancakes*. Cambridge, MA: Barefoot Books.

Child, Lauren. (2005). *But Excuse Me That is My Book*. New York: Dial.

Chocolate, Debbi. (1998). *The Piano Man*. Ill. Eric Velasquez. New York: Walker.

Chodos-Irvine, Margaret. (2006). *Best Best Friends*. San Diego, CA: Harcourt.

Cox, Judy. (1998). *Now We Can Have a Wedding*. Ill. DyAnne DiSalvo-Ryan. New York: Holiday.

Demi. (1997). *One Grain of Rice*. New York: Scholastic.

Demi. (2004). *The Hungry Coat*. New York: McElderry.

dePaola, Tomie. (1979). *Oliver Button Is a Sissy*. New York: Harcourt.

dePaola, Tomie. (2003). *Trouble in the Barkers' Class*. New York: Putnam.

Eriksson, Era. (2005). *A Crash Course for Molly*. New York: R & S Books.

Estes, Kristyn Rehling. (1999). *Manuela's Gift*. Ill. Claire B. Cotts. San Francisco: Chronicle.

Fatio, Louise. (1954). *The Happy Lion*. Ill. Roger Duvoisin. New York: McGraw-Hill.

Fleming, Candace. (2003). *Boxes for Katje*. Ill. Stacy Dressen-McQueen. New York: Farrar, Straus & Giroux.

Foley, Greg. (2007). *Thank You, Bear*. New York: Viking.

Frazee, Marla. (2003). *Roller Coaster*. San Diego, CA: Harcourt.

Ginsburg, Mirra. (1999). *Mushroom in the Rain*. Ill. Jose Aruego and Ariane Dewey. New York: Aladdin.

Graham, Bob. (2001). *Let's Get a Pup! Said Kate*. Cambridge, MA: Candlewick.

Gregory, Nan. (1997). *How Smudge Came*. Ill. Ron Lightburn. Markham, Ontario: Fitzhenry & Whiteside.

Heide, Florence Parry, and Gilliland, Judith Heide. (1992). *Sami and the Time of the Troubles*. Ill. Ted Lewin. New York: Clarion.

Henkes, Kevin. (1996). *Lilly's Purple Plastic Purse*. New York: Greenwillow.

Hoban, Russell. (1970). *A Bargain for Frances*. Ill. Lillian Hoban. New York: Harper & Row. Text copyright © 1970 by Russell Hoban. Copyright renewed 1992 by Russell Hoban. Used by permission of HarperCollins Publishers.

Hoban, Russell. (1995, 1968). *A Birthday for Frances*. Ill. Lillian Hoban. New York: HarperCollins.

Hughes, Shirley. (1987). "Alfie Gives a Hand." In *All About Alfie*. New York: Lothrop.

Khan, Rukhsana. (1998). *The Roses in My Carpets*. Ill. Ronald Himler. New York: Holiday.

Lee, Milly. (1997). *Nim and the War Effort*. Ill. Yangsook Choi. New York: Farrar.

Lester, Helen. (1999). *Hooway for Wodney Wat*. Ill. Lynn Munsinger. Boston: Houghton Mifflin.

Lionni, Leo. (1970). *Fish Is Fish*. New York: Pantheon.

Lipkind, William, and Mordvinoff, Micolas. (1951). *Finders Keepers*. New York: Harcourt.

Marshall, James. (1972). *George and Martha*. Boston: Houghton Mifflin.

McCully, Emily Arnold. (2003). *Picnic*. New York: HarperCollins.

McKissack, Patricia. (2000). *The Honest-to-Goodness Truth*. Ill. Giselle Potter. New York: Atheneum.

Ness, Evaline. (1966). *Sam, Bangs and Moonshine*. New York: Holt.

O'Connell, Rebecca. (2003). *The Baby Goes Beep*. Ill. Ken Wilson-Max. Brookfield, CT: Roaring Brook.

Offill, Jenny. (2007). *17 Things I'm Not Allowed to Do Anymore*. Ill. Nancy Carpenter. New York: Schwartz & Wade.

O'Neill, Alexis. (2002). *The Recess Queen*. Ill. Laura Huliska-Beith. New York: Scholastic.

Polacco, Patricia. (1992). *Mrs. Katz and Tush*. New York: Bantam.

Raschka, Chris. (1993). *Yo! Yes?* New York: Orchard.

Scieszka, Jon. (1989). *The True Story of the Three Little Pigs*. Ill. Lane Smith. New York: Viking.

Shannon, David. (1998). *No, David!* New York: Scholastic.

Steig, William. (1971). *Amos & Boris*. New York: Farrar.

Stevenson, James. (1977). *Could Be Worse!* New York: Greenwillow.

Torres, Leyla. (1993). *Subway Sparrow*. New York: Farrar.

Van Allsburg, Chris. (1988). *Two Bad Ants*. Boston: Houghton Mifflin.

Van Allsburg, Chris. (1993). *The Sweetest Fig*. Boston: Houghton Mifflin.

Viorst, Judith. (2001*). Super-Completely and Totally the Messiest*. Ill. Robin Preiss Glasser. New York: Atheneum.

Wiesner, David. (2006). *Flotsam*. New York: Clarion.

Willems, Mo. (2003). *Don't Let the Pigeon Drive the Bus*. New York: Hyperion.

Willems, Mo. (2004). *The Pigeon Finds a Hot Dog!* New York: Hyperion.

Willems, Mo. (2006). *Don't Let the Pigeon Stay Up Late*. New York: Hyperion.

Wong, Janet S. (2007). *Dumpster Diver*. Ill. David Roberts. Cambridge, MA: Candlewick.

Zolotow, Charlotte. (1968). *The Quarreling Book*. Ill. Arnold Lobel. New York: Harper.

CHAPTER NINE

MIKEY, Age 3

Tissue paper collage inspired by Eric Carle

At preschool, Mikey (age 3) created this tissue paper collage in the style of Eric Carle. The teacher had read a variety of Carle's books. Following a nature walk around the school, the students made their pictures to show what they had observed. When Mikey was three years old, he made this picture using a variety of different media including twigs with tempera paint on them and potatoes to make the potato print birds.

Supporting Children's Aesthetic and Creative Development

Aesthetic development denotes a person's increasing sensitivity to and appreciation of beauty in art and in nature. This ability to respond to the beautiful is sometimes termed a skill of *impression*. It is paired with the skill of *expression,* the ability to create. Davenport (1999) states, "Research shows that including visual arts, music, dance and drama in the school curriculum provides a tool for teaching literacy" (p. 15). She advocates that this type of approach to instruction is essential if significant gains are to be made in student progress. The arts contribute to the cognitive development of the mind, making learning more complete. Various studies have shown that children demonstrate more positive attitudes toward learning when arts programs are implemented. Performance, or creative activity, provides a base for children's aesthetic development as well as being a valid educational experience itself.

AESTHETIC AND CREATIVE DEVELOPMENT IN YOUNG CHILDREN

Art and music, including dance and movement, are indispensable elements of any curriculum for young children. The arts give children a choice of ways in which they can express their thoughts and feelings. Children may also find that they can understand an idea expressed through music, art, or drama that they might not have understood through words alone. For many children, their experiences with art parallels with their experiences with text. Alejandro writes that "When we read and write, we use the same critical thinking and decision-making brain power that we use when we paint or respond to paintings" (1994, p. 13). In addition, the arts provide a means of expression for what Krogh terms "the widest possible diversity." She notes that "children can move in response to the same music whether they are in a wheelchair or are totally mobile. Or they can use the same art materials to create objects or pictures that portray their own or others' cultures" (Krogh, 1994, p. 522). As a teacher, you judge whether there is enough freedom in an activity to meet various needs or whether you must make adjustments so that all can participate.

Child-care professionals and teachers should work to help children enjoy participating in the arts, use their imaginations and creative potential, and progress toward more complexity in aesthetic values. A successful arts program introduces new forms of art to children, expanding their skills of both expression and impression, but it does so gradually, allowing the children to accommodate the new information and gain control over new techniques. It also encourages children to use their creative potential.

Creative Potential

Fleith (2000) points out that a misconception about young children's inability to think productively has led to an "overemphasis upon recall and reproduction to the neglect of problem solving, creative thinking and decision making in the early years" (p. 149). Sousa, MacLin, and MacLin (2004) agree and state that creativity is a cognitive activity that results in a new or novel way of viewing a problem or situation. It is a process in which the learners first become aware of personal gaps in knowledge, problems, or disharmonies and then set about resolving inconsistencies. They look for new relationships among existing information. They make, test, modify, and perfect hypotheses and, finally, communicate their results to others. Torrance (1970) believes that sensitivity to problems may be aroused either through self-initiated activities or through a structured sequence of activities. Creative learning can take place in any subject area.

In the arts, a 3-year-old exhibits creative learning as he attempts to make a snake from modeling clay, only to have it separate in segments as he rolls it out. He has encountered a problem. The teacher helps, not through telling him what to do or through doing it for him but by asking questions that stimulate his thinking. Where is it breaking? Why do you suppose that's the place it breaks? What could you do differently? The child then hypothesizes that keeping the clay thicker, not rolling it so rapidly, using both hands to roll, or moving his hands along the snake as he works might help. He tries his ideas and reports to the teacher when his snake is finished.

Creativity has been characterized as involving divergent thinking, fluency in the production of ideas, flexibility, originality of ideas, and elaboration. Teachers and child-care professionals can encourage creative thinking by establishing an atmosphere of acceptance in the classroom and by asking questions and structuring activities that permit a variety of responses. Creativity is viewed as a process as well as a product and as a quality that all people have to some degree. As you plan activities in the arts, you will need to provide opportunities for children to use creative thinking. You will also need to know the general capabilities of the children you are teaching.

Development in Art

A sequence of development in art is fairly predictable; however, as with other developmental sequences, the age levels that correspond with each stage are approximations. Most children first begin scribbling at about 2 years of age, although some may start a few months earlier. Their activities with crayon on paper are basically a physical activity. Lowenfeld and Brittain (1987) divide the scribbling stage into three segments. The first is *disordered scribbling.* Children simply move the crayon or pencil in wide sweeps across the paper. About 6 months after they have begun scribbling, they move into *controlled scribbling.* Now they are beginning to gain some control over their markings and to experience the outcome visually. They may repeat motions, resulting in patterns of lines or circles, and often become engrossed in the activity. At about 3½ years of age, they move into *naming of scribbling.* As the title implies, they begin telling what the scribble signifies—This is my mommy, or I'm eating lunch. This is an important step in their development because they have begun to think in terms of pictures rather than motions. The drawings themselves, however, may differ little from earlier scribbles.

By age 4, most children can create shapes that resemble round or rectangular objects. Size relationships are more likely to be determined by the order in which children created each object and the medium they are using than by any attempt for accurate representation. They may also exaggerate size to show what is important to them. Also, color is not chosen for accuracy. It may be determined by preference or simply by the colors available for use (Chapman, 1978).

Around age 4½ or 5, children reach the *early expressive* stage. They begin to develop their ideas for drawings or paintings before they begin the actual work. They may look to adults for guidance and use their own previous work or that of peers as models. They may practice a skill to gain mastery over it, sometimes repeating a picture or sculpture. They are generally able to tell about their work and may include more detail in the work if they are encouraged to reenact an experience or discuss a theme.

In the early elementary grades children begin to develop more complexity in their work. In pictures, they frequently place all figures along a baseline, but by the end of third grade they are beginning to use overlapping shapes to show distance. They begin to be aware of relative size, being dissatisfied now if their flowers are as tall as their houses. They often use the stereotyped notion of proper colors—green leaves, brown tree trunks—although they will respond to structured observations and opportunities to mix colors. They enjoy art activities based on imaginative themes (Brewer, 2006).

Teachers and child-care professionals can assist children in developing artistic ability in several ways. They can provide a variety of media and give children ample time to experiment. Children need to see how paint runs together before they can begin to master its use. They need to try several ways to put legs on their clay figures or to use the sides as well as the points of their crayons.

Adults can give suggestions that encourage children to solve their own problems. This means refusing to draw the dog for the child who complains of being unable to do it and asking instead what elements make up the dog or what is special about the dog that the child might want to emphasize.

As children show their work, teachers and child-care professionals can comment objectively on what has been done: You've used thick, straight lines and then wavy ones that contrast one another, or You've mixed several interesting new shades of color. This introduces vocabulary for talking about art and allows the adult to show that all efforts are valued. Differences in style of art are to be expected and are desirable.

You can share adult art with children. Seeing different styles reinforces the idea that one style is not better than another and introduces children to art they might not see otherwise. Professional art can be used for talking about the process employed but should not be used as a model for children to copy.

Development in Music

In music and movement, as in art, some abilities and responses are governed by the children's physical and motor development. Young children sing between middle C and G or A, the middle range on a piano. Gradually they add a tone or two below C and by age 8 will have added a tone or two above G. From initial stages of not matching melodic tones at all, children move to a stage where they engage in directional singing. They approximate the tones, moving in the direction of the melody. Then, with practice, they become more accurate in singing tunes within a range of four or five notes. McDonald writes, "Not surprisingly, the most tuneful young singers come from home and/or caregiving environments that have provided many experiences and opportunities for singing and listening to music" (1979, p. 25).

Children respond to music from very early ages and seem to respond most markedly to music with strong rhythm or melody. Babies have a wonderful sense of rhythm and will bounce to rhythm at a very early age. They respond to slow, long narrative songs that help them relax into sleepiness (Honig, 2004). Toddlers will sing along with favorite tunes and enjoy moving their bodies gracefully and dreamily to slow dance music. At ages 3 and 4, children can respond to music through walking, running, clapping, and other physical movements. At first they may repeat the same movement throughout the rhythmic experience, but gradually they will begin to experiment. Often a child-care professional or teacher will use a drum or other instrument to follow the rhythm of the children's actions rather than as the impetus for rhythmic movements (McDonald & Simons, 1989).

Children of ages 4 and 5 are developing in coordination and can add hopping and skipping to their repertoire of movement. They enjoy using rhythm instruments such as triangles, bells, blocks, and rhythm sticks. They can use these instruments in response to music and may also use them to illustrate stories, making judgments about appropriate pitch, rhythm, and tempo.

As children mature and engage in musical experiences, they move more accurately with the rhythm and develop more self-control in the use of rhythm instruments. With instructions that help them explore body movements, they use space, time, and weight variations in their response to music and in dramatizations. Teachers and child-care professionals help children gain these concepts by engaging them in directed movement activities. For example, to explore space, instruct children to find a space where they will not touch anyone else when arms are outstretched. Then they make themselves use as little of the space as possible and then as much as possible. Adding the element of time, they can move slowly, using all their space; move rapidly, using the lower half of their space; or be a frightened mouse moving in their space; or be an angry bear moving in their space.

Many of the teaching strategies that support development in art apply to development in music and movement also. Just as children need time to experiment with a variety of media, they also need time to experiment with singing, instruments, and movement. Children need an area where they can use rhythm instruments and tone bars in an unstructured setting and where they can listen to the sounds, try different rhythms or melodies, or sing. Some teachers provide such an area for use during times when other "sound-producing" activities are in progress. Others have special rooms for musical experimentation. There also should be times when children use rhythm instruments in a group response to music or literature.

Children should have the opportunity to sing often, both for enjoyment and to learn to reproduce a melody. Songs to be taught should be within the vocal range of the children. The most easily learned songs have repetition of melodic lines or refrains. Teachers can help children recognize the directionality of the music and introduce the concept of musical notation by moving their hands to indicate the movement of the melody or by showing the movement with lines on the chalkboard. Duration of notes can be shown by hand movements or written symbols, with long motions or lines indicating notes to be held and short motions or lines indicating eighth or quarter notes.

Provide a variety of musical selections for listening activities. You can maintain interest in listening to music by having children respond rhythmically as they listen and by sharing selections several times so that children become familiar with them.

Child-care professionals and teachers can give children the vocabulary to talk about music and movement just as they can with art. They may comment objectively on children's responses—You are marching in a steady rhythm, or The tones you are using all have a high pitch. They may also use the vocabulary as they share adult music. Many vocabulary items are appropriate for use in several of the arts; therefore, as children hear them used in more than one context, they gain a clearer conception of the meaning of the terms.

Teachers of young children have the opportunity to engage them in activities that will foster their aesthetic and creative development and build self-confidence in both expression and impression. The satisfaction that children experience as they participate in these types of activities is a reward for the teacher as well as for the students.

GOALS FOR TEACHING

As in other areas, teaching goals for aesthetic and creative development can be categorized as long-term developmental goals, general goals for an age or grade level, and specific goals for individual children. The long-term goals are those behaviors or competencies that are developed over time and considered desired patterns of behavior. A long-term goal for aesthetic and creative development is that children will use, experiment with, and gain control over a variety of art media. It is a goal that will take several years to be achieved.

A general goal for second grade is that children will identify at least three different musical instruments by engaging in a special pattern of movement for each of the instruments as they listen to selections such as the classic *Peter and the Wolf*. Schoolwide curriculum guides may well suggest specific materials. In the absence of curriculum guides or in addition to them, teachers develop their own general goals for their classes.

A specific goal is one for an individual child: Julio will use sand blocks to match the rhythm of John's movement. At age 5, Julio is becoming aware of the rhythms around him. He is beginning to explore the use of rhythm instruments, though he still needs to develop self-control in using them. Experiences in matching the rhythm of another child's movement will develop his awareness of rhythm and will give him reason to control his use of rhythm instruments, such as sand blocks.

Literature contributes to the achievement of all three types of goals. This chapter focuses on selected long-term developmental goals common to the preschool and primary years. Literature offers opportunities for you to help children grow toward the following goals for aesthetic and creative development.

Children will respond favorably to diverse styles of art and music.

Children will exhibit a sensory awareness of their environment.

Children will use, experiment with, and gain control over a variety of art media.

Children will sing in tune within their vocal range and will respond to music and literature with movement and rhythm instruments.

Children will use their imaginations as they participate in art, music, and movement.

Children will enjoy experiencing the work of others and participating in the arts themselves.

The first two goals are for skills of impression, the next three are for skills of expression, and the last combines the two.

As with other areas, these goals, such as, the goal that children will enjoy experiencing the work of others and participating in the arts themselves, can be correlated with national and regional standards. Standards may state that students will engage in self- or group-expression by creating original or interpreting works of art. Specific descriptors within the standards may also be given for dance, the visual arts, theatre, and music. As you look at standards for your region or school district, look for ways in which these goals and the specific standards mesh.

OPPORTUNITIES BOOKS OFFER

Helping Children Develop Favorable Attitudes Toward Diverse Styles of Art

For children of preschool and primary-school age, art appreciation is basically developing a favorable attitude toward various art forms and various styles in art. Do not expect that children, any more than adults, will like all forms equally. It is important, however, that they be open to art that is new to them and that they recognize the validity of different modes of expression. You can help children achieve this openness by presenting the idea that art is a personal form of expression, by exposing children to a wide range of art, and by involving children with art in ways that give them a basis for relating to it.

Presenting Art as Personal Expression One way to show art as personal expression is to share books that demonstrate the concept directly. In Peter Reynolds *Ish* (2004), Ramon loves to draw, "Anytime. Anything. Anywhere." When his older brother makes fun of one of his pictures and points out that it doesn't look like a real vase of flowers, Ramon responds by crumpling up all his previous work. However, his younger sister has collected and displayed the discarded papers on her bedroom walls. When Ramon shares that the picture of the vase doesn't look like the real thing, she tells him that it looks "vase-ISH." Soon Ramon is drawing lots of things that are "ish" and reveling in his creations.

This book might be combined with Allen Say's *Emma's Rug* (1996) because it, too, presents an artist creating based on individual vision. Emma carries a small shaggy rug that was given to her when she was born and says that she sees the pictures she later draws and paints by staring at the rug. When her mother washes the rug, Emma thinks she can no longer create but soon realizes that she can visualize images all around her. Both books show the artist as creating what he or she "sees," whether it is seen in that fashion or at all by other people. Have children look back over some of their own paintings and drawings to see if what they drew was important to them. Then let them look at one or two paintings by well-known artists and tell what they think might have been important to that artist at that time.

Books are available like *Ish* that show children as capable, developing artists. Ti Marie in *Painted Dreams* (Karen Lynn Williams, 1998) uses paints she has taken from the trash and whatever other materials she can find to draw on the wall behind the stall where her mother sells vegetables, in this story set in Haiti. Her picture, which includes the tomatoes and onions they are selling, draws the attention of people passing by and helps convert them into customers.

In *The Art Lesson* (1989) by Tomie dePaola, the young protagonist, named Tommy, is distressed when his first-grade teacher tells the children that they are to copy the Pilgrim she has drawn on the board and that they are permitted only one sheet of paper. His cousins have told Tommy that artists do not copy and that they

In The Art Lesson, Tomie dePaola shares his own experiences as an early artist.
(From *The Art Lesson* by Tomie dePaola, copyright © 1989 by Tomie dePaola. Used by permission of G. P. Putnam's Sons, A Division of Penguin Young Readers Group, A Member of Penguin Group (USA) Inc., 345 Hudson Street, New York, NY 10014. All rights reserved.)

must "practice, practice, practice." Tommy goes on strike but eventually manages to reach a compromise. The last illustration shows a gray-haired Tommy, still drawing. Do they think they will still be drawing when they have gray hair? And is the author/illustrator writing about and illustrating something that is important to him?

A week later you could share *I Am an Artist* (Collins, 1994). "I am an artist when I look at a bird until I feel feathery too, and at an orange until I know what it is to be perfectly round" (n.p.). The poetic text presents the idea that art is a process and a way of living and seeing. Creativity can be inspired by the world around us, and art is everywhere. Although *Ish* can be used successfully with children from 4 or 5 on (when they begun to decide what they will draw before beginning), *I Am an Artist* is more appropriate for second- and third-graders who are able to think abstractly.

A second way of showing art as personal expression is to compare the work of two or more artists when they are using the same or similar subject matter. Songs and folktales often have several illustrated versions. *Over in the Meadow* by Olive A. Wadsworth, for example, has been illustrated by Ezra Jack Keats (1985, 1999), by John Langstaff (1989), by Louise Voce (2000), and by Anna Vojtech (2002), among others. After children have participated in the telling or singing of the rhyme or song, let them look at the pictures in the books, holding the books side by side so that the text matches. Children can see how each of the illustrators chooses to portray the characters and the action. Keats's collage portraying the subject of each verse, for example, contrasts with Vojtech's soft watercolor illustrations of owl mother and babies.

Having children tell which they prefer will demonstrate that not only do artists portray subjects differently but that others react to their work differently.

Reading chapter books enables children to make images of book characters in their own minds. At times, chapter books appropriate for primary grades contain illustrations. Children could sketch the character before being shown the illustrations in the book. This same strategy can work with picture books. Have them describe what they imagined; then show how the illustrator portrayed those same characters.

You and the children could select one animal and then see how that animal is shown in several books of fiction. If you choose pigs, you might compare the appearance of pictures in illustrations from various books. View the more standard-looking pigs in Davis Wiesner's *The Three Pigs* (2001). See how Wiesner's watercolor and digitized illustrations compare with the line drawings of Arthur Geisert in *Oink* (1991), the cartoon style of Mo Willems's *Today I Will Fly!* (2007), the pen-and-ink outlines with watercolor washes of Felicia Bond in *If You Give a Pig a Pancake* (Numeroff, 1998), the charcoal and gouache illustrations of Ian Falconer's *Olivia Forms a Band* (2006), and the retro look in the beginning-to-read book, *Mercy Watson: Princess in Disguise* (DiCamillo, 2007). All the books you choose should be appropriate to the age level of the children. With young children it is generally better to compare only two books at a time. A third, fourth, and fifth may be added later, one at a time. Children can see that artists use different media and different styles to show these different pig characters. Let the children use a variety of media themselves to create pigs of their own, perhaps placing them on a mural.

Exposing Children to a Wide Range of Art   Helping children see the diversity in the art in picture books and encouraging them to select different media and different styles in their own art demonstrates that differences are expected and valued. It also introduces children to a range of two-dimensional art forms. As you select literature to share, keep a record of the methods of illustration that children are seeing. You may want to select several books from this list for comparison. If some forms have not been presented, you will want to find good literature that fills the gap. Some illustrators are known for their work with certain media or with certain styles. Others vary considerably according to the text they are illustrating. As a beginning, look at some of the following books to familiarize yourself with media and styles of art found in books for young children.

Media
Collage
> Fleming, Denise. (2006). *The Cow Who Clucked.* New York: Holt.
> Rappaport, Doreen. (2001). *Martin's Big Words.* Ill. Bryan Collier. New York: Hyperion.

Pencil drawings
> McCarty, Peter. (2002). *Hondo and Fabian.* New York: Holt.
> Van Allsburg, Chris. (1981). *Jumanji.* Boston: Houghton Mifflin.

Woodcut
> Azarian, Mary. (1998). *Snowflake Bentley.* Boston: Houghton Mifflin.
> Emberley, Barbara. (1967). *Drummer Hoff.* Ill. Ed Emberley. Upper Saddle River, NJ: Prentice Hall.

Scratchboard
> Kay, Verla. (1999). *Iron Horses.* Ill. Michael McCurdy. New York: Putnam.
> Pinkney, Brian. (2005). *Hush, Little Baby.* New York: Amistad/HarperCollins.

Photography

Ancona, George. (1998). *Fiesta Fireworks!* New York: Lothrop.
McMillan, Bruce. (2001). *Days of the Ducklings*. Boston: Houghton Mifflin.

Pastels

St. George, Judith. (2002). *So You Want to Be an Inventor.* Ill. David Small. New York: Philomel.
Van Allsburg, Chris. (1985). *The Polar Express*. Boston: Houghton Mifflin.

Gouache

Cousins, Lucy. (2007). *Maisy Big, Maisy Small: A Book of Maisy Opposites.* Cambridge, MA: Candlewick.
Wildsmith, Brian. (1964). *Brian Wildsmith's Mother Goose*. New York: Franklin Watts.

Watercolor

Muth, Jon J. (2005). *Zen Shorts.* New York: Scholastic.
Yolen, Jane. (1987). *Owl Moon*. Ill. John Schoenherr. New York: Philomel.

Acrylics

Shannon, David. (1998). *No, David!* New York: Scholastic.
Winter, Jeanette. (2000). *The House that Jack Built.* New York: Putnam.

Oil Paint

Ryan, Pam Muñoz. (2001). *Mice and Beans.* Ill. Joe Cepeda. New York: Scholastic.
Zelinsky, Paul O. (1986). *Rumpelstiltskin*. New York: Dutton.

Style of Art

Realistic or Representational

Henkes, Kevin. (2004). *Kitten's First Full Moon.* New York: HarperCollins.
Say, Allen. (2005). *The Kamishibai Man.* Boston: Houghton Mifflin.

Impressionistic

Juster, Norton. (2005). *The Hello, Goodbye Window.* Ill. Chris Raschka. New York: Hyperion.
McCully, Emily. (1992). *Mirette on the High Wire.* New York: Putnam.

Expressionistic

Bunting, Eve. (1994). *Smoky Night.* Ill. David Diaz. San Diego, CA: Harcourt.
Soto, Gary. (1995). *Chato's Kitchen.* Ill. Susan Guevara. New York: Putnam.

Cartoon

Arnold, Tedd. (1997). *Parts.* New York: Dial.
Cronin, Doreen. (2005). *Wiggle.* Ill. Scott Menchin. New York: Atheneum.

Abstract

Kalman, Maira. (2002). *Fireboat: The Heroic Adventures of the John J. Harvey.* New York: Putnam.
Seeger, Laura Vaccaro. (2003). *The Hidden Alphabet.* Brookfield, CT: Roaring Brook.

Surrealistic

Browne, Anthony. (2001). *Voices in the Park.* New York: DK Publishing.
Wiesner, David. (1991). *Tuesday.* New York: Clarion.

Let children react to the art in picture books. Let them express their opinions about the quality of the paintings. Share some illustrations that you anticipate the children will Like immediately; then share some examples of more complex styles of art. The illustrations for *Ben's Trumpet* (Isadora, 1979) are almost art deco, more abstract than most art for children. The story line is slight; a little boy hears the music from a nearby club and longs to play the trumpet himself. Children could be asked to tell whether or not seeing the illustrations made the story better for them than just listening to it. They might look at specific pictures as they respond, calling attention to what they liked or telling why the illustrations were not helpful to them. They should be guided to look at the illustrations carefully but not guided into saying they like whatever is presented.

Recommended Literature About Art

Brown, Laurene Krasny. (1986). *Visiting the Art Museum.* Ill. Marc Brown. New York: Dutton.

Browne, Anthony. (2000). *Willy the Dreamer.* New York: Walker.

Catalanotto, Peter. (2001). *Emily's Art.* New York: Atheneum.

Hurd, Thacher. (1996). *Art Dog.* New York: HarperCollins.

Katz, Susan. (2002). *Mrs. Brown on Exhibit and Other Museum Poems.* Ill. R. W. Alley. New York: Simon & Schuster.

Laden, Nina. (1998). *When Pigasso Met Mootisse.* San Francisco: Chronicle.

Locker, Thomas. (1995). *Sky Tree: Seeing Science Through Art.* New York: HarperCollins.

Mayhew, James. (1998). *Katie and the Mona Lisa.* New York: Orchard.

McDonnell, Patrick. (2006). *Art.* Boston: Little Brown.

Mickelthwait, Lucy. (2004). *I Spy Shapes in Art.* New York: Greenwillow.

Scieszka, Jon. (2005). *Seen Art?* Ill. Lane Smith. New York: Viking.

Wallace, Nancy Elizabeth. (2006). *Look! Look! Look!* Tarrytown, NY: Marshall Cavendish.

Involving Children with Art Make a practice of involving children with art in ways that will enable them to relate to it personally. As they look at a painting, drawing, or illustration in a book, have them imagine themselves someplace in the picture. What can they see from where they are standing? Do they hear any sounds? If so, what do they hear? If they could move around inside the painting, where would they go?

You might, for the fun of it, talk about what might happen if they really could enter a painting—or if the contents of a painting entered our world. *The Incredible Painting of Felix Clousseau* (Agee, 1988) is about an artist whose paintings become real. It concludes with Clousseau returning to his studio—and walking back into a painting. *Katie's Sunday Afternoon* (Mayhew, 2005) has a similar motif—Katie jumps into the painting—and is one of several books in which the young protagonist hops into artwork hanging in the museum. Children might create stories about a painting or about a single illustration from a book.

Another technique for heightening children's artistic awareness is to pair a picture book with music. *The Yellow Umbrella* (Liu, 2001) comes with a classical-style music CD that is just perfect for paging through this wordless picture book. Illustrator Jae Soo Liu presents a high-rise view of colorful umbrellas carried by children on a rainy walk to school. Composer Dong II Sheen gracefully glides between rhythms and sounds, such as a train or the sprinkling of rain.

Showing videos about illustrators of children's books can help primary-grade children see the artists as real people. Weston Woods Studio has videos about many illustrators. The Reading Rockets Web site contains information about and free video clips of various authors and illustrators. They can be viewed at www. readingrockets.org and burned to a CD for later viewing or for putting in a center with the illustrator's books. Children often want to explore the artistic process that these illustrators describe.

Consider involving children in an art project before showing them a book that uses certain ideas or techniques. For example, let children decorate a plain white paper cup and paper plate, dishes that they may use at lunch or snack time if they choose. Talk with them about what they might do, whether making designs or drawing pictures. When the project is complete, share with them *The Pot that Juan Built* (Andrews-Goebel, 2002). Using the rhyming pattern of The House that Jack Built, this story focuses on Juan Quezada, one of the best-known potters in Mexico. He uses only natural materials to form and paint his pots. This book is designed for different levels of reading expertise because it presents information about Quezada in a way that can be read as a story or as an information book. By hearing about Juan Quezada, children will have a point of reference for looking at the art of another person and another culture.

As children see and become involved with a variety of artistic styles and media, both through their own work and through observations and discussion of the work of others, they are learning that diversity in art is to be both valued and enjoyed.

Sharpening Children's Awareness

Much of literature, especially poetry, provides readers with a verbal description of authors' perceptions of their environments. Virginia Wright-Frierson, for example, writes vivid descriptions of the scenes she illustrates. In *A North American Rain Forest Scrapbook* (Wright-Frierson, 2003), readers walk alongside this nature artist as she observes, draws, paints, and writes about the majesty of America's own rain forest in Washington's Olympic Peninsula. Individuals who are sensitive to the world around them share their insights and reactions in evocative language. Reading such literature to children fosters a sharpened awareness. Children see a model of keen observation. They hear a detailed description or a mood captured in metaphor. As a teacher, you can select books that present the sensory awareness of the author. You can also select books that describe activities the children can repeat and others that can be a stimulus for activities, which will enhance sensory awareness.

Sharing in the Awareness of Others   Look at both prose and poetry to find books in which authors write in sensory terms and illustrators convey the beauty they observe. An example of a book in which an author has shown the wonder and beauty of a shared event is the Caldecott Medal winner *Owl Moon* by Jane Yolen (1987). A young girl and her father go owling on a moonlit winter night. Bundled up in warm clothing, they trudge through the snow "whiter than the milk in a cereal bowl." Along the way they see various animals, but their hope is to spy an owl. The child knows that she must be silent as her father imitates the call of the Great Horned Owl. From out of the darkness the sound and the bird swoop through the trees. The watercolor palette of shades of blue provide a sense of the winter's cold, and the double-page spreads depict the vastness of the landscape filled with trees that greet them. Sharing this book with children brings them to an appreciation of the various senses in experiencing and describing a place or an event.

Look for literature that highlights the various senses. *Snow* by Uri Shulevitz (1998) also uses spare text to describe a December landscape and to cast a spell of winter magic. No snow, is the prediction. Or it will surely melt, is the observation of a woman with an umbrella. But when a boy and his dog spy a single snowflake, they rush outside in gleeful anticipation. One snowflake turns into two, two turns into three, and before long the snow is "dancing, playing,/there and there,/floating, floating through the air" (n.p). Through Shulevitz's chilly gray paintings, children can feel the change in the temperature and the thrill of a winter day. This book emphasizes the visual.

Eve Merriam's "A Matter of Taste" (1962) asks questions that children will answer even before *you* ask.

> What does your tongue like the most?
>
> Chewy meat or crunchy toast?
>
> A lumpy bump pickle or tickly pop?
>
> A soft marshmallow or a hard lime drop?
>
> Hot pancakes or a sherbet freeze?
>
> Celery noise or quiet cheese?
>
> Or do you like pizza?
>
> More than any of these?
>
> *Eve Merriam, 1962, p. 16*

The onomatopoeia in the following poem, "Poem to Mud," adds to children's delight in the message as the poet explores the feel of mud.

Poem to Mud

> Mud is very nice to feel
>
> All squishy-squash between the toes!
>
> I'd rather wade in wiggly mud
>
> Than smell a yellow rose.
>
> Nobody else but the rosebush knows
>
> How nice mud feels
>
> Between the toes.
>
> *Polly Chase Boyden (1983), p. 18*

Often poems about nature will include sensory descriptions, and certain poets use such descriptions regularly. The work of Jane Yolen is filled with portrayals of and reactions to the natural world. The following books by Yolen are appropriate for young children.

COUNT ME A RHYME: ANIMAL POEMS BY THE NUMBER. (2006). Photos. By Jason Stemple. Honesdale, PA: Wordsong/Boyds Mills.

HERE'S A LITTLE POEM: A VERY FIRST BOOK OF POETRY. (2007). Ill. Polly Dunbar. Cambridge, MA: Candlewick.

LEAST THINGS: POEMS ABOUT SMALL NATURE. (2003). Photos by Jason Stemple. Honesdale, PA: Boyds Mills.

SHAPE ME A RHYME: NATURE'S FORMS IN POETRY. (2007). Photos. by Jason Stemple. Honesdale, PA: Wordsong/Boyds Mills.

SNOW, SNOW, SNOW: POEMS FOR CHILDREN. (1998). Photos by Jason Stemple. Honesdale, PA: Boyds Mills.

WATER MUSIC. (2004). Photos by Jason Stemple. Honesdale, PA: Boyds Mills.

WELCOME TO THE RIVER OF GRASS. (2001). Ill. Laura Regan. New York: Putnam.

WILD WINGS: POEMS FOR YOUNG PEOPLE. (2002). Photos by Jason Stemple. Honesdale, PA: Boyds Mills.

Other poets and who write nature poetry for children include Joyce Sidman (*The Song of the Water Boatman and Other Pond Poems,* 2005; *Butterfly Eyes and Other Secrets of the Meadow,* 2006), Douglas Florian (*Comets, Stars, the Moon and Mars: Space Poems and Paintings,* 2007; *Autumnblings,* 2003), and Valerie Worth (*Animal Poems,* 2007).

Experiencing One's Own Environment   Some books describe how artists have captured experiences that children may have had themselves. Thomas Locker combines careful scientific observation with aesthetic observation in *Sky Tree: Seeing Science Through Art* (1995). Children can see how the elements they experience every day have been portrayed by different artists and how they change both daily and seasonally. Look around the environment where you are teaching. What is there that you and the children can observe, perhaps over a period of time, in different conditions, to see the colors and the moods? Perhaps you are close to a pond or stream or want to watch a grassy field or pavement in bright sunlight, on a gloomy day, or glistening wet from rainwater. Help children record what they have seen. List their reactions after each observation; then, after several entries, read over what they have dictated and help them put their thoughts together into a single experience chart. What would they want to capture in a painting?

After reading Henry Cole's *I Took a Walk* (1998) or *On the Way to the Beach* (2003), take the children on a walk of their own. See how many different things they see and sounds they hear, perhaps emphasizing the sounds. A listening walk can be taken indoors as well as outdoors and in both large and small groups. Preschool children going in guided groups can stop and all listen to the different sounds together, discussing each sound as it is heard. Older children might go in pairs around the school, each pair noting either with words or pictures what they hear. When all have returned to the classroom, the groups compare their experiences. You will know how much responsibility your students can handle, whether they can go unaccompanied by an adult within limits, or whether the experience is more likely to be successful if you or an aide goes along.

Adapt the experiences to fit your environment. *Tracks in the Wild* (Bowen, 1998) focuses on the author's beloved home in the Minnesota north woods. Bowen provides facts and observations about the creatures that live in the area and make tracks near her home. She also shares suggestions for how to track various forms of wildlife. Think about where tracks can be found near your school or center. It may be in the dust, in mud, in snow, or in beach sand. All will suffice for children to observe the markings left by birds and insects, dogs, or chipmunks and to see the patterns and perhaps make some guesses about who was there and what was happening.

Using Books as Stimuli for Sensory Activities   Many books and poems provide stimuli for activities that require children to use their senses in discovery or exploration. As you select books, think about any possibilities there may be for using sight, sound, touch, taste, and smell. Here are some examples.

Sight.   Read *Goggles* (Keats, 1969), in which Peter and Archie look through an old pipe as they search for the dog Willie while hiding from some older boys. Then let children make spyglasses of their own by rolling paper into a tubes. Have them look around the room through the tubes, perhaps viewing it from the floor or standing on a chair to look down. They can draw what they see in this limited field of vision from several perspectives.

Share a variety of poems from *Color Me a Rhyme: Nature Poems for Young People* (Yolen, 2000); then have children observe their own backyards or the center or school play area and describe what colors they see. Then read *All Upon a Sidewalk* (George, 1974), an ant's eye view of a city sidewalk as Lasius Flavus searches for food for her queen. The illustrations show the ants' world as though seen through a magnifying glass. What do children discover as they explore with a magnifying glass? Let them tell about it, dictate a story, or record it with crayons or paint.

Another aspect of sight that can be explored through literature can be the inability to see clearly. The picture books *Glasses, Who Needs 'Em* (Smith, 1991) and *Baby Duck and the Bad Eyeglasses* (Hest, 1996) or the short chapter book, *Agapanthus Hum and the Eyeglasses* (Cowley, 1999) all focus on the topic with both the anguish and the resolve that children have in wearing eyeglasses.

Sound. Read poems that describe sounds with strong use of onomatopoeia, such as "Our Washing Machine" by Patricia Hubbell (1963). After they hear the clicks and whirrs of this machine, have them describe the sounds of other machines. Or, after looking at Ross MacDonald's *Achoo! Bang! Crash! A Noisy Alphabet* (2003), have them tell how they would make these sounds as well as create situations for other sounds. This is an excellent time for children to use a tape recorder, capturing a sound and listening to it several times, perhaps having others guess what it is.

Read *Rainbow Joe and Me* (Strom, 1999). Eloise likes to mix colors such as red and white to paint fish and red and blue to paint monkeys. Her friend Rainbow Joe tells Eloise he can mix colors, too, but Eloise's mother says that a blind man can't mix colors. One Sunday, Rainbow Joe says he has a surprise for Eloise. When he begins to play his saxophone, big red notes, little yellow notes, and deep blue notes fill the air— and every color can be seen, loud and clear. Play music for children and have them create their own collage of color of the notes they hear.

Touch. Use just one quotation from Marcia Brown's *Touch Will Tell* (1979), in which she asks if they have hugged a tree lately and felt its coat. Let children "hug" several trees, seeing if they all feel alike. Using crayons and medium-weight paper, let the children make rubbings of some of the bark. Let them see how the rubbings differ. Perhaps they will want to continue the project by making rubbings of other surfaces.

Seven Blind Mice (Young, 1992) is a variant on the fable of the blind men trying to identity an elephant. Seven differently hued blind mice attempt to determine what the "strange something" could be. Each one feels some part of the elephant and comes up with its own conclusion—one mouse thinks that it's a pillar, another, a snake, and still another, a cliff. Finally, the white mouse runs across the entire thing and concludes that it is an elephant. Let children see what they can recognize through touch. Can they identify objects? Can they touch a classmate's face and recognize the person?

Taste. Read *Bread and Jam for Frances* (Hoban, 1969), in which Frances refuses to eat anything but her favorite food, bread and jam. Let children talk about their favorite foods. Then have a taste festival, encouraging children to try several kinds of fruit, two or three kinds of cheese, and perhaps white bread, rye bread, and raisin bread. Let each child record his or her favorite food in each of the categories in a booklet. See if any class favorites emerge.

A buoyant bunny, outlined in thick ink with a fuzzy body and mismatched ears intro-
duces readers to the five senses through rhyming verses and stylized artwork.
(Reprinted with the permission of Atheneum Books for Young Readers, an imprint of Simon & Schuster
Children's Publishing Division from FIVE FOR A LITTLE ONE by Chris Raschka. Jacket illustration copyright © 2006 Chris Raschka.)

For a silly approach to food and taste, read *Arnie, the Doughnut* by Laurie Keller
(2003). This fun-filled adventure takes children to the bakery, where a chocolate-
covered doughnut named Arnie serves as a guide in describing each of the steps
involved in the creation of various confections. Arnie has no idea why people buy the
tasty treats, and when he is sold to Mr. Bing, he is shocked to discover his fate. The doughnut refuses to be eaten and devises a number of reasons why that should not happen.
The humor is probably more appropriate for primary-grade children, but they will certainly eat it up.

Smell.   Have children generate a list of odors by categories: those they like or dislike,
odors from school, or smells associated with particular holidays. Then, let them begin
their own sniff area, bringing in substances whose smells they like. The substances
can be kept in baby food jars with the lids on them but not screwed on or pressed
down tightly. This will help preserve the odor while still allowing easy access. In addition, read *You Can't Taste a Pickle with Your Ear: A Book About the Five Senses*
(Ziefert, 2002). Using a combination of clear information and gentle humor, Ziefert
introduces children to their five senses.

As a final book, read aloud Chris Raschka's *Five for a Little One* (2006), which has been illustrated using potato prints. Children can create their own page to add to a class book in response to the literature that has been shared. With all these activities, the children use their senses to explore their own environments. Literature helps heighten sensory awareness, both through providing an impetus for such exploration and through showing children how another person has experienced a part of the world.

Giving Children Experience with a Variety of Art Media

Children who are familiar with a variety of media are in a position to choose the medium that will best express their ideas and to select media that they enjoy or feel most successful in using. As well as experimenting with many forms of two- and three-dimensional art materials, children need time to use each form repeatedly so that they can gain mastery in, and explore variations for, its use.

Experimenting with Media Used by Illustrators   Providing opportunities for children to experiment with art materials does not mean that the teacher never gives assistance. One child may need help learning how to hold scissors. Another may benefit from the teacher's suggestion that the pieces of a collage be arranged before the child begins pasting any of them onto the paper. Help is given in technique, but the work is not done for the child.

One way that picture books can stimulate children to explore various media is for you to call attention to the medium used by the illustrator and to have materials available for any children who would like to try using them. Lionni's *Let's Make Rabbits* (1982), which is available in paperback and board-book formats, calls attention itself to the media in use for the story of two rabbits—one made with a pencil and the other with scissors. The tools and the actual construction processes are shown as the pencil and scissors first decide to make rabbits and then later make carrots for the rabbits they have created.

Primary-grade children may want to try folding origami swans, as Yoko does when she moves from Japan to California. In *Yoko's Paper Cranes* (Wells, 2001), Yoko decides to make and send the origami swans to her grandmother for her birthday. In *Swimmy* (Lionni, 1963), for example, children looking closely at the illustration of the "forest of seaweeds" will see that the seaweeds are constructed of imprints made by covering lace doilies with paint and then pressing them on the paper. Children can make their own object imprints by painting one side of an object and then pressing it onto paper or by using an ink or tempera paint pad or brayer to coat the object with paint. They can begin collecting objects themselves to add to the objects you provide. There is no attempt to copy the *work* of the illustrator—only the *method*.

Getting to Know Artists and Illustrators   Children might learn about an artist while they are enjoying the literature and exploring techniques, particularly if you select several books in which the same illustrator has used a different medium for different books. After *Swimmy*, share several other books by Leo Lionni. *Little Blue and Little Yellow* (1959) would lead to explorations in mixing paints, and *Inch by Inch* (1962) or *An Extraordinary Egg* (1994) would lead to collage made from cutting images out of paper that has been colored with crayon or paint, allowing patterns to be created before the shapes are cut. Children can see that some artists use a variety of techniques, just as they do.

Media in picture books that are appropriate for young children to use include crayon, colored pencil, chalk, pastels, scratchboard (use crayon resist with children), paints (tempera for all children, watercolor for primary children), pencil, photography, torn paper, collage, and combinations of these.

Children might also come to know artists through books by them or about them. They could see how artists have portrayed their own experiences in *The Raft* (2000), where Jim LaMarche draws on his childhood summer experiences using pastel drawings. They could read and talk about the collage in Eric Carle's books and then watch the DVD *Picture Writer,* in which Carle share his process of creating his illustrations. They could listen as a teacher read some of the interviews of illustrators of children's books in Pat Cummings' *Talking with Artists* (1992). They could see how Jeanette Winter paints in the style of the artist in the biographies of Georgia O'Keeffe (Jeanette Winter, 1998) and Diego Rivera (Jonah Winter, 1991). They might also want to explore the home pages of children's book illustrators on the Internet.

Illustrating One's Own Work   As children explore various media, they can be encouraged to illustrate stories that they are writing or dictating. They see the patterns of picture and text in the books they hear read to them. They also see the endpapers, the first and last pages in a book that are attached to the cover. As they see how illustrators have prepared endpapers, they can make their own for booklets they write.

Some endpapers are simply designs. In *Kitten's First Full Moon* (Henkes, 2004), the endpapers are covered with white circles against a dark gray background, which children will soon recognize as small moons. Lois Ehlert's *Snowballs* (1995) also has endpapers with small white balls. Children can make such designs with crayons or paint or might use cardboard cutouts or vegetable prints to make repetitive patterns. *Good Boy, Fergus!* (Shannon, 2006), a story about an energetic terrier that seems to always have his nose in something, shows Fergus's chew toys on the endpapers.

Some books have endpapers that relate to the story by showing a scene from it. *A Gift for Abuelitalun Regilo para Abulita* (Luenn, 1998) shows the church and graveyard where Rosita and her family go to celebrate The Day of the Dead and to honor her grandmother. David Small's illustration on the endpapers in *The Friend* (Stewart, 2004) shows Belle sitting in her bed situated in an enormous room.

Still other endpapers symbolize the story or picture things related to it. *The Little House* (Burton, 1942), in which the house experiences a city growing up around it, shows a cartoon sequence in which the mode of transportation undergoes changes, from the first small picture of a horse and rider passing the little house to the last of a horse van going by. The beginning endpapers in *Hannah is My Name* (Yang, 2004) depict Hannah's family leaving Taiwan with a cart loaded with their possessions. The final endpapers show her family riding in a taxi in San Francisco, their new home. *Olivia Saves the Circus* (Falconer, 2001) shows Olivia carrying her cat in and out the door on the endpapers. Olivia then goes to school, where she explains to her teacher and classmates how she saved the circus when all the performers got sick and she had to do their jobs, such as being Olivia the Tattooed Lady and the Flying Olivia.

Children will need to decide which type of endpaper they want to make. They might also create endpapers for books that do not have illustrated endpapers. The activity entails deciding what is essential about a story or what would symbolize it as well as the actual creation of a picture. The design of book jackets can involve the same kind of thought process, and these jackets can often be used on paper booklets that are not going to be bound in cardboard covers.

Listening to Descriptions of Techniques   Share books with children that provide information about the process that illustrators engage in when creating a book. *What Do Illustrators Do?* (Christelow, 1999) shows how an illustrator develops a book from rough sketches to finished artwork. She explains this process by following two artists as they illustrate different versions of Jack and the Beanstalk. Christelow answers the questions often posed by children such as, What materials do you use? and Is it hard to be an illustrator? The book reveals that it takes a lot of painstaking work and creativity to create the illustrations for a picture book.

You might also want to read a "how-to" book that is direct in its presentation of techniques. *Art Around the World: Loo-Loo, Boo, and More Art You Can Do* (Roche, 1998) suggests projects from various countries, giving a very brief history of the art and then showing and telling, step by step, how to use the technique. A child might choose to make an art project based on a burial mask from Peru, stained glass from France, a mosaic from Italy, or a block print from India. A section on things to know before beginning gives helpful information for preparing, cleaning up, and reading about the whole project before beginning.

Gail Gibbons' *Click!: A Book about Cameras and Taking Pictures* (1997) could be shared for the tips it gives about taking both indoor and outdoor photographs before children take photographs of their own. For primary-grade students, *Take a Look Around* (Varriale, 1999b) uses projects to introduce various photographic concepts, including shadow and light, camera angles, composition, action, and more. Books for young children about taking digital photographs haven't been published yet, but many of the techniques described in Gibbons's and Varriale's books are applicable to all types of photography.

Representing Stories Through Art   Books and book characters can be the subject of art activities. Children can be encouraged to respond to books through art. They may translate the images of the words into pictures or two-dimensional art into three-dimensional art. Characters can be made from clay, Play-doh, wire, pipe cleaners, styrofoam, or boxes.

Children are most likely to use and gain mastery over many media in art if they have the opportunity to work in art as one of their own choices and if the materials are readily available. It is useful to have a storage area for materials that children can use, getting the materials they need and being responsible for returning materials when they are finished. Many teachers label the storage containers, so that children are soon reading words such as *scissors* and *glue* and, in the process, seeing functional reading demonstrated. You will need to introduce new materials and their care either to the class as a whole or to the children in a series of small groups before you put them out for general use. New materials and techniques should be introduced gradually so that children are not overwhelmed and so that the art area is constantly changing. If children know what materials are needed, they can bring many of them from home. String, yarn, ribbon, sticks, toothpicks, straws, milk jugs, boxes, old wrapping paper, and a variety of other "beautiful junk" can be brought to school for art projects rather than being thrown away. It is one way children contribute to their classroom and make it theirs.

If you are fortunate in your school to have an art specialist, find ways to work together to connect literature and art. At times, primary-grade teachers are reluctant to provide opportunities for art exploration because of the mess that might occur. However, if there is an art room, it enables the curriculum to extend beyond the classroom and for collaboration with other teachers to occur.

Giving Children a Variety of Musical Experiences

Literature can give added dimension to children's musical experiences in the early years, contributing to their participation in singing, listening, using rhythm instruments, and movement. Many songs that are commonly taught to and enjoyed by young children are available in picture-book format and on CDs or videos. You have the option of sharing these songs as books or videos or simply as a listening experience if you play a CD or the cassette without showing the book. Teachers who are somewhat nervous about their own singing or piano playing often begin musical experiences for the children with tapes rather than by singing themselves. Cassettes and CDs are especially useful for placing in listening centers so that children can hear the words and tune again to learn it themselves or to sing along and gain practice in matching tones while engaged in an activity that, for them, is just fun.

Sharing Picture Books of Songs   In selecting picture books of songs that you plan to teach children, use the same criteria you would use for selecting other songs. Look for songs that are within the range of the children's voices, have some repetition of words or melody, and do not have large melodic intervals. "This Old Man" fits these criteria. Then judge the quality of the illustrations. The version of *Give the Dog a Bone* by Steven Kellogg (2000) is an oversized picture book with humorous illustrations featuring large characters that can be seen by a group of children. You might use the music at the back of the book as you play the song on the piano or autoharp and sing it for the children. You can point out to them that the book tells you what notes to play and sing. Present the song as a whole, not line by line. It is often helpful to show the direction of the notes with your hand or by drawing lines on the board; for example, for the first phrase of "This Old Man." One first-grader showed that she had grasped the concept of notation when she looked at six window blinds, all raised to a slightly different level, and reported, "We can sing the shades." As well as giving an introduction to notation, hand movements or lines drawn help children visualize the direction of the melody.

After you have taught the song, sing it with the children as you show the illustrations in one of the books. Children will see the words to the song on each page as they sing and will see that they are singing about the pictures also. If more than one book is shared, they will see that different artists can interpret a song differently and perhaps will want to illustrate other songs themselves. Five artists or illustrators who have each produced several picture books of songs are Nadine Bernard Westcott, Mary Ann Hoberman, Steven Kellogg, Peter Spier, and John Langstaff. You may want to look for their work.

You might also want to purchase a book or two of collections of songs for regular use with the children. *This Little Piggy: Lap Songs, Finger Plays, Clapping Games, and Pantomime Rhymes* (Yolen, 2006) comes with a CD that contains 13 songs. *Head, Shoulders, Knees and Toes: And Other Action Rhymes* (Newcome, 2002) contains more than 50 poems and songs appropriate for ages 2 and up. *Lullabies: An Illustrated Songbook* (Kapp, 1997) has the words and music to classic

lullabies, illustrated with reproductions of works in the Metropolitan Museum of Art. This book should be left where children can browse through it. *Tortillas and Lullabies/Tortillas y Cancioncitas* (Reiser, 1998) combines family traditions with the singing of lullabies. All these books combine music, art, and movement in a way that will increase children's appreciation of all.

Recommended Illustrated Song Books

Beaumont, Karen. (2005). *I Ain't Gonna Paint No More.* Ill. David Catrow. San Diego, CA: Harcourt.

Berry, Holly. (1994). *Old MacDonald Had a Farm.* New York: North-South.

Cabrera, Jane. (2003). *If You're Happy and You Know It.* New York: Holiday House.

Hoberman, Mary Ann. (2004). *Yankee Doodle.* Ill. Nadine Bernard Westcott. Boston: Little, Brown.

Katz, Alan. (2001). *Take Me Out of the Bathtub and Other Silly Dilly Songs.* Ill. David Catrow. New York: McElderry.

Kellogg, Steven. (1998). *A-Hunting We Will Go.* New York: HarperCollins.

Metropolitan Museum of Art. *A Treasury of Children Songs: Forty Favorites to Sing and Play.* (2003). New York: Holt.

Orozco, Jose-Luis (Translater). (1994). *"De Colores" and Other Latin American Folk Songs for Children.* New York: Dutton.

Peek, Merle. (1998). *Mary Wore Her Red Dress and Henry Wore His Green Sneakers.* Boston: Houghton Mifflin.

Zelinsky, Paul. (2002). *Knick-Knack Paddywhack: A Moving Parts Book.* New York: Dutton.

Sharing Literature in Audiovisual/CD-ROM Format   Literature in audiovisual format can provide musical listening experiences for children. They often enjoy listening to songs that may be too complex for them to sing. Preschoolers can listen to *The Fox Went Out on a Chilly Night* and *Clementine* in video format. After listening to the story of *Peter and the Wolf* (Prokofiev, 1982) in picture-book format, they might attempt to follow the story in pictures as it unfolds in the music and as the various instruments indicate the character and the action. Some stories transferred to film have musical accompaniments. *Where the Wild Things Are* is available in video and DVD format, with a musical score and narration by Peter Schickele.

Using Rhythm Instruments with Literature   Rhythm instruments can be used in conjunction with literature, with the children using drums, triangles, sand blocks, or rhythm sticks. Children can add rhythmic accompaniment to nursery rhymes that have a strong beat, such as "A Bear Went Over a Mountain"; use tone bars with others such as "Rain, Rain Go Away"; or make an ostinato, a background of steady pitch and rhythm, for rhymes such as "Hickory Dickory Dock." Children may use instruments to capture the rhythm of the *Train Song* (Ziefert, 2000) as the different trains pass by with a "chug-a-chug-chug and clickety-clack."

There are opportunities for varied rhythms and sounds that children might create to accompany *Rum-a-Tum-Tum* (Medearis, 1997). A young girl describes the streets of the French Quarter in New Orleans, filled with action and sound, with the rhythms of the vendors shouting and the jazz of a marching band on parade. Children could work in small groups to develop their own interpretation of particular pages.

Moving in Response to Literature   Movement is a natural response to music and to poetry and prose that has a strong rhythmic beat. Two- and 3-year-olds, still responding to their own rhythms, might move to stories or songs by adding motions rather than keeping time. Listening to *Drummer Hoff* (Emberley, 1967), for example, they might show what each of the soldiers carried as they prepared to fire the cannon. Four- and 5-year-olds can keep the rhythm with soft drumming, marching, or by striking their thighs with their hands.

Teach children several action games played while singing. *The Itsy-Bitsy Spider* (Winter, 2000), *Skip to My Lou* (Quackenbush, 1975), and *The Hokey Pokey: Another Prickley Love Story* (Wheeler, 2006) can all be learned quickly by children. After they play the games or do the actions, let children look through the books, especially Wheeler's story, which incorporates the Hokey Pokey into the plot.

Help children explore contrasts in music. After reading *Mama Don't Allow* (Hurd, 1984), in which Miles, an opossum, gets a saxophone from Uncle Waylon for a birthday present and eventually starts his own band, teach children the song "Mama Don't Allow." The words and music are in the book. Play it in the loud and rollicking way the Swamp Band plays it. Let the children dance to the music. In the book, Miles and his band get a job playing for a group of alligators on a riverboat trip. At last they have found an audience that appreciates their playing. After an evening of music and dance, however, both the band and the alligators are ready for dinner. It is then that the band discovers that *it* is the dinner as well as the entertainment. The band offers to play one more song before dinner. They play a soft Lullaby of Swampland, the alligators all fall asleep, and the band escapes. When Miles returns home, still playing the lullaby softly on his sax, his mother is pleased with the music she hears. Play some soft music or lullabies for the children. Let them move to this music and respond to the different rhythms and varying intensities of the songs. Encourage them to talk about the differences.

Think of all the books you have read that could provide a stimulus for children to move to music. They could be *Little Toot* (Gramatky, 1939), devising their own motions as the little tug boat who disliked hard work, preferring instead to glide around the harbor making fancy figure eights in the water. They could make up their own dance as Tanya does in *Tanya and the Magic Wardrobe* (Gauch, 1997). They could be Sweet Pea in *Taking a Bath with the Dog and Other Things That Make Me Happy* (Menchin, 2007) and create movements to the different things that make her happy. Each activity allows the children to create their own movements for a familiar character, and each can be matched to appropriate music. As you share literature with children, make notes for yourself about the musical possibilities of stories and poems, including possibilities for singing, listening, rhythmic response, and movement.

Stimulating Creativity in Art, Music, and Movement

If creativity does indeed involve the ability to restructure information in new ways, to see inconsistencies or gaps in knowledge and generate and test hypotheses to fill these gaps, to engage in divergent thinking, to be open and flexible, and to be able to elaborate on ideas, then certain approaches to teaching and certain materials are more likely than others to foster such behavior. Three that apply to literature as a stimulus for creativity in the arts are the use of questions and activities that lead to divergent responses, the use of books that are inventive, and the practice of encouraging children to give more than one response.

Evoking Divergent Responses   When you make suggestions for activities to expand on literature or when you pose questions about literature structure these so that they lead to many different responses on the part of the children. For example, questions that ask children What would happen if . . . ? or Tell us one thing you would do if . . . . or What else could this character have done . . . ? can be answered in a variety of ways.

There is no one right answer, although you need to require that the children be able to support their ideas.

Activities, too, should have more than one acceptable response. Several children may show their answers about how a giraffe could dance before and then after hearing *Giraffes Can't Dance* (Andreae, 2001). Gerald is a giraffe who simply can't dance. Try as he may, his long, spindly legs buckle whenever he starts to boogie. Every year he dreads going to the Great Jungle Dance, until one night he finds his own special music. Children's answers will reflect their own thinking, however, and may well draw on the book's perspective that sometimes you just need a different type of music. The object is to develop a unique idea, not to remember an answer from a book.

If you are engaging the children in movement, allow them to choose the motions themselves. *Seven Little Monsters* (1975) is a brief book by Maurice Sendak with monsters reminiscent of those in *Where the Wild Things Are* (Sendak, 1963). Each monster has a movement, such as going up, or creeping, or eating, or sleeping, and the seven are lined up in a row "making trouble." Children dramatizing this brief text can add their own interpretations to the movements. They can decide on a rhythmic accompaniment to the text and to their movements. Your reading of the text gives a structure to their responses, but you do not tell them how to move.

The criterion of providing for divergent responses is one that can be applied to any activity designed to extend a child's understanding of a book or poem. This does not mean an excuse for a child to do whatever he or she pleases, disrupting everyone else. It does mean your acceptance of their ideas, even if they are not ideas you had thought of or expected. Children using rhythm instruments to make the sounds of the Wild Things can decide which instruments give the sounds they think fit, how they should be put together, when they should be loud or soft, and how fast they should be played. It is their interpretation that is important, their feel for the book, for the mood of the "rumpus" that is the climax of the book. Allowing children to continue to play the instruments when the group is beginning a new activity or to damage the instruments from using them inappropriately is neither developing their creativity nor helping them to accept responsibility.

Recommended Books About Dance & Movement

Briggs, Anita. (2002). *Hobart.* Ill. Mary Rayner. New York: Simon & Schuster.

Colon-Vila, Lillian. (1998). *Salsa!* Ill. Roberta Collier Morales. Houston, TX: Piñata Books.

Crimi, Carolyn. (2002). *Tessa's Tip-Tapping Toes.* Ill. Marsha Gray Carrington. New York: Orchard.

Dillon, Leo & Diane. (2002). *Rap a Tap Tap: Here's Bojangles— Think of That.* New York: Scholastic.

Kinerk, Robert. (2003). *Clorinda.* Ill. Steven Kellogg. New York: Simon & Schuster.

Pinkney, Andrea Davis. (1995). *Alvin Ailey.* Ill. Brian Pinkney. New York: Hyperion.

Sis, Peter. (2001). *Ballerina!* New York: Greenwillow.

Smith, Cynthia Leitich. (2000). *Jingle Dancer.* Ill. Cornelius Van Wright. New York: HarperCollins.

Walton, Rick. (2001). *How Can You Dance?* Ill. Ana Lopez-Escriva. New York: Putnam.

Winthrop, Elizabeth. (2001). *Dumpy La Rue.* Ill. Betsy Lewin. New York: Holt.

Presenting Books That Are Inventive   Select books in which the authors and illustrators have been inventive themselves, and use these to suggest inventiveness on the children's parts. Some of these books are told in the first person, with the lead character describing his or her actions. *Dancing Larry* (Pinkwater, 2006) sees nothing wrong with joining a ballet class, but unfortunately ballet instructor Madame Swoboda refuses to allow him to do so. Larry won't admit defeat and gathers his like-minded bruin brothers to form their own ballet company. This witty picture book combines a fun story with colorful artwork. Larry is all about dance as a mode of free expression, not one of learned steps or routines. How do children dance? Some third-graders talked about enjoying moving to "fast" music; others looked at the movements and told about classes in gymnastics. Some wanted to demonstrate how they could dance when they felt happy. None attempted to copy the movements caught in the illustrations. After their own experiences, they looked at the photographs in Jim Varriale's *Kids Dance: The Students of Ballet Tech* (1999a) and broadened even further their concept of dance.

Preschoolers can add their own fantastic stories of what they might see on the way to school after they hear what Marco saw on the way home in *And to Think That I Saw It on Mulberry Street* (Geisel, 1937). Each adds a new element, just as Marco's story became more and more elaborate as he retold it.

Children can explore making words look like the ideas they represent after seeing *Carousel* (1982) by Donald Crews. In this book, the carousel is empty at first; then riders get on, the music starts, and all go around faster and faster. Then the music ends; the carousel slows and stops; the ride is over. The text is sparse, with concise phrases rather than sentences. The illustrations show the increased blurring of colors to capture the increased speed of the carousel. The music, shown by words such as "toot" and "boom," also becomes blurred as the description changes from music "playing" to music "blaring."

Look for books that help children see things in new ways. *It Looked Like Spilt Milk* (Shaw, 1947) talks about the shapes cloud formations may take, prompting children to look at the clouds themselves. What do they see? Children can use chalk to record the formations and then describe them. *Mystery* (Geisert, 2003) is set in an art museum as a piglet and her grandfather investigate the disappearance of several paintings. Clues in the illustrations give children a chance to solve the mystery along with the little piglet.

Let children expand ideas that authors and illustrators have begun. *The Biggest House in the World* (Lionni, 1968) begs to be emulated. Lois Ehlert has illustrated a Mayan Indian tale from Mexico, *Cuckoo/Cucu* (1997), with brightly colored figures. Some figures have arms and legs attached with brads, so that they appear movable. Children could explore making such characters and placing them in various ways to indicate motion. Jan Ormerod's *Ms. Macdonald Has a Class* (1996) varies the lyrics to "Old MacDonald Had a Farm" as the class visits a farm and then makes plans for a play. The children might work together to write new lyrics to this or other familiar tunes, making them fit their own lives.

Encouraging Multiple Responses   Finally, encourage children to give several responses. They might create several animals after hearing *Cuckoo* or replay *Seven Little Monsters,* each time adding new movements, or make the biggest house for a bird, the biggest house for a snake, or the biggest house for themselves. Changing ideas, adding new elements, being flexible in approach—all encourage children to use their creative abilities.

Making Aesthetic and Creative Experiences Enjoyable for Children

If you enjoy aesthetic and creative activities and show that you do, this will influence children to enjoy such activities because your behavior provides a model for them. You show that you value aesthetic experiences when you give projects such as listening to a composition your full attention, listening to the cassette or CD with the children, and responding to the music yourself.

Planning for Enjoyable Creative Experiences   You can also plan so that the experiences will be enjoyable for you. For example, you know that if you are to teach a song to young children, you will need to sing it (or play it) many times, and you will probably sing it with the children throughout the year. Therefore, it makes sense to select songs you like and that you don't think you will tire of readily. Most teachers find that they vary the songs they teach if they have taught for several years and also select different themes or topics to explore in depth or to use in learning centers.

Organize art projects so that they operate smoothly both for you and for the children. Teach children to clean up after themselves, washing out brushes and storing scissors and paste in their specified places. Children learn responsibility when they must care for the equipment they use and develop independence as they become more and more able to get what they need and to replace it when they are finished.

Show your enjoyment of the products children produce. Display them, with the children's consent, on a regular basis. Create paper frames around the work so that it is viewed as a piece of art. Comment on what they have done and are doing; however, do so in a way that emphasizes the process rather than the product: I see you found a way to make all the pieces lay flat, or How did you feel while you were the troll waiting for the Billy Goats Gruff to start across the bridge? Let children talk about their work when they seem eager to share.

Helping Children Feel Successful   Help children gain satisfaction from their experiences by selecting books and suggesting activities that match the children's developmental level. The song "Yankee Doodle" is one you could use with children of various ages. It appears in a book illustrated with woodcuts by Ed Emberley (Shackburg, 1965) that contains both a history of the song and the music for it and in one with humorous illustrations by Steven Kellogg (1996), also available as a sound filmstrip from Weston Woods. The music is performed by The Colonial Williamsburg Fife and Drum Corps.

Infants have a wonderful sense of rhythm and will bounce to rhythms at an early age. Rhythmic songs attract babies, who listen with focused attention to what you are singing. Toddlers enjoy moving their bodies gracefully and dreamily to slow dance music. They also like to pretend they are doing something such as riding a horse. They are also expanding their vocabulary and often repeat the words that they hear to songs whether they truly understand them or not.

If you are working with 3-year-olds, you might sing just the first verse and the chorus for the children rather than all the verses. They could listen to it several times and join in on any phrases they remembered. You would not expect them to match the tones accurately nor to learn all the words. You might have them follow actions for the song or walk to the rhythm of the music on the cassette that accompanies the filmstrip. Again, it is likely that, although most of them will be keeping a steady rhythm, their movement will not synchronize exactly with the music.

If you are teaching 5- and 6-year-olds, you could present an entire song. Most of these children would be able to learn the first verse and chorus. They could be drummers, with their hands keeping time as they sing, or they could use rhythm instruments. They could march like soldiers, using arm motions as well as leg movements. After looking at the Emberley illustrations, they could use a similar printing technique of their own, perhaps making a cardboard cut with a masking-tape loop on the back. They could then repeat the print of their figure, lifting it from the paper by the loop. They might talk about how Emberley used the print to show many soldiers and decide what they could show.

If you are teaching 8-year-olds, you might read the history of the song to them and what some of the words in the lyrics mean. They, too, would enjoy singing and moving to the song. If they made prints, they could use overlapping cuts as Emberley did. They might make up new lyrics to the tune, trying out each suggestion to make certain that it fit the rhythm. For this age level, you might include activities from earlier stages. Eight-year-olds enjoy marching, even though they were able to do it when they were 6.

The essential factor is that children be able to feel themselves successful in the activity. Thus, the 3-year-old singing two phrases off tune will enjoy it and will be learning about matching tones as long as you let him or her know that this is acceptable behavior. If, however, you expect all tones to be matched and all of the words to be learned, the child may well become frustrated and decide that singing is an activity to be avoided. One parent cleverly maintained her son's good feelings about his own art when a teacher might have damaged both his interest in drawing and his self-confidence. The teacher, dissatisfied with the kindergartner's crayoning, had written POOR across the paper. He came home and showed the paper to his mother, beaming. She looked at it, looked at him, and asked him to tell her about the picture. "My teacher thought it was great," he said. "How do you know?" his mother asked. "Because she put a 100 on it, and that means it's perfect. See the 0s?" The mother decided that such a good paper should go on the refrigerator door for the family to enjoy for that week. The teacher's written comment was inappropriate, both for its implication that art should be graded and for the damage it could have done to that child's image of himself and his artistic ability.

Presenting Books That Promote Understanding and Appreciation of the Arts   Some books you may choose to present will have children as protagonists engaged in the arts; others will focus on adults. Both types are useful to present to children, for together they show that creative and aesthetic endeavors are not limited to any one age group. Rosa, in *Music, Music for Everyone* (Williams, 1984), has found that music brings her pleasure. She plays the accordion and is able to bring musical entertainment to others while making money for herself by performing with three friends at a party. Sugar, in *Papa's Lucky Shadow* (Daly, 1992), learns to tap dance from her grandfather, and the two present a winning rendition of "Me and My Shadow" at the Pensioner's Club party. Both girls are supported in their love of music or dance by at least one close family member.

Emily's Art (Catalanotto, 2001) explores difficulties encountered when artistic creations are judged by others for ability rather than for expression. *The Dot* (Reynolds, 2003) relates a story of a child convinced she cannot create art until an intelligent teacher sets the young girl on a journey of self-discovery and artistic experimentation. Books such as these provide excellent starting points for children to discuss their own artwork and their own reactions to the creative process.

Kuskin takes a lighthearted approach in *The Philharmonic Gets Dressed* (1982). Just as the title implies, this book describes how the members of the orchestra begin to prepare for a concert, starting as they get dressed at home and concluding as they begin to play. In the course of the story, the reader learns about an orchestra. Share books such as these with children to show that many people gain deep satisfaction from participation in and observation of the arts.

Sustaining an Atmosphere of Acceptance   Give children a wide variety of media from which to choose and allow children to decide for themselves on many occasions what materials they wish to use in art or which movements they wish to use in response to music. Variety maintains interest and allows children to find activities that they particularly enjoy. The choice builds independence and allows for preferences and creative responses.

Finally, let children work together in response to music or literature. Many like to work with their friends, especially in the primary grades. They might make a mural of cats in stories they have heard, with each child contributing one character. They talk about their contribution and also plan how the mural will look when finished. At other times, working together is simply sharing materials or being in the same vicinity but feeling free to converse with their neighbors if they like. An atmosphere of trust and friendship transfers positive reactions to the activity being undertaken. If you can help children enjoy their aesthetic and creative activities, you will be giving them the necessary attitude for continuing to develop their skills of impression and their skills of expression.

SUMMARY

Children's growth in creative expression through art, music, and movement is in part developmental, as they gain more physical and motor control, and in part environmental, as they have opportunities to engage in artistic and musical experiences. Performance skills of singing, using rhythm instruments, drawing, painting, and dramatizing appear to provide a base for aesthetic appreciation by helping children become familiar with the techniques involved.

The following long-term goals are appropriate for the aesthetic and creative growth of young children.

Children will respond favorably to diverse styles of art and music.

Children will exhibit a sensory awareness of their environment.

Children will use, experiment with, and gain control over a variety of media.

Children will sing in tune within their vocal range and will respond to music and literature with movement and with rhythm instruments.

Children will use their imaginations as they participate in art, music, and movement.

Children will enjoy experiencing the work of others and participating in the arts themselves.

Books offer opportunities for helping children achieve these goals. Teacher Feature 9.1 (pp. 264–267) suggests appropriate teaching strategies. Children are likely to develop favorable attitudes toward diverse styles of art if they recognize that art is personal expression, if they see a wide range of styles of art in picture books, and if they relate personally to the art they are viewing. Children become aware of the sensory qualities of their environment when they hear literature in which authors give descriptions written in sensory terms and in which illustrators recreate the beauty they observe. Books also may provide the stimulus for children to explore their environment, taking special note of sensory qualities.

Children become familiar with a variety of media when they are given the opportunity to experiment with art materials. They may explore techniques used by illustrators of picture books; they may make illustrations for their own writing; they may try artistic techniques or projects described in books. Children need both initial help in learning about the media available in their classroom and time on their own to use the media.

Literature can give added dimension to children's musical experiences in the early years, contributing to their participation in singing, listening, using rhythm instruments, and movement. Children listen to songs illustrated in picture books either read or sung; they enjoy hearing, in audiovisual format, songs too complex for them to sing themselves; they use rhythm instruments in conjunction with literature; and they move in response to poetry and prose that has a strong rhythmic beat or actions that can be dramatized.

Finally, children's creativity and their appreciation of the creativity of others can be fostered through literature. Questions and activities that are based on books should evoke divergent responses, be enjoyable for the child, and allow the child to be successful. An atmosphere of acceptance and a general pattern of encouragement for multiple reactions and responses to a single book or questions are key elements in developing children's creativity and aesthetic appreciation.

Teacher Feature 9.1   Supporting Children's Aesthetic and Creative Growth

Developmental Goals	Teaching Suggestions
Children will respond favorably to diverse styles of art and music.	• Show children that art is one form of personal expression. • Show how more than one artist has interpreted the same song, tale, or character. • Let children compare how one animal appears in several books of fiction. • Help children see the diversity in artistic styles in picture book illustrations. • Encourage careful observation of illustrations. • Involve children in art projects related to techniques used or portrayed in books.
Children will exhibit a sensory awareness of their environment.	• Read prose and poetry by authors who write in sensory terms. • Let children try sensory experiences described in books. • Use literature as a stimulus for activities that require children to use their senses in discovery or exploration.
Children will use, experiment with, and gain control over a variety of art media.	• Let children experiment with selected media used by illustrators of children's books. • Encourage children to illustrate stories and poems they dictate or write. • Help children try artistic techniques described in books. • Have children respond to books through art, both two and three dimensional.
Children will sing in tune within their vocal range and will respond to music and rhythm instruments.	• Share picture-book editions of songs. • Present literature in audiovisual format for children to hear musical accompaniment and songs too complex for them to sing. • Let children use rhythm instruments in conjunction with literature. • Encourage children to move in response to poems or stories, either adding motions or moving to the rhythm.
Children will use their imaginations as they participate in art, music, and movement.	• Plan activities that will lead to divergent responses. • Present books that are inventive. • Encourage children to give more than one response.

Recommended Literature

	Ages 0–2		Ages 5–8
Liu	*The Yellow Umbrella*	Agee	*The Incredible Painting of Felix Clousseau*
Wadsworth	*Over in the Meadow*	dePaola	*The Art Lesson*
		Falconer	*Olivia and the Missing Toy*
	Ages 2–5	Geisert	*Oink*
		Mayhew	*Katie's Sunday Afternoon*
Hoban	*Books about Frances*	Reynolds	*Ish*
Numeroff	*If You Give a Pig a Pancake*	Say	*Emma's Rug*
		Williams Karen	*Painted Dreams*

	Ages 0–2		Ages 5–8
Nest	*Baby Duck & the Bad Eyeglasses*	Bowen	*Tracks in the Wild*
Raschka	*Five for a Little One*	Brown	*Touch Will Tell*
	Ages 2–5	Locker	*Sky Trees: Seeing Science Through Art*
		Wright-Frierson	*A North American Rain Forest Scrapbook*
Boyden	*"Mud"*	Young	*Seven Blind Mice*
Hoban	*Bread and Jam for Frances*		
Keats	*Goggles*		
Merriam	*"A Matter of Taste"*		
Snyder	*"Poem to Mud"*		
Yolen	*Owl Moon*		

	Ages 2–5		Ages 5–8
Ehlert	*Snowballs*	Cummings	*Talking with Artists*
Lionni	*An Extraordinary Egg*	Gibbons	*Click! A Book About Cameras and Taking Pictures*
Lionni	*Inch by Inch*	Henkes	*Kitten's First Full Moon*
Lionni	*Let's Make Rabbits*	Varriale	*Take a Look Around*
Lionni	*Little Blue and Little Yellow*	Wells	*Yoko's Paper Cranes*
Lionni	*Swimmy*		

	Ages 0–2		Ages 5–8
Kellogg	*Give the Dog a Bone*	Daly	*Papa's Lucky Shadow*
Ziefert	*Train Song*	Geisert	*Mystery*
	Ages 2–5	Hurd	*Mama Don't Allow*
		Liu	*The Yellow Umbrella*
Ehlert	*Cuckoo/Cucu*		
Emberley	*Drummer Hoff*		
Gramatky	*Little Toot*		
Ormerod	*Ms. MacDonald Has a Class*		
Quackenbush	*Skip to My Lou*		

	Ages 2–5		Ages 5–8
Andreae	*Giraffes Can't Dance*	Crews	*Carousel*
Geisel	*And to Think That I Saw It on Mulberry Street*	Gauch	*Tanya and the Magic Wardrobe*
		Hurd	*Mama Don't Allow*
Sendak	*Seven Little Monsters*	Lionni	*The Biggest House in the World*
Sendak	*Where the Wild Things Are*	Menchin	*Taking a Bath with the Dog and Other Things That Make Me Happy*
Shaw	*It Looked Like Spilt Milk*	Pinkwater	*Dancing Larry*
		Reiser	*Tortillas and Lullabies/Tortillas y Cancioncitas*
		Varriale	*Kids Dance*

(continued)

Teacher Feature 9.1　Supporting Children's Aesthetic and Creative Growth (*continued*)

Developmental Goals	Teaching Suggestions
Children will enjoy experiencing the work of others and participating in the arts themselves.	• Organize art projects so that they operate smoothly. • Show your own enjoyment of the work children produce. • Talk with children while they work, emphasizing the artistic process in your comments. • Suggest activities that match the children's developmental level. • Give children frequent opportunities to choose the media or type of response they wish to use. • Present books that promote understanding and appreciation of the arts. • Let children work together on music and art projects.

Extending Your Learning

1. Select one animal and compare how at least three illustrators have drawn it.

2. Select five Caldecott Award winners and identify as best you can the different media and styles of illustration used.

3. Start a section of your poetry collection for children in which poets use sensory descriptions.

4. Take a walk around the school and observe nature, thinking about ways you could plan a lesson around this activity using literature.

5. Select three picture books in which the illustrator has used media that children could try themselves.

6. Select three picture books that lend themselves to interpretation through music or movement. Describe how you would engage children in the activity.

Recommended Literature

Ages 2–5		Ages 5–8	
Kellogg	*Yankee Doodle*	Catalanotto	*Emily's Art*
Shackburg	*Yankee Doodle*	Reynolds	*The Dot*

REFERENCES

Professional References Cited

Alejandro, A. (1994). Like happy dreams—integrating visual arts, writing, and reading. *Language Arts*, *71*(1), 12–21.

Brewer, J. (2006). *Introduction to early childhood education* (6th ed.). Boston: Allyn and Bacon.

Chapman, L. (1978). *Approaches to art in education.* New York: Harcourt.

Davenport, G. (1999). The Arts: A Means for Developing Literacy. *Delta Kappa Gamma Bulletin*, *1*, 11–15.

Fleith, D. (2000). Teacher and Student Perceptions of Creativity in the Classroom Environment. *Roeper Review*, 22(3), 148–53.

Honig, A. (2004). Communicating with babies through music. *Scholastic Early Childhood Today*, *18*(5), 24–6.

Krogh, S. (1994). *Educating young children: Infancy to grade three.* New York: McGraw-Hill.

Lowenfeld, V., & Brittain, L. (1987). *Creative and mental growth* (8th ed.). New York: Macmillan.

McDonald, D. (1979). *Music in our lives: The early years.* Washington, DC: National Association for the Education of Young Children.

McDonald, D., & Simons, G. (1989). *Musical growth and development: Birth through six.* New York: Schirmer.

Sousa, R., MacLin, K. M., and MacLin, O. H. (2004). *Cognitive psychology* (7th ed.). Boston: Allyn & Bacon.

Torrance, E. P. (1970). *Encouraging creativity in the classroom.* Dubuque, IA: Brown.

Children's Literature Cited

Agee, Jon. (1988). *The Incredible Painting of Felix Clousseau.* New York: Farrar, Straus & Giroux.

Andreae, Giles. (2001). *Giraffes Can't Dance.* Ill. Guy Parker-Rees. New York: Orchard.

Andrews-Goebel, Nancy. (2002). *The Pot that Juan Built.* Ill. David Diaz. New York: Lee & Low.

Bowen, Betsy. (1998). *Tracks in the Wild.* Boston: Houghton Mifflin.

Boyden, Polly Chase. (1983). "Mud" in Prelutsky, Jack. *The Random House Book of Poetry for Children.* New York: Random House.

Brown Marcia. (1979). *Touch Will Tell.* New York: Watts.

Burton, Virginia. (1942). *The Little House.* Boston: Houghton Mifflin.

Catalanotto, Peter. (2001). *Emily's Art.* New York: Atheneum.

Christelow, Eileen. (1999). *What Do Illustrators Do?* Boston: Houghton Mifflin.

Cole, Henry. (1998). *I Took a Walk.* New York: Greenwillow.

Cole, Henry. (2003). *On the Way to the Beach.* New York: Greenwillow.

Collins, Pat Lowery. (1994). *I Am an Artist.* Brookfield, CT: Millbrook.

Cowley, Joy. (1999). *Agapanthus Hum and the Eyeglasses.* Ill. Jennifer Plecas. New York: Penguin.

Crews, Donald. (1982). *Carousel.* New York: Greenwillow.

Cummings, Pat. (1992). *Talking with Artists.* New York: Bradbury.

Daly, Niki. (1992). *Papa's Lucky Shadow.* New York: Simon.

dePaola, Tomie. (1989). *The Art Lesson.* New York: Putnam.

DiCamillo, Kate. (2007). *Mercy Watson: Princess in Disguise.* Ill. Chris Van Dusen. Cambridge, MA: Candlewick.

Ehlert, Lois. (1995). *Snowballs.* San Diego: Harcourt.

Ehlert, Lois. (1997). *Cuckoo/Cucu.* San Diego: Harcourt.

Emberley, Barbara. (1967). *Drummer Hoff.* Ill. Ed Emberley. Upper Saddle River, NJ: Prentice Hall.

Eric Carle: Picture Writer DVD. (2008). New York: Phiomel.

Falconer, Ian. (2001). *Olivia Saves the Circus.* New York: Atheneum.

Falconer, Ian. (2003). *Olivia and the Missing Toy.* New York: Atheneum.

Falconer, Ian. (2006). *Olivia Forms a Band.* New York: Atheneum.

Florian, Douglas. (2003). *Autumnblings.* New York: Greenwillow.

Florian, Douglas. (2007). *Comets, Stars, the Moon and Mars: Space Poems and Paintings.* San Diego, CA: Harcourt.

Gauch, Patricia Lee. (1997). *Tanya and the Magic Wardrobe.* Ill. Satomi Ichikawa. New York: Philomel.

Geisel, Theodore. (1937). *And to Think That I Saw It on Mulberry Street.* New York: Vanguard.

Geisert, Arthur. (1991). *Oink.* Boston: Houghton Mifflin.

Geisert, Arthur. (2003). *Mystery.* Boston: Houghton Mifflin.

George, Jean. (1974). *All Upon a Sidewalk.* Ill. Don Bolognese. New York: Dutton.

Gibbons, Gail. (1997). *Click!: A Book about Cameras and Taking Pictures.* Boston: Little, Brown.

Gramatky, Hardy. (1939). *Little Toot.* New York: Putnam.

Henkes, Kevin. (2004). *Kitten's First Full Moon.* New York: Greenwillow.

Hest, Amy. (1996). *Baby Duck and the Bad Eyeglasses.* Ill. Jill Barton. Cambridge, MA: Candlewick.

Hoban, Russell. (1969). *Bread and Jam for Frances.* Ill. Lillian Hoban. New York: Harper & Row.

Hubbell, Patricia. (1963). "Our Washing Machine" in *The Apple Vendor's Fair.* Ill. Julia Mass. New York: Atheneum.

Hurd, Thacher. (1984). *Mama Don't Allow.* New York: Harper.

Isadora, Rachel. (1979). *Ben's Trumpet.* New York: Greenwillow.

Kapp, Richard. (1997). *Lullabies: An Illustrated Songbook.* New York: Metropolitan Museum of Art.

Keats, Ezra Jack. (1969). *Goggles.* New York: Macmillan.

Keller, Laurie. (2003). *Arnie, the Doughnut.* New York: Holt.

Kellogg, Steven. (1996). *Yankee Doodle.* New York: Simon & Schuster.

Kellogg, Steven. (2000). *Give the Dog a Bone.* New York: SeaStar.

Kuskin, Karla. (1982). *The Philharmonic Gets Dressed.* Ill. Marc Simont. New York: Harper & Row.

LaMarche, Jim. (2000). *The Raft.* New York: HarperCollins.

Lionni, Leo. (1959). *Little Blue and Little Yellow.* New York: Astor-Honor.

Lionni, Leo. (1962). *Inch by Inch.* New York: Astor-Honor.

Lionni, Leo. (1963). *Swimmy.* New York: Pantheon.

Lionni, Leo. (1968). *The Biggest House in the World.* New York: Pantheon.

Lionni, Leo. (1982). *Let's Make Rabbits.* New York: Pantheon.

Lionni, Leo. (1994). An *Extraordinary Egg.* New York: Knopf.

Liu, Jae Soo. (2001). *The Yellow Umbrella.* La Jolla, CA: Kane/Miller.

Locker, Thomas. (1995). *Sky Tree: Seeing Science Through Art.* New York: HarperCollins.

Luenn, Nancy. (1998). *A Gift for Abuelita/Un Regalo para Abuelita.* Ill. Robert Chapman. Phoenix, AZ: Rising Moon.

MacDonald, Ross. (2003). *Achoo! Bang! Crash! A Noisy Alphabet.* New York: Millbrook.

Mayhew, James. (2005). *Katie's Sunday Afternoon.* New York: Orchard.

Medearis, Angela Shelf. (1997). *Rum-a-Tum-Tum.* Ill. James Ransome. New York: Holiday.

Menchin, Scott. (2007). *Taking a Bath with the Dog and Other Things That Make Me Happy.* Cambridge, MA: Candlewick.

Merriam, Eve. (1962). "A Matter of Taste" in *There Is No Rhyme for Silver.* New York: Atheneum. Copyright © 1962, 1990 by Eve Merriam. Used by permission of Eve Merriam.

Newcome, Zita. (2002). *Head, Shoulders, Knees and Toes: And Other Action Rhymes.* Cambridge, MA: Candlewick.

Numeroff, Laura. (1998). *If You Give a Pig a Pancake.* Ill. Felicia Bond. New York: HarperCollins.

Ormerod, Jan. (1996). *Ms. MacDonald Has a Class.* New York: Clarion.

Pinkwater, Larry. (2006). *Dancing Larry.* Tarrytown, NY: Marshall Cavendish.

Prokofiev, Serge. (1982). *Peter and the Wolf.* Ill. Charles Mikolaycak. New York: Viking.

Quackenbush, Robert. (1975). *Skip to My Lou.* Philadelphia: Lippincott.

Raschka, Chris. (2006). *Five for a Little One.* New York: Atheneum.

Reiser, Lynn. (1998). *Tortillas and Lullabies/Tortillas y Cancioncitas.* New York: Greenwillow.

Reynolds, Peter. (2003). *The Dot.* Cambridge, MA: Candlewick.

Reynolds. Peter. (2004). *Ish.* Cambridge, MA: Candlewick.

Roche, Denis. (1998). *Art Around the World: Loo-Loo, Boo, and More Art You Can Do.* Boston: Houghton Mifflin.

Say, Allen. (1996). *Emma's Rug.* Boston: Houghton Mifflin.

Sendak, Maurice. (1963). *Where the Wild Things Are.* New York: Harper.

Sendak, Maurice. (1975). *Seven Little Monsters.* New York: Harper.

Shackburg, Richard. (1965). *Yankee Doodle.* Ill. Ed Emberly. Upper Saddle River, NJ: Prentice Hall.

Shannon, David. (2006). *Good Boy, Fergus!* New York: Scholastic.

Shaw, Charles. (1947). *It Looked Like Spilt Milk.* New York: Harper.

Shulevitz, Uri. (1998). *Snow.* New York: Farrar, Straus & Giroux.

Sidman, Joyce. (2005). *Song of the Water Boatman and Other Pond Poems.* Ill. Beckie Prange. Boston: Houghton Mifflin.

Sidman, Joyce. (2006). *Butterfly Eyes and Other Secrets of the Meadow.* Ill. Beth Krommes. Boston: Houghton Mifflin.

Smith, Lane. (1991). *Glasses, Who Needs 'Em?* New York: Viking.

Snyder, Zilpha Keatley. (1969). "Poem to Mud" in *Today is Saturday.* New York: Atheneum. Copyright 1969. Used by permission of the author.

Stewart, Sarah. (2004). *The Friend.* Ill. David Small. New York: Farrar, Straus & Giroux.

Strom, Maria Diaz. (1999). *Rainbow Joe and Me.* New York: Lee & Low.

Varriale, Jim. (1999a). *Kids Dance: The Students of Ballet Tech.* New York: Dutton.

Varriale, Jim. (1999b). *Take a Look Around.* New York: Millbrook.

Wadsworth, Olive A. (1985, 1999) *Over in the Meadow.* Ill. Ezra Jack Keats. New York: Puffin.

Wadsworth, Olive A. (1989). *Over in the Meadow.* Ill. John Langstaff. New York: Voyager.

Wadsworth, Olive A. (2000). *Over in the Meadow.* Ill. Louise Voce. Cambridge, MA: Candlewick.

Wadsworth, Olive A. (2002). *Over in the Meadow.* Ill. Anna Vojtech. New York: North-South.

Wells, Rosemary. (2001). *Yoko's Paper Cranes.* New York: Hyperion.

Wheeler, Lisa. (2006). *Hokey Pokey: Another Prickly Love Story.* Ill. Janie Bynum. Boston: Little Brown.

Wiesner, David. (2001). *The Three Pigs.* New York: Clarion.

Willems, Mo. (2007). *Today I Will Fly!* New York: Hyperion.

Williams, Karen Lynn. (1998). *Painted Dreams.* Ill. Catherine Stock. New York: Lothrop.

Williams, Vera. (1984). *Music, Music for Everyone.* New York: Greenwillow.

Winter, Jeanette. (1998). *My Name Is Georgia:* A Biography in Words and Pictures. San Diego, CA: Harcourt.

Winter, Jeanette. (2000). *The Itsy-Bitsy Spider.* New York: Red Wagon.

Winter, Jonah. (1991). *Diego.* Ill. Jeanette Winter. New York: Knopf.

Worth, Valerie. (2007). *Animal Poems.* Ill. Steve Jenkins. New York: Farrar, Straus & Giroux.

Wright-Frierson, Virginia. (2003). *A North American Rain Forest Scrapbook.* New York: Walker.

Yang, Belle. (2004). *Hannah is My Name.* Cambridge, MA: Candlewick.

Yolen, Jane. (1987). *Owl Moon.* Ill. John Schoenherr. New York: Philomel.

Yolen, Jane. (2000). *Color Me a Rhyme: Nature Poems for Young People.* Photos. Jason Stemple. Honesdale, PA: Boyds Mills.

Yolen, Jane. (2006). *This Little Piggy: Lap Songs, Finger Plays, Clapping Games, and Pantomime Rhymes.* Ill. Will Hillenbrand. Cambridge, MA: Candlewick.

Young, Ed. (1992). *Seven Blind Mice.* New York: Philomel.

Ziefert, Harriet. (2000). *Train Song.* Ill. Donald Soaf. New York: Orchard.

Ziefert, Harriet. (2002). *You Can't Taste a Pickle with Your Ear: A Book About Your Five Senses.* Ill. Amanda Haley. Brooklyn, NY: Blue Apple Books.

CHAPTER TEN

BETHANY, Age 4

Don't Let the Pigeon Drive the Truck

Bethany (age 4) loved Mo Willems' story *Don't Let the Pigeon Drive the Bus* (2004) so much that she wanted to write her own. She dictated her story to her father then added her own illustrations.

Planning Your Program

As you begin to plan the literature program for your class or group of children, you will first need to familiarize yourself with the actual literature. Spend several afternoons or evenings in the library or bookstore reading picture books and chapter books and browsing through poetry for children. Look up and read any of the books mentioned in this text or that you have found in other sources that seem to you to have promise for your students. Make notes about those you plan to use. Some teachers and child-care professionals use index cards; others use loose-leaf notebooks or create databases. Whatever method you choose, the important thing is to select one that allows you to find the books again easily and to remember what strengths you saw in them.

SEEING THE POSSIBILITIES

Choose books for their literary value and for the quality of the text and the illustrations. Then think about the ways in which the literature itself, or extensions of it, support goals of early childhood education and of your curriculum in particular. You will often find that one book has many possibilities. Here are some examples.

A Book for Toddlers and Preschoolers

Many child-care professionals and teachers select *Hattie and the Fox* (Fox, 1986), for example, because of its patterned and predictable language. Hattie the hen looks out one morning and sees something in the bushes. She immediately announces to the other barnyard animals that she can see a nose. The goose, the pig, the sheep, the horse, and the cow each give their two-word responses to this information.

Hattie continues to announce what she sees, in cumulative fashion, adding a nose to the two eyes and then two ears to the two eyes and the nose. Each time the animals answer with the same phrases. Hattie gets more and more agitated as more and more of the fox is revealed. Finally, she announces that it is a fox and flies up into a nearby tree. Only then do the animals really pay attention. The cow's loud "moo" frightens the fox away, and the animals stand quietly, too startled to speak.

Following are some examples of how this book can be used to support the goals of early childhood education.

Language Development

Goal: "Children will enjoy the creative and aesthetic use of language." The patterned language, alliteration, and just plain fun of "Goodness gracious me!" make this a story children enjoy hearing over and over. They should have the opportunity to hear it more than once, either through its selection by them as an "old favorite," through an aide or other adult sharing it with small groups, or by listening to a tape as they turn the pages of the book.

Goal: "Children will become skilled listeners." Adults can enhance children's attentive listening by having them say the words they know as the book is being read. A variation is to have a child or small group of children take the part of the pig, the cow, or the horse and say just what that animal says.

As children hear this story they quickly gain control over the story structure. As you repeat it, they then can match the words they are hearing and saying to the words in print. A big-book format facilitates this with a group of children, but the same end can be achieved by sharing the book with one or two children at a time, allowing them to see the print clearly.

This is a fine story for dramatization. Children who portray the animals might decide on their own stock responses rather than using those from the book, particularly if new animals are being added to accommodate the number of children to be involved in the activity. They might decide to have a different animal approaching or to have different parts of the animal appearing first.

Intellectual Development

Goal: "Children will become skilled in a variety of thinking processes." This book encourages observation as more and more of the fox is revealed. You could begin by reading the text and showing the illustrations, having skipped the title and covered the back cover, which shows the fox. Then children could see what Hattie sees and predict with each illustration what the animal might be.

The children could find and cut out animal pictures in magazines. They could then cover all but a small part of the animal and let others guess what is there.

The children also might demonstrate their grasp of the sequence of the story—and thus gain experience in organizing—by telling or helping to tell the story using felt-board figures. Have the pieces displayed in random order. Let the children select what one will be needed next as you tell the story, or let them arrange the pieces and tell the story themselves.

Goal: "Children will engage successfully in problem solving." You might ask children why they think the other animals didn't seem to pay much attention to what Hattie was saying. What else might she have done to have gotten their help in identifying the animal in the bushes?

Personality Development

Goal: "Children will weigh evidence and make appropriate choices." After reading the book, you might suggest that the children decide what they would like to do in relation to the book. It might be a group decision, between activities such as making felt-board characters in order to retell it or making puppets. They may make individual decisions, with some choosing to make pictures using collage techniques or cut out and partially cover a picture of an animal and others creating an observational riddle. Children might decide whether they wanted to work by themselves or with others on the project.

Social and Moral Development

Goal: "Children will view a situation from more than one perspective." If children are dramatizing the story or retelling it with puppets or felt-board characters, they should have the opportunity to play several roles. They might then tell the incident as the fox would or perhaps use Hattie's point of view.

Goal: "Children will engage competently in group activities." You can help children work successfully in groups by making certain that the task is clear. Perhaps each child could identify what animal his or her puppet will be. For very young children, the task for "group" work may be to share materials and to engage in friendly talk as they work.

Aesthetic and Creative Development

Goal: "Children will use, experiment with, and gain control over a variety of art media." *Hattie and the Fox* is illustrated with a technique using tissue paper collage and conte crayon. Young children could explore making a collage picture. With toddlers and preschoolers, however, this activity is likely to be more successful if you use construction paper rather than tissue paper, because its stiffness makes it easier to cut and paste.

Goal: "Children will respond favorably to diverse styles of art and music." Children could be asked what they notice about the illustrations and encouraged to give a variety of responses. The book might be compared with *Rosie's Walk* (Hutchins, 1968), in which Rosie the hen goes for a walk, oblivious to the fact that she is being stalked by a fox. Rosie is safe in her naiveté as one misfortune after another befalls the fox, and she continues merrily on her way. Thus children would see one hen noticing danger and another totally unaware of it but both being safe in the end. They might tell how the illustrations in the two books differ, describing the different styles of art and the media used.

A Book for Primary Grades

Just as there are many possibilities for toddlers and preschool children to enjoy and respond to *Hattie and the Fox,* so too are there opportunities for primary-grade students to enjoy and respond to *Mrs. Biddlebox: Her Bad Day and What She Did About It* (Smith, 2002, 2007). Mrs. Biddlebox wakes up on the wrong side of the bunk. The birds give her a headache and there are "creakies" in her chair. However, she refuses to give in to the gloomy day, so Mrs. Biddlebox decides to "cook this rotten morning! I will turn it into a cake!" And that is what she does as she whips and whisks the bad parts of the day into dough, bakes it, and eats and eats. She finally feels better and then it's time to go to sleep.

Language Development

Goal: "Children will hear the flow of language through the rhythm and rhyme of the text." As you read the story aloud, children will hear the cadence of the words and how they are read. Have them listen for interesting words such as despicable and whiffles. Begin a word wall of words that come from literature, which they can revisit or use for their own writing.

Gloomy feelings don't stand a chance in this snappy picture book about a woman who kicks a dreary little funk with her can-do spirit.

(Book cover from MRS. BIDDLEBOX, illustrations copyright © 2007, 2002 by Marla Frazee, reproduced by permission of Harcourt, Inc.)

Goal: "Children will communicate effectively, both orally and in writing." Children might write about their own bad day and what they did about it. They could also interview each other or else a parent to discover experiences of others. One or more of these experiences could be turned into a class story and "_____'s Bad Day."

Intellectual Development

Goal: "Children will continue to acquire new concepts and refine old ones." As children read or listen to this story, they are presented with ideas about dealing with emotions. Mrs. Biddlebox bakes up a cake with all sorts of items she believes are reasonable for the bad day, such as gloom. Children can share what causes a bad day and whether it is the same for everyone. They can also create a list of problem-solving strategies that they could use for changing something negative into something positive.

Goal: "Children will develop skill in a variety of thinking processes." Read other books about characters that are having a bad day and what they did about it. Books such as *When Sophie Gets Angry. . . Really Really Angry* (Bang, 1999) or *Alexander and the Terrible, Horrible, No Good Very Bad Day* (Viorst, 1972) are two stories that would work well with *Mrs. Biddlebox.* How did those characters react to their bad day as well as to other people they encounter?

Personality Development

Goal: "Children will recognize that everyone expresses emotions in different ways." Mrs. Biddlebox made a cake and used aspects of the day as her ingredients. Have children think about the ingredients they would need to make up the best day they could possibly have. Write their ideas in recipe form. Share Todd Parr's *The Feel Good Book* (2004), which presents both silly and serious ways to feel good.

Goal: "Children will explore how different emotions are portrayed." Brainstorm a list of emotions with children. Write them on cards and place them into a bowl or bag. Individually, or in small groups, ask each child to select a piece of paper and then pantomime the emotion for the class. Challenge them further to not just do the emotion itself but to couch it within a story that they act out.

Social and Moral Development

Goal: "Children will view a situation from more than one perspective, seeing the viewpoint of another person." If you could interview Mrs. Biddlebox, what would you ask her? What can you learn from Mrs. Biddlebox? Have children write down a list of questions and have them share these in small groups. They could tape these questions as well as new understandings about Mrs. Biddlebox to play for others as well.

Goal: "Children will understand and demonstrate social behavior." Read aloud *Are You Going to Be Good?* (Best, 2005), in which Robert is told that he must practice his best manners at Great-Gran Sadie's 100th birthday party. Children can brainstorm and then role-play situations they have been in or events that they have attended where they needed to exhibit their best behavior.

Goal: "Children will engage competently in group activities." In groups of three, make a plan for how to deal with the children's next bad day. Develop a strategy for helping others deal with a bad day that you can implement in the classroom.

Aesthetic and Creative Development

Goal: "Children will evaluate how meaning is expressed through illustrations." Obtain a copy of the 2002 and 2007 versions of *Mrs. Biddlebox.* Have children discuss the different cover illustrations. Why do you think it was changed? Are there other changes that have been made in the book?

Goal: "Children will understand how colors represent different moods and emotions." How did illustrator Marla Frazee use colors to convey that *Mrs. Biddlebox* was having a bad day and then a good day? Revisit *When Sophie Gets Angry* and discuss how Molly Bang has used colors to show Sophie's anger and sense of calm. Have children create symbols for three different emotions. What colors would they use? Give children a choice of media when they do their series of illustrations.

SELECTING ACTIVITIES

Many, although not all, of these goals and activities are compatible with one another for each of the books. Given these possibilities, far more than you would actually do with any one group of children, your task becomes that of deciding which you wish to pursue. Here are three general suggestions for determining the merit of specific activities for extending books.

FIRST, THE ACTIVITY SHOULD ENHANCE THE LITERATURE, NOT DETRACT FROM IT. Toddlers or preschoolers dramatizing *Hattie and the Fox* take an active part in the story, help build the suspense, and work together in developing their understanding of it. They enjoy the predictability of the language and the plot. They are likely to want to hear the book again, to want to dramatize it in various ways, and to think positively about literature as a result. If, however, you require the children to practice individually with flash cards until they have learned the words each animal says, it is likely that many of the children will see literature as a source of frustrating work. They will not be eager to have you read more books, let alone repeat *Hattie and the Fox.* They will not have gained any deeper understanding of, or appreciation for, the literature.

SECOND, THE ACTIVITY SHOULD EMERGE NATURALLY FROM THE BOOK. *Mrs. Biddlebox* is an engaging story because of the jaunty rhyme and the expressive illustrations. This is a story that children can relate to. Everyone has gotten up on the wrong side of the bed and started the day in a bad mood. But Mrs. Biddlebox isn't willing to accept a "belly full of grumblies." She gets right to work with a pot and a broom to clear away the gloom and doom. Mrs. Biddlebox solves her problem in a unique and visual manner. The ingredients aren't what most children think would go into a cake batter—dirt, sky, and fog—but Mrs. Biddlebox whips up a tasty tart and is definitely satisfied with the end result. The emotional dilemma and quick thinking to resolve the problem naturally emerge from the story. How an author tells a story through rhyming text easily lends itself to children responding in a like manner. Identifying descriptive words in a story and brainstorming others will provide additional vocabulary for written responses to the story. Illustrations that depict a grumpy Mrs. Biddlebox at the beginning of the story but then a happy person at the end will encourage discussion about the use of color and character's expressions to convey meaning. This discussion will fuel others as children experience other stories. Although Mrs. Biddlebox stomps down the dough with "witchety delight," there is no mention in the story that she is a witch. An initial glance might suggest that this book would be appropriate for Halloween; however, the real theme is about empowerment in solving one's problem. It is important to read a book and think about what it's really about rather than to assume it's about something else and thus limit the book's potential for response by children.

THIRD, THE ACTIVITIES SHOULD MATCH BOTH THE NEEDS AND THE ABILITIES OF THE CHILDREN. Making collage illustrations with construction paper rather than tissue paper after sharing *Hattie and the Fox* allows toddlers and preschoolers to explore the artistic technique using materials they can manipulate successfully. Having second- or third-graders interview an adult or another child about his or her good- or bad-day experiences after hearing *Mrs. Biddlebox* gives the children experience in planning an interview, using oral language and listening skills, and reporting accurately, in writing, what another has said. The activities for both books relate to goals for early childhood education. Deciding which are most appropriate means knowing your children well, being able to assess and rank their needs, and knowing which needs will be met in other ways. It also means recognizing that there will be a range of needs and abilities in any group of children and that you will be planning activities for small groups or individuals much of the time. Some toddlers and preschoolers are able to cut pictures from magazines; others still need practice controlling scissors and benefit more from cutting large, less-detailed shapes. Some of your children may need help learning to work cooperatively with others. Some may need to work alone before they are ready to contribute to a group project. Being able to determine which activities should be suggested to which children is a professional skill of teaching and child-care work.

RECOGNIZING THE LARGER CONTEXT

The sharing of a single book fits within the context of all the literature the children are experiencing, and the literature fits within the context of their lives both at home and at school. Your planning will be more effective if you think of the larger picture as you make decisions about literature and literature-based activities.

The Literature Curriculum

As you select individual books and as you plan your curriculum, group some of the books into units or webs. Ideas for grouping may emerge as you look at the literature, a particular author or illustrator's work, or several books expressing a similar theme. Sometimes you may need to use reference guides to children's literature to help you find books that fit the topics you intend to develop. With *Hattie and the Fox* you might look for other stories about foxes and hens, particularly those in which the fox presents a danger to the hen. Your grouping might be *Hattie and the Fox* (Fox, 1986), *Rosie's Walk* (Hutchins, 1968), and *The Tale of Tricky Fox: A New England Trickster Tale* (Aylesworth, 2001).

You might focus on books with repetition, in which case *Hattie* could be combined with *When I First Came to This Land* (Ziefert, 1998), *The Little Old Lady Who Was Not Afraid of Anything* (Williams, 1986), and *Mr. Gumpy's Outing* (Burningham, 1971). You might even decide to engage children in games of careful observation and, after having shared *Hattie*, have them guess what they are seeing in *Just Look* (Hoban, 1996) and then find the mouse in each of the illustrations of Waber's humorous *Do You See a Mouse?* (1995).

With *Mrs. Biddlebox*, you might look at other works illustrated by Marla Frazee because she is able to effectively express emotions through her pictures. You might select books about characters that portray emotions in several stories such as David Shannon's *No, David!* (1998), *David Gets in Trouble* (2002), and *David Goes to School* (1999). There are also Mo Willem's "Pigeon" books or Ian Falconer's "Olivia" stories.

You can sequence some units throughout the school year, and the placement of these units may be a determining factor in their success. You should keep other units and books in mind but be flexible in your planning of when they will be presented. The units mentioned might come at any convenient time, whereas holiday books obviously need to be scheduled to coincide with the event. Check your general plan to make certain that you are developing a balanced literature curriculum that has both prose and poetry, fantasy and realism, and classic and modern stories.

The Child's World

Plans for bringing children and books together must always revolve around the specific children with whom you are working. The children must be able to create meaning from the books you share because they are touched by them—through the topic, the language, the emotion expressed, and the intellectual stimulation they provide. You should have books that depict a diverse set of characters, so that children both see themselves and the people they know in books and come to know and appreciate others who are different from them. You will want children to see literature in various formats—hardcover and paperback books, videos, CD-ROM retellings—and come to appreciate the strengths of each of them. And you will think not just of the world in which the child finds himself or herself at the moment, but the world the child will live in for the future. Most of all, you will want children to find literature a source of joy and knowledge, and this will guide not only your selection of books but also the way in which you share them with children.

EVALUATING YOUR LITERATURE PROGRAM

You should evaluate your literature curriculum on a daily basis and at the close of the year. Daily evaluation should be based on the specific goals and objectives of each lesson. Did the children find at least three hidden objects in each picture? Could each child think of at least two activities Curious George might do if he were in the classroom? Did the children state two ways in which two books were alike and two ways in which they were different? Did the children repeat the refrain with you as you read a book for the second time?

Evaluation at the close of the year should involve an assessment of the program and the children's development. Was the program balanced? Were the books and activities appropriate for the children? Were you using the best literature available? As you look at the children's behavior, you will discern changes that have occurred over the year and will find patterns of behavior that indicate the children's response to literature. A successful literature program should result in some or all of these behaviors:

Children will reread or look at the illustrations in books you have read to them.

Children will choose to read or look at books in their free time or as work choices.

Children will recommend books and book-related activities to one another.

Children will choose to respond to literature through art, music, movement, and drama.

Children will talk about book characters and happenings in new situations.

Children will ask you to read to them.

You will also be evaluating goals for your students in their language, intellectual, personal, social, moral, aesthetic, and creative development. Your literature program will have supported growth in all of these areas.

Extending Your Learning

1. Select one book. List the goals of early childhood education that it supports, stating your rationale for why it supports each one. Then suggest several possible units of study incorporating the book.

2. Evaluate a literature experience you have had with children. List specific criteria and describe how well each was met.

3. Reread a book that you have enjoyed and think of ways to extend it as you encourage children's responses to it.

4. Locate a professional book that discusses sharing literature with young children. What ideas can you gather to assist you in planning a future program?

REFERENCES

Children's Literature Cited

Aylesworth, Jim. (2001). *The Tale of Tricky Fox: A New England Trickster Tale.* Ill. Barbara McClintock. New York: Scholastic.

Bang, Molly. (1999). *When Sophie Gets Angry . . . Really Really Angry.* New York: Scholastic.

Best, Cari. (2005). *Are You Going to Be Good?* Ill. G. Brian Karas. New York: Farrar, Straus & Giroux.

Burningham, John. (1971). *Mr. Gumpy's Outing.* New York: Holt.

Fox, Mem. (1986). *Hattie and the Fox.* Ill. Patricia Mullins. New York: Macmillan.

Hoban, Tana. (1996). *Just Look.* New York: Greenwillow.

Hutchins, Pat. (1968). *Rosie's Walk.* New York: Collier.

Parr, Todd. (2004). *The Feel Good Book.* Boston: Little, Brown.

Shannon, David. (1998). *No, David!* New York: Scholastic.

Shannon, David. (1999). *David Goes to School.* New York: Scholastic.

Shannon, David. (2002). *David Gets in Trouble.* New York: Scholastic.

Smith, Linda. (2002, 2007). *Mrs. Biddlebox: Her Bad Day and What She Did About It.* Ill. Marla Frazee. San Diego, CA: Harcourt.

Viorst, Judith. (1972). *Alexander and the Terrible, Horrible, No Good, Very Bad Day.* New York: Atheneum.

Waber, Bernard. (1995). *Do You See a Mouse?* Boston: Houghton Mifflin.

Williams, Linda. (1986). *The Little Old Lady Who Was Not Afraid of Anything.* Ill. Megan Lloyd. New York: Crowell.

Ziefert, Harriet. (1998). *When I First Came to This Land.* Ill. Simms Taback. New York: Putnam.

Appendix

The Caldecott Medal

The Caldecott Medal is awarded annually to the illustrator of the most distinguished American picture book for children. The winner is selected by a committee of the Association for Library Service to Children of the American Library Association.

1938. *Animals of the Bible* by Helen Dean Fish, ill. by Dorothy P. Lathrop, Lippincott. **Honor Books:** *Seven Simeons* by Boris Artzvbasheff, Viking; *Four and Twenty Blackbirds* by Helen Dean Fish, ill. by Robert Lawson, Stokes.

1939. *Mel Li* by Thomas Handforth, Doubleday. **Honor Books:** *The Forest Pool* by Laura Adams Armet, Longmans; *Wee Gillis* by Munro Leat, ill. by Robert Lawson, Viking; *Snow White and the Seven Dwarfs* by Wanda Gag, Coward-McCann; *Barkis* by Clare Newberry, Harper & Row; *Andy and the Lion* by James Daugherty, Viking.

1940. *Abraham Lincoln* by Ingra and Edgar Parin D'Aulaire, Doubleday. **Honor Books:** *Cock-A-Doodle-Doo* by Berta and Elmer Hader, Macmillan; *Madeline* by Ludwig Bemelmans, Viking Press; *The Ageless Story,* ill. by Lauren Ford, Dodd, Mead.

1941. *They Were Strong and Good* by Robert Lawson, Viking Press. **Honor Book:** *April's Kittens* by Clare Newberry, Harper & Row.

1942. *Make Way For Ducklings* by Robert McCloskey, Viking. **Honor Books:** *An American ABC* by Maud and Miska Petersham, Macmillan; *In My Mother's House* by Ann Nolan Clark, ill. by Velino Herrera, Viking Press; *Paddle-to-the-Sea* by Holling C. Holling, Houghton Mifflin; *Nothing at All* by Wanda Gag, Coward-McCann.

1943. *The Little House* by Virginia Lee Burton, Houghton Mifflin. **Honor Books:** *Dash and Dart* by Mary and Conrad Buff, Viking Press; *Marshmallow* by Clare Newberry, Harper & Row.

1944. *Many Moons* by James Thurber, ill. by Louis Slobodkin, Harcourt. **Honor Books:** *Small Rain: Verses from the Bible* selected by Jessie Orton Jones, ill. by Elizabeth Orton Jones, Viking; *Pierre Pigeon* by Lee Kingman, ill. by Arnold E. Bare, Houghton Mifflin; *The Mighty Hunter* by Berta and Elmer Hadar, Macmillan; *A Child's Good Night Book* by Margaret Wise Brown, ill. by Jean Charlot, W. R. Scott; *Good Luck Horse* by Chih-Yi Chan, ill. by Piao Chan, Whittlesey.

1945. *Prayer for a Child* by Rachel Field, ill. by Elizabeth Orton Jones, Macmillan. **Honor Books:** *Mother Goose,* ill. by Tasha Tudor, Walck; *In the Forest* by Marie Hall Ets, Viking; *Yonie Wondernose* by Marguerite de Angeli, Doubleday; *The Christmas Anna Angel* by Ruth Sawyer, ill. by Kate Seredy, Viking.

1946. *The Rooster Crows* (traditional Mother Goose), ill. by Maud and Miska Petersham, Macmillan. **Honor Books:** *Little Lost Lamb* by Golden MacDonald, ill. by Leonard Weisgard, Doubleday; *Sing Mother Goose* by Opal Wheeler, ill. by

Marjorie Torrey, Dutton; *My Mother Is the Most Beautiful Woman in the World* by Becky Reyher, ill. by Ruth Gannet, Lothrop.

1947. *The Little Island* by Golden MacDonald, ill. by Leonord Weisgard, Doubleday. ***Honor Books:*** *Rain Drop Splash* by Alvin Tresselt, ill. by Leonard Weisgard, Lothrop; *Boats on the River* by Marjorie Flack, ill. by Jay Hyde Barnum, Viking; *Timothy Turtle* by Al Graham, ill. by Tony Palazzo, Viking; *Pedro, the Angel of Olivera Street* by Leo Politi, Scribner's; *Sing in Praise: A Collection of the Best Loved Hymns* by Opal Wheeler, ill. by Marjorie Torrey, Dutton.

1948. *White Snow, Bright Snow* by Alvin Tresselt, ill. by Roger Duvoisin, Lothrop. ***Honor Books:*** *Stone Soup* by Marcia Brown, Scribner's; *McElligot's Pool* by Dr. Seuss, Random House; *Bambino the Clown* by George Schreiber, Viking; *Roger and the Fox* by Lavinia Davis, ill. by Hildegard Woodward, Doubleday; *Song of Robin Hood* ed. by Anne Malcolmson, ill. by Virginia Lee Burton, Houghton Mifflin.

1949. *The Big Snow* by Betta and Elmer Hader, Macmillan. ***Honor Books:*** *Blueberries for Sal* by Robert McCloskey, Viking Press; *All Around the Town* by Phyllis McGinley, ill. by Helen Stone, Lippincott; *Juanita* by Leo Politi, Scribner's; *Fish in the Air* by Kurt Wiese, Viking.

1950. *Song of the Swallows* by Leo Politi, Scribner's. ***Honor Books:*** *America's Ethan Allen* by Stewart Holbrook, ill. by Lynd Ward, Houghton Mifflin; *The Wild Birthday Cake* by Lavinia Davis, ill. by Hildegard Woodward, Doubleday; *The Happy Day* by Ruth Krauss, ill. by Marc Simont, Harper & Row; *Bartholomew and the Oobleck* by Dr. Seuss, Random House; *Henry Fisherman* by Marcia Brown, Scribner's.

1951. *The Egg Tree* by Katherine Milhous, Scribner's. ***Honor Books:*** *Dick Whittington and His Cat* by Marcia Brown, Scribner's; *The Two Reds* by Will, ill. by Nicolas, Harcourt; *If I Ran the Zoo* by Dr. Seuss, Random House; *The Most Wonderful Doll in the World* by Phyllis McGinley, ill. by Helen Stone, Lippincott; *T-Bone, the Baby Sitter* by Clare Newberry, Harper & Row.

1952. *Finders Keepers* by Will, ill. by Nicolas, Harcourt. ***Honor Books:*** *Mr. T. W. Anthony Woo* by Marie Hall Ets, Viking; *Skipper John's Cook* by Marcia Brown, Scribner's; *All Falling Down* by Gene Zion, ill. by Margaret Bloy Graham, Harper & Row; *Bear Party* by William Pene du Bois, Viking; *Feather Mountain* by Elizabeth Olds, Houghton Mifflin.

1953. *The Biggest Bear* by Lynd Ward, Houghton Mifflin. ***Honor Books:*** *Puss in Boots* by Charles Perrault, ill. and tr. by Marcia Brown, Scribner's; *One Morning in Maine* by Robert McCloskey, Viking; *Ape in a Cape* by Fritz Eichenberg, Harcourt; *The Storm Book* by Charlotte Zolotow, ill. by Margaret Bloy Graham, Harper & Row; *Five Little Monkeys* by Juliet Kepes, Houghton Mifflin.

1954. *Madeline's Rescue* by Ludwig Bemelmans, Viking Press. ***Honor Books:*** *Journey Cake, HO!* by Ruth Sawyer, ill. by Robert McCloskey, Viking; *When Will the World Be Mine?* by Miriam Schlein, ill. by Jean Charlot, W. R. Scott; *The Steadfast Tin Soldier* by Hans Christian Andersen, ill. by Marcia Brown, Scribner's; *A Very Special House* by Ruth Krauss, ill. by Maurice Sendak, Harper & Row; *Green Eyes* by A. Birnbaum, Capitol.

1955. *Cinderella, or the Little Glass Slipper* by Charles Perrault, tr. and ill. by Marcia Brown, Scribner's. ***Honor Books:*** *Book of Nursery and Mother Goose Rhymes,* ill. by Marguerite de Angeli, Doubleday; *Wheel on the Chimney* by Margaret Wise Brown, ill. by Tibor Gergely, Lippincott; *The Thanksgiving Story* by Alice Dalgliesh, ill. by Helen Sewell, Scribner's.

1956. *Frog Went A-Courtin'* ed. by John Langstaff, ill. by Feodor Rojankovsky, Harcourt. **Honor Books:** *Play with Me* by Marie Hall Ets, Viking; *Crow Boy* by Taro Yashima, Viking.

1957. *A Tree Is Nice* by Janice May Udry, ill. by Marc Simont, Harper & Row. **Honor Books:** *Mr. Penny's Race Horse* by Marie Hall Ets, Viking; *1 Is One* by Tasha Tudor, Walck; *Anatole* by Eve Titus, ill. by Paul Galdone, McGraw-Hill; *Gillespie and the Guards* by Benjamin Elkin, ill. by James Daugherty, Viking; *Lion* by William Pene du Bois, Viking.

1958. *Time of Wonder* by Robert McCloskey, Viking. **Honor Books:** *Fly High, Fly Low* by Don Freeman, Viking. *Anatole and the Cat* by Eve Titus, ill. by Paul Galdone, McGraw-Hill.

1959. *Chanticleer and the Fox* adapted from Chaucer and ill. by Barbara Cooney, Crowell. **Honor Books:** *The House That Jack Built* by Antonio Frasconi, Harcourt; *What Do You Say, Dear?* by Sesyle Joslin, ill. by Maurice Sendak, W. R. Scott; *Umbrella* by Taro Yashima, Viking.

1960. *Nine Days to Christmas* by Marie Hall Ets and Aurora Labastida, ill. by Marie Hall Ets, Viking. **Honor Books:** *Houses from the Sea* by Alice E. Goudey, ill. by Adrienne Adams, Scribner's; *The Moon Jumpers* by Janice May Udry, ill. by Maurice Sendak, Harper & Row.

1961. *Baboushka and the Three Kings* by Ruth Robbins, ill. by Nicolas Sidjakov, Parnassus Imprints. **Honor Book:** *Inch by Inch* by Leo Lionni, Obolensky.

1962. *Once a Mouse . . .* by Marcia Brown, Scribner's. **Honor Books:** *The Fox Went Out on a Chilly Night* by Peter Spier, Doubleday; *Little Bear's Visit* by Else Holmelund Minarik, ill. by Maurice Sendak, Harper & Row; *The Day We Saw the Sun Come Up* by Alice E. Goudey, ill. by Adrienne Adams, Scribner's.

1963. *The Snowy Day* by Ezra Jack Keats, Viking Press. **Honor Books:** *The Sun Is a Golden Earring* by Natalia M. Belting, ill. by Bernarda Bryson, Holt, Rinehart & Winston; *Mr. Rabbit and the Lovely Present* by Charlotte Zolotow, ill. by Maurice Sendak, Harper & Row.

1964. *Where the Wild Things Are* by Maurice Sendak, Harper & Row. **Honor Books:** *Swimmy* by Leo Lionni, Pantheon; *All in the Morning Early* by Sorche Nic Leodhas, ill. by Evaline Ness, Holt, Rinehart & Winston; *Mother Goose and Nursery Rhymes,* ill. by Philip Reed, Atheneum.

1965. *May I Bring A Friend?* by Beatrice Schenk de Regniers, ill. by Beni Montresor, Atheneum. **Honor Books:** *Rain Makes Applesauce* by Julian Scheer, ill. by Marvin Bileck, Holiday; *The Wave* by Margaret Hodges, ill. by Blair Lent, Houghton Mifflin; *A Pocketful of Cricket* by Rebecca Caudill, ill. by Evaline Ness, Holt, Rinehart & Winston.

1966. *Always Room for One More* by Sorche Nic Leodhas, ill. by Nonny Hogrogian, Holt, Rinehart & Winston. **Honor Books:** *Hide and Seek Fog* by Alvin Tresselt, ill. by Roger Duvoisin, Lothrop; *Just Me* by Marie Hall Ets, Viking Press; *Tom Tit Tot* by Evaline Ness, Scribner's.

1967. *Sam, Bangs & Moonshine* by Evaline Ness, Holt, Rinehart & Winston. **Honor Book:** *One Wide River to Cross* by Barbara Emberley, ill. by Ed Emberley, Prentice Hall.

1968. *Drummer Hoff* by Barbara Emberley, ill. by Ed Emberley, Prentice Hall. **Honor Books:** *Frederick* by Leo Lionni, Pantheon; *Seashore Story* by Taro Yashima, Viking; *The Emperor and the Kite* by Jane Yolen, ill. by Ed Young, World.

1969. *The Fool of the World and the Flying Ship* by Arthur Ransom, ill. by Uri Shulevitz, Farrar. **Honor Book:** *Why the Sun and Moon Live in the Sky* by Elphinstone Dayrell, ill. by Blair Lent, Houghton Mifflin.

1970. *Sylvester and the Magic Pebble* by William Steig, Windmill. **Honor Books:** *Goggles!* by Ezra Jack Keats, Macmillan; *Alexander and the Wind-Up Mouse* by Leo Lionni, Pantheon; *Pop Corn & Ma Goodness* by Edna Mitchell Preston, ill. by Robert Andrew Parker, Viking Press; *Thy Friend, Obadiah* by Brinton Turkle, Viking Press; *The Judge* by Harve Zemach, ill. by Margot Zemach, Farrar.

1971. *A Story, A Story* by Gail E. Haley, Atheneum. **Honor Books:** *The Angry Moon* by William Sleator, ill. by Blair Lent, Atlantic; *Frog and Toad Are Friends* by Arnold Lobel, Harper & Row; *In the Night Kitchen* by Maurice Sendak, Harper & Row.

1972. *One Fine Day* by Nonny Hogrogian, Macmillan. **Honor Books:** *If All the Seas Were One Sea* by Janina Domanska, Macmillan; *Moja Means One: Swahili Counting Book* by Muriel Feelings, ill. by Tom Feelings, Dial; *Hildild's Night* by Cheli Duran Ryan, ill. by Arnold Lobel, Macmillan.

1973. *The Funny Little Woman* retold by Arlene Mosel, ill. by Blair Lent, Dutton. **Honor Books:** *Anansi the Spider* adapted and ill. by Gerald McDermott, Holt, Rinehart & Winston; *Hosie's Alphabet* by Hosea, Tobias and Lisa Baskin, ill. by Leonard Baskin, Viking; *Snow White and the Seven Dwarfs* translated by Randall Jarrell, ill. by Nancy Ekholm Burkert, Farrar; *When Clay Sings* by Byrd Baylor, ill. by Tom Bahti, Scribner's.

1974. *Duffy and the Devil* by Harve Zemach, ill. by Margot Zemach, Farrar. **Honor Books:** *Three Jovial Huntsmen* by Susan Jeffers, Bradbury; *Cathedral: The Story of Its Construction* by David Macaulay, Houghton Mifflin.

1975. *Arrow to the Sun* adapted and ill. by Gerald McDermott, Viking. **Honor Book:** *Jambo Means Hello* by Muriel Feelings, ill. by Tom Feelings, Dial.

1976. *Why Mosquitoes Buzz in People's Ears* retold by Verna Aardema, ill. by Leo and Diane Dillon, Dial. **Honor Books:** *The Desert Is Theirs* by Byrd Baylor, ill. by Peter Parnall, Scribner's; *Strega Nona* retold and ill. by Tomie dePaola, Prentice Hall.

1977. *Ashanti to Zulu: African Traditions* by Margaret Musgrove, ill. by Leo and Dianne Dillon, Dial. **Honor Books:** *The Amazing Bone* by William Steig, Farrar; *The Contest* retold and ill. by Nonny Hogrogian, Greenwillow; *Fish for Supper* by M. B. Goffstein, Dial Press; *The Golem* by Beverly Brodsky McDermott, Lippincott; *Hawk, I'm Your Brother* by Byrd Baylor, ill. by Peter Parnall, Scribner's.

1978. *Noah's Ark* by Peter Spier, Doubleday. **Honor Books:** *Castle* by David Macaulay, Houghton Mifflin; *It Could Always Be Worse* by Margot Zemach, Farrar.

1979. *The Girl Who Loved Wild Horses* by Paul Goble, Bradbury. **Honor Books:** *Freight Train* by Donald Crews, Greenwillow; *The Way to Start a Day* by Byrd Baylor, ill. by Peter Parnall, Scribner's.

1980. *Ox-Cart Man* by Donald Hall, ill. by Barbara Cooney, Viking. **Honor Books:** *Ben's Trumpet* by Rachel Isadora, Greenwillow; *The Treasure* by Uri Shulevitz, Farrar; *The Garden of Abdul Gasazi* by Chris Van Allsburg, Houghton Mifflin.

1981. *Fables* by Arnold Lobel, Harper & Row. **Honor Books:** *The Bremen-Town Musicians* by Ilse Plume, Double-day; *The Grey Lady and the Strawberry Snatcher* by Molly Bang, Four Winds; *Mice Twice* by Joseph Low, Atheneum; *Truck* by Donald Crews, Greenwillow.

1982. *Jumanji* by Chris Van Allsburg, Houghton Mifflin. ***Honor Books:*** *A Visit to William Blake's Inn: Poems for Innocent and Experienced Travelers* by Nancy Willard, ill. by Alice and Martin Provensen, Harcourt; *Where the Buffaloes Begin* by Olaf Baker, ill. by Stephen Gammell, Frederick Warne; *On Market Street* by Anita Lobel, Greenwillow; *Outside Over There* by Maurice Sendak, Harper & Row.

1983. *Shadow* by Blaise Cendrars, ill. by Marcia Brown, Scribner's. ***Honor Books:*** *When I Was Young in the Mountains* by Cynthia Rylant, ill. by Diane Goode, Dutton; *A Chair for My Mother* by Vera Williams, Morrow.

1984. *The Glorious Flight: Across the Channel with Louis Bleriot* by Alice and Martin Provensen, Viking. ***Honor Books:*** *Little Red Riding Hood* by Trina Schart Hyman, Holiday; *Ten, Nine, Eight* by Molly Bang, Greenwillow.

1985. *St. George and the Dragon* retold by Margaret Hodges, ill. by Trina Schart Hyman, Little, Brown. ***Honor Books:*** *Hansel and Gretel* retold by Rika Lesser, ill. by Paul Zelinsky, Dodd; *Have You Seen My Duckling?* by Nancy Tafuri, Greenwillow; *The Story of Jumping Mouse* by John Steptoe, Lothrop.

1986. *The Polar Express* by Chris Van Allsburg, Houghton Mifflin. ***Honor Books:*** *The Relatives Came* by Cynthia Rylant, ill. by Stephen Gammell, Bradbury; *King Bidgood's in the Bathtub* by Audrey Wood, ill. by Don Wood, Harcourt.

1987. *Hey, Al* by Arthur Yorinks, ill. by Richard Egielski, Farrar, Straus & Giroux. ***Honor Books:*** *The Village of Round and Square Houses* by Ann Grifalconi, Little, Brown; *Alphabatics* by Suse MacDonald, Bradbury; *Rumpelstiltskin* by Paul Zelinsky, Dutton.

1988. *Owl Moon* by Jane Yolen, ill. by John Schoenherr, Philomel. ***Honor Book:*** *Mufaro's Beautiful Daughters* by John Steptoe, Lothrop.

1989. *Song and Dance Man* by Karen Ackerman, ill. by Stephen Gammell, Knopf. ***Honor Books:*** *Goldilocks* by James Marshall, Dial; *The Boy of the Three-Year Nap* by Dianne Snyder, ill. by Allen Say, Houghton Mifflin; *Mirandy and Brother Wind* by Patricia McKissack, ill. by Jerry Pinkney, Knopf.

1990. *Lon Po Po: A Red Riding Hood Story from China* by Ed Young, Philomel. ***Honor Books:*** *Hershel and the Hanukkah Goblins* by Eric Kimmell, ill. by Trina Schart Hyman, Holiday; *Bill Peet: An Autobiography* by Bill Peet, Houghton Mifflin; *Color Zoo* by Lois Ehlert, Lippincott; *The Talking Eggs* by Robert San Souci, ill. by Jerry Pinkney, Dial.

1991. *Black and White* by David Macaulay, Houghton. ***Honor Books:*** *"More More More," Said the Baby: Three Love Stories* by Vera B. Williams, Greenwillow; *Puss in Boots* by Charles Perrault, ill. by Fred Marcellino, Farrar/Michael di Capua.

1992. *Tuesday* by David Wiesner, Clarion. ***Honor Book:*** *Tar Beach* by Faith Ringgold, Crown.

1993. *Mirette on the High Wire* by Emily Arnold McCully, Putnam. ***Honor Books:*** *The Stinky Cheese Man* by John Scieszka, ill. by Lane Smith, Viking; *Working Cotton* by Sherley Williams, ill. by Carole Byard, Harcourt; *Seven Blind Mice* by Ed Young, Philomel.

1994. *Grandfather's Journey* by Allen Say, Houghton Mifflin. ***Honor Books:*** *In the Small, Small Pond* by Denise Fleming, Holt; *Owen* by Kevin Henkes, Greenwillow; *Peppe the Lamplighter* by Elisa Bartone, ill. by Ted Lewis, Lothrop; *Raven: A Trickster Tale from the Pacific Northwest* by Gerald McDermott, Harcourt; *Yo! Yes!* by Chris Raschka, Orchard.

1995. *Smoky Night* by Eve Bunting, ill. by David Diaz, Harcourt. ***Honor Books:*** *John Henry* by Julius Lester, ill. by Jerry Pinkney, Dial; *Swamp Angel* by Anne Isaacs, ill. by Paul O. Zelinsky, Dutton; *Time Flies* by Eric Rohmann, Crown.

1996. *Officer Buckle and Gloria* by Peggy Rathmann, Putnam. ***Honor Books:*** *Alphabet City* by Stephen T. Johnson, Viking; *The Faithful Friend* by Robert San Souci, ill. by Brian Pinkney, Simon & Schuster; *Tops and Bottoms* by Janet Stevens, Harcourt; *Zin! Zin! Zin! A Violin!* by Lloyd Moss, ill. by Marjorie Priceman, Simon & Schuster.

1997. *Golem* by David Wisniewski, Clarion. ***Honor Books:*** *Hush! A Thai Lullaby* by Minfong Ho, ill. by Holly Meade, Orchard; *The Graphic Alphabet* by David Pelletier, Orchard; *The Paperboy* by Dav Pilkey, Jackson/Orchard; *Starry Messenger* by Peter Sis, Farrar.

1998. *Rapunzel* by Paul O. Zelinsky, Dutton. ***Honor Books:*** *The Gardener* by Sarah Stewart, Farrar; *Harlem* by Walter Dean Myers, ill. Christopher Myers, Scholastic; *There Was an Old Lady Who Swallowed a Fly* by Simms Taback, Viking.

1999. *Snowflake Bentley* by Jacqueline Briggs Martin, ill. Mary Azarian, Houghton Mifflin. ***Honor Books:*** *No, David!* by David Shannon, Scholastic; *Tibet: Through the Red Box* by Peter Sis, Farrar; *Snow* by Uri Shulevitz, Farrar; *Duke Ellington: The Piano Prince and His Orchestra* by Andrea Davis Pinkney, ill. Brian Pinkney, Hyperion.

2000. *Joseph Had a Little Overcoat* by Simms Taback, Viking. ***Honor Books:*** *A Child's Calendar* by John Updike, ill. Trina Schart Hyman, Holiday House; *Sector 7* by David Wiesner, Clarion; *When Sophie Gets Angry—Really, Really Angry* by Molly Bang, Scholastic; *The Ugly Duckling* by Hans Christian Andersen, ill. Jerry Pinkney, Morrow.

2001. *So You Want to Be President?* by Judith St. George, ill. David Small, Philomel. ***Honor Books:*** *Casey at the Bat* by Ernest Lawrence Thayer, ill. Christopher Bing, Handprint; *Click, Clack, Moo: Cows That Type* by Doreen Cronin, ill. Betsy Lewin; *Olivia* by Ian Falconer, Atheneum.

2002. *The Three Pigs* by David Wiesner, Clarion. ***Honor Books:*** *The Dinosaurs of Waterhouse Hawkins* by Barbara Kerley, ill. Brian Selznick, Scholastic; *Martin's Big Words* by Doreen Rappaport, ill. Bryan Collier, Jump at the Sun/Hyperion; *The Stray Dog* by Marc Simont, HarperCollins.

2003. *My Friend Rabbit* by Eric Rohmann, Roaring Brook Press. ***Honor Books:*** *The Spider and the Fly* by Mary Howitt, ill. Tony DiTerlizzi, Simon & Schuster; *Hondo & Fabian* by Peter McCarty, Holt; *Noah's Ark* by Jerry Pinkney, SeaStar/North-South Books.

2004. *The Man Who Walked Between the Towers* by Mordicai Gerstein. Roaring Brook Press/Mill brook Press. ***Honor Books:*** *Ella Sarah Gets Dressed* by Margaret Chodos-Irvine, Harcourt; *What Do You Do with a Tail Like This?* by Steve Jenkins and Robin Page, Houghton Mifflin; *Don't Let the Pigeon Drive the Bus* by Mo Willems, Hyperion.

2005. *Kitten's First Full Moon* by Kevin Henkes. Greenwillow/HarperCollins Publishers. ***Honor Books:*** *The Red Book* by Barbara Lehman, Houghton Mifflin Company; *Coming on Home Soon* by Jacqueline Woodson, G.P. Putnam's Sons/Penguin Young Readers Group; *Knuffle Bunny: A Cautionary Tale* by Mo Willems, Hyperion Books for Children.

2006. *The Hello, Goodbye Window* by Norton Juster, ill. Chris Raschka. Michael deCapua Books/Hyperion. ***Honor Books:*** *Rosa* by Nikki Giovanni, ill. Bryan

Collier, Henry Holt & Company; *Zen Shorts* by Jon J. Muth, Scholastic Press; *Hot Air: The (Mostly) True Story of the First Hot Air Balloon Ride* by Marjorie Priceman, Atheneum Books for Young Readers/Simon & Schuster; *Song of the Water Boatman and Other Pond Poems* by Joyce Sidman, Houghton Mifflin.

2007. *Flotsam* by David Wiesner, Clarion. **Honor Books:** *Moses: When Harriet Tubman Led Her People to Freedom* by Carole Boston Weatherford, ill. Kadir Nelson, Hyperion; *Gone Wild: An Endangered Animal Alphabet* by David McLimaus, Walker.

2008. *The Invention of Huge Cabret* by Brian Selznick, Scholastic. **Honor Books:** *Henry's Freedom Box* by Ellen Levine, ill. Kadir Nelson, Scholastic; *First the Egg* by Laura Vaccaro Seeger, Roaring Brook; *The Wall: Growing up Behind the Iron Curtain* by Peter Sis Farrar/Frances Foster; *Knuffle Bunny Too: A Case of Mistaken Identity* by Mo Willems, Hyperion.

Author/Illustrator/Title Index

Subject Index